The Politics of Marxism

LIVERPOOL JOHN MOORES UNIVERSITY
Aldham Robarts L.R.C.
TEL. 0151 231 3701/3634

D1643121

LIVERPOOL JMU LIBRARY

3 1111 01243 3320

The Politics of Marxism

The Critical Debates

Jules Townshend

Leicester University Press
London and New York

LEICESTER UNIVERSITY PRESS
A Cassell imprint
Wellington House, 125 Strand, London WC2R 0BB
215 Park Avenue South, New York, New York 10003

First published in Great Britain

© Jules Townshend 1996

Apart from any fair dealing for the purposes of research or private study, or criticism or review, as permitted under the Copyright, Designs and Patents Act 1988, this publication may not be reproduced, stored or transmitted, in any form or by any means or process, without the prior permission in writing of the copyright holders or their agents. Except for reproduction in accordance with the terms of licences issued by the Copyright Licensing Agency, photocopying of whole or part of this publication without the prior written permission of the copyright holders or their agents in single or multiple copies whether for gain or not is illegal and expressly forbidden. Please direct all enquiries concerning copyright to the publishers at the address above.

Jules Townshend is hereby identified as the author of this work as provided under Section 77 of the Copyright, Designs and Patents Act 1988.

British Library Cataloguing-in-Publication Data
A catalogue record for this book is available from The British Library.

Library of Congress Cataloging-in-Publication Data
Townshend, Jules, 1945–
    The politics of Marxism: the critical debates/Jules Townshend.
        p.   cm.
    Includes bibliographical references.
    ISBN 0-7185-1420-3 (hb).–ISBN 0-7185-0004-0 (pb)
    1. Communist state–History. 2. Communism–History. 3. Post-
communism.   I. Title.
JC474.T74   1996
320.5'322–dc20   95-20512
                                                                              CIP

ISBN 0-7185-1420-3 (hardback)
      0-7185-0004-0 (paperback)

Typeset by BookEns Ltd, Royston, Herts.
Printed and bound in Great Britain by Biddles Limited, Guildford and King's Lynn

Contents

Preface

This book is about the conflict between theory and reality: the theory, Marxism; the reality, capitalism. This reality is what Marxism, throughout its relatively brief history, has sought to explain and change. Here politics enters. Only through political action could capitalism be transformed.

The underlying problem for Marxist politics has been twofold. First, capitalist reality has not fully conformed to Marxist theory. It has exhibited an unforeseen capacity for self-regeneration. Second, the working class has by and large refused to enact its role as capitalism's gravedigger, as predicted by Marx. As Isaac Deutscher once remarked, the 'basic predicament' of classical Marxism lay in the 'discrepancy and the divorce between the Marxist vision of revolutionary development and the actual course of class struggle and revolution'.[1] Consequently, Marxists have had to adapt their theory and political practice, as paradigmatically expressed in *The Communist Manifesto*; hence the debate and argument.

The urge to write this book stems from wanting to do the obvious, to reflect a dominant feature of Marxist politics: its incessant and passionately intense argument over the 'what is to be done' question. Fate had it that Marx was a genius who proclaimed his own relative unimportance in the process of historical transformation – ostensibly, he did not want to put the world to rights, he wanted it to right itself. Yet he spawned a political movement that loudly proclaimed his importance and whose members quarrelled among themselves over the meaning of what he and Engels meant. Commentaries on major Marxists, and Marxist analyses of the political, economic and social world, are abundant. A few works deal with specific Marxist political debates. But no relatively comprehensive treatment of the cut and thrust of Marxist argument exists. However, the limits of the book's ambitions must be hastily added. It does not analyse all the key political debates, but those which are covered are, it is hoped, at least symptomatic of characteristic tensions, weaknesses and lacunae within Marxism. Neither is the book concerned with rival conceptions about politics, as exemplified by the Poulantzas–Miliband debate over the nature of the state in the early 1970s, which do not clearly indicate different implications for political practice.

Furthermore, this coverage of debates is made in the full knowledge that the notion of the 'political' within Marxism is presented in a circumscribed fashion. Technical debates over philosophy and economics, for example, have largely been omitted, yet they were generally prompted by political considerations. The selection criteria have been determined by either historical or theoretical importance, or by accessibility of material. And debates between Marxists come within the book's purview, while those between Marxists and non-Marxists do not. The working definition of what constitutes 'Marxism' has been broadly defined as 'the theory and practice of the proletarian revolution'.[2] While the debates analysed in Chapters 2 and 14 could be seen strictly as falling outside the purposes of this book, even the non-Marxist protagonists (using the above definition) were, or are, deeply preoccupied with Marxist questions and wrote primarily with a Marxist audience in mind.

This book has also been prompted by the desire to make sense of the key debates within the history of Marxist politics in a relatively balanced way, exploring the strengths and weaknesses of opposing positions. This re-evaluation becomes especially relevant at a time when Marxist politics is undergoing a deep – and some would argue terminal – crisis. The hope is that this work will help in the understanding of that crisis, and contribute to a re-assessment of the Marxist political tradition. The advantages of hindsight, and the academic luxury of not having to answer in imperative mode the 'what is to be done' question, are fully acknowledged.

The contributions of others to the writing of this book are also fully acknowledged. My thanks go to Jerry Agnew, Colin Barker, David Beetham, Valerie Bryson, Paul Cammack, Glyn Daly, John Dumbrell, Norman Geras, Donna Hunter, Paul Kennedy, Phil Mole, Colin Mooers, Maureen Ramsay, Geraldine Skinner and Mike Tyldesley. I would also like to thank Alec McAulay for his help in the early stages of the planning of this project. All the aforesaid are hereby absolved from any guilt by association with the end product.

NOTES

1. *The Prophet Outcast, Trotsky: 1929-1940*, Oxford University Press, Oxford (1970), 514.
2. H. Draper, *Karl Marx's Theory of Revolution, Volume 2*, Monthly Review Press, New York (1978), 27.

To Saoirse and a world worthy of her name

1
Marx's Problematic Legacy

Marx said that 'Revolutions are the locomotives of history.'[1] His own thought, and the ideology and movement created in his name, was the progeny of two revolutions that threw mid-nineteenth-century Europe into turmoil. The French Revolution of 1789 called into question the whole way Europe was governed. It inspired many populations subject to the yoke of absolutism – either home-grown or foreign – to struggle for some form of democracy and national self-determination. The Industrial Revolution, starting in late eighteenth-century England, began transforming the social and economic landscape, particularly of France and Germany.

Marx's ideas developed in the early 1840s as a critique of both these revolutions. His standpoint, he claimed, was not based upon some abstract postulate. Rather, it was an 'immanent' one: although both revolutions represented enormous progress for humankind, they failed to live up to their promise – the expansion of human freedom. The French Revolution offered political freedom on the one hand, yet, in espousing the rights of private property, impoverished it on the other. The Industrial Revolution promised freedom through the conquest of nature by science and technology and untold wealth. Yet it delivered dire poverty to the very people producing that wealth. This gap, between declaration and deed, could be overcome, Marx argued, by the 'material force' of the proletariat. He shared the dream of human freedom with the two major ideologies given a large impetus by these revolutions – liberalism and socialism – but with a sharp difference. He maintained that his notion of freedom was grounded on modern historical development, whose mainspring was capitalism. Indeed, he sought to recast the language of politics in its contemporary liberal or socialist form, turning it away from transcendental, eternal, abstract verities and values. The universalism inherent in liberalism's abstract individualism, apart from upholding the principle of private property, was ultimately conservative, concealing class cleavages and thereby the class dynamic, deemed fundamental to historical change.

'Utopian' socialism, on the other hand – grounded on will-power, imagination and moral indignation – was deficient for other reasons. It was ineffectual, flying in the face of history, or accommodating to the capitalist status quo, or divisive, depending on one's choice of utopia, or potentially despotic, resulting in the imposition of ideals on a recalcitrant population.[2] Marx saw himself and Engels as bringing sanity to the socialist movement.[3]

Marx's historical principle in relation to freedom separated him from these two ideologies in another sense. Their limitations lay precisely in the fact that they were 'ideological', unconscious reflections of class interests and forces. Marx explicitly tied his theoretical (and practical) endeavours to the working class's struggle for freedom. Through such a struggle, he argued, universal freedom would be achieved. For Marx, thought was inseparably bound up with the practical problems of social existence, although it 'appeared' not to be so. Thus, although liberalism appealed to universal principles, it was a reflection of the practical needs of the bourgeoisie. Crucially, just as liberalism was the ideology of the bourgeoisie in its struggles with feudalism – at least in its triumphant period – so Marx considered his own thought as deliberately aiding the proletariat in its quest for liberation against the bourgeoisie. He saw himself as a partisan theorist of this newly emerging ruling class.

Unlike the 'utopian' socialists, he held that the relationship between his theorizing and proletarian political practice was profoundly democratic. Workers' emancipation could only be achieved by themselves, as a process of their own activity. Thus, all knowledge had to be tested in the light of this struggle for self-emancipation. Theorizing was a process of 'practical-critical' activity.[4] He saw his own writings as a contribution to the collective reflexivity of the proletariat in its emancipatory endeavour.

His argument rested upon a spinal assumption: social, economic and political conditions were in the process of being generated that would both enable and impel working-class self-emancipation. Hence, there existed a happy historical coincidence, where freedom would become realized in the dissolution of capitalism, independently of the imaginings and arguments of philosophers. As he put it:

> In the measure that history moves forward, and with it the struggle of the proletariat assumes clearer outlines, [socialists and communists] no longer need to seek science in their minds; they have only to take note of what is happening before their eyes and to become its mouthpiece.[5]

Marx saw himself merely as giving voice to this historical movement that would realize human freedom, making explicit what was implicit in the historical process, and thereby aiding the working-class cause. Many of his writings were concerned directly or indirectly to demonstrate the inevitability of this process. In a letter to a friend he claimed that one of his intellectual innovations was 'to prove' that the 'class struggle necessarily leads to the *dictatorship of the proletariat*'.[6] Knowledge of the overall trajectory of modern society could 'shorten and lessen' its 'birth-pangs'.[7]

Here we come to Marx's problematic legacy. His theorizing was *doubly* problematic. In one sense it was *intentionally* so. The striving to unite theory and practice made it so. Practice was always context-dependent, and the context in which political action took place was always subject to change. Despite his attempt to highlight the underlying forces at work in history, he was fully aware of contingent factors which did not correspond to his simplifying assumptions. Hence the need to modify analysis in the light of changed circumstances was always a possibility, requiring the study, for example, of the development of national and world economies, class structures and class capacities, levels of class consciousness especially among the proletariat, forms of state and the actual political activity of the protagonists in the class struggle itself, all of which were subject to various mutations. Equally, decisive failures and successes in the struggle for proletarian self-emancipation yielded lessons that had to be learnt.

Yet his legacy was also *unwittingly* problematic. His rejection of philosophizing, liberalism and other forms of socialism rested upon the twin assumption that capitalism was in a process of dissolution and that the proletariat as part of this process would become a new hegemonic class, creating a global communist order. What if the evidence pointed in a different direction? What if capitalism had far more economic, social and political resources than he had imagined? What if the working class proved coy in accepting the mantle of a future ruling class?

THE FOUNDATIONS OF MARXIST POLITICS: *THE COMMUNIST MANIFESTO*

The background

Debates between Marxists over the 'what is to be done' question will be treated in this book as a long, if convoluted, footnote to *The Communist Manifesto*. This pamphlet was first published in London, in February 1848, on the eve of the European revolutions. It was to become the founding document of Marxist politics, although at the time of publication it had a limited readership. While many of the positions advanced in this pamphlet were more closely argued elsewhere, it was the most comprehensive, comprehensible and widely read statement outlining the rationale of Marxist politics. Most of the major debates subsequently, either explicitly or implicitly, were inspired by this document: arguments either confirmed its central premises or amended them in some way.

The *Manifesto*, written between December 1847 and January 1848, was commissioned by the newly formed Communist League.[8] It was established in June 1847 as a result of a merger between the League of the Just – an organization with conspiratorial traditions, consisting of predominantly *émigré* German artisans, with branches in England, France, Switzerland and Germany – and Marx and Engels's Correspondence Society, composed of renegade intellectuals, based in Brussels. This new organization was set up on the understanding, at Marx's insistence, that it abandon its conspiratorial outlook and allow him and Engels to produce a public manifesto for the League. Marx in fact became its author, although he incorporated some of Engels's ideas as formulated in *The Principles of Communism* (October 1847).

It was written against a background of economic and political unrest in Europe. The effects of the industrial revolution were being increasingly felt on mainland Europe, with the rural and urban petty bourgeoisies driven into poverty and unemployment. And, as in England, a newly created urban proletariat was sinking into deeper misery. Famine stalked urban and rural Europe from 1844 as a result of crop failures, intensified by the commercial crisis of 1847. This was the decade of the 'Hungry Forties'. These material problems had a highly politicizing effect. There was a groundswell of opinion throughout Europe wanting to reconstitute the framework of government in order to effect some sort of social and economic change. These stirrings led to calls for increased democracy, with or without a monarchy in Western Europe, and in turn inspired demands for national self-determination in Central and Eastern Europe.

The *Manifesto* encapsulated in accessible form the results of Marx's intense intellectual transition between 1843 and 1845. The story of this 'pre-Marxist' emergence through a series of theoretical confrontations with Hegel, the Young Hegelians, Feuerbach and British political economy has often been told.[9] This period could be viewed as a deep reflection upon his journalistic experiences, between 1842 and 1843, mainly as editor of the *Rheinische Zeitung*, a liberal newspaper funded by Rhineland capitalists. The paper was continually at loggerheads with the Prussian authorities, who eventually closed it down in March 1843.

The first conclusion he drew was that human freedom could not ultimately be realized within the framework of the state, as argued by Hegel, whose views were semi-officially endorsed by the Prussian state. Although Marx remained indebted to Hegel throughout his life, taking on board his 'dialectic', suitably shorn of its philosophically idealist premises, he rejected Hegel's thesis that the modern state, especially in its Prussian incarnation, was built on rational principles designed to promote human freedom. Marx, in his unpublished *Critique of Hegel's Philosophy of Right*, written in 1843, attempted to show that Hegel's concept of the state, and the reality it sought to justify, was unable to articulate the general interest of society. It could not reconcile particular interests and give them a universal form through the bureaucracy, which he described as the 'universal class'. Rather, the bureaucracy, like the rest of the state, was a particular interest in society, characterized by careerism. And the state itself was dominated by a particular interest: private property. The only way in which the state could truly represent the common interest was if it ceased to be separate from society. This could only be achieved through '*unrestricted* active and passive *suffrage*', which would in turn lead to the abolition of private property.[10] Marx seemed to be implying that the state had a necessary independence from society as long as it represented only minority interests, especially of private property. With 'active' and 'passive' universal suffrage the state would lose its independence, when accountable to the propertyless majority, which would seek to eliminate private property. And with the elimination of private property the state itself would lose its 'political', repressive character. As he stated a little later in his article 'On the Jewish question', only when man's 'social forces' were no longer separated in the form of 'political force' would 'human emancipation be completed'.[11]

The second conclusion he drew from his journalistic experiences was that freedom could not be achieved through reasoned argument with those in power. The law passed by the Rhenish parliament in 1842, criminalizing the taking of wood from private land, and the censorship and final closure of the newspaper by the Prussian authorities were object lessons in politics. Self-interest, not reason, was its regulative principle. The world was not one big debating society. However, this experience did not make him into a cynic, but into a realist. There had to be a conjoining of the ideal with self-interest. He rapidly came to a solution to this problem between 1843 and 1844. The answer lay in proletarian communism. The proletariat was the only class which genuinely had the common interests of humanity at heart. It was dehumanized by private property, and could only regain its humanity through the abolition of private property. It was a 'universal' emancipatory class because its sufferings were 'universal' and claimed no 'particular right', since it was 'the object of no particular injustice but of injustice in general'. It could not 'emancipate itself without emancipating itself from all other spheres of society and thereby emancipating these other spheres themselves . . . . It is the complete loss of humanity and thus can only recover itself by a complete redemption of humanity.'[12] This dehumanizing process Marx analysed in greater detail in his *Economic and Philosophic Manuscripts*, which were notebooks penned in the summer of 1844.[13] Marx soon took a less humanistic and more, but not exclusively, 'sociological' view of the working class's universality in *The German Ideology*, as a potentially global class which would abolish all distribution systems where only a minority benefited.[14]

In coming to this proletarian solution he was no doubt influenced by his visits to working men's clubs in Paris, where he had temporarily settled in the autumn of 1843, and later by the struggles of the Silesian weavers in 1844 and the English Chartists as relayed by Engels, who was to become Marx's lifelong collaborator in 1844. Engels's intellectual contribution to the foundation of Marxism was mainly in alerting Marx to the importance of political economy (and some of its theoretical weaknesses) and in providing information about the newly formed English working class.[15]

In this 1843–5 period Marx arrived at a third general inference. Again, it stemmed from his observation that interest rather than morality was the driving force in politics. It consisted of a conceptual leap in understanding the relationship between knowledge and the world. Ideas did not have an independent existence from the world, as portrayed by Hegel and his followers. Rather, they sprang from the 'material life-process' of men.[16] And in this real world, thinking and doing were not separated: ideas and human activity directed towards the satisfaction of material needs constantly modified each other. Marx sought to demonstrate that communism developed from the 'material life-process' of the working class. Not only did the working class have an interest in communism as a result of being dehumanized by capitalism, it also had the potential capacity to create this new society. In *The German Ideology*, Marx and Engels sought to show that interests and their contradictions were constituted by class, which was generated by the process of material production, especially the division of labour.[17]

This work represented Marx and Engels's first attempt to develop a materialist conception of history, grounded upon the interactive development of the forces and relations of production. The purpose of this theory was to show that the material conditions engendered by capitalism were conducive to the creation of world communism through proletarian revolution. And with the establishment of such a world these conditions, which generated obfuscating ideologies, would disappear. Social relations would become transparent.[18]

Marx, along with Engels, saw his lifelong intellectual task as providing the proletariat with this 'scientific', i.e. non-speculative, empirically based, world view, facilitating its self-emancipation. This job of enlightenment involved an analysis of capitalism's inherent weaknesses – economic and social – that would lead to its disintegration. Second, it entailed the debunking of mystifying theories that impeded the proletariat in its struggle for freedom.

Key ideas

The *Manifesto* signalled Marx and Engels's first public attempt to aid the self-emancipation of the proletariat. It told a simple story about how it would slay the capitalist dragon, ushering in a classless society of communism in which 'the free development of each is the condition for the free development of all'.[19] Although the story had a strong moral undercurrent, the *Manifesto* proposed to show that solid empirical grounds existed for believing this story. This would imbue the proletariat with a confidence in, and an awareness of, its own historic destiny.

The core of their argument was that capitalism had an in-built tendency to self-destruct and create the necessary conditions for a classless society. Although capitalism was a phenomenally dynamic system, it was subject to epidemics of over-production. These became more acute as the possibilities exploiting new and old markets became more limited.[20] Capitalism also fostered the development of a classless society through the simplification of classes, compelling peasants, artisans and other members of the petty bourgeoisie to become proletarianized, i.e. members of a propertyless class that could only survive through the sale of its labour (later changed to 'labour power') to the capitalist.[21] This class would inevitably become the majority class in society. Unlike previous ruling classes in history, the proletariat was the 'independent movement of the majority in the interests of the immense majority'.[22] Capitalism, in creating the proletariat, made its own 'gravedigger'. The proletariat had a fundamental interest in overthrowing capitalism owing to the sheer meaninglessness and intensity of work as appendages of machines and its growing absolute impoverishment.[23] Thus, because it could not improve its lot within capitalism, it had to overturn it. It therefore abolished its own 'mode of appropriation and thereby every other previous mode of appropriation'.[24] Thus, the proletariat, unlike previous ruling classes, would not be extending its own form of appropriation, i.e. exploitation. Rather, it would be eliminating it altogether, creating a classless society. Finally, it had the potential strength to overthrow capitalism: not merely was it becoming a majority class, its feeling of its own strength grew as it became more concentrated.[25] Moreover, its organizational capacities and class awareness developed through the 'dialectic' of struggle, first in the form of the struggles of individuals, then those of trade unions and finally those of political parties.[26] Its political education was also fostered by the bourgeoisie itself, which enlisted it to fight its battles against feudalism. This process was helped further by renegade bourgeois intellectuals joining it, such as Marx and Engels.[27]

The immediate objective of the proletariat was to 'win the battle of democracy', thereby raising it 'to the position of ruling class'.[28] Such struggles, starting on a national basis, would assume international dimensions. Once in power, the proletariat would 'wrest by degrees all capital from the bourgeoisie' and 'centralise all instruments of production in the hands of the State'.[29] However, where the bourgeoisie was not in power, as in Germany, a two-stage revolution was in order. The first priority of the proletariat was to align with the bourgeoisie to bring about a successful revolution against the feudal aristocracy. This would be the 'prelude to an immediately following proletarian revolution'.[30] Quite clearly, then, strategy was condition-dependent.

Revolution also required a revolutionary party. To prevent any elitist and conspiratorial tendencies, the party would not 'set up any sectarian principles of their own, by which to shape and mould the proletarian movement'. Its 'theoretical conclusions' were 'in no way based on ideas or principles that have been invented, or discovered, by this or that would-be universal reformer. They merely express, in general terms, actual relations springing from an existing class struggle, from a historical movement going on under our very eyes.'[31] The aim of communists was to unite national and international working-class struggles, representing the 'interests of the movement as a whole'.[32] Apart from being the most 'resolute' section of working-class parties, they were superior in understanding 'the line of march, the conditions, and the ultimate general results of the proletarian movement'.[33] In other words, their job was to render explicit what was immanent in the historical process, culminating in communism.

This historically grounded form of argument enabled them to avoid getting drawn into moral discourse when dealing with various objections to communism. Hence, in response to the objection that communists wanted to abolish hard-earned, self-acquired property, they replied that capitalism had already achieved this for most of the population. In any case, capital was a collective product and its conversion into common property merely meant losing its class character.[34] And as for communism meaning losing the incentive to work, capitalism should have collapsed long ago, since those who work 'acquire nothing, and those who acquire anything, do not work'.[35] Again, in response to the claim that communists want to abolish culture, they retorted that bourgeois culture for the masses meant being trained 'to act as a machine'. In any case, the cultural notions of the bourgeoisie were the product of their 'economic conditions of existence'.[36] Retorting to the charge that communists wanted to abolish the family, they claimed that bourgeoisie was already bringing this about: capitalism had virtually eliminated the proletarian family, with all its members having to work, or women becoming prostitutes.[37] And among the bourgeoisie itself wife-swapping and prostitution were common. Further, employers often used their position to seduce female employees.[38] As for the anti-nationalist tenor of communism, capitalism itself was abolishing national differences.[39] Finally, religious and philosophical objections were not worth countering because they derived from the ruling ideology of the ruling class, which would inevitably seek to resist communism, a historical movement produced by changing material conditions in society.[40]

The main thrust of Marx and Engels's critique of other forms of socialism was likewise informed by a materialist analysis. 'Feudal' and 'petty bourgeois socialism' was the product of a decaying aristocracy and petty bourgeoisie respectively.[41] German, ' "true" socialism' was a petty bourgeois reaction to the rise of the German bourgeoisie and a revolutionary proletariat.[42] 'Bourgeois socialism' aimed at redressing social grievances in order to preserve bourgeois society.[43] Finally, 'critical-utopian socialism and communism', in offering utopian blueprints to relieve proletarian suffering, reflected a period when this class was in its political infancy, without historical initiative.[44] They were, however, highly appreciative of the criticisms offered of capitalist society, and indeed took on board some of the ideals of this school of thought, principally the abolition of the division of labour.[45]

THE PROBLEMATIC LEGACY

The *Manifesto* was a precipitate document. In the first part Marx and Engels seemed to assume that they were playing to a full proletarian house. Yet the proletariat in the mid-nineteenth century constituted only a small fraction of the world's population. Does this rather obvious fact demonstrate that the attempt to restore sanity in the socialist movement could only be achieved through tunnel vision? The answer can only be in the affirmative if their method of analysis is ignored. They worked at two levels: one is what we shall call 'tendential', where they examine the underlying tendencies of a phenomenon, i.e. world society. Their specific analysis derived from an economic model of capitalism. The other level of analysis is what we will call 'conjunctural', which acknowledges the existence of actual, empirical 'impurities' in the model in the form of political and social factors, which are in some way 'autonomous' from, or interact with, the economic model (which of course is often itself 'impure', embracing noncapitalist modes of production).[46] Marx and Engels assumed that the world would increasingly conform over time to the model appropriate to the 'tendential' level of analysis, with capitalism spreading over the planet and a two-class model emerging. Nevertheless, political practice had to be based upon concrete analysis, which invariably entailed the 'conjunctural' perspective. If this key analytical distinction is taken into account, then their discussion of the necessity of a bourgeois revolution in Germany and an agrarian revolution in Poland, rather than proletarian revolutions, becomes explicable. And, if the proletariat is in a minority situation, the question of alliances with other classes becomes an important one.[47]

The fact that the world was in a constant state of flux, especially as a result of the advent of capitalism – 'all that is solid melts into air'[48] – and that the class struggle itself was ever-changing, meant that concrete analysis had to be continually updated. This aspect of Marx and Engels's necessarily problematic legacy – the need for constant revision – was amply displayed by Marx and Engels from the 1848 revolutions until their deaths in 1883 and 1895 respectively. In the preface to the German edition of the *Manifesto*, they asserted that its 'general principles' were still correct, although their 'practical application' depended 'everywhere and at all times, on the historical conditions for the time being existing'.[49]

Revisions occurred in two broad areas. The first concerned class alliances. Marx and Engels had strongly supported the German bourgeoisie in 1848, even at the expense of the working-class movement, hoping that it would overthrow the monarchy, thereby imitating the French bourgeoisie of 1789. After the failures of 1848, they no longer confidently argued, as they had in the *Manifesto*, that 'each step of the bourgeoisie was accompanied by a corresponding political advance of that class'.[50] They now clearly recognized that an automatic correlation between economic and political power did not necessarily exist, something which Marx himself had noted in his 'A critique of Hegel's Philosophy of Right, introduction' in 1843.[51] For Germany Marx now recommended what he termed 'permanent revolution', by which he meant that revolution would be uninterrupted until the proletariat came to power. The need for revolutionary stages – first bourgeois, then proletarian – as suggested in the *Manifesto*, was thereby eliminated. Nevertheless, this process was still a 'protracted' one. In their 'Address to the Central Committee to the Communist League' (March 1850) Marx and Engels argued that the proletariat ought to support the democratic petty bourgeoisie (including the peasantry) in achieving its aims. Yet at the same time the proletariat had to form its own independent political and military organization, so that it could displace the petty bourgeoisie when it came to power. Furthermore, petty bourgeois attempts to secure their own position through bribing the workers had to be exposed through demonstration of their commitment to private property. This involved continually going beyond petty bourgeoisie demands on the property question, revealing to the proletariat that it was not seriously committed to making inroads into private property. And as Marx had assumed in 1843, they held that the proletariat's progress to power would be facilitated by proletarian revolution in France.[52]

Marx and Engels, however, did not totally eliminate the bourgeoisie from the progressive historical script after 1848. Especially in the 1860s they supported Polish and Irish independence movements, in which it played a key role. National independence, in Poland's case, would strike a blow against Russia, the bastion of reaction in Europe, and in Ireland's case it would help to break down the English bourgeoisie's ideological control over the proletariat through instilling a sense of national superiority.[53]

As a result of their reflections on the revolutions of 1848, they also paid attention to the possibility of a worker–peasant alliance in countries such as Germany and France, where the proletariat was still in a minority. Although they had ignored this question in the *Manifesto*, they drew up

'The demands of the Communist Party in Germany' in March 1848, which included four demands that favoured the peasantry.[54] They never wavered in their commitment to such an alliance where peasants formed the majority of the population.[55] Marx towards the end of his life gave much thought to the situation of the Russian peasantry and tentatively concluded that the prevailing form of common land ownership 'may' provide the 'starting point for a communist development', if a Russian revolution sparked off a proletarian revolution in the West.[56]

The other area where they revised their political strategy was over the question of the transition to communism. In effect they still continued to talk about 'winning the battle of democracy', i.e. the democratization of the state. They became much clearer over time that the conduct of this 'battle' was heavily dependent upon the political terrain. Marx, in a speech to the Hague Congress of the First International in 1872, explicitly stated: 'We do not claim ... that the road leading to this goal [of seizing political power] is the same everywhere.'[57] This goal could be achieved peacefully in the United States and Britain, and possibly Holland, where 'institutions, customs and traditions' were propitious to such a strategy. Yet in most Continental countries, 'force' would be necessary, because the state constituted a large, military-bureaucratic machine. Here, the state assumed some degree of autonomy from the economically dominant class, as exemplified by the Second French Empire of Louis Napoleon (1852–70). Such a form of government was only 'possible at a time when the bourgeoisie had already lost, and the working class had not yet acquired, the faculty of ruling the nation'.[58] In the same year as this speech, in the preface to the German edition of the *Manifesto*, Marx and Engels noted, quoting from Marx's *The Civil War in France*, that the vital lesson of the Paris Commune of 1871 was that the working class 'cannot simply lay hold of the ready-made state machinery, and wield it for its own purposes'.[59] Yet even in these countries Marx and Engels maintained that universal suffrage remained a crucial lever of communist transition.[60]

A subsidiary, yet nevertheless significant, revision concerned the whole time-scale of proletarian revolution.[61] Gone was the easy confidence of the *Manifesto* in fairly imminent revolution, although we must remember that it was essentially a propaganda document. Marx, in addressing the Central Committee to the Communist League in September 1850, argued that the organization had to tell the workers: 'If you want to change conditions and make yourself capable of government, you will have to undergo fifteen, twenty or fifty years of civil war.'[62] Thus, Marx began to take a much longer view of how proletarian revolution would unfold.

At this point we come to the question of how Marx's legacy was problematic in an unwitting sense. The world did not alter as expected. Capitalism developed at different speeds in different countries, and was internationally far more antagonistic than he supposed. Further, it showed more sustained dynamism and resilience than he presumed.[63] And either as a cause or as an effect of this, the working class, with the possible exception of Russia, failed to live up to hegemonic expectations as projected by Marx. It has been far more prepared to work within capitalism, through reformist methods, than to organize its overthrow.[64] Through economic and political reforms workers developed a stake in capitalism. Divisions within it may have been greater than Marx and Engels suspected, based upon locality, occupation, status and nationality.[65] And he saw the gender divisions within the working class as either unimportant or fairly easily surmountable. Additionally, its leadership became heavily bureaucratized.[66] Indeed, the whole question of working-class leadership, which seemingly had been happily resolved in the *Manifesto*, became far more problematic. What does a revolutionary party do if the working class does not tend to unify and readily embrace its ideas? Finally, modern capitalism did not 'tend' towards the two-class model. Rather, there has been the rise of a new urban middle class.[67] Indeed, Marx towards the end of his life acknowledged this fact, thereby undermining his binary vision of capitalist social development.[68] So the historically teleological scenario depicted in the *Manifesto*, of capitalism unconsciously and inevitably generating universal human freedom through class simplification and polarization causing proletarian revolution, of the 'real' and the 'good' coalescing, has to be treated with caution.

At the methodological level – crucial when considering the 'what is to be done' question – there is the problem of how the 'tendential' and 'conjunctural' levels of analysis intermesh, so that in practice underlying trends can be identified and combined with existing 'surface' phenomena. Difficulties arise especially if the latter includes struggles that do not obviously centre on class. Indeed, this issue raised a further question, which Engels touched upon towards the end of his life, but never satisfactorily answered, of how the non-economic factors – e.g. political and ideological – shaped the economic.[69] This in turn touches on the 'structure/agency' difficulty in Marxist theory as a 'sociology of change' or as a 'dialectic of liberation', i.e. the extent to which revolutions can be made through human volition, irrespective of whether 'objective conditions' have fully matured.[70]

In sum, Marx and Engels's followers faced a twofold problem. First, they had to analyse the conditions thrown up by capitalism and the class struggle quite different from those the founding fathers had envisaged. Second, the theoretical equipment they possessed was either faulty in some ways or quite difficult to handle, not merely owing to its complexity, but also stemming from certain conceptual lacunae and ambiguities. All this left plenty of scope for debate. And this is what this book is about. To extend and bend the 'revolution-as-locomotive-of-history' metaphor with which we began the chapter, Marx and Engels and their disciples were clear about the train's ultimate destination: communism. But various dilemmas cropped up on the way, prompting controversy. What if working-class passengers pulled the emergency cord before reaching the destination, because capitalism did not seem such a bad place after all? Indeed, was the train going towards communism in any case? (The revisionist debate, Chapter 2.) What if workers in various carriages started to argue among themselves on the basis of different national identities? (The national question, Chapter 3.) What if the terrain was exceedingly hostile, with capitalists and workers from different countries killing each other? (Imperialism and war, Chapter 4.) Should the ticket collector let on board peasants or members of the bourgeoisie, and could workers in the rear coaches, stuck in an economically backward country, swap seats with those in the more advanced carriages? (Strategic debates in Russia, prior to and during 1917, Chapter 5.) What sort of leadership and organization do the workers require to fend off hostile attacks? (The question of party organization in Russia, before 1917, Chapter 6.) Would workers on the capitalist–communist border be able to use the capitalist, parliamentary locomotive, or would they have to construct their own? (The nature of the transitional state, Chapters 7 and 11.) What happened if the train just got over the border and most of the carriages became uncoupled, leaving most of the proletariat behind in capitalist territory? (The debate over socialism in one country, Chapter 8.) How should the workers left behind organize themselves against particularly clever and vicious anti-working-class organizations? (The fight against fascism, Chapter 9.) Did any of the train really cross over into communist territory after all? (Categorizing the former Soviet Union, Chapter 10.) Would workers at the rear of the train in economically less developed countries be able to move faster to communism if they were somehow more detached from their capitalist environment, and should the strategy of force be used, virtually irrespective of political conditions? (Underdevelopment and guerilla warfare, Chapter 12.) What happened if the women on board wanted their own carriages, which they might even decide to uncouple from the train? (The question of women's oppression, Chapter 13.) What if workers ceased to identify themselves as a class, or were a far smaller proportion of the population than originally thought, or what if popular struggles were less obviously centred on issues of class? (The question of the retreat from class, Chapter 14.) Finally, did this train run into some buffers on a railway siding, short of its destination? (The future of Marxist politics, Chapter 15.)

Before we proceed to outline and analyse these debates, a brief overview of the historical background contained within each section of the book will be given. This will situate the debates more clearly within the overall development of Marxist politics. The first section (Chapters 2, 3 and 4) covers the period of the Second International, from its inception in 1889 to its eventual demise in 1914. Under the leadership of the German Social

Democratic Party, this International soon came under the influence of the Marxism of the late Engels and Karl Kautsky. Their Marxism had to acknowledge that the labour movement in Germany and much of Western Europe, although it had developed rapidly, both economically and politically, in this period, had become integrated into capitalist society. They both had to take into account in their subtly, yet significantly, different ways the political importance of parliamentary democracy for the working class. Proletarian integration into bourgeois society was clearly evidenced in August 1914, when most of the constituent parties of the International rallied behind their respective governments in the ensuing world war. The International's moment of truth had arrived. On paper it had been committed to turning the imperialist war into civil wars that would overthrow capitalism. Indeed, two of the three major debates on revisionism and the national question analysed in this section were symptomatic of the need to address the question of adaptation to capitalism. As such they called into question two postulates of the *Manifesto*: the irreconcilability of class struggle and the diminution of the importance of national identity within the working class. The third debate on imperialism and war challenged the *Manifesto*'s assumption that national antagonisms would decrease.

The First World War was a watershed in the history of Marxism. It marked a period of decay and renewal. The war destroyed the Second International and with it the German SPD's political, and Kautsky's ideological, hegemony. Yet it created conditions for the Russian revolution of October 1917, where there was no firmly established parliamentary democracy, or proportionately large working class. The Bolshevik success decisively moved the magnetic field of Marxism from Germany to Russia. Lenin's Marxism replaced Kautsky's as the new orthodoxy and a Third International was created in 1919 under Soviet tutelage. This International's Marxism was far more militant, anti-parliamentary, anti-reformist, anti-imperialist and vanguardist in political style than the Second. The second section (Chapters 5, 6 and 7) accordingly analyses a number of debates surrounding the Russian revolution. Arguments about the shape and role of the Marxist party, strategic options and the nature of socialist democracy became significant for the theory and practice of the Third - and, indeed, the Fourth - International.

The third section (Chapters 8 and 9) deals with the conflict between Trotsky and Stalin and his followers. While early on in the International's history the main debates were over the tactical question of abstentionism in relation to parliament and the strategic issue of how to combat imperialism, the differences between Stalin and Trotsky were significant for the history of Marxist politics. The first issue concerned Stalin's espousal of 'socialism in one country', which Trotsky saw as a revision of the Bolshevik's internationalist strategic premise: permanent revolution.

The second major question was over how to combat fascism, in Germany and elsewhere. Trotsky maintained that the International increasingly became an instrument of Soviet foreign policy, rather than a vehicle for global revolution. This accusation was graphically validated in 1943, when Stalin, in seeking closer cooperation with the United States in fighting Hitler, wound up the International. Trotsky had in the meantime established his own Fourth International in 1938 in an attempt to keep the authentic Bolshevik tradition alive.

The fourth section (Chapters 10 to 15) covers the post-war period. Early on, communism grew rapidly, as a result of Soviet expansionism not merely in Eastern and Central Europe, but also in colonial and semi-colonial countries, such as China and North Korea, and later Cuba and Vietnam. In Western Europe it was strong in France and especially Italy. Given the monolithic nature of the communist movement before and after the Second World War, few notable debates occurred within it. Creative theoretical developments within Marxism had occurred for the most part in a way that did not directly tie into political practice. So-called 'Western Marxism', starting with Gramsci and Lukács, was essentially philosophical in tone,[71] and although it had political implications, these were not concretely spelt out. The major political debate in the early post-war period was between Trotskyists over the class nature of the Soviet Union and its satellite states.

The major event in the history of communism, apart from its downfall in the Soviet Union and Eastern Europe between 1989 and 1991, was the Soviet Communist Party leader, Khrushchev, denouncing Stalin's cult of personality and the Soviet invasion of Hungary in 1956. This created huge splits within Western Communist Parties in particular and weakened many members' inner faith, built on a previous deification of Stalin and a worship of Soviet political and economic system. Trotskyist and Maoist organizations grew rapidly in the 1960s out of the student revolt, inspired by China's cultural revolution in 1966 and the Cuban revolution of 1959, and the activities of one of its leaders, Che Guevara. Both types were highly voluntarist in style, and unable to establish themselves as significant political forces in Europe or the Americas as the Communist Parties had done. Meanwhile, Communist Parties, partly in response to the Hungarian invasion and to the later Soviet invasion of Czechoslovakia in 1968, began to distance themselves from the Soviet Union in the 1970s, by embracing the doctrine of 'Eurocommunism'. At a formal level major Western Communist Parties unequivocally committed themselves to achieving political power through constitutional means. In the 1980s Communist Parties, as well as other Marxist political parties, went into decline in the West. This was partly the result of ebbing working-class militancy and the success of the neo-liberal project in consolidating the power of capital. Equally crucial as an explanation was the rise of new social movements that began in the 1960s, concerned with issues of sex, gender, peace, race and ecology, which were often seen by Marxist organizations as peripheral to the class struggle. At present the political fortunes of Marxism are depressed. Whether this will be its permanent state will be discussed in the last chapter.

NOTES

1. K. Marx, 'The class struggles in France: 1848 to 1850' in K. Marx and F. Engels, *Selected Works* (hereafter *SW*), Vol. 1, Foreign Languages Publishing House, Moscow (1962), 217.
2. See H. Draper, *Karl Marx's Theory of Revolution, Vol. 4*, Monthly Review Press, New York (1990).
3. Engels, in his preface to the English edition of the *Manifesto*, stated that Marx and he deliberately called themselves 'communists' in the 1840s in order to distinguish themselves from middle-class socialists, who merely tinkered with capitalism. H. Draper, *Karl Marx's Theory of Revolution, Vol. 1*, Monthly Review Press, New York (1977), 97.
4. K. Marx, 'Theses on Feuerbach' in *The German Ideology*, Lawrence and Wishart, London (1965), 659.
5. K. Marx, *The Poverty of Philosophy*, Progress Publishers, Moscow (1955), 109.
6. K. Marx and F. Engels, Marx to Weydemeyer, 5/3/1852, in *Selected Correspondence*, Progress Publishers, Moscow (1965), 69 (Marx's emphasis).
7. Preface to the first German edition of *Capital, Vol. 1*, Progress Publishers, Moscow (1965), 10.
8. K. Marx and F. Engels (F. L. Bender, Ed.), *The Communist Manifesto* (hereafter *CM*), Norton, New York (1988).
9. See, for example, D. McLellan, *The Young Hegelians and Karl Marx*, Macmillan, London (1969); R. N. Hunt, *The Political Ideas of Marx and Engels, Vol. 1*, Macmillan, London (1974), Chapters 1–2, *passim*; H. Draper, *Karl Marx's Theory of Revolution, Vol. 1*, Monthly Review Press, New York (1977), Chapters 1–10, *passim*.
10. K. Marx, *Early Writings*, Penguin, Harmondsworth (1975), 191.
11. Marx, *Early Writings*, 234.
12. K. Marx, 'Towards a critique of Hegel's Philosphy of Right: introduction' in D. McLellan (Ed.), *Early Texts*, Blackwell, Oxford (1971), 125–6. See also K. Marx and F. Engels, 'The holy family' (1845), *Collected Works, Vol. 4*, Lawrence and Wishart, London (1975), 37; K. Marx and F. Engels, *The German Ideology* (hereafter *GI*), Progress Publishers, Moscow (1968), 86–7.
13. See Marx, *Early Writings*, 259–400.
14. *GI*, 47, 86–7.
15. T. Carver, *Marx and Engels: the Intellectual Relationship*, Harvester, Brighton (1983), 49–50. Although there is some dispute over their implicit philosophical differences over the duration of their partnership, their political differences will be treated here as minimal, although detailed argument, beyond the scope of this work, is required to establish this point. The political use that subsequent Marxists made of Engels's philosophy is another matter.

Major works, apart from Carver's, on the Marx–Engels relationship include: N. Levine, *The Tragic Deception: Marx Contra Engels*, Clio Books, Santa Barbara, CA (1975); S. H. Rigby, *Engels and the Formation of Marxism*, Manchester University Press, Manchester (1992). See also J. Rees (Ed.), *The Revolutionary Ideas of Frederick Engels*, International Socialism, second series, no. 65 (December 1994).

16. *GI*, 38.
17. *GI*, 44.
18. See G. A. Cohen, 'Karl Marx and the withering away of social science' in *Karl Marx's Theory of History: a Defence*, Clarendon Press, Oxford (1978).
19. *CM*, 75.
20. *CM*, 60-1.
21. *CM*, 56.
22. *CM*, 65.
23. *CM*, 61, 66.
24. *CM*, 65.
25. *CM*, 63.
26. *CM*, 63.
27. *CM*, 64.
28. *CM*, 74.
29. *CM*, 74.
30. *CM*, 86.
31. *CM*, 67.
32. *CM*, 67.
33. *CM*, 67. See also K. Marx, *The Poverty of Philosophy*, Progress Publishers, Moscow (1955), 109.
34. *CM*, 68-9.
35. *CM*, 70.
36. *CM*, 71.
37. *CM*, 71.
38. *CM*, 72.
39. *CM*, 73.
40. *CM*, 73.
41. *CM*, 76-8.
42. *CM*, 79-81.
43. *CM*, 81.
44. *CM*, 83. See also *The Poverty of Philosophy*, 109.
45. V. Geoghegan, *Utopianism and Marxism*, Methuen, London (1987), 33.
46. This kind of distinction is expressed in A. Gilbert, *Marx's Politics: Communists and Citizens*, Martin Robertson, Oxford (1981), 5-13.
47. H. Draper, *Karl Marx's Theory of Revolution, Vol. 2*, Monthly Review Press, New York (1978), 38.
48. *CM*, 58.
49. *CM*, 43.
50. *CM*, 57.
51. *Early Writings*, 254.
52. K. Marx, *The Revolutions of 1848* (D. Fernbach, Ed.), Penguin, Harmondsworth

(1973), 319–30.

53. See Chapter 3.

54. *The Revolutions of 1848*, 109–10.

55. Gilbert, *op. cit.*, 219. See also H. Draper, *Karl Marx's Theory of Revolution, Vol. 2*, Monthly Review Press, New York (1978), Chapters 12–13, *passim*.

56. Preface to the 1882 Russian edition of the *Communist Manifesto*, 45.

57. K. Marx, *The First International and After* (D. Fernbach, Ed.), Penguin, Harmondsworth (1974), 324.

58. 'The civil war in France', *SW*, 1, 518.

59. *CM*, 44.

60. See Marx, 'Introduction to the programme of the French Workers' Party', *The First International and After*, 376–7; and Engels, 1895 introduction to 'The class struggles in France: 1848–1850', Marx and Engels, *SW, Vol. 1* (1962), 130.

61. J. Hoffman, 'The Communist Manifesto' in M. Forsyth, M. Keens-Soper and J. Hoffman (Eds.), *The Political Classics: from Hamilton to Mill*, Oxford University Press, Oxford (1993), 199.

62. *The Revolutions of 1848* (D. Fernbach, Ed.), Penguin, Harmondsworth (1973), 341.

63. L. Trotsky, 'On the ninetieth anniversary of the *Communist Manifesto*' in *CM*, 142.

64. See, for example, Trotsky, *op. cit.*

65. See, for example, C. Johnson, 'The problem of reformism in Marx's theory of fetishism', *New Left Review*, 119 (1980); R. Blackburn, 'Marxism: theory of proletarian revolution' in R. Blackburn (Ed.), *Revolution and Class Struggle*, Fontana, Glasgow (1977), 60.

66. See, for example, Blackburn, *ibid.*, 39.

67. Trotsky, *op. cit.*, 142.

68. Marx, *Theories of Surplus Value*, Lawrence and Wishart, London (1972), Chapter 19, Section 14, 62–3.

69. Marx and Engels, *SW, Vol. 2*, Engels to J. Bloch (1890), 488.

70. See, for example, S. Moore, 'Marx and Lenin as historical materialists' in T. Nagel and T. Scanlon (Eds), *Marx, Justice and History*, Princeton University Press, Princeton (1980), 213.

71. P. Anderson, *Considerations on Western Marxism*, New Left Books, London (1976), 49.

2
The Revisionist Debate

PROBLEMS AND ISSUES

The revisionist debate within the German Social Democratic Party, the leading party within the predominantly Marxist Second International (1889–1914), at the end of the nineteenth century went to the heart of many key difficulties contained in Marx's political project, as indicated in Chapter 1. The first major problem, to which in a sense all the rest were ramifications – as far as the revisionist debate was concerned – had to do with Marx's teleological conception of history, namely that it had a goal. But what if history was moving in a different direction, so as to falsify this assumption? Second, a difficulty arose stemming from a potential tension between his tendential and conjunctural analysis, between the *predictive* proposition implicit in historical teleology and his *method* of analysing economic, social and political phenomena that allowed for contingency. Although Marx was often categorical about the inevitability of communism, his research, because it rested on thorough empirical investigation, led him to change his mind on certain important questions, such as the future of the middle class under capitalism and the nature of revolution in Russia. Third, a potential conflict arose between Marx's economic determinism and his idea of human agency, which allowed individuals, and particularly classes, a certain autonomy of action, through 'practical-critical' activity. Marx's economic determinism also posed another problem: how did the superstructure of law, state and ideology relate to the economic base? Fourth, Marx's idea that communism was inevitable permitted him to avoid the question of whether it was morally desirable, and enabled him to pour scorn on all those pre-'scientific' socialist theories that were imbued with moralism and utopianism. Yet what if the determinist theory, upon which this 'inevitability' rested, was flawed? Would this not then put the moral appeal of socialism centre stage? Fifth, Marx saw his theory as an essential tool in the emancipation of the working class, enabling it to achieve its innate potential as a ruling class that would liberate the whole of humanity. But what if the working class consistently displayed neither the inclination nor the capacity to overthrow capitalism, and instead sought to work within it? Equally, what if the theory which predicted that capitalism would face ever greater slumps was questionable? Would not certain answers to these questions signal the need to articulate another type of political strategy, uniting a different sort of theory with a different sort of practice?

CONTEXT

What were the pressures on the SPD that led it to address these problem areas, and induced Bernstein and others to suggest that Marxism required a wholesale revision? First, social and economic conditions in the late nineteenth century were unfavourable to an immediate confirmation of Marx's cataclysmic scenario, with capitalist society splitting into two warring classes, in which the proletariat would overthrow the bourgeoisie as a result of growing economic crises. Germany in the 1890s had joined the world industrial superleague. Economic expansion had also brought forth a large and affluent middle class and a 'labour aristocracy' of well-paid skilled workers. In southern Germany the continued existence of a large peasant population confounded Marx's prediction that the peasantry were doomed to extinction as a result of the development of large-scale farming. The question that arose for the SPD was whether it should seek the electoral support of the peasantry. Moreover, owing to the relatively liberal political system in this area, the party had begun in the early 1890s to make significant electoral headway, which created the possibility of practical legislative gains through collaboration with other parties, thereby compromising the official party ideology of self-imposed political isolation.

Other revisionist pressures existed. First, the SPD, founded in 1875, had been driven underground by Bismarck's Anti-Socialist Laws of 1878–1890, creating a paradoxical effect on the party. It became radicalized and more susceptible to Marxist theory.[1] Yet in the face of a strong state and a growing economy, working within the system rather than against it seemed a far more attractive proposition. Indeed, this feeling of revolutionary impotence manifested itself in the organization of the party. It was a 'state within a state'. It contained a network of self-help organizations – temperance societies, orchestras, theatres, cycling clubs, gymnasia, news-papers, etc. An important implication of this type of party organization was that it gave members a feeling that socialism could be built in the present, rather than after the revolution. Thus, much energy was directed towards creating an alternative society within capitalism, rather than overthrowing it. In sum, as far as the party was concerned, its embrace of revolutionary Marxist theory that would guide day-to-day action was weak.

Moreover, given the strength of the state and the existence of a democratic facade, electoral activity was an attractive proposition. By 1890 the SPD was the largest party in Germany. The effect of this success was to make the party increasingly into an electoral machine, with a bureaucratic and conservative organization, involving the possible dilution of Marxist theory in the process. Another bureaucratic tendency was at work: the party in the 1890s relied increasingly on the growing trade union movement for members and voters. Here again a bureaucracy was emerging, committed to caution and making immediate practical gains out of capitalism.[2]

Outside the party two intellectual forces seemed to indicate the need to revise Marxism. First, there had emerged a strong, ethically oriented, neo-Kantian movement in the universities, in reaction to the dominant climate of evolutionary positivism, especially the application of Darwinian evolutionary concepts to the understanding of human social evolution. Although Bernstein never became a convert, and claimed that he was not influenced by its ethics, he did acknowledge that he was influenced by its generally critical spirit.[3] Second, Eugen von Bohm-Bawerk, an Austrian economist, rejected Marx's labour theory of value. He expounded a marginal utility theory based on subjective consumer preferences. The value of commodities was equated with their price, rather than with an abstract notion of the amount of 'socially necessary' (or average) labour time embodied in them.[4] For Bohm-Bawerk and his followers, therefore, exploitation was not something inherent in the labour process, involving the creation by workers of surplus value for the capitalist. If it occurred at all it was due to imperfections in the market, in the process of distribution, where certain bargainers got an unfair advantage.

All these pressures found their simplest expression in a desire by Bernstein and other revisionists to amend the Erfurt Programme of 1891.[5] The programme contained three sections: the first was written by Karl Kautsky, the leading theoretician of the SPD, and the other two sections by Eduard Bernstein, who became the leading revisionist. The first part reiterated the cataclysmic revolutionary scenario depicted in the *Communist Manifesto* and *Capital, Volume 1*. As a result of capitalist development, society would be divided into two battling classes, the proletariat and the bourgeoisie, with other classes such as the petty bourgeoisie (artisans and peasants) being wiped out. An increasingly impoverished, but better organized proletariat, would eventually be victorious. The job of the SPD, as part of a wider international workers' movement, was to lead the political struggle in Germany, in order to transform capitalist property relations for the benefit of all through socialized ownership.

The second part of the programme called for various reforms within the existing (capitalist) society: universal suffrage, referendums, freedom of assembly, freedom of religious worship, state, secular education for all children, a free legal system, free medicine and graduated income tax. And the third part was devoted to the protection of workers in the workplace, the eight-hour day, the abolition of children's employment, at least one and a half rest days per week, state insurance and the right to organize. The problem with the programme was that there was no obvious or necessary link between the first part and the other two sections. Why should the achievement of all the political and economic reforms of capitalism called for in the second and third parts inevitably lead to the proletarian socialist revolution clearly implied in the first part?

REVISING MARX

Bernstein (1850–1932) was strongly influenced during his exile in England (1888–1901) by Engels (whose later writings he interpreted in a particularly reformist fashion), the Fabians and progressive liberals, such as J. A. Hobson. He expounded his revisionist views in a series of articles, entitled 'The problems of socialism', published between 1896 and 1898. He later developed his ideas in a book, *The Presuppositions of Socialism and the Tasks of Social Democracy*, published in 1899, and translated into English under the title *Evolutionary Socialism*.[6] His overall purpose in revising Marxism was to bring theory into line with the 'facts' of contemporary capitalism, stripping it of its 'ideological' elements, and thereby making it more 'scientific'. The results of such an enterprise, he hoped to demonstrate, would be more consistent, first, with the demands for individual political and economic rights within capitalism contained in parts two and three of the Erfurt Programme and, second, with the implicit direction of the actual practice of the SPD. Thus Bernstein, through his 'revision' of Marxism, aimed to bring about a more coherent unity of theory and practice. And strategically, to achieve these reforms, he wanted an explicit alliance of workers and the progressive middle class and to work more obviously within the existing political order. Hence Marxism had to be made more pragmatic and liberal 'friendly'.

His starting point was a critical examination of the Marxist end-point, as depicted in part one of the Erfurt Programme, of a revolution with the proletariat triumphant, ushering in a communist society. He stated that this final goal of revolution meant 'nothing' to him, and the movement for piecemeal reforms 'everything'.[7] His message was: concentrate on winning reforms and forget about revolution, because there is no final purpose, or *telos*, in history, which is not a predictable and inevitable process. History is the result of cumulative changes. The final goal has no finality. Reformers are always presented with new and unforeseen needs and tasks.

However, he was polemicizing to make a point. He accepted the notion of a *telos*, believing that an immanent principle operated in history, namely the principle of cooperation. This was manifested in the diminution of the anarchy of capitalism as a result, for example, of cartelization, the increased possibility of the socialization of production, cooperatives and social reform. Thus, he defined socialism as the 'movement towards – or the state of – an order of society based upon the principle of association'.[8]

He rejected the Marxian *telos* because it was premised upon a faulty method – the dialectic. It led to a view of history that was *a priori* and tendentious. The facts were made to fit a theory of history that moved by dialectical antithesis, rather than theory fitting the facts of historical evolution. 'Actual evolution is really always bringing forth new arrangements, forces, facts, in the face of which that presentation [in *Capital*] seems insufficient and loses to a corresponding extent the capability of serving as a sketch of the coming evolution.'[9]

Marxism's seemingly economically determinist presuppositions also rendered the notion of a final goal implausible. Humankind's growing control over the socio-economic environment, through increased knowledge of it, meant that the 'iron laws of history' became increasingly limited in their power.[10] And if socialism was not inevitable, voluntarist elements had to be activated by making it ethically appealing. Socialism ought to have a universal appeal that should attract workers as well as the middle classes in order to build up an alliance between these classes.

Bernstein claimed, further, that the evidence did not support the cataclysmic scenario, as manifested in an economic collapse. The facts refuted Marx's predictions. The concentration of production in advanced capitalist countries had occurred extremely slowly in commerce and industry. And in Germany the reverse had occurred in agriculture. Furthermore, the facts did not confirm the view that economic crises were intensifying. From the mid-1870s, Bernstein noted, commercial crises had been virtually absent. Whether periodic crises would return was an 'abstract deduction'.[11] He argued that the growth of credit and cartels had helped to stabilize the situation, and that the enormous extension of the world market allied with improved communications and transport had mitigated trade disturbances.

His desire to be 'concrete' expressed itself in his critique of the labour theory of value. The theory entailed 'quite a series of abstractions and reductions' that made the theory hard to demonstrate; for example, in determining the value of a commodity, skilled labour had to be reduced to unskilled labour. The labour theory of value was 'nothing more than a key, an abstract image, like the philosophical atom endowed with a soul'.[12] Capitalism was not therefore inherently exploitative. Any 'exploiting tendencies' could be removed by reform.[13]

Another element of Marxist economics that he rejected was the distinction between productive and unproductive labour. This enabled Bernstein to put his 'progressive alliance' on a sounder footing, by not alienating the liberal bourgeoisie. Merchants, bankers and their staff, who for Marx exemplified unproductive labour, were 'from their very nature indispensable to the social life of modern times'.[14]

Consonant with this desire for an alliance, he sought to show that class polarization, intended to create a revolutionary 'big bang' according to Marxist theory, was a damp squib. The facts showed that workers were not experiencing increased impoverishment. If anything, they were becoming embourgeoisified. The middle classes had not been wiped out by big business. Statistics demonstrated the capacity of small businesses to survive. Moreover, many of the middle class had become the managers and shareholders of big business. Neither had the peasantry disappeared. Indeed, they prospered.

The growth of democratic institutions attenuated the class struggle further, because they helped to remove bourgeois privileges through social reform, and to improve the lot of the working class. Finally, outside the state itself the revolutionary imperative was obviated by the growth of trade unions and cooperatives.

The culmination of the 'big bang' – the dictatorship of the proletariat – he also could not accept. First, he contended that the working class was too heterogeneous, in terms of different types of occupation, work and income, to create anything more than a moderate feeling of class solidarity.[15] It did not, therefore, possess the potential cohesiveness to become a ruling class. Second, since Germany was moving towards a democracy, which he defined as the 'suppression of class government, though it is not yet the suppression of classes', there was little point in having a dictatorship of the proletariat, because the state was becoming increasingly responsive to the needs of the majority of the population.[16] Indeed, socialism was the fulfilment of the liberal project. It aimed to make a worker into a citizen 'and thus to make citizenship universal'.[17]

Moreover, he denied the necessity of violence implied in the notion of proletarian dictatorship. Liberal democratic institutions were sufficiently flexible: 'they did not need to be destroyed, but only further developed. For that we need organisation and energetic action, but not necessarily a revolutionary dictatorship.'[18]

In sum, although Bernstein may have thought that he was revising or modifying Marxism, he challenged its central tenets: its dialectical method, the inherent instability of capitalism, the class nature of the state and society, the centrality of the class struggle in achieving socialism and the idea of the working class running society. He may have genuinely thought that he was applying radical surgery to save Marxism. His opponents vehemently argued that such an operation would kill the patient.

ROSA LUXEMBURG

While there were a number of rebuttals of Bernstein, Rosa Luxemburg

(1871–1919) wrote the most renowned one, perhaps because of its cogent, hard-hitting style and its unambiguous reaffirmation of revolutionary Marxist principles. Her pamphlet *Social Reform or Revolution* (1899) has become a Marxist classic.[19]

The essence of her reply was, first, to insist upon the fundamental connection between the final goal, which she described as the attaining of proletarian power, and the day-to-day practical tasks of social reform, democratizing the capitalist state and building the trade union and cooperative movements. Put another way, she wanted to show that part one of the Erfurt Programme had to be neither jettisoned nor rewritten, and that its realization critically depended upon the struggle to achieve the minimum demands outlined in the second and third parts. Second, she insisted upon the strategic importance of the final goal, owing to the inherent contradictions of capitalism, which would ultimately lead to its collapse.

She took Bernstein at his word when he said that the final goal meant 'nothing' to him, and the movement 'everything'. She analysed this statement from the point of view of its consequences. If reforms became ends in themselves, then this would lead to opportunism, i.e. the sacrificing of long-term objectives for short-term gains, thereby immobilizing workers in their struggles as a class to set up a workers' state. She saw opportunism as an expression of the working class's momentary weakness, a temporary lack of confidence in achieving the final aim.[20] Moreover, if the struggle for reforms was an end in itself, then there was no need for theory at all. However, she did admit that theory was only required if one accepted the idea of the necessity of the long-term goal. Crucially, for Luxemburg, Marxist theory could demonstrate to workers how to achieve their historic mission as a hegemonic class by linking it up with day-to-day struggles. 'For social democracy there exists an indissoluble tie between social reforms and revolution. The struggle for reforms is its *means*; the social revolution its *goal*.'[21] Thus, the significance of the fight for reforms was owing to the effect it had on the organization, combativity and class-awareness of the proletariat. It was its *subjective* impact on the working class that was crucial, not the effect on the objective structure of capitalism.[22]

In order to understand this historic goal and how it was to be achieved, the working class required not only theory, but also the correct theory. *Contra* Bernstein, this entailed a dialectical comprehension of social, economic and political reality, or, more specifically, a dialectical understanding of capitalism. Such a view of capitalism had two features. First, it is a system riven with contradictions, ultimately ineradicable through reform. In her pamphlet, she repeatedly comes back to this point. The reason for this is precisely that the contradictions *are systemic*. Production, exchange, credit, investment, etc., are all bound up with one another. Hence, a specific problem – say, a shortage of markets – could not be seen to exist on its own, but, for example, as symptomatic of a crisis of profitability. Thus, specific palliatives to remedy individual problems would be to little avail. Indeed, methodologically, Bernstein looked at capitalism from the point of view of the individual capitalist, who could only see the problem as lack of markets, which could be solved through the extension of credit. However, while credit may help to stimulate trade, equally it could exacerbate crisis. Moreover, crises were not something which were avoidable through credit. Rather, they were part and parcel of capitalist development, caused the depreciation of capital and were followed by a recovery of investment.[23]

Second, a dialectical understanding of capitalism revealed a 'dualism of the socialist future and the capitalist present, of capital and labour, of the bourgeoisie and the proletariat'.[24] Capitalism, with its in-built contradictions, was a historically doomed system. Thus, she saw the dualism of the dialectic as accurately reflecting the future development of capitalism culminating in a socialist society.

She therefore had to demonstrate the 'historic necessity' of socialism. Arguing from within the Marxist tradition, she took it for granted that 'social being determines consciousness', and that therefore the preconditions for socialist consciousness among the proletariat lay in its struggles against capitalism. Thus, if capitalism was not inscribed with contradictions that generated proletarian opposition to it, if it was evolving, or reformable, into a relatively conflict-free system, then socialism would have no material basis. It would no longer be 'objectively necessary'. Its foundation would be 'pure reason'.[25]

Thus, she had to show that capitalism could not overcome its contradictions. She challenged Bernstein's argument that credit, trusts and cartels had stabilized the system. The expansion of credit was of little help because it provoked over-production and speculation. And it accentuated capitalism's contradictions by, for example, stretching production to the limit, but paralysing the exchange process at the slightest loss of commercial confidence. Luxemburg asserted that credit exacerbated all of capitalism's major contradictions, between the mode of production and exchange, between the mode of production and appropriation, between property relations and production relations, and between the social character of production and private ownership.[26]

Trusts and cartels were ineffective as well. They only increased the profits of one industry at the expense of others. They intensified international competition, because they encouraged firms to sell expensively in the domestic market and cheaply abroad. They aggravated the contradictions between producer and consumer, between capital and labour, and finally between the international character of the capitalist economy and the national character of the capitalist state, because the growth of trusts was always accompanied by a general tariff war.[27]

Above these specific arguments against Bernstein's 'adaptation' of capitalism thesis, she posited the existence of objective limits to capitalist expansion. She asserted that there were definite limits to the expansion of the world market, a point that became the focus of her later book, *The Accumulation of Capital* (1913).

As for the question of the absence of commercial crises since the mid-1870s, she contended that they did not have to occur every ten years. This periodicity was purely external and accidental to the dynamics of capitalism. The present period was transitional between the growth and decline of capitalism. When capitalism reached greater maturity, the regular periodicity of crises would return. In the second edition of *Social Reform or Revolution* (1908), she reinforced this position by pointing to the world economic crisis of 1900.[28]

On one final empirical issue, she questioned Bernstein's thesis that small and medium-sized capitalists had not been decimated by big capital. She held that ascendent and descendent tendencies existed. The latter would finally predominate, since, first, the stakes, i.e. initial outlay, required to compete would increase with the growth of capital accumulation, to such an extent that small capitalists would be unable to get into the game. Or if they could, as innovating capitalists, the time in which they could remain competitive would get shorter as production methods became more quickly capital-intensive.[29]

At a theoretical level, she rejected Bernstein's critique of the labour theory of value that it was an 'abstraction'. It really existed in a commodity economy. Money was the most developed form of abstract human labour. She did not, however, discuss his opposition to Marx's distinction between productive and unproductive labour.

As for the social dynamics of capitalism, she held that class polarization would not disappear, because all reforms of capitalism, which Bernstein argued would attenuate the class struggle, were ultimately ineffectual. The four paths of reform – the trade unions, cooperatives, state welfare measures and the political democratization of the state – led nowhere.

Trade union activity by itself was ultimately self-defeating: all gains would be wiped out as the world market started to contract, or as a result of changes in production techniques.[30] Such struggles were about the distribution of income, not about transforming the ownership of the means of production, and the size of the cake to be distributed was dependent on how production (i.e. profits) was faring. This form of activity, she concluded in a phrase that upset many trade union leaders, was a labour of Sisyphus.[31] Nevertheless, she recognized the value of trade union struggles in fostering the organization and class consciousness of workers.[32]

Neither could cooperatives transform the structure of capitalism. They were small units of socialized production within capitalism, and were therefore governed by its laws of competition, with attendant effects upon wages and conditions. Further, evidence indicated that producer cooperatives could not be successful in the most important areas of industry, especially heavy industry. They could only survive where they had assured markets, especially where they were linked to consumer cooperatives and produced goods to meet immediate and local needs.[33]

Nor could the gradual introduction of social and labour legislation be interpreted as an incremental advance towards socialism. Such measures constituted not a reduction of capitalist ownership, but a protection or normalization of capitalist exploitation. She argued that exploitation was 'extra-legal': 'No law obliges the proletariat to submit itself to the yoke of capitalism.'[34]

Finally, she challenged Bernstein's view that socialism could be brought about through the extension of parliamentary democracy. He maintained that with the growth of democracy, which he assumed as inevitably bound up with industrialization, socialism would occur as the state became coextensive with society. Though the democratization of parliament represented a *formal* merging of state and society, between form and content there was a crucial difference. The bourgeoisie was only committed to democracy as long as it suited its interests. It was becoming increasingly less so, especially in Germany, as it became more imperialistic and militaristic, and felt threatened by the rising labour movement.[35] She offered another reason why socialism could not be attained by legal means. Apart from extra-legality of exploitation, she pointed out that every legal constitution was the product of a previous social revolution.[36] An attempt to bring about fundamental social changes by working within a political framework created by a victorious class of a previous revolution would not achieve the socialist objective. It would lead to a different goal: the reform of capitalism. She also concluded, against Bernstein, that the violence he so desperately sought to avoid was endemic to the historical process. It had been employed by all classes in history that had come to power.[37] For the proletariat it would be no different.

Thus, Bernstein's rejection of proletarian hegemony was unrealistic. The unreformability of capitalism and the inherently class nature of the state, however democratic, indicated that the working class could only improve its conditions of existence on a permanent basis if it had political power. Liberal institutions did not have the flexibility attributed to them by Bernstein. Therefore the 'final goal' of proletarian dictatorship still remained *the* historical imperative. Nevertheless, she was not indifferent to the struggle for democracy within a capitalist state: 'it creates the political forms (self-government, electoral rights, etc.) which will serve the proletariat as springboards and fulcrums in its transformation of bourgeois society. Second ... it is indispensable because only in it, in the struggle for democracy and the use of its rights, can the proletariat become conscious of its class interests and its historical task.'[38]

COMMENTARY

Historically, the outcome of the debate was that Bernstein lost the battle, but in effect won the war. A motion condemning revisionism was carried by 215 votes to 21 after a three and a half day debate at the SPD's Hanover Congress in 1899. There were no formal changes to the strategy and tactics of the SPD. Nevertheless, as the centre-right veteran, Ignaz Auer, wrote to Bernstein, 'My dear Ede, one does not formally decide to do what you ask, one doesn't say it, one *does* it.'[39] There already existed a good deal of congruity between Bernstein's theory and the practice of the pragmatic right-wing bureaucracy, headed by Ebert, Noske and Legien, that was taking over the party. It wanted to integrate the SPD more closely into 'official' German political life. It achieved its objective in August 1914. Despite the party's formal position to the contrary, it supported the German war effort.

To assess the points raised in the debate: Bernstein clearly picked on a basic weakness of Marxism's historical teleology. Yet his alternative teleology – the principle of cooperation – as expressed in the growing adaptation of capitalism is equally problematic. Today, there are still generalized booms and slumps, areas of regional, sectoral and national economic growth and decay, as well as international conflicts over resources. And despite much international economic cooperation, there is no guarantee that such efforts will always be successful.

As for Luxemburg's argument that, if no final goal to history existed, theory was unnecessary, Bernstein could be defended on the grounds that he was only making theoretically explicit the practice of piecemeal reform, and that it would be irrational not to have a theory of reform, because one would have no way of estimating the possibilities of the success of such a practice.

On the question of Luxemburg's linking of the struggle for reforms to the final goal, it may be true that working-class consciousness can only develop in a revolutionary direction as a result of the struggle for reforms, but, as experience has shown, such reformist struggles do not *necessarily* point in this direction. The weight of historical evidence up to now is that workers on the whole have become incorporated into capitalism for whatever reason. Yet to reverse the argument, this need not in the future be *necessarily* true either. Certainly, there is always ample evidence, looked at globally, of workers in opposition to capitalism, even if they have not acted to overthrow it.

Methodologically, Bernstein certainly touched upon one of the weak spots of the dialectic in its teleological form. Yet, insofar as the dialectical approach insisted upon seeing capitalism as a contradictory phenomenon, it is stronger than his essentially non-antagonistic perspective. There is far greater plausibility in conceiving capitalism in systemic or holistic terms, in which different parts are interconnected, and in viewing specific problems as symptomatic of an underlying malaise. Nevertheless, there still remains the question of the precise dynamics of the capitalist totality. Indeed, Luxemburg's tendential analysis of capitalism was confirmed only in one period during this century, the 1930s, although the possibility of capitalist 'melt down' can never be ruled out.

As for Bernstein's corollary argument that, if Marxism's teleological perspective is questionable, then moral suasion in winning people to socialism becomes crucial, pushed to its extreme the importance of self-interest in political life gets ignored. So too does the way in which individuals and classes seek to further their interests through the use of moral argument. Yet although Bernstein's position seems a-sociological, it is still a moot point whether workers will necessarily become revolutionary through self-interest, as a result of social conditioning, or a belief that reforms are possible, or because of the uncertainties of, or sacrifices entailed in, a revolution.

On the empirical issue of whether credit, cartels and improved communications have stabilized capitalism, the question remains open. Certainly, speculation caused by the pyramiding of credit was a major factor in the 1929 Wall Street crash.[40] Possibly governments of today are better able to anticipate such occurrences, yet stock markets do crash, as occurred in 1987. Little research has been carried out to show whether cartels and improved communications strengthen or weaken the system. Similarly, little systematic research has been carried out concerning the centralization and concentration of capital. Intuitively, it would seem that although in certain industries, especially manufacturing, much concentration and centralization have taken place, there is still plenty of scope for small capitalists in the service sector.

As for Luxemburg's argument about limits to the expansion of markets, there appears to be little evidence that these have been reached. And finally, on the question of the periodicity of economic crises, it may be hard to pick out a discernible pattern, although they do occur, and their depth cannot always be predicted or controlled.

The differences over the labour theory of value are far from settled to this day. Strikingly, however, the theory is perhaps the one aspect of Marxism, apart from its determinism, that non-Marxists have the least sympathy with, in comparison with other elements of the theory, such as alienation, ideology, state and historical methodology.

Moving on to the social terrain of capitalism, both were right and wrong on the issue of class polarization and simplification. The social tendencies depicted in the *Communist Manifesto* have not occurred. Yet that a class struggle exists is hard to deny. Such a struggle does not have to consist of workers taking the initiative against employers. As the post-1979 Tory Governments have demonstrated, it can take the form of employers and governments severely restricting the activities of the labour movement through legislation, state coercion and control of the media.

As to the efficacy of reforms, trade unions and cooperatives in transforming capitalism into socialism, although both had different definitions of socialism, the experience of reforms in the twentieth century has demonstrated, first, that they have not abolished capitalism, and, second, that the health of the welfare state is dependent upon the health of the capitalist economy and the balance of class struggle. Yet the question of the permanence of reforms and whether there is 'space' for them is a complex one, because the relation between economics and politics under capitalism is itself complex. Certain reforms or welfare state measures might not be directly beneficial to the capitalist economy, but on the other hand they can be essential to the political stability of the system.

Finally, can capitalism be changed into socialism through the democratization of the 'bourgeois' state? Here it would seem that Luxemburg has the evidence of history on her side. In Italy in the 1920s, Germany in the 1930s and Chile in 1973, when capitalist property relations were under threat, liberal democracy was jettisoned.

At one level, then, Luxemburg had realism and logic on her side, as far as a relatively rapid transition to socialism was concerned. The bourgeoisie will ultimately use 'its' state to defend its interests, through force if necessary. Thus, if the working class was to institute a socialist order it would have to establish its own form of state. Whether such a state would be created from scratch or would consist of a drastically modified bourgeois state is another matter. On the other hand, she did not directly answer Bernstein's point about the capacity of the proletariat to become a ruling class. She assumed that this would be developed as a result of its involvement in liberal democracy and through its reformist struggles.

The debate was, in some ways, finely balanced. Bernstein more accurately reflected the reformist temper of the European working class, and teased out the strategic implications of abandoning Marxism's teleological assumption. However, he was less accurate in his account of capitalism's historical trajectory as a smooth-growing, conflict-free system. If Luxemburg presented more cogent arguments and was more sensitive to the contradictoriness of capitalism, she nevertheless underestimated its resilience and was over-optimistic about the development of the proletariat's hegemonic capacities.

The immediate impact of the revisionist debate within the German SPD in the late nineteenth century was small. Yet its significance for Marxism was enormous. Politically, it was a harbinger to the split between Lenin and Kautsky after the Russian Revolution, over the question of the state in the transition to socialism, analysed in Chapter 7. This difference was itself a precursor to the debate between Eurocommunists and their critics in the 1970s, considered in Chapter 12. Historically, the debate led to a pluralized Marxism. No longer was there Marxism in general. It had to be preceded by an adjective, such as 'revisionist', 'revolutionary' or 'orthodox'.[41] Theoretically, the debate foreshadowed the postmodernist criticism of Marxism as a 'grand narrative', explored in Chapter 14.

NOTES

1. D. McLellan, *Marxism after Marx*, Macmillan, London (1979), 22. The main commentaries on the revisionist debate are: P. Gay, *The Dilemma of Democratic Socialism*, Collier Books, New York (1970); L. Colletti, *From Rousseau to Lenin*, New Left Books, London (1972), Chapter 2, *passim*; H. Tudor and J. M. Tudor (Eds), *Marxism and Social Democracy*, Cambridge University Press, Cambridge (1988).
2. C. E. Schorske, *German Social Democracy, 1905-1917*, Harvard University Press, Cambridge, MA (1955), 13.
3. E. Bernstein, *Evolutionary Socialism* (hereafter *ES*), Schocken, New York (1961), 222; S. E. Bronner, *Socialism Unbound*, Routledge, New York (1990), 60; R. Fletcher, *Revisionism and Empire*, Allen and Unwin, London (1984), 132.
4. M. C. Howard and J. E. King, *A History of Marxian Economics, Vol. 1*, Macmillan, Basingstoke (1989), 50-5.
5. See the English translation of the Programme in B. Russell, *German Social Democracy*, Allen and Unwin, London (1965), 137-41 (first published 1896).
6. A new edition has recently been published which includes the previously omitted chapter on the dialectic: H. Tudor (Ed.), *The Preconditions of Socialism*, Cambridge University Press, Cambridge (1993).
7. Tudor and Tudor, *op. cit.*, 20.
8. *ES*, 96. Cf. Gay, 75.
9. *ES*, 208-9.
10. *ES*, 15-16.
11. *ES*, 91.
12. *ES*, 38; cf. Colletti, *From Rousseau to Lenin*, 45-108.
13. *ES*, xxv.
14. *ES*, 37.
15. *ES*, 103.
16. *ES*, 143.
17. *ES*, 147-8; cf. Gay, 211, McLellan, 31.
18. *ES*, 163-4.
19. R. Luxemburg, *Selected Political Writings* (edited and introduced by Dick Howard), Monthly Review Press, New York (1971), 129 (hereafter *SPW*). Although she does not spell this point out, what she probably meant was that in order to achieve short-term gains, class collaboration could be entailed, and this would dilute workers' class consciousness, and therefore reduce impetus to struggle for revolution. Other critics of Bernstein include Belfort Bax, Parvus, Plekhanov, Kautsky, Victor Adler and Franz Mehring. See Tudor and Tudor, *op. cit.*
20. *SPW*, 132-4.

21. *SPW*, 52.
22. There is a tension between what she says here and her idea that social reforms and democracy actually consolidate bourgeois rule, which suggests either that all reforms possess this danger and therefore should not be struggled for, or that social reforms and democracy could be of a lasting nature, because the bourgeois required them for political, rather than directly economic reasons. *SPW*, 85.
23. *SPW*, 91-2.
24. *SPW*, 101.
25. *SPW*, 58-9.
26. *SPW*, 62.
27. *SPW*, 63-5.
28. *SPW*, 67-9.
29. *SPW*, 71.
30. *SPW*, 75.
31. *SPW*, 103.
32. *SPW*, 86.
33. *SPW*, 102-3.
34. *SPW*, 117.
35. *SPW*, 110-12.
36. *SPW*, 115.
37. *SPW*, 115.
38. *SPW*, 119.
39. J. Joll, *The Second International*, Routledge and Kegan Paul, London (1975), 94.
40. See J. K. Galbraith, *The Great Crash, 1929*, Penguin, Harmondsworth (1961).
41. G. Haupt, 'Marx and Marxism' in E. Hobsbawm (Ed.), *The History of Marxism, Vol. 1*, Harvester, Brighton (1982), 285.

3
The National Question

PROBLEMS AND ISSUES

The national question caused a great deal of political and theoretical trouble for late-nineteenth-century Marxists within the Austro-Hungarian and Russian Empires. That national and cultural oppression was wrong and should be opposed, and that nationalism in essence was a bourgeois phenomenon, they were all agreed. What divided them was whether nations were entitled to independent statehood. This was an issue for which the founding fathers had left them ill-prepared.[1]

First, Marx and Engels often saw the national question as a non-problem. Capitalism would 'denationalize' the working class. In the *Manifesto* they argued: 'Modern industrial labour, modern subjection to capital, the same in England as in France, in America as in Germany, has stripped [the worker] of every trace of national character.'[2] This homogenized workforce had a common interest in the overthrow of international capital. Thus, workers of different nations of the world would supposedly have little difficulty in uniting. Moreover, while they saw nationalism as an expression of the early bourgeoisie's need for expanded markets, modern capitalist development was generally reducing antagonisms between 'peoples'. Again the *Manifesto*: 'National differences and antagonisms between peoples are daily more and more vanishing, owing to the development of the bourgeoisie, to freedom of commerce, to the world-market, to uniformity in the mode of production and in the conditions of life corresponding thereto.'[3] By the late nineteenth century, however, events had not borne out these confident predictions, especially within the Austro-Hungarian and Russian Empires. Here, there were struggles between 'peoples', and workers often put national loyalties before those of class in their desire for an independent state.

Second, as a result of this highly economistic and optimistic view that nationalism would disappear, they were unable to understand the psychological causes of nationalism, especially the way in which ethnic identity was such a powerful supra-class phenomenon. In relation to the ethnic underpinnings of nationalism, group or community feelings have often transcended those of class. In other words, they could not conceive of nationalism as an 'autonomous force', partly explicable at least in non-class terms.[4]

Third, when Marx and Engels did regard it as a problem, they were unable to provide their late-nineteenth-century followers with a set of consistent, ready-made answers. They did not give automatic support for national self-determination. Rather, their attitude was instrumental, determined by whether national movements fostered or hindered the attainment of their ultimate objective: world proletarian revolution.

In making a judgement about whether to support national movements, Marx and Engels took into account three conflicting factors. The first was whether a nation had the capacity to construct a strong centralized state – i.e. a capacity for statehood – that would promote capitalist development and thereby create a proletariat necessary for its overthrow. Thus, on the basis of the statehood criterion, Marx and Engels refused to support certain nationalities on the grounds that they were 'non-historic'. During the 1848 revolutions, they deemed the 'Southern Slavs' – Czechs, Slovaks, Ukrainians, (Ruthenians), Romanians, Croats, Slovenes, Dalmatians, Moravians and Serbs – to be 'historyless'. They were doomed to extinction through assimilation by more vigorous 'historic' peoples, such as Germans and Russians.[5]

Yet from the 1860s onwards, as a result of their political involvement in the First International, they also backed the nationalism of oppressed nations, logically regardless of whether they were 'historic'. Such nationalism would, they held, undermine the chauvinism of workers in oppressing nations, and hence foster the international working class unity. A successful national movement would, moreover, erode the confidence of ruling classes and undermine the material bases for their rule. Thus, in the 1860s Marx and Engels supported movements for immediate national independence. They viewed Irish independence as a precondition for proletarian revolution in England. 'Any nation that oppresses another forges its own chains.'[6] Irish independence would weaken the material strength of the English 'landed oligarchy', because Ireland was an important source of its wealth. Further, Ireland served as a pretext for a large standing army that could be used against English workers in the event of a revolutionary upheaval. More significantly, Marx saw Ireland as a source of ideological enslavement of the English worker to the English aristocracy and bourgeoisie, instilling a sense of superiority over Irish workers, and turning 'himself into a tool of the aristocrats and capitalists of his country *against* Ireland, thus strengthening their domination *over* himself'.[7] Thus, if Ireland became independent, at least one source of ideological control would disappear.

The third consideration was whether national struggles prevented certain powers from carrying out reactionary foreign policies, which thwarted historically progressive national-democratic movements. In the 1860s they backed Polish self-determination, because it would weaken Russia, whose foreign policy retarded movements in Central Europe for modern democratic statehood and therefore the development of capitalism in Europe.[8]

Therefore, the reason why Marx and Engels left their followers with theoretical difficulties was not only the absence of a psychological dimension, but also the flexibility of their position. Their economistic perspective meant that the national question either was not important because economic development was eroding the national identity of workers, or was crucial in creating a superstructure that hastened capitalist economic development and therefore conditions for proletarian revolution. If a nation could not do this it was 'non-historic' and would inevitably be economically and culturally assimilated by the 'great' nations. On the other hand, from a more directly political perspective, they supported the national independence movements of Ireland or Poland, irrespective of size and progressiveness, on the grounds that such movements would foster international proletarian unity and/or help to dislodge the ruling class of the oppressor nation.

BAUER VERSUS STALIN ON NATIONAL-CULTURAL AUTONOMY

Followers of Marx first had to address the national question within the Austro-Hungarian Empire in the late nineteenth century. The Empire contained before 1914 fifteen different nationalities, most of whom felt oppressed by the German and Magyar (Hungarian) minorities. In particular, national middle classes were disadvantaged because theirs was not the official language. Owing to national divisions by the 1890s the central parliament of the Empire had reached deadlock, through filibustering by representatives of national parties. This enabled the unrepresentative Imperial bureaucracy to control the political life of the Empire.

National issues also divided the fast-developing working classes, to such an extent that the Czechs established their own trade unions in Bohemia, based on the principle of nationality. The leaders of the All-Austrian SPD, founded in 1889, realized that the problems would not be solved by sermons on proletarian solidarity. At the same time, to acquiesce totally to national aspirations would seem to hinder the proletarian struggle, dividing workers against each other, and obscuring the fundamental conflict between capital and labour. Moreover, they held that if national separation occurred, workers could easily find themselves isolated in a state dominated by their respective national bourgeoisies in alliance with the church, military and landed interests. Finally, although Marx and Engels had opposed federalism,[9] party leaders felt that they were keeping to their spirit, if not their letter: to preserve the territorial integrity of the Empire would aid capitalist economic development.[10]

At the famous All-Austrian SPD Congress at Brunn (now Brno, in the Czech Republic) in 1899, the party called for the transformation of the Hapsburg Empire into a democratic, multinational state, divided into autonomous self-administered regions, which were to deal with internal questions such as language and schools. Boundaries were to be drawn up on a linguistic and cultural basis, and minority rights protected by law.

A firm link therefore remained between autonomy and territoriality, which could easily be a source of friction between the nationalities within the Austro-Hungarian Empire, wanting their own nation-states with clear boundaries. In order to 'depoliticize' the issue still further, and to enable workers of different nationalities to unite more easily in their economic struggles, Karl Renner and Otto Bauer expounded the idea of what became known as 'national-cultural autonomy', resting autonomy on the principle of personality. This notion also had an added virtue: it was consistent with Marx's notion that workers had no country.

Otto Bauer

The theory of Bauer (1881–1938) became more significant than Renner's. His *The National Question and Social Democracy* (1907) is considered the most important work on the national question produced by the Austro-Marxists, especially because it attempted to grapple with the question, albeit imperfectly, in a non-economic reductionist manner, filling a theoretical gap left by Marx and Engels.[11] And it became historically noteworthy: Bauer became the target of criticism by Lenin and Stalin, two future leaders of the Soviet state.

In order to preserve the Austro-Hungarian multinational state, while simultaneously making concessions to nationalist sentiment, he defined a nation in such a way as to play down the territorial principle: 'The nation is the totality of men bound together through a common destiny into a community of character.'[12] National-cultural communities could, then, be established independent of territory.

Having uncoupled nationality from territoriality, and therefore, he hoped, headed off the demand for a nation-state, Bauer then made a concession to nationalism by blending it with socialism. He called for workers and peasants who had been culturally excluded to be given the right to participate in a national culture: 'We must start from the fact that only socialism will give the whole people a share in the national culture.'[13] Departing from the orthodox Marxist position that world socialism would eliminate national differences, and that therefore all nations were in a sense ultimately 'non-historic', Bauer argued that it would lead to a flowering of national diversity. A socialist society 'will distinguish whole peoples from each other by the diversity of national education and civilisation, in the same way as at present only the educated classes of the different nations are distinguished'.[14]

As for practical policies, he believed that national-cultural aspirations would and should be met in an evolutionary and constitutional way: 'The new Constitution will not be created by a great legislative act, but by a series of provincial and local laws.'[15] He sharply separated politics from culture: 'Each nation should govern itself and be free to meet its own cultural needs from its own resources: the state should confine itself to watching over those interests that are common to all its nations and are neutral as between them.'[16]

Stalin's critique

Marxism and the National Question (1913), authored by Joseph Stalin (1879–1953), became Soviet orthodoxy in the 1920s at least for nations *outside* the Soviet Union. It was undoubtedly inspired by Lenin. In all probability he wanted a member of a Russian minority to write a riposte to the Austro-Marxists (Stalin was a Georgian).[17] Stalin's position was broadly similar to Lenin's views on national-cultural autonomy in this period.[18]

In the wake of the growth of national feeling within the Russian Empire after the failure of the 1905 revolution, the principle of national-cultural autonomy had found some resonance among Caucasian social democrats and Jewish political parties, most notably the Bund. Lenin wanted to avoid what he saw as the decentralizing federalist implications for the Russian Social Democratic Labour Party (RSDLP) embedded in the Bauer-inspired proposals. Moreover, he wished to halt any diversion away from the central political task of the RSDLP and the Russian working class: the democratization of the Tsarist state.

Stalin's pamphlet fully reflected Lenin's concerns. He sought to curb nationalist demands, implicit in Bauer's broad definition of a nation as a 'community with a common destiny'. He offered a far more restrictive definition: 'A nation is a historically constituted, stable community of people, formed on the basis of a common language, territory, economic life and psychological make-up manifested in a common culture.'[19] Unlike Bauer's formulation, common territory and economic life were essential ingredients of nationhood. Accordingly, he questioned the Jewish right to nationhood on the basis of Bauer's definition. 'Can it be seriously maintained that petrified religious rites and fading psychological relics affect the "destiny" of these Jews more powerfully than the living social, economic and cultural environment that surrounds them?'[20] He saw economic life and territorial contiguity as powerful assimilating factors. The Bund, therefore, could not claim that Russian Jews constituted a nation.

Certainly, Stalin argued, there was good reason to oppose all manifestations of national oppression. It stunted the development of the proletariat's intellectual capacities, through, for instance, the repression of language.[21] Second, if national persecution arose, workers would be diverted from the class struggle. Moreover, it glossed over the distinct class interests of the proletariat. Finally, it enabled rulers in multinational empires, such as Austria-Hungary and Russia, to divide and rule.

However, the answer, he argued, lay not in national-cultural autonomy. This accentuated national differences at a time when they were disappearing with the development of capitalism, and when peoples were being dispersed to different parts of Russia. And most crucially, such a demand encouraged a split in the workers' movement – both political and economic – on federal principles. Instead, supporting the right of nations to self-determination was the best remedy in combating national oppression, i.e. 'no one has the right *forcibly* to interfere in the life of the nation, to *destroy* its schools and institutions, to *violate* its habits and customs, to *repress* its language, or *curtail* its rights.'[22] Thus, all nations should have equal rights.

Stalin maintained that national-cultural autonomy was inapplicable to Russia. The right to full self-determination was necessary to ensure harmony between workers of different nations within Russia. The national question dominated Austro-Hungarian politics, because it immobilized parliament, the hub of political life. However, in Russia there was no parliament, and the agrarian problem was the central political issue. Democracy was the answer. It would destroy the remnants of feudalism, and in the process it could grant national self-determination.[23] Evidence showed that even under capitalism, when states were democratized, as in Switzerland and the USA, nationalities could live in harmony.

Apart from democracy, the national question could be resolved, according to Stalin, through regional autonomy, *if* nations decided to stay within the framework of Russia. This could apply to such areas as Poland, Lithuania and Ukraine, where according to the territorial principle there existed a 'definite population inhabiting a definite territory'.[24] People would therefore not be divided according to nations, and the possibility of future class divisions would be opened up. Such a proposal had an added advantage: it facilitated the development of the wealth of that region because it would not be hindered by a centralized administration. Problems for minorities in these areas could be solved through democracy, which, Stalin thought, would give them equal rights to language, equal access to education, etc. Finally, the same principle of regional autonomy could be applied to party organization. It would not have the same corrosive impact upon party unity as federalism, based on national-cultural lines.

LUXEMBURG VERSUS LENIN ON SELF-DETERMINATION

Rosa Luxemburg's views on the national question acquired international significance after Lenin's blistering critique of them in his pamphlet *The Right of Nations to Self-Determination* (1914). Her arguments against national self-determination were used by the Jewish Bundists and by what he dubbed the 'liquidators' within the RSDLP, who wanted to give up underground activity and work on a strictly legal basis. Later, they were also taken up by the Bolshevik left – notably Bukharin and Piatakov – during the First World War. After the October Revolution, the newly formed People's Commissariat for the Affairs of the Nationalities had a 'Luxemburgist' majority on it.[25] Moreover, many communists in areas of national minorities were influenced by her ideas.

Lenin strongly polemicized against Luxemburg's *The Problem of Nationality and Autonomy* (1909). She called for the removal of article 9 of the RSDLP's programme, which demanded that Russia be made a democratic republic in which 'all nationalities forming the state have the right to self-determination'. Her position had developed in the early 1890s, when she vehemently criticized the Polish Socialist Party (PPS) for its nationalist or 'social patriotic' obsession with Polish independence.

In this text she deployed many of the epithets found in Marx's polemical locker. The demand for national self-determination was 'utopian', 'metaphysical', giving 'no practical guidelines for the day to day politics of the proletariat, nor any practical solution of nationality problems'.[26] She implied that each nationality problem in the Russian Empire was different, and that therefore the Russian proletariat could not support a general solution. Such a demand was incompatible with the principles of historical materialism, which rejected any notion of 'eternal truths'. Ideas were the product of particular material–social circumstances, and these were ever-changing. Thus, a position on the national question could not be developed on an *a priori* basis, but only out of the 'concrete circumstances of each case, which differ from country to country'.[27] Second, the principle of national self-determination under capitalism was as utopian as the right to work. She commented sardonically: 'The "right" of a nation to freedom as well as the "right" of workers to economic independence are, under existing social conditions, only worth as much as the "right" of each man to eat off gold plates.'[28]

Her case flowed from her economic perspective. She maintained that the requirements of capitalist development had transcended existing national boundaries. Nation-states were no longer the best form for the further growth of productive forces. Imperialism was necessary for the continued development of capitalism, and did not respect national independence: 'the modern development of capitalism cannot be reconciled with the true independence of all nationalities'.[29] The development of powerful capitalist states had created 'world powers', which condemned 'all small nations to political impotence'.[30] 'The big-power economy and politics ... turn the politically independent formally equal small European states into mutes on the European stage and more often into scapegoats.'[31]

Given the unreality of national independence in the modern world, she proposed, instead of national self-determination, what she saw as the more realistic and practical demand of national autonomy. Paragraph 9 of the RSDLP's programme would be replaced 'by a concrete formula, however general, which would provide a solution of the national question in accordance with the proletariat of particular nationalities'.[32] National autonomy was essential to the 'political and spiritual maturity' of the working class. This required national self-government, especially national control over schools and religious worship, as well as freedom to use its own native language.

Although national autonomy was essentially bourgeois, she believed that its realization would develop working-class organization, education and consciousness. 'The riper the bourgeois institutions grow ... the broader grows the battlefield and the bigger the number of firing lines wherefrom the proletariat conducts the class struggle. The more unrestrictedly and efficiently the development of bourgeois society proceeds, the more courageously and surely advances the consciousness, political maturity and unification of the proletariat as a class.'[33]

LENIN'S CRITIQUE

Concrete analysis of the issue, both in Russia and elsewhere, led Lenin (1870–1924) to opposite conclusions to Luxemburg. Lenin argued that, first, the task of nation-building, globally, was incomplete. In Eastern Europe, Asia and the Middle East it had still to be achieved. Multinational states, such as the Habsburg Empire, were a sign of economic backwardness.[34] In these regions imperialism and/or absolutism, which prevented nation-building, and therefore the political framework for an expanding capitalism, still had to be overcome. Lenin maintained that national independence aided capitalist development.[35] Moreover, all struggles of oppressed nations, Lenin asserted, had a general 'democratic content', which he assumed would create the necessary terrain for the development of working-class capacities.[36] This led Lenin to make an axiomatic distinction between the rights of the oppressed and oppressor nations. Luxemburg neglected his distinction and therefore ignored the nationalism of the Great Russians, which was 'the principal obstacle to democracy and to the proletarian struggles'. And, equally, she failed to support the bourgeois nationalism of oppressed nations.

Furthermore, he emphatically stated that he did not mean that all oppressed nations *ought* to fight for secession. They merely had the *right* to secession. Hence, he did not reject the Polish Social Democrats' opposition to nationalism: that was *their* right. Rather, they were wrong 'to deny the necessity of including the recognition of the right to self-determination in the programme of the *Russian* Marxists'.[37] The right of nations to secede in no way precluded '*agitation* against secession by Marxists of a particular *oppressed* nation, just as the recognition of the right of divorce does not preclude agitation against divorce in a particular case'.[38]

Dealing specifically with Russia, Lenin wanted to demonstrate the cardinal importance of the principle of national self-determination. The Greater Russian minority dominated the peripheral nations, who constituted the majority. These nations were more oppressed in Russia than in neighbouring states. Capitalism was more mature in these areas than at the centre, so they provided greater possibilities for bourgeois revolutions.[39] In addition, these nations would inevitably draw inspiration from national movements outside Russia as they were often members of the same nation. Not to raise the demand for self-determination, therefore, played into the hands of Greater Russian chauvinists and the terrorist Black Hundred gangs that vigorously supported the domination of these peripheral nationalities.

Russian Marxists therefore had to support the right of nations to self-determination in order to create a situation of trust between the Russian proletariat and that of oppressed nations within the Russian Empire, and hence to unify these proletariats, as in the case of Norwegian and Swedish workers, when Norway seceded from Sweden in 1905.[40]

Closely following Marx's views on Ireland, as outlined earlier, he believed that equal rights of all nations to self-determination were a necessary precondition of international working-class unity. If workers of any one nation gave 'the slightest support to the privileges of [their] "own" national bourgeoisie', they would inevitably arouse distrust among workers of other nations. 'It will weaken the international class solidarity of the workers and divide them, to the delight of the bourgeoisie.'[41]

However, in supporting the right to self-determination, Lenin did not believe – in keeping with Marx's view that bigness is best – that in practice smaller nations would not exercise this right. They would see the economic advantages of being attached to a larger state.[42] And therefore in reality they would become assimilated to the larger body over time as economic ties grew.[43] Thus, the demand for equality of nations, aimed at generating trust between workers of nations, was in effect the other side of the assimilation coin. Lenin hoped that he had synthesized the economic and political sides of the national question. Although the demand for the right of national self-determination was abstract, it had the practical effect of uniting workers of different nationalities and at the same time promoting larger economic units.

Thus, paradoxically, as far as Russia was concerned, the demand for the right of self-determination was the best way to combat nationalism in reality. And he was adamant that such a demand was the most appropriate method of preventing nationalism *within* the RSDLP. Any lesser demand, such as Luxemburg's national autonomy, failed to distinguish between the nationalism of oppressed and oppressor nations, and therefore would not establish a position of equality and trust between workers of different nationalities within the party.[44]

COMMENTARY

In terms of their immediate practice, all the theories considered here were found wanting. These theories were unable to go fully with the 'flow' of history. In this respect, Bauer's theory of cultural autonomy was the biggest casualty. After the First World War many, but not all, of the nations that composed the Austro-Hungarian Empire wanted and got full political sovereignty, if only to protect their cultures.[45] Bauer by 1918 fully endorsed the demand of these nations for self-determination. As for Stalin's position, insofar as it was close to Lenin's, it was not fully operationalized within the Soviet Union when he became leader of the Soviet state in the late 1920s.

The application of Lenin's theory after the Russian revolution was made more difficult as a result of his change of strategic direction in 1917. As a result of his analysis of the world political and economic situation, and of that within Russia, he concluded after the February Revolution that a proletarian and peasant revolution was possible and desirable. It would, he hoped, detonate workers' revolutions in the West. Workers in the West would then be able to support the Russian proletariat to create a fully socialist society. The demand for national self-determination prior to February 1917, within the context of Russia becoming a bourgeois republic, was relatively unproblematic. But now that Lenin saw Russia as the catalyst for global socialist revolution, the Western capitalist powers were likely to do their level best to douse the fires of proletarian revolution in Russia. Moreover, the bourgeoisies of national minorities were hardly likely to want to integrate with a proletarian state. Indeed, they were more likely to side with Western capitalism against the Soviets, a point Rosa Luxemburg was quick to make.[46]

In this situation Lenin's policy of self-determination, which aimed to synthesize the economic development demands of size with the political requirements of international proletarian unity, became increasingly difficult to follow. The survival of the revolution became the overriding prerogative, requiring a politically and economically unified territory under central control, whatever national aspirations might be.[47] Lenin and the Bolsheviks of course hoped that such policy reversals would only be temporary, until European socialist revolutions had occurred, thereby removing all the military, political and economic pressures which were undermining the revolution. Thus, Lenin in 1918, on the grounds of expediency, accepted federalism despite his previously expressed opposition to the principle.[48] During the Civil War (1918-20) he in effect endorsed the annexation of Ukraine and Bashkiria, and later, in 1922, the forcible absorption of Georgia, despite his deep misgivings and his desire for national sensibilities to be handled with delicacy. Indeed, the national question and particularly Stalin's handling of the Georgian affair troubled him until his death. In his 'Testament' of December 1922, he attacked what he termed 'Great Russian chauvinism' within the Communist Party.[49]

Nevertheless, there were those on the left of the party, such as Bukharin, or in Communist Parties amidst the oppressed nationalities, such as Piatakov, leader of the party in Ukraine, who took a principled stand against nationalism on the basis of Luxemburg's view that self-determination could not be realized under modern capitalism in its imperialist form. In 1919 they added to this argument, drawing an anti-nationalist conclusion from the change in Lenin's strategic position in 1917. It was in the interests of the world proletariat that the Soviets be defended, even if this entailed the denial of national rights. Again, advancing an argument similar to Luxemburg's, Bukharin called for the self-determination of the workers of each nationality, which in effect justified local Communist Parties' opposition to nationalism.[50] Stalin in this period also held a similar position,[51] and Trotsky displayed a strong hostility to nationalism.[52]

Ultimately, however, both the Leninist and the Luxemburgist positions were defeated by Stalin and his followers as the Russian revolution became more isolated. Stalin, in opposing the aspirations of the national minorities, combined the 'class' ideology of the Russian proletariat with that of Russian nationalism. At the Twelfth Party Congress in April 1923 he said:

> That the Great Russian proletariat must be put in an inferior position vis-à-vis the formerly oppressed nations is absurd ... the political basis of proletarian dictatorship lies primarily and chiefly in the central industrial regions and not the border regions which are peasant countries ... the right of self-determination cannot and must not be a barrier to preventing the working class from expressing its right to dictatorship.[53]

As a result of the failure of the Russian revolution to spread to Western Europe, its growing isolation and the need for the regime to consolidate itself, Lenin's policy of self-determination within Russia became a dead letter (although it was strongly promoted *outside* the Soviet Union in order to combat imperialism), as did the notion of self-determination for the working class as Stalin and the bureaucracy gradually increased its grip on all aspects of Russian life in the 1920s.

Moving on to assessing the particular debates, in the Bauer–Stalin controversy, Bauer's position was certainly unrealistic. He attempted to 'depoliticize' the national issue just at a time when it was becoming intensely political. To separate educational, cultural and linguistic questions from power and class was not possible, given that the control over this 'ideological apparatus' is such an important element in controlling the minds of populations by ruling classes. Furthermore, nationality formed the basis of a great deal of discrimination within the Austro-Hungarian Empire. Bauer also removed national culture from any class anchorage. He ignored the possible class content of culture, and the way in which ruling classes manipulate national identities and symbols for their own benefit.

Yet his theory had its strengths: it exhibited a multi-causal approach that incorporated a psychological aspect, and that helps us to understand why nationalism seems to flourish in all sorts of different economic conditions. Bauer's historically dynamic approach was certainly an advance on Engels's concept of 'history-less' peoples, and it did not have the nationally repressive implications of Stalin's static definition of a nation.

Stalin's theory also introduced a psychological element, but his limiting definition of nationhood had a drawback: if peoples could not meet all the stipulated definitions they could be denied national rights. Further, he did not clearly distinguish between the nationalism of oppressor and oppressed nations.[54]

As for the weaknesses in Luxemburg's approach, they were quite obvious. Her economism assumed that because capitalism had reached a highly developed imperialist phase, with global socialism on the immediate historical agenda, the national question had become irrelevant. Even within the terms of her own economism, she had, unlike Lenin, no concept of 'uneven development', and so was unable to see that 'bourgeois' nation-building was still important in developing the forces of production. Further, given her highly Eurocentric analysis, and her failure to distinguish clearly between the nationalism of the oppressor and oppressed, she was not, unlike Lenin, able to develop a flexible position and link it (albeit imperfectly) to a strategy of proletarian revolution, as he was later to do in the struggle against imperialism. However, her theory came into its own after the October Revolution in the sense that her hostility to nationalism and her constant emphasis on it as a bourgeois phenomenon made sense to Communist Parties in the oppressed areas that were opposed to their local bourgeoisies, which were exercising their national rights to undermine the revolution. Nevertheless, her argument could be used to suppress all national rights, as Piatakov, party boss of Ukraine in the early 1920s, did.

The strength of Lenin's position is fairly obvious: it was far more flexible and adaptable. Nevertheless, in the situation of civil war and foreign encirclement, with the survival of the revolution at stake, even he was unable to protect consistently the right of nations to self-determination. Yet his appreciation of the force of nationalism in the modern world, and its potential as an ally of the proletariat against imperialism, was an undoubted strength.

Finally, while the question of the right to national self-determination was the real difference between these protagonists, a similarity of their *initial* positions ought to be noted. They were all opposed to national oppression, and they believed that the working class could benefit through participation in struggles against it. Moreover, Stalin and Lenin were not all that far from Luxemburg: they were prepared to support nations choosing national autonomy rather than national independence. The key difference was that Luxemburg, along with Bauer (before 1918), did not want to make independent statehood into a *right*.

NOTES

1. Marx's and Engels's followers were not helped by their terminological confusion. See W. Conner, *The National Question in Marxist-Leninist Theory and Strategy*, Princeton University Press, Princeton, NJ (1984).
2. K. Marx, *The Communist Manifesto* (hereafter *CM*), 65.
3. *CM*, 73.
4. See J. M. Blaut, *The National Question: Decolonising the Theory of Nationalism*, Zed Books, London (1987), Chapter 2, *passim*. See also J. Schwartzmantel, *Socialism and the Idea of the Nation*, Harvester/Wheatsheaf, Hemel Hempstead (1991), 198.
5. See R. Rosdolky, *Engels and 'Nonhistoric' Peoples: the National Question in the Revolutions of 1848*, Critique Books, London (1987). There were also nations whose 'history' was in a sense in temporary abeyance, as with India. British imperialism was in the process of preparing India for capitalist statehood, especially through the railway system. See Marx and Engels, *On Colonialism*, Foreign Languages Printing House, Moscow (n.d.), 87–8.
6. Quoted by I. Cummins, *Marx and Engels and National Movements*, Croom Helm, London (1980), 115.
7. K. Marx and F. Engels, *On Britain*, Foreign Languages Publishing House, Moscow (1962), 552.
8. Cummins, *op. cit.*, 98.
9. *Ibid.*, 38.
10. R. Loew, 'The politics of Austro-Marxism', *New Left Review*, 118 (1979), 20. See also Schwartzmantel, *op. cit.*, 152.
11. E. Nimni, *Marxism and Nationalism*, Pluto Press, London (1991), Chapters 6 and 7, *passim*.
12. T. Bottomore and P. Goode, *Austro-Marxism*, Clarendon Press, Oxford (1978), 107.
13. *Ibid.*, 110.
14. *Ibid.*, 107.

15. Quoted by M. Lowy, 'Marxism and the national question' in R. Blackburn (Ed.), *Revolution and Class Struggle: a Reader in Marxist Politics*, Fontana, Glasgow (1977), 150.

16. L. Kolakowski, *Main Currents of Marxism, Vol. 11*, Clarendon Press, Oxford (1978), 288.

17. E. H. Carr, *The Bolshevik Revolution, Vol. 1*, Penguin, Harmondsworth (1966), 425.

18. See V. I. Lenin, 'Critical remarks on the national question' in *Collected Works, Vol. 20*; H. B. Davis, *Nationalism and Socialism: Marxist and Labor Theories of Nationalism to 1917*, Monthly Review Press, New York (1967), 164, although there were important differences. See Nimni, *op. cit.*, 93.

19. B. Franklin (Ed.), *The Essential Stalin* (hereafter *EST*), Croom Helm, London (1973), 60.

20. *EST*, 63.

21. *EST*, 69.

22. *EST*, 70.

23. *EST*, 79.

24. *EST*, 80.

25. M. Leibman, *Leninism under Lenin*, Merlin Press, London (1975), 274.

26. H. B. Davis (Ed.), *The National Question: Selected Writings of Rosa Luxemburg* (hereafter *NQ*), Monthly Review Press, New York (1976), 109.

27. *NQ*, 112.

28. *NQ*, 123.

29. *NQ*, 133.

30. *NQ*, 129.

31. *NQ*, 129–30.

32. *NQ*, 153.

33. *NQ*, 279. She later made it clear that she was opposed to national self-determination in a bourgeois sense. It was only realistically possible in a non-oppressive form in a world socialist system. Davis, *The National Question*, 290.

34. Although Lenin opposed cultural autonomy, he supported the Brunn Programme – indeed, Renner's and Bauer's views never became official party policy. He sympathized with the desire of the Germans, Hungarians and Slavs to maintain Austro-Hungarian integrity in order to preserve their independence against more powerful neighbours.

35. V. I. Lenin, *The Right of Nations to Self-determination* (hereafter *RNSD*), Progress Publishers, Moscow (1967), 11.

36. *RNSD*, 24.

37. *RNSD*, 41.

38. *RNSD*, 62.

39. *RNSD*, 18.

40. *RNSD*, 35.

41. *RNSD*, 23–4.

42. V. I. Lenin, *Selected Works*, Lawrence and Wishart, London (1969), 159. See also H. B. Davis, *Towards a Marxist Theory of Nationalism*, Monthly Review Press, New York (1978), 61; R. Munck, *The Difficult Dialogue: Marxism and the National Question*, Zed Books, London (1986), 72.

43. N. Harris, *National Liberation*, I. B. Taurus, London (1990), 68–71.
44. *Ibid.*, 63–4.
45. Schwartzmantel, *op. cit.*, 206.
46. *NQ*, 294–5.
47. Harris, *op. cit.*, 97.
48. Munck, *op. cit.*, 80.
49. *Ibid.*, 84.
50. *Ibid.*, 60.
51. J. P. Nettl, *Rosa Luxemburg, Vol. 2*, OUP, Oxford (1966), 858.
52. Munck, *op. cit.*, 84.
53. Harris, *op. cit.*, 113.
54. Although he can be seen to be groping towards this position. See *EST*, 72–3.

4

Imperialism and War

PROBLEMS AND ISSUES

How to combat imperialism and war? These two interconnected questions were a major preoccupation of the Second International, from its inception in 1889 until its demise in August 1914 with the outbreak of the First World War. Indeed, the question proved insoluble for the Second International. It collapsed in that fateful month precisely because most of its constituent parties totally contradicted previous anti-war resolutions and supported their respective governments in the world conflict. Now that the war had broken out, its strategic implications for workers' movements of the belligerent powers had to be assessed.

Two fundamentally different strands of thought can be detected on this question. One was reformist, most clearly articulated by Karl Kautsky. He maintained that a policy of national defence ought to be pursued, while simultaneously demanding an equitable peace, without annexations, free trade, democratized governmental institutions and an international organization of states. It rested on the assumption that the war was not a *necessary* outcome in the development of world capitalism. Imperialism did not have to be warlike in its essence. The war, then, could be seen as a problem in itself, not as something which would automatically provide the basis of an anti-capitalist movement. Further, it was not conceived within a teleological framework, signifying a vital landmark in human history, i.e. the 'birth pangs' of a communist society.

The other strand of thought was revolutionary. It was comprehensively developed at a theoretical level during the war, by Bukharin and Lenin.[1] They viewed it from a teleological perspective: the war was integrally bound up with the development of capitalism in its imperialist phase and it signalled the last and highest stage of capitalism. The war was therefore central to a revolutionary strategy. The domestic crises that the war would inevitably produce should be transformed into a class war against the bourgeoisies of the belligerent countries, bringing about an international

49

workers' revolution. This was in effect merely a reaffirmation of the Second International's Basle Resolution of 1912, and part of the earlier Stuttgart Resolution of 1907. The crux of the debate revolved around the relationship between capitalism and war. More specifically, the issue was whether capitalism was essentially pacific, or whether it had developed deeply ingrained warlike tendencies.

Marx's and Engels's writings offered little help in enabling the protagonists in the debate to make their case. Symptomatic of this fact is that Lenin, who used quotations from Marx and Engels as polemical trump cards, made far fewer references to their work in his writings on war and imperialism then he normally did. One reason for this was that they were writing in a different historical period, one in which various national bourgeoisies were still in the process of attaining statehood and where war was not generalized on a global scale, but usually fought on a one-to-one basis. Their attitude was determined by the effect that a war would have on the long- and short-term interests of the working class. Thus, they took the side of the belligerent most likely to promote capitalism and therefore the development of the working class, i.e. the side of the bourgeoisie in its 'progressive' phase. Accordingly, during the 1848 revolutions they backed the idea of a 'revolutionary war' against Russia, whose influence was retarding the development of independent, democratic statehood in East and Central Europe, which was crucial to the development of capitalism in these areas.[2] They supported the North during the American Civil War (1861-5) because the eradication of slavery would foster the development of the proletariat. In the Franco-Prussian War they wanted the victory of the latter because it would aid German unification and therefore the promotion of German capitalism. Furthermore, a French defeat would lead, they argued, to the fall of Louis Napoleon and the establishment of a republican government, which in turn would facilitate the development of working-class political organization and consciousness.

Second, Marx and Engels could not provide definitive answers because they had an ambiguous attitude about whether bourgeoisies had inherently belligerent propensities. They noted that they used violence in order to achieve independent statehood, or to extend markets in capitalistically underdeveloped countries such as India. Yet they were uncertain about whether bourgeoisies were inherently warlike against *each other*. They were imbued with a great deal of free-trade optimism and had faith in the capacity of capitalism to eliminate distinctions between peoples, as indicated in Chapter 3.[3] They also maintained that wars for capitalists were too costly to pursue. Marx, for example, held that the French financial oligarchy was always in favour of peace, because war depressed the stock exchange.[4] However, Engels in *Anti-Dühring* believed that militarism was dominating and 'swallowing Europe' and that it bore the 'seeds of its own destruction', because competition in arms spending would 'hasten financial collapse' and universal compulsory military service would train workers in the use of weaponry, a skill that would be eventually turned against their respective bourgeoisies.[5] This self-destruct scenario would seem to have influenced the shape of the Stuttgart and Basle Resolutions, which called upon workers to turn a future imperialist war into a series of anti-capitalist civil wars, and Lenin's position. This was also Kautsky's view in his *Road to Power* (1909). He predicted that a 'world war was ominously imminent, and war means also revolutions'. He could 'quite definitely assert that a revolution that war brings in its wake, will break out either during or immediately after the war'.[6]

KARL KAUTSKY

The volte-face by Kautsky (1854–1938) just prior to, and during, the war, in which he moved from an ostensibly revolutionary to a reformist position, was determined by an overriding strategic consideration. A war would (and did) in his opinion divert workers away from the parliamentary route to socialism. It made war rather than domestic issues the central political focus, thereby preventing the SPD from playing its trump electoral cards.

Second, any attempt to implement the Stuttgart and Basle Resolutions would divide the workers' movement, given the extent of their patriotism, and such a division would prevent it from becoming a cohesive ruling class in the event of an opportunity for it to come to power.[7] Thus, he called upon workers to 'Struggle for peace, class struggle in peace-time'.[8]

In order to justify his position, he sought to demonstrate that imperialism was not an expression of capitalism in its death throes and that war was essentially irrational for capitalism. He developed this position in a famous article, 'Der Imperialismus', published in September 1914.[9] His key argument was that inter-imperialist conflict was not endemic among the major capitalist powers. He admitted that imperialism itself was necessary to capitalism: 'the growing ability of capitalist industry to expand constantly increases the pressure to extend the agricultural zone that provides industry not only with foodstuffs and raw materials, but also with consumers.'[10] Industrial capitalists, owing to economic expansion, were compelled increasingly to go beyond national boundaries in search of foodstuffs and raw materials. Nevertheless, this form of economic necessity, according to Kautsky, did not rule out the possibility of non-conflictual forms of domination among the imperialist powers themselves.

> What Marx said of capitalism can also be applied to imperialism: monopoly creates competition and competition monopoly. The frantic competition of giant firms, giant banks and multi-millionaires obliged the great financial groups, who were absorbing the small ones, to think

up the notion of the cartel. In the same way, the result of World War between the great imperialist powers may be a federation of the strongest, who renounce their arms race.[11]

He then speculated that this war was not an expression of world capitalism in deep, terminal crisis, and that after it was over there could occur another phase, one of peaceful imperialism.

> From the purely economic standpoint it is not impossible that capitalism may still live to see another phase, the translation of cartelisation into foreign policy: a phase of *ultra-imperialism*, which of course we must struggle against as energetically as we do against imperialism, but whose perils lie in another direction, not in that of the arms race and the threat to world peace.[12]

He postulated that the imperialist powers might find it in their interests not to fight each other. Opposition to capitalist exploitation was growing in the more developed agrarian zones, such as East Asia and India. There was also the possibility of internal opposition from the proletariat within the imperialist countries, owing to the huge tax burden engendered by the inter-imperialist conflict. And finally, some section of the capitalist class could object to conflictual imperialism, because arms expenditure diverted resources away from capital accumulation. For all these reasons capitalism could be non-conflictual. In effect, therefore, Kautsky, especially as a result of his theory of ultra-imperialism, uncoupled the struggle against the war from the struggle against capitalism.

BUKHARIN AND LENIN

Both Lenin and Bukharin (1888–1938) were concerned with the non-revolutionary implications of Kautsky's position. It obscured 'the profundity of the contradictions of imperialism and the inevitable revolutionary crisis to which it gives rise', and therefore did not prepare the international working class for the possibility of revolution.[13] Lenin and Bukharin maintained that inter-imperialist conflict was intrinsic to capitalism in its monopoly phase, and that the world war, an expression of this conflict, signalled that capitalism was moving rapidly in a moribund direction. Hence, there would be no 'business-as-usual' situation, as suggested by Kautsky, following the war, where Marxists could return to their pre-war, evolutionary parliamentary strategy.

The object of their argument was: first, to emphasize the intensity and global nature of capitalist conflict through their respective explanations of imperialism; second, to show the impossibility of a lasting, inter-imperialist peace; and, third, in Lenin's case, to demonstrate that world capitalism was ceasing to be progressive.

Explaining imperialism

Bukharin in *Imperialism and World Economy* (1915) and Lenin in *Imperialism, the Highest Stage of Capitalism* (1916) offered broadly similar explanations of imperialism. They worked from Marx's basic postulate that under capitalism there arose a fundamental contradiction between the developing social forces of production and their private ownership. This contradiction in the twentieth century had assumed global proportions. The social division of labour, the concentration of productive units and the centralization of capital into monopolies now had international implications. These monopolies enlisted their respective governments to protect their foreign interests, especially, but not exclusively, in the less developed regions of the world, leading to inter-imperial conflict.

Further, they both attached great significance to Hilferding's concept of finance capital, i.e. 'capital controlled by banks and employed by industrialists'.[14] In his seminal work, *Finance Capital* (1910),[15] he had identified finance capital as the major trend under contemporary capitalism. It consisted of the coalescence of financial, industrial and commercial capital under the control of the banks. The latter, in order to protect their loans and investments, encouraged this form of monopolization. Moreover, they promoted tariff protection and the defence of markets through the expansionist policies of their respective states.

Bukharin employed the concept to underline the intensity of international capitalist conflict. He described imperialism as the 'policy of finance capital'. Imperialism was the product of the twin processes of the 'nationalization' and the 'internationalization' of the capitalist economy. State capitalist trusts (i.e. alliances of finance capitalists with the state) had arisen as a response to international competition.[16] They developed on a national basis, because they could enlist the aid of the state to give them protection. This in turn fostered monopoly. A tendency existed for the transformation of the 'entire national economy *into one gigantic combined enterprise under the tutelage of the financial kings and the capitalist state, an enterprise which monopolises the national market*'.[17]

The internationalization of capital intensified the competition between these state capitalist trusts, which manifested itself at three levels. First, increased competition for international markets resulted from the growth of mass production methods and from the search for super-profits that could be gained from international trade.[18] Second, international competition arose from the growing need for raw materials as urbanization within the imperialist heartlands increased.[19] Third, competition for fields of foreign investment had become much stronger. This was engendered by the over-production of capital, arising from the increased turnover of capital, the by-product of technical progress. Cartels exacerbated this process, because they limited investment through

LIVERPOOL JOHN MOORES UNIVERSITY
LEARNING SERVICES

limiting production. And finally, capital exports became more significant, owing to the need for finance capitalists to circumvent tariff barriers.[20]

For Bukharin this economic competition translated itself into military competition. The 'national' groups of finance capitalists found 'their final argument in the force and power of the state organization.... A mighty state military power is the last rump in the struggle of the powers. The fighting force in the world market thus depends upon the power and consolidation of the "nation", upon its financial and military resources.'[21]

Lenin too gave a pivotal role to finance capital in his explanation of the necessity for violent inter-imperialist conflict. Kautsky had defined imperialism in terms of the annexation of agrarian zones, in order to satisfy the needs of industrial capitalism. Lenin, on the other hand, saw finance capital and not industrial capital as the root cause of imperialism. He argued that the former wanted not only agrarian areas, but any other areas suitable for investment, including industrial countries. This occurred because in 'a few countries capitalism has become "overripe" and (owing to the backward state of agriculture and the poverty of the masses) capital cannot find a field for "profitable" investment'.[22] Moreover, now that the world had been divided up among the imperialist powers, finance capitalists were interested in a *redivision* of the planet.[23] According to Lenin, this was what the First World War was all about. Kautsky in effect detached the politics of imperialism from its economics.[24]

Lenin was just as keen as Bukharin to stress the intensity of the economic conflict. He could agree with Kautsky (and Bukharin) that imperialism was in part engendered by industry's need for raw materials. However, he underscored the competitiveness of this situation: 'The more capitalism is developed, the more strongly the shortage of raw materials is felt, the more intense the competition and the hunt for sources of raw materials throughout the whole world, the more desperate the struggle for the acquisition of colonies.'[25]

The impossibility of ultra-imperialism

Kautsky was a sufficiently orthodox Marxist to connect imperialism to (especially industrial) capitalism. This systemic connection he was prepared to admit, but not one between imperialism and war, as his theory of ultra-imperialism aimed to demonstrate. For Bukharin and Lenin, on the other hand, the contradictions of capitalism were too deep-seated to permit the cartelization of foreign policy.

Bukharin asserted that although the development of a single world trust was a theoretical possibility, in practice it was unlikely. The precondition for such an unusual eventuality would be comparative equality in the world market between the state capitalist trusts. Otherwise it would not be in the interest of all to join a 'mega' trust. Such equality was hard to conceive. It presupposed an equality in production costs between each trust.[26] In reality, low-cost trusts would be reluctant to enter into such an agreement. Second, it assumed an equality of economic policies between states, but some states were politically stronger than others and could therefore obtain more favourable tariff agreements.[27] Finally, even if such equality existed between these trusts at any one point in time, each one would have plans to become unequal in order to dominate the others.[28]

Thus, after the war had finished he contended that every agreement or fusion between these trusts would only lead to 'bloody struggles on a new scale'. For 'anyone acquainted with the history of the struggle among cartels within the boundaries of one country knows how often, when the situation changed, when the market conditions changed, agreements dissolved like soap bubbles.'[29] And even if centralization was theoretically possible, where one trust devoured all others, it would be prevented by the proletariat, which was profoundly opposed to the imperialist conflict generated by such a process.[30]

Lenin, in opposing the ultra-imperialist thesis, developed Bukharin's notion that uneven economic development between different capitalist powers was inevitable, thereby undermining any possibility of sustained inter-imperialist cooperation.[31] Finance capital, rather than lessening 'the unevenness and contradictions inherent in the world economy', increased them.[32]

From this perspective he examined the foreign policies of the three leading economic powers: Germany, Britain and the United States. Germany had rapidly expanding productive forces, but few colonies. The United States was in a similar position. Britain, on the other hand, had a large number of colonies, from which she derived substantial 'booty', but relatively undynamic productive forces.[33] Being a latecomer on the imperial scene, German and American finance capital was engaged in *redividing* the world on the basis of a new relation of forces that is being changed by methods *anything* but peaceful'.[34] Lenin posed the question rhetorically: 'what means other than war could there be *under capitalism* to overcome the disparity between the development of the productive forces and the accumulation of capital on the one side, and the division of the colonies and spheres of influence for finance capital on the other?'[35] Thus, the possibility of inter-imperialist peace after the war was chimerical. Peace and capitalism could not coexist. Therefore to struggle for peace had to be a struggle against capitalism.

Lenin also rejected the argument justifying a defensive war, while simultaneously calling for peace, which relied on Marx's case for supporting a 'progressive' capitalist side. Objective conditions had changed since Marx's day.[36] Relatively harmonious free-trade capitalism had given way to conflict-ridden monopoly, finance capitalism to generalized world conflict in the attempt to redivide the world. A new epoch had arrived. All the major states were engaged in aggressive predatory conflict. Capitalism had now become uniformly reactionary. Thus, defensive wars in the name of progressive capitalism were impossible.

In addition, he asserted that capitalism was no longer economically progressive. It tended towards technological stagnation, as a result of the monopolies retarding the application of new inventions.[37] Equally significantly, finance capitalism was leading to parasitism. Britain, for example, was becoming a rentier state, living off its foreign investments.[38]

In sum, for Lenin there could be no peace or progress after the war. The war was indeed *the* crisis of capitalism. Accordingly, the working classes of the belligerent powers had to turn the imperialist war into a series of civil wars, with socialism as the object.

COMMENTARY

This chapter has focused on the argument between Marxists during the First World War about the interrelationship between imperialism and war. In other periods Marxists have looked at imperialism with other issues and strategic considerations in mind. Before the First World War, they examined imperialism with reference to the so-called 'colonial question', in the inter-war period in relation to anti-colonial movements, and in the post-Second World War era in connection with economic strategies in developing countries, as will be discussed in Chapter 11.

As for the debate during the First World War, the question was not whether imperialism was linked to capitalism. Kautsky, as much as Lenin and Bukharin, saw it as bound up with capitalism's development. The real issue was an interconnected one of whether imperialism was inherently conflict-ridden, and whether the First World War represented the 'death agony' of capitalism.

Their differing analyses of imperialism were partly determined by their different strategies for socialism. Kautsky's was based upon a peaceful, parliamentary road, which saw violence as positively harmful to this endeavour. He saw the world war as an event which compelled socialists to put their long-term goals into temporary abeyance, because it diverted attention away from social issues required to raise class consciousness. Further, if the struggle for socialism could be put into cold storage, then it would be hard to admit that it represented the terminal crisis of capitalism. There had to be another stage. Another consequence of Kautsky's parliamentary strategy was that it placed little emphasis on the need to develop an international strategy.

Lenin's position in particular was the complete antithesis of Kautsky's. He linked the struggle against the war with the struggle for socialism on an international scale. This was something he attempted practically in

October 1917, as will be discussed in the next chapter. He opposed Menshevik policies, supporting the provisional government in continuing the war. He denied the legitimacy of defensive wars in the imperialist epoch. Consistent with the Stuttgart and Basle Resolutions, he was able in Russia to turn the imperialist war into a civil war in October 1917, and in 1918 took Russia out of the war with the treaty of Brest-Litovsk.

In terms of the strengths and weaknesses of their respective positions, Kautsky's theory of ultra-imperialism has had some plausibility. Imperialist powers did and do cooperate. They united to contain Russia after the Revolution; they united to share out the colonial spoils of war after defeating Germany in the First World War, as embodied in the League of Nations Mandate system; different powers cooperated under the aegis of the United States in the Vietnam War in the 1960s, as they did more recently in the Gulf War of 1989–90. Moreover, at a theoretical level, as Anthony Brewer suggests, there is no necessary *a priori* reason why finance capitalists would want to call upon their respective governments to annex territory, if the motive for capital export itself is to circumvent tariff barriers, i.e. to penetrate national markets from within.[39]

On the other hand, Kautsky's perspective would seem to be unrealistic, underplaying the dynamic, and often violent, nature of capitalist competition, as well as the instability of the world political system. The Treaty of Versailles, after the end of the First World War, was anything but equitable in relation to the losers, especially Germany. The victors levied enormous tribute from Germany and took her colonies, thereby laying the foundations for another world war.

Nevertheless, the post-Second World War bipolar pattern of international relations, the rise of US hegemony in relation to other imperialist states and the balance of nuclear terror greatly reduced the possibility of violent inter-imperial conflict for at least 45 years.

However, Bukharin's and Lenin's theory of uneven development, which emphasized the way in which changes of relative economic strength in the international arena accompany changes in political strength, would seem to possess some plausibility. The recent collapse of the Soviet Empire was in part owing to its failure to compete militarily because of its economic decline. Moreover, the rise of Germany and Japan as key international players has much to do with their growing economic strength.

Nevertheless, Lenin's position in particular did contain a central weakness, which stemmed from his teleological assumption. It suggested that imperialism was the highest stage of capitalism and was about to collapse. This led him to overdraw his 'composite picture' of world capitalist relations. The major imperialist powers had demonstrably different economic and social structures as well as different economic policies. Moreover, his use of Britain, a parasitic rentier state, to show that capitalism was no longer progressive was quite clearly an over-generalization. In a sense the example of Britain tended to conflict with his theory of uneven development, which suggested that while Britain might be economically stagnating, Germany and Japan were economically dynamic. Indeed, the notion of the imperialist epoch as the final epoch of capitalism, and especially the First World War as symptomatic of its inevitable demise, proved faulty. It underestimated the continued resilience and dynamism of capitalism, its capacity to survive wars and slumps. Of course, whether the system can always continue to do so, remains an open question.

NOTES

1. Luxemburg had developed a revolutionary position on the possibility of an imperialist war a good deal earlier. See L. Basso, 'An analysis of classical theories of imperialism', *The Spokesman*, Winter (1974–5), 139. And in *The Accumulation of Capital* (1913) she saw the revolutionary implications of the capital accumulation process (see 466–7), but this work was more in the nature of an economic treatise than an overtly strategic-political text.
2. V. G. Kiernan, in T. Bottomore (Ed.), *A Dictionary of Marxist Thought*, Blackwell, Oxford (1983), 519.
3. See pages 34–5.
4. Kiernan, *op. cit.*, 519. On the other hand it has been suggested that Marx supposed that capitalists were innately bellicose: 'The international relations of capitalist countries are always the result of foreign policies in pursuit of criminal designs, playing upon national prejudices and squandering in piratical wars the peoples' blood and treasure.' Quoted by V. Kubalkova and A. Cruikshank, *Marxism and International Relations*, Oxford University Press, Oxford (1989), 34. However, this does not necessarily imply that capitalist powers would be warlike against each other, but rather against capitalistically underdeveloped countries.
5. F. Engels, *Anti-Dühring*, Progress Publishers, Moscow (1969), 204–5.
6. Quoted in V. I. Lenin, *Collected Works, Vol. 21*, Progress Publishers, Moscow, (1974), 95.
7. See M. Salvadori, *Karl Kautsky and the Socialist Revolution, 1880–1938*, New Left Books, London (1979), especially Chapter 5 *passim*.
8. Kautsky, 'Internationalism and the war' in J. Riddell (Ed.), *Lenin's Struggle for a Revolutionary International*, Monad Press, New York (1984), 149.
9. Published in English as 'Ultra-imperialism', *New Left Review*, 59 (1970), 41–6.
10. *Ibid.*, 41.
11. *Ibid.*, 46.
12. *Ibid.*, 46.
13. V. I. Lenin, *Imperialism, the Highest Stage of Capitalism*, Progress Publishers, Moscow (1966), 10 (hereafter *I*).
14. Quoted, Lenin, *I*, 43.
15. English translation, *Finance Capital* (T. Bottomore, Ed.), Routledge and Kegan Paul, London (1981).

16. N. Bukharin, *Imperialism and World Economy*, Merlin Press, London (1972), 118 (hereafter *IWE*).
17. *IWE*, 73–4.
18. *IWE*, Chapter 5 *passim*.
19. *IWE*, Chapter 6 *passim*.
20. *IWE*, Chapter 7 *passim*.
21. *IWE*, 109. See also 54, 86–7, 107, 125, 142–3.
22. *I*, 58. We can note here that Lenin should not be construed as an under-consumptionist. He explicitly rejected Hobson's underconsumptionism, which denied the 'inevitability of imperialism', *I*, 103.
23. *I*, 85; see also Bukharin, *IWE*, 121.
24. *I*, 86.
25. *I*, 66–7.
26. *IWE*, 136.
27. *IWE*, 137.
28. *IWE*, 138.
29. *IWE*, 141.
30. *IWE*, 142.
31. *I*, 110–11.
32. *I*, 88.
33. *I*, 89–91.
34. *I*, 91.
35. *I*, 91–2.
36. *I*, 72.
37. *I*, 92.
38. *I*, 93.
39. A. Brewer, *Marxist Theories of Imperialism: a Critical Survey*, Routledge, London (1990), 132.

5
Revolutionary Strategies

PROBLEMS AND ISSUES

The next three chapters are devoted to arguments surrounding the Russian Revolution and its aftermath. Patently, social, economic and political conditions in Russia corresponded neither to those considered conducive to proletarian revolution, as stipulated in the *Manifesto*, nor to those existing in Western Europe, the heartland of the Second International. Debate among Russian Marxists was therefore inevitable. This chapter will cover the key strategic issues, and the next will deal with the question of political organization.

That Russian Marxists prior to and during 1917 were constantly preoccupied with the problem of strategy was not surprising. There was no natural 'fit' between their 'scientific' socialist beliefs and the objective situation in Russia. According to the general principles underlying Marx's theory of history, outlined in the *Manifesto* and elsewhere, socialism was only possible in advanced capitalist countries, and Russia was not one of them.

The 'problem' of socialism in Russia had exercised Marx himself towards the end of his life. Departing from any over-simple theory of history he may have had, he suggested that Russia could take a unique road to socialism, which did not entail capitalist industrialization. Traditional peasant communes (or *obshchina*) could provide the bases of a socialist society, provided they were supported by successful proletarian revolutions in the West.[1]

However, the onset of capitalist industrialization from the 1880s enabled Marxists to adopt a more straightforward Marxist or 'European' position, followed by the Second International, and particularly by the German SPD: socialism could eventually come through proletarian revolution. Plekhanov, who became known as the 'father' of Russian Marxism, in order to apply the European scenario to Russian conditions, developed a two-stage scenario. Borrowing heavily from Marx's writings on

Germany in the 1848–50 period, he argued that although Russia was semi-feudal, the proletariat in the absence of a strong, revolutionary bourgeoisie could none the less carry out the latter's historical mission. The proletariat could be a 'hegemonic', or leading, force in a bourgeois revolution. It could establish a constitutional regime with political liberties. After an indeterminate length of time in which the economy would further develop and the proletariat could acquire greater political and administrative capacities to become a ruling class, a second socialist, genuinely proletarian, revolution would follow.[2]

This two-stage formula raised more questions before and during 1917 than it solved. How would the bourgeois and proletarian revolutions relate to one another? Was there not a contradiction between the bourgeois democratic form of the forthcoming revolution and the class interests of the leading social agency in that revolution, the proletariat? How much capitalist economic development after the bourgeois revolution was required before a proletarian revolution was a possibility? Should the Russian bourgeoisie be written off as a revolutionary force, in the same way that Marx had written off the German bourgeoisie after the 1848 revolutions? What were the revolutionary capacities and aspirations of the peasantry, which constituted the overwhelming bulk of the Russian population? Finally, given that Russia was a police state, to what extent could a revolutionary party model itself on European lines, in an open, democratic way?[3]

In answering these strategic questions Russian Marxists had to face a further problem that derived from a tension in Marx's own analysis of the revolutionary process itself, which required a delicate synthesis of 'objective' and 'subjective' elements, as alluded to in Chapter 1.[4] As we shall see, this tension between the 'objectivist' and 'subjectivist' perspectives was reflected in the strategic positions adopted by various groupings within the Russian Social Democratic Labour Party (RSDLP), founded in 1898. Three strands of opinion developed during the revolution of 1905, which Lenin later called the 'dress rehearsal' for the October Revolution in 1917: the Bolshevik (or 'majority') and Menshevik (or 'minority'), and the position of Trotsky. The terms Bolshevik and Menshevik were used after the RSDLP's second congress in 1903.

Following Russia's setbacks in her war with Japan (January 1904 to August 1905), there arose a groundswell of opinion demanding constitutional, democratic reform. This culminated in 'Bloody Sunday' on 9 January 1905, when over a hundred demonstrators were killed, which unleashed a rash of strikes throughout the Russian Empire. As a result of pressure from virtually all sections of the population, the Tsar in October 1905 promised an assembly (the State Duma) and full civil liberties, which divided the opposition. Unrest continued among significant sections of the proletariat (especially in St Petersburg, where a Soviet was created) and the peasantry, and among national minorities in the Baltic and Poland. By December, however, the Tsar had regained the initiative after he had suppressed the St Petersburg Soviet and crushed an uprising in Moscow. We can examine the Bolshevik, Menshevik and Trotsky positions in terms of what they thought was possible, and their respective assessments of the key social agents of change.

The Mensheviks

While the Mensheviks and the Bolsheviks agreed that only a bourgeois revolution was an immediate possibility, they differed about what type of bourgeois revolution was possible, and about the alliance of social forces that would bring it about. On the latter issue, the Mensheviks, led by Martov, believed that the proletariat should cooperate with the bourgeoisie in order to achieve reform. They abandoned Plekhanov's idea (as did Plekhanov himself!) of the hegemony of the proletariat in a democratic revolution, and maintained that important sections of the bourgeoisie were progressive.[5] They argued that, as in Europe, a new state middle class had evolved in Russia with progressive tendencies. Although landowners might be reactionary, this was not true of the urban industrial and commercial bourgeoisies. Thus, they wanted the bourgeoisie to make their own revolution, with assistance from the proletariat, which should play more of a supportive role than a leading one. Once the bourgeoisie was in power, the proletariat should then become the party of extreme opposition.[6] The Mensheviks also argued that the proletariat should not seek to cooperate with peasantry. In keeping with Marx's general lack of sympathy with the peasantry (although, as we have noted in Chapter 1 and in this chapter, he was not opposed in principle to worker–peasant alliances and had a favourable view of the Russian peasantry), they maintained that it was a conservative force: 'It was upon the peasants that oriental despotisms sustained themselves unchanged for thousands of years.'[7]

In response to the events of the winter of 1905, the Mensheviks at a conference held in April and May in the following year agreed in principle on the desirability of an armed uprising, but believed it to be impracticable. No effective workers' organization existed that could organize one, although it could occur spontaneously. In any case, the Mensheviks were wary of any workers' militancy that could drive the liberal bourgeoisie into the arms of reaction. The conference supported the idea of a provisional government or a constituent assembly, either of which would be the product of a successful armed uprising, or the result of the 'direct revolutionary pressure from the people'. Once the bourgeoisie was in power, the working class would become the 'party of extreme revolutionary opposition'.[8] Because they tended to adopt the more 'objectivist' view of the revolutionary process, believing that the forthcoming bourgeois revolution would lead to the further development of the productive forces, which would eventually create the preconditions for a workers' revolution, they tended to be a little indifferent about the 'superstructural' outcomes of that revolution. They did, however, accept that in the unlikely event of a workers' revolution in Western Europe being sparked off by a Russian revolution, the working class, led by the RSDLP, could seize power and pursue a maximum, socialist programme.

The Bolsheviks

Lenin's and the Bolsheviks' strategic differences with the Mensheviks were profound. They had sharply contrasting estimations of the revolutionary capabilities of the bourgeoisie and the peasantry. Lenin saw the liberal bourgeoisie as a timid bunch, far more likely to imitate their German counterparts of 1848 than their French forebears of 1789.[9] Their timidity was compounded, according to Lenin, by the fact that the Russian proletariat was relatively much larger than that existing in mid-nineteenth-century Germany. The bourgeoisie would therefore be far more inclined to side with the Tsar, and to rely on the existing army and bureaucracy to protect its interests against the working class. Moreover, because a substantial proportion of the liberal bourgeoisie were landowners, it would automatically oppose any proposals for thorough land reform. It would therefore be opposed to the interests of the poorer peasants, whom Lenin regarded as a vital force in the forthcoming democratic revolution, because they would see a radical, republican form of democracy as more likely to give them land.

The poorer peasantry was crucial to his wider strategy. He rejected the Mensheviks' virtual indifference to what form of democracy was preferable. He wanted to extend the boundaries of the democratic revolution as far as possible, in order to prepare the proletariat 'for the future complete victory'.[10] The less favourable result of a revolution would be a Prussian-style constitutional monarchy, which would be preferred by the bourgeoisie, because of its cowardice and opposition to the working class. Working-class rights would be restricted, thereby hindering the development of their political capacities, and, given such a regime's support from liberal landowners hostile to radical land reform, agricultural development would be retarded. Lenin instead wanted a democratic republic committed to the nationalization of land. Peasants could then devote their surplus resources to improving productive technique rather than paying off former landlords for the transfer of land. Thus, land nationalization would foster the rapid growth of efficient capitalist agriculture. This was important for two reasons. First, it would, in aiding the development of industry, generate a large proletariat, essential to a future socialist revolution. Second, it would create an agrarian proletariat, which would be a natural ally of the urban proletariat.[11] Thus, a democratic republic established by workers, in which the poorer peasants played a key part, was far more desirable than a constitutional monarchy. Moreover, Lenin felt that such a democratic form of revolution was far more likely to inspire revolutions in Europe.

Lenin advanced the slogan, 'the revolutionary democratic dictatorship of the proletariat and peasantry'. It entailed the organization of an armed uprising, led by the RSDLP and the formation of a provisional government, committed to a minimum programme: abolition of monarchy, establishment of basic democratic rights and civil liberties, nationalization of land and workplace reforms, such as the eight-hour day. He maintained that the organization of an armed uprising was vital. Without one the Tsar would have room for manoeuvre in granting reforms. Equally important, in line with a more 'subjectivist' view of revolution, such an uprising would also develop the revolutionary initiative of the proletariat in preparation for a subsequent socialist revolution. There was an 'indissoluble link' between the bourgeois and socialist revolutions.[12]

Trotsky

A distinctive position, which assumed enormous significance in 1917, was articulated by Trotsky – the theory of 'permanent revolution'. Put simply, the theory suggested that a revolution in Russia would be a continuous, uninterrupted one that would not stop at the bourgeois, democratic stage, as postulated by the Bolsheviks and Mensheviks. Rather, it would inevitably move into a maximalist, socialist phase under the dictatorship of the proletariat.

How did Trotsky arrive at this conclusion? It stemmed from his analysis of class forces in Russia and Europe. In *Results and Prospects* (1906), he rejected what he regarded as Marxist formalism and an over-reliance on historical analogies derived from the French Revolution of 1789: 'Marxism is above all a method of analysis – not an analysis of texts, but analysis of social relations.'[13] Hence, few parallels could be drawn between the respective histories and socio-economic structures of Russia and Europe. The Russian bourgeoisie was not the French bourgeoisie of 1789. It constituted a comparatively small proportion of the population. Although a significant amount of industrialization had occurred in Russia, the bourgeoisie had not grown commensurately. Economic development had been undertaken primarily by foreign capital in alliance with the state. The resultant large-scale factory system had helped to create a proportionately large working class. Between the proletariat and the autocracy 'stood a capitalist bourgeoisie, very small in numbers, isolated from the "people", half-foreign, without historical traditions, and inspired only by the greed of gain'.[14] Thus, in his estimation of the Russian bourgeoisie's revolutionary capacities Trotsky sided with Lenin against the Mensheviks. Yet in his assessment of the peasantry he stood closer to the Mensheviks. At best it could play only a supporting role in relation to the proletariat. Peasants were too 'unorganised, scattered, isolated from the towns ... stupid, limited in their horizons to the confines of their respective villages'.[15]

As for his analysis of the proletariat, he was even more optimistic about its revolutionary capacities than Lenin. In creating Soviets in the 1905 Revolution, it had demonstrated that it had replaced the bourgeoisie as the new, hegemonic, 'national' class. However, he did not believe, as did Lenin and the Mensheviks, that it would merely want to achieve the minimum programme of overthrowing the Tsar and the establishment of a democratic republic. Its political domination would be 'incompatible with its economic enslavement'.[16] It would inevitably pursue a maximal, socialist programme once it had overthrown the Tsar. Given that the peasantry was only interested in land ownership, the only way in which such a programme could be achieved was if the Russian working class could inspire through its actions a socialist revolution in Europe. Support from the European working class would enable it to combat the forces of reaction inside Russia.[17] Thus, Trotsky attempted to synthesize the 'subjectivist' and 'objectivist' views of revolution: the dynamics of class consciousness would take workers beyond a 'bourgeois' form towards a socialist one. The socialism option would become a possibility owing to changes in the 'objective' world situation, in which workers in the West would be transforming the capitalist mode of production into a socialist one.

Leading Mensheviks and Bolsheviks came close to Trotsky's position in the Autumn of 1905, as a result of the successful insurrectionary activities of the Russian proletariat.[18] However, after the failure of the Moscow rising in December 1905, largely organized by the Bolsheviks, the Mensheviks increasingly pinned their hopes on the liberal bourgeoisie to bring about political and social change.[19] Lenin reverted to his own two-stage theory.[20]

To compare and contrast the three revolutionary strategies in 1905: the Mensheviks advocated a two-stage revolution, first bourgeois, then proletarian, led by the bourgeoisie with the proletariat in support. They were indifferent to whether this bourgeois revolution took the form of a constitutional monarchy or a democratic republic. Lenin and the Bolsheviks also held to a two-stage theory, but differed from the Mensheviks, first, on the question of agency. The bourgeois revolution would have to be made by an alliance of the proletariat and peasantry. Second, they specifically demanded a democratic republic. Trotsky, on the other hand, rejected the stages theory of revolution, and wanted the implementation of a maximum, socialist programme. This could be achieved by the proletariat, supported by the peasantry and the European proletariat.

1917: THE TWO REVOLUTIONS

After a successful uprising by the Petrograd[21] military detachments and a population driven to desperation by the sacrifices imposed upon them by the war, the Tsar abdicated in early March 1917. A Provisional Government was established, headed by Prince Lvov, with the liberal Kadet (Constitutional Democrat) Party as the major influence. This government only took power after much coaxing by the re-emerged Petrograd Soviet, which was under the control of the Social Revolutionaries and Mensheviks. The Soviet was the real power, but according to the Menshevik (and at the time Bolshevik) two-stage theory of revolution, a bourgeois government had to come to power. Thus, in reality a dual power situation had arisen, with the Petrograd Soviet and Provisional Government sitting uneasily side by side.

Menshevik policy

The Menshevik policy had not changed from late 1905. There had to be a government by the bourgeoisie for the bourgeoisie. Accordingly, workers' militancy must not drive it into the arms of reaction. Yet at the same time the Soviets in Petrograd and elsewhere had to maintain their independence from the bourgeoisie, so that they could become an effective opposition once the bourgeoisie had come to power.[22] The Mensheviks were thus prepared to support the Provisional Government, provided it played its historical part in demolishing the old semi-feudal order, entailing, as a first step, the convening of a Constituent Assembly.

Of crucial significance for future events, the Mensheviks agreed with the Kadets that Russia's participation in the First World War must continue, and that no separate peace should be made with the Central Powers. They justified this policy of 'revolutionary defencism' on the grounds that now that the Tsar had been overthrown, Russia was a progressive state, and could not let down the democracies of France and Britain by coming to terms with the autocracies of Germany and Austria-Hungary. Simultaneously, the Mensheviks called for a universal 'democratic peace' without annexations and indemnities. They hoped to make this policy effective by persuading socialist parties in the belligerent states to put pressure on their respective governments, and by using official government channels to get Russia's allies to seek peace.

Support for the war had a vital implication for domestic policy. Reforms had to be put into abeyance until this 'democratic peace' had been achieved. Until then maximum unity between classes had to be maintained in order to sustain the war effort. Peasant or working-class militancy had to be suppressed, contained or restrained. The Mensheviks opposed workers seizing the factories. To end the economic chaos created by the war, they proposed the state regulation of industry, rather than the transfer of property ownership. Similarly, they opposed peasant seizure of land. Instead, it should be redistributed in an orderly fashion, according to principles decided upon by a Constituent Assembly.

The Mensheviks were strongly committed to these policies, and when the Kadet ministers resigned in July 1917, as a result of the failure of Kerensky's war offensive, leading moderate members joined the Provisional Government. But Menshevik policies became increasingly unpopular. Support for the Bolsheviks grew rapidly in the summer of 1917. Their policies were encapsulated in the slogans of 'Bread, Peace and Land', and later 'All Power to the Soviets'. After the Bolsheviks had played a key role in organizing Petrograd resistance to General Kornilov's attempted coup in August 1917, their support was such that especially in urban centres they were in a position to take power.

Lenin and the Bolsheviks

Until Lenin's arrival in April 1917 at the Finland Station in Petrograd, via Germany in a sealed train, the Bolsheviks in Russia had broadly supported the Menshevik policy of continuing the war and accepting the dual power situation. His arrival changed all this. He told a crowd gathered at the Finland Station, preoccupied with Russia's domestic concerns: 'The Russian revolution made by you has prepared the way and opened a new epoch. Long live the world-wide socialist revolution!'[23] Later that day, to everyone's astonishment, he rejected his previous two-stage formula, and declared: 'We don't need a parliamentary republic, we don't need bourgeois democracy, we don't need any government except the Soviets of Workers, Soldiers and Farm-Labourers Deputies.'[24]

Mensheviks and Bolsheviks were shocked. They called him a 'madman' a 'Blanquist' and an 'anarchist'. They believed, in common with Lenin's earlier position, that in the present situation it was impossible to go further than creating a bourgeois revolution. And because the forces of production had to be further developed, a socialist revolution could only occur at some time in the future. They saw the Soviets as a pressure group upon the Provisional Government to ensure that it did not go over to the side of reaction, and that it completed the bourgeois revolution.

Why Lenin's volte-face?

Lenin's volte-face was not a snap decision. As early as 1915, he argued from his analysis of the world war and imperialism that the world was objectively ripe for socialism. The crisis of capitalism was at hand, as indicated in Chapter 4: 'The epoch of capitalist imperialism is one of ripe and rotten capitalism, which is about to collapse, and which is mature enough to make way for socialism.'[25] In March 1917, he believed that the Russian proletariat could play a vital catalytic role in this development. In the *Farewell Letter to Swiss Workers*, he stated: 'To the Russian proletariat has fallen the great honour of *initiating* the series of revolutions which are arising from the imperialist war with objective inevitability.'[26] He had in effect adopted Trotsky's thesis of permanent revolution.

Conditions inside Russia were ripening to enable the Russian working class to carry out this role. In his famous *April Theses* he argued:

> The specific feature of the present situation in Russia is that the country is *passing* from the first stage of the revolution – which owing to the insufficient class consciousness and organization of the proletariat placed power in the hands of the bourgeoisie – to its *second* stage, which must place power in the hands of the proletariat and the poorest sections of the peasants.[27]

Accordingly, he called upon the Soviets to stop playing second fiddle to the bourgeois Provisional Government, which entailed continuing support for the war. Such a government, he argued, could not bring about a 'democratic peace', because it was a capitalist government. Imperialism and war were part and parcel of the capitalist system. Thus, the government could not but participate in the imperialist war. The conflict was not between progressive and reactionary government, as proposed by the Mensheviks. The Provisional Government had secret annexationist aspirations and was supported by British and French financiers. Only a proletarian and peasant government with true internationalist aspirations could bring about a real peace, by encouraging foreign workers to turn the imperialist war into a civil war. A policy of revolutionary defencism should be replaced by one of revolutionary defeatism.[28]

On the domestic front, such a government was vital in satisfying the needs and aspirations of Russia's masses. The Provisional Government was in reality pro-Tsar. It was doing little to reform the state or land ownership and it delayed the convening of a Constituent Assembly. Only if the Soviets took power could these demands be met and the immediate problems of famine and economic dislocation be solved. The purpose of Soviet power was therefore to make the bourgeois revolution more thorough.

Hence, Lenin repeatedly stressed that the policies he recommended were not socialist in themselves. 'It is not our *immediate* task to "introduce" socialism, but only to bring social production and distribution of products at once under the *control* of the Soviets of Workers' Deputies.'[29] Measures nationalizing land, banks and capitalist syndicates 'do not in any way constitute the "introduction" of socialism.... Without such measures, which are only a step towards socialism and which are perfectly feasible economically, it will be impossible to heal the wounds caused by the war and to avert impending collapse.'[30] Russia was far too economically backward for the introduction of socialism. Nevertheless, if the Russian revolution ignited socialist revolutions in Europe, then Russian workers could be assisted in bringing about socialism in Russia.[31]

One final but important point can be made about Lenin's rationale for the Soviet seizure of power: the idea that Soviets could be a vehicle for socialism, rather than a bourgeois parliament, was something rather novel for Bolsheviks and Mensheviks alike. Lenin saw them less as pressure groups and more as embryonic institutions of workers' and peasants' self-government; that is, as congruent with what he held to be the Marxist theory of the dictatorship of the proletariat.[32]

COMMENTARY

Both Lenin's and the Mensheviks' positions had their strengths and weaknesses. Both could be labelled 'utopian' and 'realistic'. The argument between them highlighted the tension within Marx's own theory of revolution, which attempted to marry subjective and objective factors through a theory of praxis.

The Mensheviks were certainly hidebound by doctrinal rigidity. Owing to their 'objectivist' Marxism, they were unable to comprehend fully the dynamics of the revolutionary process in 1917. They wanted the bourgeoisie to carry out a progressive role. In the context of Russia in 1917, this entailed supporting the war effort and the containment of social change, in order not to drive the bourgeoisie into the camp of reaction. Their strict adherence to an abstract historical schema, and their 'orthodox' Marxist attitude towards the peasantry, prevented them from developing policies in line with working-class aspirations, and led them to underestimate the revolutionary importance of the peasantry. Thus, they could not keep abreast of events, especially once the Tsar had been toppled. Moreover, they did not fully face up to the implication of the proletariat playing a key role in a bourgeois revolution as Trotsky had done, namely that it would want to transcend the bourgeois framework.

Lenin, by contrast, while he was equally committed to Marxist theory, was far more flexible in applying it, taking into account changes in both the domestic and international scenes and trying to combine the 'objectivist' and 'subjectivist' sides of Marxism. As a result of the First World War and his study of imperialism, his analytical starting point became the world context and the possibility of world socialism. He viewed Russian events within this framework, while the Mensheviks remained locked within a domestic perspective and the belief that the revolution could not transcend the bourgeois stage. Lenin, however, from his analysis of the international situation and the revolutionary process in Russia, where the hegemonic capacities of the proletariat were clearly evident and the revolutionary potential of the peasantry was revealed, drew a different conclusion. Given the failure of the Provisional Government to implement radical social change in line with the wishes of the majority of the Russian population, a

Soviet government committed to the policies of bread, peace and land could make the bourgeois revolution more thorough, yet at the same time lay the basis for a socialist state, in a double sense: first, through the increased state control of the economy; second, by inspiring workers' revolutions in the West, which would then enable the Russian proletariat to move to a socialist stage. Thus, Lenin, via a less schematic route, came to Trotsky's conclusion: the need for permanent revolution, in which the distinction between the bourgeois and socialist phases became blurred by the dynamics of the revolutionary process.

Lenin's emphasis on concrete analysis, as opposed to the formalistic, abstract stages schema of the Mensheviks, underlined his greater realism in another way. Consistent with his more 'subjectivist' Marxism, it allowed greater room for political leadership. The Marxist party did not have to 'tail' the masses, or the bourgeoisie, waiting upon events, waiting for 'history' to flow along its predestined course. Rather, Lenin saw the party as a major creative factor in 'making' events: after February 1917 the revolution had not run its full course and, with the correct leadership, the party could radicalize the revolution for the benefit of the proletariat and peasantry, and move Russia along a transitional path between capitalism and socialism.

Yet if Lenin proved to be more realistic in his understanding of the events of 1917, arguably in the light of hindsight the Mensheviks were more realistic in their estimation of the revolution's outcome. Trotsky said in 1917: 'Were Russia to stand all on her own in the world, then Martov's reasoning [that Russia was not ripe for socialism] was correct.'[33] And for many years after 1917, for whatever reason, Russia was indeed 'all on her own in the world'. With the failure of the Russian revolution to spread to the rest of the world, 'objective' factors within the world capitalist environment put a stop to the socialist aspirations of the Bolsheviks and sections of the Soviet working class. The fragile balance between the 'objective' and 'subjective' elements in Lenin's theory of the Russian Revolution was further disturbed by the effects of civil war and famine on workers' revolutionary consciousness and self-organizational capacities. The consequences of these events for the Soviet regime are considered in Chapter 10.

NOTES

1. *CM*, 45. See also T. Shanin (Ed.), *Late Marx and the Russian Road*, Routledge and Kegan Paul, London (1984); E. Kingston-Mann, *Lenin and the Problem of Marxist Peasant Revolution*, Oxford University Press, New York (1985), 30–1.
2. See 'Manifesto of the Russian Social-Democratic Labour Party' (1898), drafted by Plekhanov, in G. Zinoviev, *History of the Bolshevik Party*, New Park Publications, London (1973), 201–3.

3. This question will be discussed in the next chapter.
4. See page 12.
5. N. Harding (Ed.), *Marxism in Russia*, Cambridge University Press, Cambridge (1983), 35-6.
6. *Ibid.*, 35; E. H. Carr, *The Bolshevik Revolution, Vol. 1*, Penguin, Harmondsworth (1966), 51.
7. Quoted T. Cliff, *Lenin, Vol. 1*, Pluto Press, London (1975), 220.
8. A. Ascher, *Pavel Axelrod and the Development of Menshevism*, Harvard University Press, Cambridge, MA (1972), 58.
9. See Cliff, *op. cit.*, 143.
10. Lenin, 'Two tactics of social democracy in the democratic revolution', *Selected Works*, Lawrence and Wishart, London (1969), 78.
11. N. Harding, *Lenin's Political Thought, Vol. 1*, Macmillan, London (1977), 215-18.
12. Carr, *op. cit.*, 26.
13. Trotsky, *The Permanent Revolution* and *Results and Prospects*, New Park Publications, London (1962), 196 (hereafter *PRRP*).
14. *PRRP*, 138.
15. *PRRP*, 188-9.
16. *PRRP*, 233.
17. *PRRP*, 246-7.
18. See, for example, Lenin, *Collected Works, Vol. 9*, Progress Publishers, Moscow (1961), 237.
19. T. Shanin, *Russia, 1905-07: Revolution as a Moment of Truth*, Macmillan, Basingstoke (1986), 219.
20. M. Leibman, *Leninism under Lenin*, Merlin Press, London (1975), 81.
21. The name St Petersburg was changed during the First World War, as it was considered too Germanic.
22. See T. Cliff, *Lenin, Vol. 2*, Pluto Press, London (1976), 87-8.
23. *Ibid.*, 120.
24. *Ibid.*, 121.
25. Quoted in N. Harding, *Lenin's Political Thought, Vol. 2*, Macmillan, London (1981), 39-40.
26. Little Lenin Library, Vol. 8 (n.d.), 45.
27. Foreign Languages Printing House, Moscow (1970), 6.
28. See B. Pearce, 'Lenin and Trotsky on pacifism and defeatism', *Labour Review*, 6 (1961), 29-40.
29. *Ibid.*, 8.
30. Little Lenin Library, Vol. 8, 46.
31. Leibman, *op. cit.*, 181.
32. See *The State and Revolution*, in V. I. Lenin, *Selected Works*, Lawrence and Wishart, London (1969).
33. Quoted in I. Getzler, *Martov*, Cambridge University Press, Cambridge (1967), 220.

6
The Revolutionary Party, 1903–1904

PROBLEMS AND ISSUES

Few participants in the debates within the RSDLP over party organization would have assumed that they were involved in an historical event. Much heat was generated, but most of it was owing to Lenin's 'hard' attitude towards comrades who were legendary figures in the Russian revolutionary movement. By 1905, the fiercely contested organizational questions of the 1903–4 period had lost their intensity. The Mensheviks agreed with Lenin's proposals on party membership, and Lenin concurred with the Mensheviks on the need for a broad democratic party.[1] Moreover, after 1905, fundamental divisions between the Mensheviks and Bolsheviks moved more into the domain of strategy. The October Revolution of 1917, however, lent the 1903–4 debates fresh significance. Critics of the revolution and its outcome saw Lenin's 'Jacobinism' first manifested in this period, as well as the seeds of Stalin's one-party rule.

The difficulties faced by Russian Marxists in party-building stemmed from two things. First, political and economic conditions in Russia were not conducive to constructing a broad democratic party along Western, especially German, lines. Second, Marx's writings on the party could only go part of the way to getting to grips with the problem.

Marx, although in some respects vague in his conception of the party, nevertheless established some clear principles about its structure and function. It was a vital weapon of proletarian self-emancipation: the 'constitution of the proletariat into a political party is indispensable to ensure the triumph of the social revolution and of its ultimate goal: the abolition of classes'.[2] It had to overthrow the political power of the bourgeoisie. Second, Marx saw the party as the independent creation of the proletariat itself, whose structure and function had to be grounded upon the idea of self-emancipation. Thus, consistent with this notion, the party had to be broad and democratic. Otherwise it was in danger of becoming an isolated sect. Third, as indicated in Chapter 1, in enabling the working class to become aware of its collective self-interest, and consistent with the self-emancipatory principle, the party should not shape the movement according to sectarian principles. Rather, the party merely had to render explicit to the working class what was immanent in the historical process, namely that the logic of capitalism and their struggles against it would culminate in the classless society of communism.[3]

Although Marx had firm principles as to how a party should function, he and Engels never created their own party, again in accord with the idea of proletarian self-emancipation. They joined existing parties, and were certainly not permanently wedded to any party as a matter of principle. Indeed, Marx seemed to think that any political party could not be of an enduring nature: 'Any political party, whatever its nature and without exception, can only hold the enthusiasm of the masses for a short time, momentarily.'[4] Marx's own political activities preceded the establishment of modern political parties, i.e. relatively stable, bureaucratic, vote-gathering organizations. Perhaps this lack of institutional fixity as well as his direct or indirect involvement in various parties led him to entertain numerous definitions of the term 'party', ranging from a group of his followers to the historical movement of the working class.[5]

Political, economic and social conditions of late nineteenth and early twentieth centuries could hardly have been more inauspicious for Russian Marxists attempting to replicate Marx's theory and practice of party-building or to copy the mass democratic German SPD model. The working class, both politically and economically, was organizationally undeveloped. Thus, Marxist intellectuals could not do what Marx had done: join an existing proletarian political organization. Instead, one had to be created. The question then became how these intellectuals were going to build a Marxist party that would be genuinely part of, and represent the vanguard of, the working class. Second, there was the problem of how the scattered circles of Marxist intellectuals were going to become a cohesive and durable body in the face of severe police repression. In this period the average life of such a circle was about five months. Indeed, soon after the founding conference of the RSDLP in 1898 most of the leadership were arrested. In these circumstances and in the absence of democratic rights there was no way in which the RSDLP could immediately become a mass electoral organization, like the German SPD. Finally, the question of what type of party depended upon what sort of strategy was implicitly or explicitly envisaged: namely, what role would the proletariat have in the forthcoming bourgeois revolution? Clearly, if it was to have a leading, 'hegemonic', role, then it had to be a well-organized party, prepared for armed combat, as Lenin envisaged. On the other hand, such organizational imperatives would not arise if the bourgeoisie was to lead its own revolution, with the proletariat playing an independent but supportive role, which became the Menshevik strategy after 1905.

THE SECOND CONGRESS OF THE RSDLP AND AFTER

The second congress of the RSDLP, attended by 60 delegates representing 26 different organizations in Russia, took place in late July 1903, starting in Brussels and finishing in London. The object of the congress was to unite these organizations into a single party. Although Lenin's demand that the veteran revolutionaries – Axelrod, Zasulich and Potresov – be removed from the editorial board of *Iskra* caused the most rancour, the more significant division during and after the congress was to do with what shape the party should take: should it be a close-knit, highly organized one, or should it be broader and looser? More specifically, the issues, which were interrelated, boiled down to the definition of membership and the degree of centralization.

Lenin

In essence, Lenin's objective was to build a strong, stable, proletarian combat party that could effectively resist police repression, challenge the Tsarist state and assert the 'hegemony of the proletariat' in the forthcoming revolution. This could only be achieved if the party had a certain type of function and structure. If the working class was to become a hegemonic class it would have to be highly politicized. Workers could not achieve this level of awareness spontaneously through economic struggles: 'Class political consciousness can be brought to the workers *only from without*, that is, only outside the sphere of relations between workers and employers.'[6] He was in effect separating the 'thinking' from the 'doing'. Yet, although later critics were to make much of this statement, seeing in it the origins of Stalinism, Lenin's opponents at the time were more vexed by what he had to say about the implications of this proposition for party organization. He suggested that if it was going to undertake this politicizing role, it should be highly centralized, with a clearly circumscribed membership. During and after the congress Lenin was in effect spelling out the implications already developed in his pamphlet, *What Is to Be Done?*, which at the time was seen as a relatively non-controversial document, a reaffirmation of old guard orthodoxy against the Economists, who maintained that the working class was politically immature and that the political fight against the Tsar should be left to the middle classes.[7] In order for the proletariat to undertake its 'hegemonic' task, which included 'carrying out [a] nation-wide armed uprising',[8] he called for a party of 'professional revolutionaries' which (a) could generalize the 'exposures' of the oppression of the population by the Tsarist autocracy,[9] (b) would not lag behind the spontaneous upsurges of the masses,[10] and (c) would avoid being picked up by the secret police.[11] The party's immediate activity should be centred on the establishing of a newspaper, which would act as a 'collective organizer'.

Not surprisingly, at the congress Lenin was keen to emphasize commitment to the party. He wanted to restrict membership to those who accepted 'the party's programme' and supported it 'by material means and by personal participation in one of the Party's organisations'. Although it seemed like hair-splitting, Martov (1873–1923), leader of what became the Menshevik wing of the RSDLP, offered what they believed to be an alternative, broader formulation of membership: a member was one who accepted the party's programme and 'supports it by material means and by regular personal assistance under the direction of one of the party organisations'.[12] He wanted membership to be sufficiently wide to include those who could help the party, but were not in a position to join an illegal organization, such as those under police surveillance, older workers, those with families or intellectuals in sympathy with the party. Lenin's motion was defeated by 28 votes to 22.

What became clear after the Congress was that Lenin in his own mind linked the issue of membership with that of centralization. In January 1904, he published *A Letter to a Comrade on Our Organisational Tasks*. He maintained that in the existing circumstances the party had to be organized on extremely hierarchical principles: the central committee should have enormous powers in directing lower committees, which in turn controlled the disposition of individual members.[13] In this way the amateurish 'circle spirit' could be eliminated through tight central control. This would, Lenin hoped, apart from protecting it from the secret police, change the social composition of the party. It would become less attractive to bourgeois intellectuals, and more attractive to workers: '*In words*, Martov's formulation defends the interests of a broad strata of the proletariat, but *in fact* it serves the interests of the *bourgeois intellectuals* who fight shy of proletarian discipline and organization.'[14] The intelligentsia were characterized '*by and large precisely by individualism* and incapacity for discipline and organization'.[15] A tightly disciplined party would appeal to workers, who appreciated the value of discipline as a result of factory life.

Mensheviks, Trotsky and Luxemburg

The criticisms of Lenin's position from the Mensheviks, Trotsky and Luxemburg all had one thing in common: they all underlined, following Marx, the importance of the principle of proletarian self-emancipation. For Axelrod, the RSDLP as currently constituted was merely 'an organisation of partisans of the proletariat among the revolutionary intelligentsia'.[16] Lenin's organizational scheme would subordinate workers 'to the leadership of the radical intelligentsia'.[17] Axelrod, along with Martov, argued, in contrast to Lenin, that the only way such an intelligentsia could implant itself in the working class was if the party had looser membership rules and a looser form of centralism that would encourage workers' self-activity.[18]

Similarly, Luxemburg in *Organisational Questions of the Russian Social Democracy* (1904) and Trotsky in *Our Political Tasks* (1904) stressed, in contrast to Lenin, the principle of working-class self-activity. They both argued that he hermetically sealed the party from the working class, the 'thinking', directing element from the 'doing' element. This rigid separation between vanguard and class eliminated the interplay between both, which was necessary for proletarian self-emancipation. For Luxemburg the working class could only emancipate itself by learning from its own mistakes: 'Historically, the errors committed by a truly revolutionary movement are infinitely more fruitful than the infallibility of the cleverest central committee.'[19] Moreover, in the light of her experience of the German SPD, she held that too much influence held by a central committee could become a conservative force, dampening the tactical creativity of the working class.[20]

In the same vein, Trotsky saw Lenin's conception of the party as one in which it 'thinks for the proletariat'. And, adding a new word to the rich Marxist lexicon, he asserted that Lenin's proposals were 'substitutionist': 'In the internal politics of the Party these [substitutionist] methods lead ... to the Party organisation "substituting" itself for the Party organisation, and finally the dictator substituting himself for the Central Committee.'[21]

Both Luxemburg and Trotsky rejected Lenin's argument that intellectuals ought to be subject to tight discipline. They viewed intellectuals from a historical angle and concluded for different reasons that Russian intellectuals were far more inclined to discipline and centralism than their West European counterparts, where a more developed social democracy created the conditions for opportunism.[22] Luxemburg felt that because the proletarian movement was only in a nascent phase in Russia, there was plenty of room for experimentation. Opportunism was 'to a large extent a by-product and experimentation of socialist activity seeking to advance over a terrain that resembles no other in Europe'.[23] Finally, Trotsky challenged Lenin's favourable contrasting of the discipline workers gained in factories with the individualism of petty bourgeois intellectuals. Factory and 'political revolutionary discipline' were different. Indeed, the party's task was to rouse the proletariat against factory discipline, which 'replaces the work of human thought with the rhythm of physical movements', and to unite it 'against this brutalising mortal discipline in a single army linked to hand and shoulder by community of political consciousness and revolutionary enthusiasm. Such discipline does not yet exist in the Russian proletariat; factory and machine give it this quality much less spontaneously than union disputes or conflicts.'[24]

1905 AND AFTER

Lenin's reaction to the events of 1905 underlined just how flexible his attitude was towards the structure and function of the party, although he never wavered in his belief in the need for a strong, combat party that could take on the might of the Tsarist state and enable the proletariat to exercise its 'hegemony'.[25] His views between 1905 and 1907, when the period of reaction fully set in, were much more in line with Marx's own position and therefore far closer to those of his opponents. He recognized that he had 'bent the stick' in 1903 in his arguments with the Economists.[26] As a result of the major role that the working class played in the 1905 revolution, he stressed to a greater extent the self-emancipatory principle: 'the elementary instinct of the working class movement is able to correct the conceptions of the greatest minds'.[27] 'Undoubtedly, the revolution will teach us, and will teach the masses of the people. But the question that now confronts a militant political party is: shall we be able to teach the revolution anything?'[28] 'In the course of the fight, events themselves will suggest to the working masses the right tactics to adopt.'[29] 'The working class is instinctively, spontaneously social-democratic.'[30]

His faith in working-class self-activity led him to change his mind on the question of membership, with virtually open recruitment. He wanted young workers to swamp out the intellectuals or the 'committeemen', as he called them. 'Enlarge the committee threefold by accepting young people into it, set up half a dozen or a dozen sub-committees, "co-opt" any and every honest and energetic person. Allow every sub-committee to write and publish leaflets without any red tape.... Do not fear their lack of training.'[31]

On the question of centralism, the 'days of freedom' that followed in the wake of the October Revolution of 1905, Lenin was in full agreement with Menshevik proposals for a democratic centralist organization at the re-unification congress of 1906 held in Stockholm. Democratic centralism was understood by both sides to mean full freedom of discussion about policy, but maximum unity of action in implementing policy. Soon after the congress, Lenin stated that work still had to be done 'to apply the principles of democratic centralism in Party organisation, to work tirelessly to make the local organisations the principal organisational units of the Party in fact and not merely in name, and to see to it that all the high standing bodies are elected, accountable and subject to recall'.[32]

However, with the onset of reaction during and after 1907, Lenin put up the shutters. He reverted to his earlier, highly centralist position, underlining the importance of a powerful underground organization. He accused the Mensheviks of 'liquidationism', because although they were in principle in favour of secret activity, they recommended that every opportunity be used to exploit legal methods, especially the press and trade unions. The struggle on this organizational issue culminated in the irrevocable split between the Bolsheviks and Mensheviks in January 1912.

COMMENTARY

A number of difficulties arise in assessing the strengths and weaknesses of the Bolshevik and Menshevik conceptions of the party. As already noted, Lenin in some respects had a pragmatic attitude towards the organization and membership of the party. He could in effect agree with his critics on the question of membership and centralism in certain circumstances. Thus, particularly on the issue of the relationship between Lenin and Stalin, we have to bear in mind *which* of Lenin's conceptions of the party is under consideration.

A second difficulty is that if we assess their competing ideas about the party in terms of success, as, for example, measured by the degree of party implantation in the working class, we still do not know whether to attribute this to party organization or to party strategy. Hence, while the Bolsheviks in 1905 had a more proletarian membership than the Mensheviks, in the 1912–14 period had a more proletarian periphery[33] and in October 1917 had the mass backing of the proletariat, this could just as easily be attributable to party strategy as to party organization.[34]

If the criterion of success is invoked it has to be measured against the strategic goals they set themselves. The Mensheviks, according to their own lights, were successful in the February Revolution of 1917, in the sense that they played an important role in toppling the Tsar. They had achieved what they wanted: a bourgeois revolution. The Bolsheviks, according to their strategic goals, after Lenin's arrival in Russia in 1917 saw the need for a further revolution. Certainly, the Bolsheviks' estimation of the workers' and peasants' desire for change was more accurate than the Mensheviks'. And in the Bolshevik Party, Lenin had built an instrument that could harness these discontents for another successful revolution.

Not only did the Mensheviks not have much enthusiasm for another revolution, their stages theory and more 'European' approach meant that they put far less emphasis on leadership and tight organization. After the 1905 revolution they hoped that the bourgeoisie would make its own revolution, and that a 'European' situation would prevail, where civil and democratic rights would enable them to create a mass democratic parliamentary party in opposition to the bourgeoisie. Only at this stage would the question of leadership assume real importance. Lenin, on the other hand, adopted a far more 'Russian' approach, paying far greater attention to the specific political, social and economic conditions prevailing in Russia. The problem of stable organization in the face of police repression had to be addressed, and so too did the fact that the bourgeoisie was unlikely to lead a successful revolution. In these circumstances discipline and leadership were at a premium. Without these qualities the party would not survive, let alone organize a successful revolution.

Does Lenin's flexible view of the party absolve him from all charges of 'substitutionism'? To cite *What Is to Be Done?* as proof is to neglect his later express reservations about applying its formulations to other circumstances. Moreover, such citation fails to take into account how the events of 1905 wrought crucial changes in his thinking about party and class. And it could be argued that his *The State and Revolution* is one of the great celebrations of workers' self-activity.[35]

Nevertheless, the 'substitutionist' doubt remains: at the second congress of the Communist International in July 1920, he argued that a substantial coincidence between the dictatorship of the proletariat and that of the party existed because in the capitalist epoch only a minority of workers could attain class consciousness.[36] In 1921, against the Workers' Opposition he claimed that 'the dictatorship of the proletariat is impossible except through the Communist Party'.[37] In the same year he also went against the grain of the self-emancipatory principle when he stated: 'Even when the proletariat has to live through a period of being declassed, it can still carry out its task of conquering and retaining power.'[38] A virtue out of a necessity? Quite possibly. Yet he was speaking after the historical circumstances in Russia, of economic devastation, political and military encirclement, had blown the revolution way off course. This merely highlights a tension in Marx's original position, which assumed a neat fit between his understanding of capitalism and its future evolution on the one hand and workers' spontaneous self-activity on the other, the compatibility between knowledge and spontaneity. Marxists could be seen as non-impositional because they understood the 'line of march', merely making what was implicit in the class struggle explicit. A difficulty arises if 'history' is 'marching' in a different direction, breaking the tie between those who know the 'real' long-term interests of the working class and the working class's own definition of its interests, which may be very short term indeed. The temptation for Lenin to become a 'substitutionist' in order to protect the beleaguered Soviet beach-head of socialism became overwhelming.

NOTES

1. N. Harding (Ed.), *Marxism in Russia*, Cambridge University Press, Cambridge (1983), 32.
2. Quoted in D. McLellan, *Introduction to the Thought of Karl Marx*, 2nd edn, Macmillan, London (1980), 202.
3. See page 8.
4. McLellan, *op. cit.*, 201.
5. *Ibid.*, 196; M. Johnstone, 'Marx and Engels and the concept of the party' in R. Miliband and J. Saville (Eds), *Socialist Register, 1967*, Merlin Press, London, 122.

6. V. I. Lenin, *What Is to Be Done?* (hereafter *WITBD*), Progress Publishers, Moscow (1969), 78–9. Lenin's emphasis.
7. N. Harding, *Lenin's Political Thought, Vol. 1*, Macmillan, London (1977), Chapter 7 *passim*.
8. *WITBD*, 172.
9. *WITBD*, 89.
10. *WITBD*, 95–6.
11. *WITBD*, 11.
12. Harding, *Lenin's Political Thought*, 190.
13. See M. Leibman, *Leninism under Lenin*, Merlin Press, London (1975), 39.
14. V. I. Lenin, 'One step forwards, two steps back', *Collected Works, Vol. 7*, Progress Publishers, Moscow (1965) 267.
15. *Ibid.*, emphasis added.
16. Quoted in S. M. Schwartz, *The Russian Revolution of 1905*, University of Chicago Press, Chicago (1967), 209.
17. Quoted in *ibid.*, 210.
18. *Ibid.*, 205–6.
19. R. Luxemburg, *The Russian Revolution and Leninism or Marxism?* University of Michigan Press, Ann Arbor, MI (1961), 108. 'Leninism or Marxism?' was not the original title of 'Organisational questions … '.
20. *Ibid.*, 102.
21. L. Trotsky, *Our Political Tasks*, New Park Publications, London (n.d.), 77. See also T. Cliff, 'Trotsky on substitutionism' in *International Socialism*, 2 (1960); N. Geras, 'Lenin, Trotsky and the Party' in *The Literature of Revolution*, Verso, London (1986).
22. Luxemburg, *op. cit.*, 106; Trotsky, *op. cit.*, 107.
23. Luxemburg, *op. cit.*, 106.
24. Trotsky, *op. cit.*, 103–4; see also Luxemburg, *op. cit.*, 90.
25. A pragmatism underlined by the fact that he was reluctant to have *What Is to Be Done?* reprinted in foreign languages after the Revolution unless an introduction was written to demonstrate that the pamphlet arose out of a specific context and that its ideas were not directly and universally applicable in other contexts. See T. Cliff, *Rosa Luxemburg*, Socialist Review Publishing, London (1968), 48; see also Harding, *Lenin's Political Thought*, 161; L. Menashe, 'Vladimir Illych Bakunin: an essay on Lenin', *Socialist Revolution*, 18 (1973), 31.
26. T. Cliff, *Lenin, Vol. 1*, Pluto Press, London (1975), 67.
27. Quoted in J. Molyneux, *Marxism and the Party*, Pluto Press, London (1978), 59.
28. *Ibid.*, 60.
29. Quoted in Harding, *Lenin's Political Thought*, 234.
30. Quoted in Molyneux, *op. cit.*, 59.
31. Quoted in Cliff, *Lenin, Vol. 1*, 172.
32. Quoted in Leibman, *op. cit.*, 51.
33. D. Lane, *The Roots of Russian Communism*, Van Gorcum, Assen (1969), 50.
34. E. Acton, *Rethinking the Russian Revolution*, Edward Arnold, London (1990), 158.

35. For a contrary view, see A. J. Polan, *Lenin and the End of Politics*, Methuen, London (1984).
36. A. Carlo, 'Lenin and the Party', *Telos*, 17, Fall (1973), 36.
37. Quoted in R. Miliband, 'Lenin's The State and Revolution' in R. Miliband and J. Saville (Eds), *Socialist Register, 1970*, Merlin Press, London, 312.
38. Quoted in T. Cliff, 'Trotsky on substitutionism'.

7
Soviet or Parliamentary Democracy? Lenin versus Kautsky

PROBLEMS AND ISSUES

The debate between Lenin and Kautsky over the significance and meaning of Soviet (or council) and parliamentary democracy has, among Marxists, reverberated to this day, especially between Trotskyists and members of former Communist Parties in the West. It raised fundamental questions about what strategy workers ought to adopt and what form their rule ought to take. Historically, the debate epitomized the differences between Second and Third International Marxism, between an essentially evolutionary and pacific Marxism happy to work within the confines of the bourgeois, parliamentary state, and a revolutionary Marxism aimed at its violent dismemberment and its replacement by a more direct form of democracy. However, the concept of 'dictatorship of the proletariat' became corrupted under Stalin, identified with dictatorship of the Party. Indeed, it led major Western European Communist Parties in the 1980s, wishing to distance themselves from Stalinism, to drop the term from their political programmes. Equally significant, the Kautsky–Lenin debate raised a specific question: was the Bolshevik Revolution a truly Marxist one? Kautsky's evaluation of the Bolsheviks in *The Dictatorship of the Proletariat* (1918) was, along with Rosa Luxemburg's *The Russian Revolution*, one of the earliest Marxist critiques of the October Revolution.

Kautsky penned his famous critique of the October Revolution in early August 1918, before what he believed to be imminent German and Austrian revolutions. He wanted to prevent these uprisings from coming under communist influence.[1] He was writing in the wake of the Bolsheviks' exclusion of rival parties, such as the Left and Right Social Revolutionaries and the Mensheviks, from the Soviets, their restrictions on suffrage and the press and their disbanding of the Constituent Assembly in January 1918. Lenin wrote *The Proletarian Revolution and the Renegade Kautsky* between

October and November 1918. It was perhaps one of the angriest polemics in the history of Marxism, written when the fate of the Revolution hung by a thread. The Bolsheviks were under siege from armies of 14 different countries. Kautsky's critique, from Lenin's viewpoint, could only serve further to isolate the Revolution.

Both sides in the debate could claim that their positions had some pedigree in the works of Marx and Engels because, as with many other political questions, the founding fathers had left what would appear to be a confusing legacy. On this issue, some of the ambiguities were more apparent than real. They were consistent and relatively clear in the sense that the term 'dictatorship of the proletariat' merely meant the class rule of the proletariat in the transition from capitalism to communism, and was interchangeable with the term 'rule of the proletariat' or the 'political power of the working class'.[2] Thus, it did not necessarily entail, as both Kautsky and Lenin wrongly assumed, the unrestricted use of force. Further, it did not mean the rule of an individual or a party. And equally significantly, it did not refer exclusively to a governmental form, as followers of the nineteenth-century French revolutionary, August Blanqui, maintained, but primarily (although not exclusively) to the class content of the state, i.e. the class basis of political power.[3] The ambiguity seemed to arise because they were flexible about what precise *form* such a dictatorship should take and the strategy to achieve it. This stemmed from their anti-utopianism, and from their commitment to workers' *self*-emancipation. Marx and Engels firmly resisted the temptation to provide a clear blueprint of the type of state that workers should develop, or to indicate that there was only one kind of strategy that should be pursued. Whatever conclusions they drew were based upon their observations of workers making efforts to emancipate themselves in different contexts. These efforts assumed different forms.

Thus, on the one hand they often had reservations about 'bourgeois' democracy, especially 'parliamentary cretinism', the illusion that parliament had a real influence on society.[4] Yet, on the other hand, as a result of their familiarity with the Chartist struggles, they saw within the British context the revolutionary implications of universal (male) suffrage in enabling workers to attain 'political power'. Indeed, in *The Communist Manifesto* they generalized upon this experience and saw workers in Europe becoming a ruling class through winning the 'battle of democracy'.[5] Hence, the proletariat could rule through attaining a simple majority. As indicated in Chapter 1, in 1872 Marx contemplated a peaceful transition to socialism in countries where militarism and bureaucracy were not pronounced features of political life.[6]

Suffrage was important not only in an instrumental sense. It was vital in developing the capacity of the working class to become a ruling class. In discussing the significance of universal suffrage in mid-nineteenth-century France, Marx noted: 'Universal suffrage had fulfilled its mission, the only function it could have in a revolutionary period. The majority of the people had passed through the school of development it provided.'[7]

Engels, after Marx's death, influenced by the astounding electoral success of the German SPD in the 1890s, extolled the virtues of a parliamentary *strategy*. In his preface to the 1895 edition of Marx's *Class Struggles in France*, he maintained that the SPD had transformed the franchise 'from a means of deception ... into an instrument of emancipation'.[8] It provided an accurate estimate of the balance of class forces, thereby preventing premature attempts to overthrow the bourgeoisie. Elections also helped the party to reach wider audiences, and parliament could be used as a propaganda platform. Barricades and street fighting were to a 'considerable extent obsolete', in contrast to the situation in the Europe of 1848. Now soldiers were better organized and had better weapons. Successful surprise attacks by conscious minorities leading unconscious majorities were no longer possible. The 'utilisation of universal suffrage' was the new method of struggle. 'Long, persistent work' was necessary so that the masses 'may understand what is to be done'. This entailed 'slow propaganda and parliamentary activity'.[9] Nevertheless, he did not want workers to 'renounce their right to revolution', which could at some stage entail the use of force.[10] He still expected a 'decisive day' of reckoning with the bourgeoisie. The purpose of increasing the vote for the SPD was to demonstrate the legitimacy of workers' rule and undermine the confidence of the bourgeoisie. He stated elsewhere: 'On the day the thermometer of universal suffrage registers boiling point among the workers, both they and the capitalists will know what to do.'[11] This would seem to suggest that the utilization of suffrage was merely *one* weapon in the class struggle. He saw this electoral strategy within the framework of a 'democratic republic', which he regarded as the 'highest form of state' in which 'the last decisive struggle between the proletariat and bourgeoisie can be fought out'.[12] Yet he left open the precise nature of the socialist transition, after workers had taken political power.

Nevertheless, Marx and Engels unequivocally favoured the total, and if need be violent, dismantling of the bourgeois state machine in the transition from capitalism to communism. In his eulogy on the Paris Commune, *The Civil War in France*, Marx held that the Commune represented the 'destruction of the State power which claimed to be the embodiment of that unity independent of, and superior to, the nation itself, from which it was but a parasitic excrescence ... its legitimate functions were to be wrested from an authority usurping pre-eminence over society itself, and restored to the responsible agents of society.'[13] State functionaries and armed forces were now to be directly accountable to, and recruited from, the people. Indeed, the Commune was a 'Revolution against the *State* itself', with its coercive aspects disappearing, as a conflict-free classless society emerged.[14]

The Marx–Engels theoretical corpus on the state therefore provided more than adequate quotable ammunition for both Lenin and Kautsky to justify their positions, although, as suggested, their position was far clearer than appeared at first sight. There emerged as a result of their analyses of the proletariat's struggles in revolutionary situations, especially in Europe of 1848 and Paris of 1871, an implicit distinction between the strategy advocated towards the state in a pre-revolutionary situation and the form of state developed in a post-revolutionary situation. Few followers of Marx and Engels made this distinction, and few before 1917 upheld the idea of a commune state. Lenin only became a convert to the idea in early 1917, possible influenced by Bukharin.[15]

KAUTSKY'S CRITIQUE

The central focus of Kautsky's critique of the Bolsheviks was that they had offended Marxist principles with reference to the preconditions for revolution, the role of force and the strategic and institutional model of proletarian rule.

Kautsky argued that the political preconditions for a socialist revolution in Russia simply did not exist. These in turn depended upon certain economic preconditions. Large-scale factory production was essential to the generation of the 'will' to socialism among workers. Such a productive form had enormous socializing powers, thereby overcoming the forces of individualism associated with small-scale production.[16] Well-developed capitalist relations of production were necessary, so that the overwhelming majority of the population would actually want socialism, thereby ruling out the need for force, which occurred only if it was desired by a minority.[17]

In addition, capitalist production relations were vital for 'superstructural' reasons: they undermined the 'absolute rule' of bureaucracies, which were not responsive to industrial changes. Parliamentary government achieved this by making them accountable to the wider population.[18] Such a form of government, with its attendant civil and democratic liberties, generated a precondition upon which he focused most of his attention. For Kautsky, the real question was whether the Russian proletariat was 'strong and intelligent enough to take in hand the regulation of society'; that is, whether it had the capacity to become a ruling class.[19] 'Socialist production' was only possible 'if the proletariat has acquired experience in self-government, in trade unions, and on town councils, and has participated in the making of laws and the control of government'.[20] 'Democracy' provided the framework within which workers developed these skills in their struggles against the capitalist class. Moreover, with workers in control under a 'democracy', the working day could be reduced to allow them more time to consider larger political questions.

'Democracy' had an added virtue: following Engels, he maintained that a proper appraisal of class forces could be made, so that 'reckless and premature attempts at revolution' could be avoided, as could the use of force.[21]

In the absence of such political and economic preconditions, Kautsky contended, the Bolsheviks came to rely heavily on force, and in this sense their revolution was closer to the French Revolution of 1789; that is, a bourgeois revolution. Their dependency on force was all the greater because they had 'staked all on the card of the general European Revolution'.[22] This card had not turned up. The use of repression, according to Kautsky, led them to distort the whole meaning of Marx's concept of the 'dictatorship of the proletariat', a term which in any case he rarely used. It referred to a *'condition'*, not a form of government, an automatic consequence of universal suffrage where workers had a natural majority, for a class could rule, but it could not govern, i.e. administer. In discussing the Paris Commune, where the power of government was subject to universal suffrage, he noted that 'the dictatorship of the proletariat was [for Marx] a condition which necessarily arose in a real democracy, because of the overwhelming numbers of the proletariat'.[23] It amounted to the 'sovereignty' of the proletariat.

The Bolsheviks, in creating a governmental dictatorship, as opposed to a class dictatorship based upon democracy, were unable to protect minorities, which occurred in democracies because even majority parties had an interest in protecting minority parties, for at some stage they too could become a minority party. Moreover, minorities were the key to intellectual progress.[24] A second consequence of dictatorship was that it provoked civil war, which further delayed the introduction of socialist production.[25] Nevertheless, although he rejected the Bolshevik dictatorship based upon Soviets, he argued that the latter had their place in the class struggle as working-class combat organizations.[26] They could not, however, be organs of government. That was the job of parliament.

Given his attachment to the idea of parliamentary democracy, not surprisingly he strongly opposed the Bolsheviks' dispersal of the Constituent Assembly in January 1918. True, the elections held in November 1917 did not in January 1918 accurately reflect the wishes of the electorate, owing to the split between the Left and Right Social Revolutionaries in this period. However, the proper solution to this problem was to hold fresh elections in constituencies where Social Revolutionaries had been elected.[27]

Kautsky concluded that the Bolsheviks were formulating a new Marxist theory to legitimate their strategy and policies in circumstances inappropriate for the construction of socialism. They were making a virtue out of a necessity. This 'new theory', the Bolsheviks were suggesting, could be applied to the rest of Europe. Instead, he argued, they should have honestly explained the situation: they were left with no choice but 'dictatorship or abdication'.

LENIN'S REBUTTAL

Lenin in his reply held that he was not advocating a 'new theory', but one based upon the 'fundamental principles of Marxism'.[28] He concentrated upon the question of the meaning of the 'dictatorship of the proletariat'. He saw the Soviets as its concrete form, the logical outcome of the class struggle, in which their role could not be restricted to that of a combat organization. He rejected what he regarded as Kautsky's general, abstract conception of democracy, which glossed over its class content. A distinction had to be made between bourgeois and proletarian democracy. Even in supposedly 'purely' democratic modern states, the bourgeoisie always had constitutional loopholes, enabling troops to be despatched against workers.[29] Indeed, minorities were not necessarily protected; for example, blacks in the United States were being lynched.[30]

Kautsky's idea of 'pure' democracy stemmed from his false juxtaposition of dictatorship and democracy, deploring the former and commending the latter. He forgot to ask the question: democracy for whom, i.e. for what class? However democratic the form of government, the class in power, which controlled the state apparatus, necessarily dictated to other classes, and dictatorship implied violence, because it was part and parcel of class rule. Indeed, Lenin defined dictatorship as 'rule based directly upon force and unrestricted by any laws'.[31] Violence was the necessary outcome in any society which contained antagonistic classes, however democratic the government. Hence, even if the proletariat formed a majority, force against the bourgeoisie, which would resist measures attempting to achieve social equality, was inevitable.[32]

Kautsky, argued Lenin, in order to avoid the issue of proletarian violence, misinterpreted Marx's notion of the 'dictatorship of the proletariat', in defining it as a 'condition of domination'. Its natural majority within a democracy would supposedly enable the proletariat to rule without violence. Lenin, on the other hand, insisted that for Marx dictatorship of the proletariat referred to the form of *state*, not to the 'condition of domination'. The state, especially its administrative and military apparatus, through which the working class, like other ruling classes, exercised its dictatorship, was the significant fact. Different forms of state were associated with different forms of class rule. Thus, the working class on coming to power would have to destroy the bourgeois state and create a new one appropriate to its rule. This entailed the maximization of participation in the running of the state, especially its administration and armed forces. Thus, proletarian democracy, in contrast to bourgeois democracy, involved a vast expansion of democracy.[33] Yet clearly for Lenin this kind of democracy was intrinsically bound up with proletarian dictatorship.

Accordingly, Lenin objected to Kautsky's use of the Paris Commune as an example of a 'condition of domination' by the proletariat through universal suffrage. Marx in *The Civil War in France* had noted that the bourgeois state had been destroyed,[34] and that although universal suffrage existed, the Commune was nevertheless a dictatorship, employing force against the bourgeoisie.[35] Indeed, peaceful revolution, which Kautsky sought to legitimate, was no longer possible in the era of monopoly capitalism. Unlike the era of pre-monopoly capitalism, which lasted until the 1870s, it was characterized by the universal development of state bureaucracies, militarism and violence.

In the light of his notion of proletarian dictatorship, not surprisingly he justified the breaking up of the Constituent Assembly on the grounds that it represented the bourgeoisie, and that the Soviets were the 'highest type of democracy', more accurately reflecting the interests of the oppressed in their struggles against the bourgeoisie. Moreover, the elections to various Congresses of Soviets held in January and after unequivocally reflected a shift to the left among the masses.[36] Second, on the question of the franchise, of depriving the 'exploiters of the franchise', it was a '*purely Russian* question, linked to the specific need to break the resistance of the Russian bourgeoisie'.[37] Similarly, the exclusion of various parties, 'from the Cadets to the Right Socialist-Revolutionaries', was a specifically Russian question, relating to the nature of the Russian bourgeoisie's resistance to proletarian rule.[38]

COMMENTARY

Lenin in this pamphlet steered clear of Kautsky's argument that Russia lacked the objective and subjective preconditions for proletarian revolution. Lenin had previously hoped that the absence of at least certain material preconditions could be remedied as a result of the Russian Revolution inspiring proletarian revolutions in the West, so that they could in effect be imported. Nevertheless, on the question of subjective preconditions – that is, the capacity of the proletariat to become a ruling class – Lenin was silent. A little later he became fully aware of this problem. In a report to the party congress in March 1919, he suggested that, as a result of the 'low cultural level' of the working class, 'the Soviets, which by virtue of their program are organs of government *by the working people*, are in fact organs of government *for the working people* by the advanced section of the proletariat, but not the working people as a whole'.[39] While Kautsky had a strong point in indicating the absence of the subjective preconditions, his solution to this problem, parliamentary democracy, was not without its dangers from a revolutionary perspective, especially of working-class incorporation into the bourgeois state.

On the issue of Lenin's accusation that Kautsky had an abstract conception of democracy, stressing the importance of majority rule, and thereby failing to note the class content of democracy, evaluation is complex. Marx and Engels did not use the terms 'proletarian democracy' and 'bourgeois democracy', and made no explicitly qualitative distinction between them. Marx talked about 'winning the battle for democracy' and along with Engels saw the possibility of universal suffrage as a lever of social revolution. Yet in the passages where they underlined the strategic value of universal suffrage they avoided the question of the precise shape of the state in the transition from capitalism to communism. However, where they did discuss it a commune state would appear to be what they had in mind. The important lesson of the Paris Commune was that 'the working class cannot simply lay hold of the ready-made State machinery, and wield it for its own purposes'.[40] This was consistent with Marx's desire to overcome political alienation, i.e. the separation of state from society.

The Paris Commune represented the radical extension of democracy into the executive arm of the state, subordinating it to society. Here Lenin was closer to Marx than Kautsky, who was fixated with parliamentary democracy, not merely in a strategic sense, but as the political form of socialist transition. Thus, on the issue of the disbanding of the Constituent Assembly, within the framework of the proletarian revolution, Lenin's justification, on the grounds that the Soviets represented a higher form of democracy, would appear to be close to Marx, at least in a theoretical sense.

Moreover, given what Marx and Engels had to say about the Paris Commune and the way in which the hierarchical and militaristic state had to be smashed, Lenin was on firm ground in assuming that under twentieth-century conditions, with the growth of militarism and bureau-cracy, much state smashing would be required. Within the Marxist theory of the state, then, Lenin's position *vis-à-vis* the Russian state could be justified. The violent overthrow of that state did not have to be attributable, as Kautsky suggested, to immature preconditions.

In one sense, therefore, Kautsky's counterposing of democracy and dictatorship, which assumed that, if the state was democratic, violence in the socialist transition would be unnecessary, was a false antithesis. While applauding the democratic form of the Commune, Marx was sharply critical of its mistake in not marching on Versailles, and allowing the 'Party of Order' to 'try its strength at the ballot box'.[41] Hence, it failed to put down the 'slaveholders' rebellion'. Again, Engels, commenting on Marx's suggestion about the possibility of a peaceful revolution in England, stated that Marx 'certainly never forgot to add that he hardly expected the English ruling classes to submit, without a "proslavery rebellion", to this peaceful and legal revolution'.[42] And as Marx himself wrote, a socialist government on coming to power would need 'immediately [to] take the necessary measures for intimidating the mass of the bourgeoisie sufficiently to gain time ... for permanent action'.[43] Not only were violent measures against the bourgeoisie a distinct possibility, but Engels at least had few illusions about 'pure democracy' in a revolutionary situation where the *'whole of the reaction'* would *'group around pure democracy'* as they did in France and Germany in 1848.[44] Thus, Marx and Engels in effect seemed to reject the possibility of a non-violent, 'bourgeois' democratic social and economic revolution.

As for the weight that Marx and Engels put on the concept of the 'dictatorship of the proletariat', Kautsky had little textual evidence to show that it was merely incidental in their work. They used it frequently in two post-revolutionary periods, 1850–2 (after the 1848 revolutions), and 1871–5 (after the Paris Commune), when they were seeking to collaborate with, and distinguish themselves from the Blanquists and other elitist revolutionaries.[45] Equally, Marx clearly held the concept of proletarian dictatorship to be important: 'What I did that was new was to prove ... that the class struggle necessarily leads to the *dictatorship of the proletariat*.'[46]

Nevertheless, whilst Kautsky may have had little theoretical warrant in contrasting dictatorship unfavourably with democracy in Marx and Engels's writings, he was closer to the mark in describing Bolshevik *practice*, which consisted of decreasing democracy and increasing dictatorship.[47] Not only were there restrictions on the press, disenfranchisements and the exclusion of bourgeois parties from the Soviets; the banning of parties sympathetic to the revolution, the Left Social Revolutionaries and the Mensheviks also occurred – one of Kautsky's points to which Lenin failed to respond. A formidable, democratically unaccountable police apparatus, the Cheka, was also in the process of construction, which Lenin by November 1918 saw as 'directly exercising the dictatorship of the proletariat'.[48] Indeed, he increasingly identified the dictatorship of the proletariat with the 'revolutionary elements of the class', i.e. with the Communist Party. Thus, in practice, it came not to mean, as Marx and Engels thought it should, a workers' state and government both democratic in form, but a one-party state and government.

In a sense, therefore, Lenin's theoretical identification of the dictatorship of the proletariat with the form of state, and not a form of government, took the critical focus off the type of government that was being built in the Soviet Union. While it could be argued in Marxian terms that ruling classes in the past, consisting of minorities, could allow different governmental forms (e.g. democratic or autocratic) to coexist with certain state forms, for the proletariat, i.e. the majority, to rule, *both* the state and governmental forms had to be democratic.[49] A necessary relationship between the class content of proletarian rule and its form had to exist. Indeed, Kautsky could with some justification claim that insofar as Lenin increasingly came to construe the dictatorship of the proletariat to mean dictatorship by the Party and unaccountable, repressive parts of the state, he was effectively making a virtue out of a necessity, i.e. justifying repressive, one-party rule. Yet Kautsky was equally at fault in suggesting that the term referred to the working class ruling, but not governing. That the working class would be doing both was precisely the point behind Marx's insistence upon the democratization of all state and governmental institutions.[50]

NOTES

1. K. Kautsky, *The Dictatorship of the Proletariat* (hereafter *DP*), University of Michigan, Ann Arbor, MI (1964). Introduction by John H. Kautsky, xv.
2. See H. Draper, *The Dictatorship of the Proletariat from Marx to Lenin*, Monthly Review Press, New York (1987), 24–6. For other discussions about the nature of proletarian dictatorship in the works of Marx and Engels see M. Johnstone, 'Marx, Blanqui and majority rule' in R. Miliband and J. Saville (Eds), *Socialist Register, 1983*, Merlin Press, London; J. Ehrenberg, *The Dictatorship of the Proletariat*, Routledge, New York (1992); E. Balibar, *On the Dictatorship of the Proletariat*, New Left Books, London (1977); H. Draper, *Karl Marx's Theory of Revolution, Vol. 3*, Monthly Review Press, New York (1986).
3. Draper, *Dictatorship of the Proletariat from Marx to Lenin*, 35.
4. See M. Levin, 'Marx, Engels and the parliamentary path' in M. Cowling and L. Wilde (Eds), *Approaches to Marx*, Open University Press, Milton Keynes (1989), 152.
5. *CM*, 74.
6. See page 11.
7. 'The class struggles in France: 1848 to 1850' in K. Marx, *Surveys from Exile* (Ed. D. Fernbach), Penguin, Harmondsworth (1973), 134.
8. Marx and Engels, *Selected Works, Vol. 1*, 129.
9. *Ibid.*, 134.
10. *Ibid.*, 136.
11. Marx and Engels, *Selected Works, Vol. 11*, 322.
12. *Ibid.*, 321.
13. Quoted in D. McLellan, *Introduction to the Thought of Karl Marx*, Macmillan, London (1980), 221.
14. R. Miliband, 'Marx and the state' in R. Miliband and J. Saville (Eds), *Socialist Register, 1965*, Merlin Press, London, 290.
15. See S. F. Cohen, *Bukharin and the Bolshevik Revolution*, Vintage Books, New York (1975), 42.
16. *DP*, 12. Cf. Marx, *Capital, Vol. 1*, Progress Publishers, Moscow (1965), Chapter 32 *passim*.
17. *DP*, 38.
18. *DP*, 26.
19. *DP*, 23.
20. *DP*, 96.

21. *DP*, 36.
22. *DP*, 64.
23. *DP*, 45.
24. *DP*, 33.
25. *DP*, 52–5.
26. *DP*, 74.
27. *DP*, 68.
28. V. I. Lenin, *The Proletarian Revolution and the Renegade Kautsky* (hereafter *PR*), Progress Publishers, Moscow (1967), 57.
29. *PR*, 21.
30. *PR*, 21–2.
31. *PR*, 13.
32. *PR*, 27–30.
33. *PR*, 23.
34. *PR*, 17.
35. *PR*, 16.
36. *PR*, 48.
37. *PR*, 31, Lenin's emphasis.
38. *PR*, 49.
39. Quoted in Draper, *The Dictatorship of the Proletariat from Marx to Lenin*, 136.
40. 1872 preface to *The Communist Manifesto* (Ed. F. C. Bender), 44.
41. Marx and Engels, *Selected Works*, Vol. 11, 514.
42. Quoted in Draper, *op. cit.*, 55.
43. Marx and Engels, *Selected Correspondence*, Progress Publishers, Moscow (1965).
44. *Ibid.*, 382, Engels's emphasis.
45. Draper, *op. cit.*, 23.
46. Marx to Weydermeyer, 5 March 1852, in Marx and Engels, *Selected Works, Vol. 11*, 452, Marx's emphasis.
47. F. Claudin, 'Democracy and dictatorship in Lenin and Kautsky', *New Left Review*, 106 (Nov/Dec 1977), 73.
48. Quoted in Draper, *op. cit.*, 104.
49. R. Miliband in 'Marx and the state', 289–90, in a slightly different way makes this point against Draper, *op. cit.*, 26. Draper may perhaps have had to concede the force of Miliband's point if he himself drew the appropriate conclusion from his own statement that 'for Marx, the "class rule of the proletariat" was equivalent to the complete and thoroughgoing democratization of society': *Karl Marx's Theory of Revolution, Vol.* 3, 117; see also 298–301.
50. See, for example, Marx, 'Conspectus of Bakunin's "Statism and Anarchy" ', in *The First International and After* (Ed. D. Fernbach), Penguin, Harmondsworth (1974), 333–8.

8
Socialism in One Country or Permanent Revolution?

PROBLEMS AND ISSUES

By 1924 the fragile strategic formula that had undergirded the October Revolution was under severe strain. As indicated in Chapter 5, Lenin, departing from the previous Bolshevik tradition, had put socialism on the immediate agenda. He reasoned that Russia in 1917 was moving towards an anti-capitalist revolution, and that it was the 'weakest link' in the imperialist chain. A proletarian revolution in Russia, with the support of the poor peasants, would therefore break this chain, inspiring revolution within the imperialist heartlands. This would enable the Russian proletariat to overcome problems of economic backwardness and move towards socialism. However, the remainder of the imperialist chain proved more durable. Although successful workers' struggles occurred in Germany, Hungary and Italy between 1918 and 1920, they were short-lived. The failure of the Bulgarian revolution in June 1923, and then more importantly the last-minute decision by the German Communist Party four months later to abandon insurrection, left the Bolsheviks stranded as the revolutionary tide ebbed. Incantations declaiming the centrality of the West European proletariat to their socialist project were demoralizing to a population that had undergone so many hardships since the outbreak of the First World War in 1914, and not pleasing to a rising Soviet bureaucracy, pragmatic in outlook and nationalist in aspiration. Thus, conditions were ripe for a new formula, which downplayed dependence on the European proletariat and told the Soviet population that their sacrifices for socialism were not in vain.

Although Bukharin had expounded the idea of 'socialism in one country' as early as November 1922,[1] the term became more closely associated with Stalin, who began popularizing it in December 1924. As hopes of international proletarian revolution receded, issues of economic development became more obviously paramount. The period of War Communism (1918–21), with the state controlling the commanding heights of industry and the distribution process, was superseded by the New Economic Policy (NEP), allowing for a limited market in agricultural produce and other goods. Both policies were *ad hoc*, and the serious issue of how the Soviet Union should industrialize remained. Stalin argued that it ought to occur within a self-sufficient, autarkic framework: economic integration with the West would make the Soviet Union 'into an appendage of the world capitalist system'.[2]

The issue was not merely about economic policy. It became interwoven with rivalry over Lenin's succession, after his death in January 1924. Stalin and initially Zinoviev and Kamenev, the other members of the so-called 'triumvirate', aimed to discredit Trotsky, who was seen by many as Lenin's heir apparent. Stalin sought to damage Trotsky ideologically and to highlight his supposed differences from Lenin, whose authority was unquestionable. In 1924 the term 'Trotskyism' was coined, with pejorative connotations. Rivalry continued even after Trotsky's expulsion from the Soviet Communist Party in 1927 and his exile to the Turkish island of Prinkipo in 1929, and only ended with his assassination in 1940 by one of Stalin's agents. From the time of his expulsion until his death his demonization performed a useful function for Stalin: it served to delegitimate opposition to Stalin's leadership within the Soviet Union and the Comintern. And in the Moscow trials of 1936–8, involving mass purges of old Bolsheviks, Kamenev, Zinoviev and Bukharin were executed on the grounds of conspiring with Trotsky, who was supposedly in league with Hitler (and the Emperor of Japan), to restore capitalism in the Soviet Union.

SOCIALISM IN ONE COUNTRY: STALIN'S ARGUMENT

Stalin first made his case for socialism in one country in 'The October Revolution and the tactics of the Russian communists', published in December 1924, having rejected the theory only a few months earlier.[3] In one sense the article was a response to Trotsky's discrediting of Kamenev and Zinoviev in his pamphlet *The Lessons of October*, which was written with the failure of the German 'October' (1923) very much in mind. They had initially opposed the idea of armed insurrection in October 1917. Stalin sought to undermine Trotsky by showing how he differed from Lenin and by exposing the flaws in his concept of permanent revolution. Stalin also had a more serious political point: to persuade party members to accept his policy innovation of socialism in one country, although he endeavoured to couch it in the language of Lenin.

First, Stalin, in noting one 'peculiarity' of the Russian revolution, claimed that Lenin's conception of the dictatorship of the proletariat entailed an alliance with the 'labouring masses of the peasantry'.[4] Maintaining this worker–peasant alliance and stressing the importance of the peasantry for building socialism was crucial to Stalin's vision of socialism in one country, since this class constituted 80 per cent of the population. Trotsky, according to him, when he formulated his theory of permanent revolution in 1905, 'forgot all about the peasantry as a revolutionary force'.[5] After quoting from an article by Lenin in 1915, criticizing Trotsky for denying the revolutionary importance of the peasantry, he then referred to Trotsky's 1922 introduction to *1905*, where he held that after the Russian Revolution the proletariat would enter into 'hostile collision' with the 'broad masses of the peasants' as it increasingly eliminated bourgeois property rights.[6] Hence, for the Russian proletariat an international revolution was imperative. Lenin, on the other hand, saw the proletariat as leading the peasantry. The revolution for him drew 'its strength primarily from among the workers and peasants of Russia itself', but for Trotsky '*only* from the arena of world revolution'.[7] Trotsky, according to Stalin, presented the revolution with a bleak prospect: 'to vegetate in its own contradictions and rot away while waiting for the world revolution'.[8]

The second important 'peculiarity' of the October Revolution had a more direct bearing on his argument for socialism in one country. A proletarian dictatorship had occurred in a capitalistically underdeveloped country. This could be explained by Lenin's theory of uneven development, as adumbrated in his 1915 article, 'On the slogan for a United States of Europe'.[9] The uneven development of world capitalism had led to the clashes between the imperialist powers and had also created opportunities for proletarian revolution where it was weakest, for 'the victory of socialism ... first in several or even in one capitalist country, taken singly'.[10] The October Revolution had confirmed Lenin's 'theory of the proletarian revolution of the victory of socialism in one country', even if it was underdeveloped. Trotsky, on the other hand, contradicted Lenin by holding in effect that the 'victory of socialism' had to be 'simultaneous' in the advanced countries of Europe.

Stalin then made a crucial distinction between the types of support required from the European working class and their relevance for the 'victory of socialism' in the Soviet Union. The Western working classes were only essential in the military sense: they obstructed intervention by their respective governments. Accordingly, they were only pivotal to the '*complete* victory of socialism, for *complete* security against the restoration of the old order'.[11] In providing a continuous counterweight to capitalist military intervention, they were helping the Soviets 'to push on with the organisation of socialist economy', even without revolutions.[12] Trotsky, on the other hand, argued in *A Program of Peace* (1917) that a 'genuine advance of the socialist economy' in Russia was only possible after such revolutions. Thus, with no revolutions occurring in Western Europe the only choice, on the basis of Trotsky's argument, was either to 'rot away or to degenerate into a bourgeois state'.[13] Lenin, however, had clearly indicated that the NEP would lay the 'foundation of a socialist economy'. Moreover, in an unfinished article, 'On co-operation', which he wrote towards the end of his life, he maintained that Russia had all that was 'necessary and sufficient' to build a 'complete socialist society'.[14] Trotsky, then, had little 'faith in the strength and capabilities of our revolution, lack of faith in the strength and capabilities of the Russian proletariat'.[15]

Stalin's later article, 'On the problems of Leninism', published in January 1926, reiterated his case concerning West European proletarian cooperation with the Soviet Union. In essence, this was not required for the 'victory of socialism' in the Soviet Union, because in the resolution of the internal contradiction between the proletariat and the peasantry technical backwardness was not an 'insuperable obstacle'.[16] Nevertheless, international cooperation, presumably through proletarian revolutions in Western Europe, was essential for the 'complete, final victory' of socialism in one country to prevent foreign intervention.

In sum, Stalin made European, and indeed world, revolution into an optional extra for the construction of socialism in the Soviet Union. His doctrine helped to insulate the Soviet population from the demoralizing implications of the failure of such revolutions to materialize. And, finally, it undermined Trotsky's ideological authority derived from his theory of permanent revolution.

PERMANENT REVOLUTION: TROTSKY'S ARGUMENT

Trotsky was slow to rebut Stalin's critique. In a letter to the Central Committee of the Soviet Communist Party in January 1925 he replied that the formula of permanent revolution 'applies wholly to the past' and denied that he was pessimistic about 'socialist reconstruction' in the face of non-revolution in the West. Despite this difficulty, 'the economic and political resources of the Soviet dictatorship are very great'.[17] His tardiness of riposte may be explicable for a number of reasons: to prove his loyalty to the party, especially as he had joined it only in 1917, his failure to contemplate Stalin as a serious rival and his preoccupation with other matters as chairman of the Main Concessions Committee, the electrochemical board and scientific-technical board of industry. Equally, he may not have seen the immediate and long-term significance of Stalin's ideological novelty, which became clearer in retrospect, after he had been expelled from the party. The effect that it had on the Comintern's position in relation to the Chinese Revolution in 1927, which facilitated the massacre of thousands of Chinese communists by the bourgeois Kuomintang, began to make its implications visible. Later, after his views on the 'betrayal' of the Russian Revolution had clarified, he saw the doctrine of socialism in one country as central to the 'historic mission of the Soviet bureaucracy'.[18] Thus, although the initial policy difference between Stalin and Trotsky, as R. B. Day has suggested, may have been over the question of economic integration with the West, this became subsumed within a larger political debate.[19]

Trotsky, defending himself in *The Permanent Revolution* (1930), resisted the accusation that he had 'underestimated' or 'ignored' the peasantry. In replying to Radek, who had taken up Stalin's criticism, he quoted from *1905* to demonstrate that he had considered the peasantry vital in the forthcoming revolution, and that the proletariat had to form an alliance with this class. Trotsky's point was that it could not play an '*independent political role*'.[20] Rather, it would support the proletariat, because this class would, initially, be instrumental in bringing about a democratic revolution, giving peasants political rights and recognizing their expropriation of land. Moreover, in the 1905 period there were, in effect, few differences between him and Lenin. Although the latter had advocated a democratic dictatorship of the proletariat and peasantry, this was an 'algebraic' formulation, and he explicitly stated that the proletariat had a hegemonic role in relation to the peasantry.[21] Trotsky also observed that Lenin had recognized a similar potential conflict of interests between the proletariat and peasantry, once the bourgeois revolution had been completed. Lenin also shared the view, in 1905 and 1917, that help from the West European proletariat was indispensable to the achievement of socialism in Russia; otherwise the Russian proletariat would remain isolated in a sea of petty bourgeois peasants.[22]

Trotsky, however, devoted more attention to the question of the possibility of socialism in one country. First, he rejected the proposition that Lenin had endorsed such a notion. He observed that Lenin in a 'United States of Europe' passage quoted by Stalin was referring to this possibility in Western Europe, rather than Russia.[23] More importantly, Lenin, as his subsequent writings confirmed, invested the term socialism with two meanings. The first, short term and used in this article, referred to a workers' state controlling production. This was not in fact socialism, Trotsky suggested, but its 'legal premise'.[24] The second meaning was long term, involving a time-scale of generations as well as a 'material-productive and social content'.[25] For Trotsky the longer-term definition was the more crucial, because socialism was grounded on a high productivity of labour. Without this, quoting Marx, 'want' merely became 'generalized'.[26]

Second, Stalin misconstrued Lenin's law of uneven development. It supposedly buttressed the idea that socialism occurred in isolated countries, rather than as a 'single, simultaneous and universal act' of workers in different countries. While this was trivially true – revolutions, such as the Russian, took place in separate countries – the law also postulated that uneven development upset, but did not eliminate, the growing bonds of international economic interdependence. As a result of this increasing global division of labour, socialism in one country was impossible, because only on an international basis could a well-developed productivity of labour exist, essential for socialism.[27]

Third, he held that Stalin had misinterpreted Lenin's article 'On co-operation', which purportedly claimed that all the 'conditions' necessary for socialism existed in Russia. Lenin was referring merely to the 'socio-organizational forms' of the transition from petty commodity production to a collective economy, and not to 'material-productive conditions'. By implication Lenin maintained that dramatic technological advances were necessary in order to create the material conditions needed to overcome the cultural backwardness of the population. Trotsky concluded that these advances required a revolution in, or some form of economic cooperation with, the capitalist West.[28]

Trotsky then demonstrated through copious quotation that Lenin and the Bolsheviks in 1917 and after had consistently clung to the perspective that socialism could not be sustained without revolutions in the West. For example, Lenin stated in November 1918: 'The complete victory of the socialist revolution is unthinkable in one country, but demands the most active cooperation at least of several advanced countries, among which Russia cannot be numbered.'[29] Trotsky was particularly fond of quoting the 1921 programme of the Young Communist League: 'Russia, although it possesses enormous natural resources, is, nevertheless, from an industrial point of view, a backward country, in which a petty bourgeois population predominates. It can arrive at socialism only through the world proletarian revolution, which epoch of development we have now entered.'[30]

Stalin's conception of socialism in one country, he argued, had more in common with the German Social Democrat Georg Vollmar, who expounded a theory of 'The isolated socialist state' in 1878, than with Lenin. Given that in the era of imperialism the productive forces had outgrown national boundaries, and that socialism depended on high levels of productivity, deriving from a well-developed international division of labour, the concept of 'national socialism' or socialism in one country was an oxymoron, a contradiction in terms. And it was 'reactionary', going against the grain of history.[31]

Whether Stalin liked it or not, the Soviet Union was part of the world economy, and its economic planning calculations were based upon foreign trade figures.[32] These in turn were determined by the Soviet productivity of labour relative to the world economy. Thus, 'the intervention of cheaper capitalist commodities ... constitutes perhaps the greatest immediate menace to the Soviet economy', not military intervention.[33] The Ford tractor was 'just as dangerous as a Cruesot gun'.[34] Hence, there was a 'life and death struggle between two social systems', with the constant threat of capitalist restoration in the Soviet Union. While 'socialist construction' in the Soviet Union was a vital factor affecting the outcome of this struggle, the 'fate of the world economy as a whole' was of 'decisive significance'.[35] This meant that the question of 'world economic and political struggle' could not be ignored. Trotsky said in effect that Soviet economic development depended, at least in the short term, on trade with the West, in order to import foreign technology, thereby boosting labour productivity. The existence of abundant natural resources was not sufficient to build socialism.[36] The Soviet Union would not win in the economic struggle against world capitalism through autarky. He also argued that class contradictions within the Soviet Union could not be solved internally, since these contradictions depended 'directly' on the European and world class struggle.[37] He was implying that the proletariat in its struggle with the Russian peasantry would be more or less powerful, depending on the extent to which the world, and especially European, proletariat was successful in its class struggle.

Trotsky, in challenging the idea that socialism in one country was possible, also had to deal with the accusation that his insistence on international revolution meant a lack of faith in the 'inner forces of the revolution'. He answered this charge in two ways. First, he offered numerous quotations from Lenin between 1918 and 1921 to demonstrate that the Soviet revolution would 'perish' unless revolutions occurred rapidly in Europe.[38] Second, the doctrine of socialism in one country had led Stalin to declare in 1926 that socialism had been 90 per cent completed. Given the appalling conditions that existed in the Soviet Union, such a revelation was hardly an inspiration to further sacrifice.[39]

Finally, Trotsky dealt with the impact of socialism in one country upon the strategy for world revolution. First, this doctrinal innovation transformed the role of the Comintern, from a spearhead of world revolution to an 'auxiliary', its mission being 'to protect the USSR from intervention and not to fight for the conquest of power'.[40] The Comintern therefore became a *'pacifist'* instrument whose object was to prevent capitalist countries from militarily intervening in the Soviet Union.[41] Prophetically, Trotsky deduced that if socialism in one country was possible, it would spell the 'liquidation of the Communist International', since it was no longer integral to the construction of Soviet socialism.[42] Another effect on Comintern policy was to encourage 'social-patriotism'. If the Soviet Union had sufficient resources to build socialism, then for industrially advanced countries, such as Germany, this was even more apparent. Such an ideology led to the breakdown of international proletarian solidarity, as occurred in August 1914.[43]

Just as crucially, the theory led to an indifference towards the tempo of class struggle, which was decisive in revolutionary situations, such as in Germany in 1923, in Britain in 1926 and in China from 1925 to 1927.

Trotsky held that such a theory 'accustoms us to regard these errors [of leadership] with indulgence, as if we had all the time we want at our disposal. A profound error! Time is a decisive factor in politics.'[44]

The disastrous policy pursued by the Comintern towards China induced Trotsky to bring all colonial and semi-colonial countries within the ambit of his theory of permanent revolution.[45] Chinese communists were put under the leadership of the bourgeois Kuomintang. This led to the massacre of thousands of communists and trade unionists by the Kuomintang in Shanghai in April 1927 and by the Left Kuomintang in the Hunan province in the July. Although before these massacres he had supported a 'stagist' theory of revolution in China – that is, Lenin's 1905 formula of a democratic dictatorship of the proletariat and the peasantry – afterwards he adopted the October Revolution strategy of proletarian dictatorship supported by the urban and rural poor.[46] This dictatorship, in fulfilling the tasks of the democratic revolution, would make 'deep inroads into the rights of bourgeois property', through bringing about an agrarian revolution.[47] Hence, 'the democratic revolution grows over into the socialist revolution and thereby becomes a *permanent* revolution'.[48] He now claimed that the October experience could be universalized to include all colonial and semi-colonial countries.

The theoretical underpinning of this universalization lay in the 'law of uneven and combined development', implicit in his *Results and Prospects*, but explicitly articulated in the first chapter of *The History of the Russian Revolution*. In essence, Trotsky posited, because capitalism was a global totality, the tempo of social change in specific countries was uneven. The pattern of economic development of backward countries was not a mere replication of the advanced ones. As a result of being tied into the world economy, they could omit intermediate stages, especially through borrowing up-to-date technology. Such development had the effect of 'combining' advanced with archaic social structures.[49] Trotsky assumed that world capitalism was 'objectively' ripe for socialism and that democratic, anti-imperialist struggles led by the proletariat in colonial and semi-colonial countries could legitimately 'grow over' into socialist struggles. They would either ignite, or be part of, a worldwide socialist struggle.[50]

The generalization of permanent revolution was also a response to the Comintern's own strategic generalization of the 'bloc of four classes' (urban petty bourgeoisie, sections of the 'capitalist' bourgeoisie, workers and peasants) which had initially been applied to China.[51] This rested upon the assumption that the October experience was irrelevant, particularly because unlike their Russian counterpart, colonial and semi-colonial bourgeoisies were oppressed by imperialism. Inevitably, Trotsky's universalized theory of permanent revolution became a cornerstone of the programme of the Fourth International eventually founded in 1938.[52]

COMMENTARY

The point at issue between Stalin and Trotsky was not whether socialism could and should be built in the Soviet Union. It was about whether it could be 'completed' without either some form of economic cooperation with Western capitalism in the short term or proletarian revolutions in the West in the medium to longer term. For Stalin, such revolutions were vital only in the sense that they would provide the country with permanent military security. For Trotsky they were just as vital economically, not merely in creating the material abundance of socialism, but in preventing internal conditions conducive to capitalist restoration.

In his arguments, with reference to positions advanced by Marx and Lenin, Trotsky was generally the more orthodox. Stalin was definitely heterodox in claiming that socialism had been 90 per cent completed in 1926 (and fully by 1936), largely ignoring the importance of material (and political!) preconditions. His definition emphasized the state control of the economy, economic planning and the 'absence' of class conflict, and relegated the importance of material conditions. Similarly, in downplaying the need for international proletarian cooperation and the centrality of the international division of labour for the construction of socialism, he was departing from Marx.

As for who was closer to Lenin, there is little doubt that in 1917 he had effectively endorsed Trotsky's thesis of permanent revolution, whatever his earlier reservations.[53] And Stalin's use of Lenin's 'law of uneven development' in support of socialism in one country was, as Trotsky indicated, misplaced: in the passage quoted by Stalin, he was clearly referring to the economically advanced European states, rather than a backward Soviet Union.[54] And Lenin clearly endowed the law with a conceptually richer content than Stalin, although whether he would have fully accepted Trotsky's gloss on this law remains an imponderable question.

On the issue of the peasantry, at one level Stalin may have exaggerated the differences of attitude towards the peasantry that might have existed between Lenin and Trotsky, especially in 1905.[55] In 1917 they both assumed that the peasantry, as a petty bourgeois class, could play no independent historical role, and that its interests were potentially hostile to those of the proletariat, although its poorer sections in alliance with the proletariat were crucial in the transition from capitalism to socialism in the Soviet Union. Yet Lenin clearly had a much greater interest in the peasantry. And, significantly, Trotsky remained silent about whether he endorsed Lenin's view in 'On co-operation' that peasants, under proletarian leadership, could build socialism through cooperatives.[56]

In the Lenin quotation game Stalin generally found fewer supporting quotations, while Trotsky was spoilt for choice. Nevertheless, Lenin's article 'On co-operation' did imply that 'complete socialism' could be achieved in the Soviet Union without outside assistance. Yet the actual purpose of the article has to be considered. As with many pieces written by Lenin, it was clearly not an academic treatise on the meaning of 'complete socialism' – indeed, in the same article he sharply rounded on Marxist 'pedants', who were guided by theory rather than an awareness of a reality pregnant with transformational possibilities, which did not fit into their preconceived intellectual schemas.[57] Here, Lenin was characteristically engaging in the arts of persuasion, aiming to move people, in this case enthusing the Soviet population about cooperatives, and overcoming some traditional Marxist prejudices against them. Thus, since his writings are particularly situation-dependent, a quotation from him is hardly a trump card when used in a different context.

Yet if Stalin could find few quotations from Lenin to legitimize his doctrinal innovation, his position certainly reflected Lenin's preoccupation towards the end of his life with building some form of socialism in the Soviet Union. Equally, his argument had undoubted immediate political strengths. Trotsky, in retaining the 1917 formula, was merely promising more of the same, in circumstances where the European working class had proved an unreliable ally. Stalin's new formula gave the rising bureaucracy a sense of purpose and the war-weary, poverty-stricken population a feeling of hope that their collective successes were not conditional upon international revolution.[58] The idea also had a strong pull on members of the Comintern, who were expected to defend the 'bastion' of world socialism.[59] In addition, Stalin's self-sufficient, 'do-it-yourself' socialism gave the Soviet Union greater leverage vis-à-vis the West, in the short term, in comparison to Trotsky's advocacy of technological development through economic integration.[60] Indeed, a tension existed between Trotsky's policies for Soviet economic development (short term) and his strategy of permanent revolution (longer term) insofar as the latter was hardly likely to foster Western goodwill. Moreover, economic growth did occur under isolationist policies, contrary to Trotsky's prognostications,[61] although as we know, this was at enormous human cost to the peasantry.[62] Further, the Soviet regime survived much longer than he expected, in the absence of world revolution, without a restoration of capitalism as defined in orthodox Marxist terms. Nevertheless, unlike Stalin he was very conscious of the degenerative effects that isolation would bring, especially of inequality, bureaucracy and lack of democracy.

In the longer term Trotsky's prediction that the Soviet Union, without world revolution, would not be able to compete with the capitalist West has been validated. So too has his prophecy about the changing role of the Comintern, from the vanguard of world proletarian revolution into an instrument of Soviet foreign policy, and its ultimate demise in 1943, as a result of Stalin's deal with Roosevelt, the United States President. Yet at this point his success, in a strict temporal sense, as a historical forecaster stops.[63] The whole assessment upon which he based his theory of permanent revolution proved illusory. The working class was not the hegemonic force in movements for independence in Africa and Asia, let alone for socialism, in the post-war period. Often urban intelligentsias played a key role, with peasant support.[64] In addition, self-styled 'Marxist' regimes in China and Eastern Europe, as well as Cuba, were hardly exemplars of proletarian self-emancipation. And proletarian revolutions failed to occur in the West. Hence, Trotsky's endeavour to universalize the 1917 strategic formula was debatable.[65] National social, economic and political structures have to be adequately reconnoitred in order to see whether they fit into the October 1917 strategic template. Interestingly, Trotsky, before the debacle of 1927, had seen the Chinese Revolution unfolding in a way different from the Russian.[66] He had adopted Lenin's 1905 stages strategy of a democratic dictatorship of the proletariat and the peasantry. While the stages strategies applied in Spain in the 1930s and elsewhere[67] were disasters or failures, whose form was prompted by the needs of Soviet foreign policy, the choice of a stagist, meant in the broadest sense of the term, or a 'permanent' strategy is a matter of empirical calculation. And this is derived from a concrete assessment of domestic and international class forces, rather than almost *a priori* reasoning, based upon the teleological, 'epochal' assumptions of Lenin's *Imperialism*.

An argument can therefore be made that Stalin's conception of socialism in one country had, especially for those colonial and semi-colonial countries that took the 'socialist' route, much greater historical purchase in the absence of permanent revolution. However these post-colonial regimes were classified, the state for a certain historical period was able to play a key role in independent economic development.[68]

NOTES

1. S. Cohen, *Bukharin and the Bolshevik Revolution*, Vintage Books, New York (1975), 149.
2. Quoted in R. B. Day, *Leon Trotsky and the Politics of Economic Isolation*, Cambridge University Press, Cambridge (1973), 120.
3. In *The Foundation of Leninism* (April/May 1924) he stated: 'For the final victory of socialism, for the organisation of socialist production, the efforts of one country, particularly of a peasant country like Russia, are insufficient; for that, the efforts of the proletarians of several advanced countries are required.' Quoted in I. Deutscher, 'Socialism in one country', in T. Ali (Ed.), *The Stalinist Legacy*, Penguin, Harmondsworth (1984), 95.
4. J. Stalin, 'The October Revolution and the tactics of the Russian Communists', *Selected Writings* (hereafter *ORT*), Greenwood Press, Westport, CT (1970), 12.
5. *ORT*, 14.
6. *ORT*, 15.

7. *ORT*, 15, Stalin's emphasis.
8. *ORT*, 16.
9. V. I. Lenin, *Selected Works*, Lawrence and Wishart, London (1969), 153–6.
10. *ORT*, 18.
11. *ORT*, 20, Stalin's emphasis.
12. *ORT*, 20.
13. *ORT*, 22.
14. *ORT*, 22. See Lenin, *Selected Works*, 690–5.
15. *ORT*, 23.
16. *On the Problems of Leninism*, Foreign Languages Printing House, Moscow (1953), 192.
17. *Errors of Trotskyism*, Communist Party of Great Britain, London (1925), 373–4.
18. L. Trotsky, *Revolution Betrayed*, New Park Publications, London (1967), 292.
19. Day, *op. cit.*, 6.
20. L. Trotsky, *The Permanent Revolution* (hereafter *PR*), New Park Publications, London (1962), 60, Trotsky's emphasis.
21. *PR*, 74.
22. L. Trotsky, *The History of the Russian Revolution* (hereafter *HRR*), *Vol. 3*, Sphere Books, London (1967), 355–8.
23. L. Trotsky, *The Third International after Lenin* (hereafter *TI*), Pathfinder Press, New York (1970), 29.
24. *HRR*, 366.
25. *TI*, 27.
26. *RB*, 295.
27. *TI*, 22.
28. *TI*, 33–4. See also *HRR*, 380.
29. *HRR*, 374.
30. *TI*, 38–9; *HRR*, 382.
31. *TI*, 43, 52, 70.
32. *TI*, 46–7.
33. *TI*, 47.
34. *TI*, 48.
35. *TI*, 49.
36. *PR*, 156.
37. *TI*, 65.
38. *TI*, 12–14.
39. *TI*, 66–8.
40. *TI*, 61. See also *PR*, 27.
41. *TI*, 62, Trotsky's emphasis.
42. *PR*, 27.
43. *TI*, 70.
44. *TI*, 255.
45. M. Lowy, *The Politics of Combined and Uneven Development: the Theory of Permanent Revolution*, Verso, London (1981), 86; J. Molyneux, *Leon Trotsky's Theory of Revolution*, Harvester Press, Brighton (1981), 42.
46. Lowy, *op. cit.*, 82–3.
47. *PR*, 154.

48. *PR*, 154, Trotsky's emphasis.
49. L. Trotsky, *The History of the Russian Revolution, Vol. 1*, Sphere Books, London (1967), 22-3.
50. *PR*, 154-5.
51. Lowy, *op. cit.*, 83.
52. L. Trotsky, *The Death Agony of Capitalism and the Tasks of the Fourth International* (1938), Socialist Labour League, London (1972), 41-3.
53. E. H. Carr, *Socialism in One Country, 1924-1926, Vol. 2*, Macmillan, London (1959), 37.
54. Stalin, *Selected Works*, 155. For further criticisms of Stalin's gloss on the law of uneven development, see F. Claudin, *The Communist Movement: from Comintern to Cominform*, Penguin, Harmondsworth (1975), 71-3.
55. Although Lenin admitted later that Trotsky was correct in 1905. Molyneux, *op. cit.*, 36.
56. Lenin, *Selected Works*, 691.
57. Lenin, 'On co-operation', *Selected Works*, 695. See also 'Our revolution', *op. cit.*, 696.
58. R. Lew, 'Maoism, Stalinism and the Chinese Revolution', in T. Ali (Ed.), *The Stalinist Legacy*, Penguin, Harmondsworth (1984), 276.
59. *Ibid.*
60. Interestingly, the Soviet regime was far from autarkic in the early 1930s, with more than 50 per cent of UK and US machinery exports going to the Soviet Union. R. Blackburn, 'Fin de siecle: socialism after the crash' in Blackburn (Ed), *After the Fall*, Verso, London (1991), 199.
61. Indeed, he later became proud of the Soviet Union's economic achievement. Trotsky, *Revolution Betrayed*, 7.
62. Something of an irony given Stalin's charge against Trotsky that he had 'ignored' the revolutionary potential of the peasantry.
63. Although a distinction can be made between permanent revolution as a strategy and as a prediction, thereby rescuing it as a strategy (Molyneux, *Leon Trotsky's Theory of Revolution*, 43), such a move can be questioned, unless by 'strategy' is merely meant the 'aim' of world proletarian revolution (*ibid.*, 46): in what sense would the strategy be effective, if the predictions hitherto have been so woefully inaccurate? Was the only flaw in Trotsky's prediction a matter of empirical detail or 'betrayal' by the Soviet bureaucracy or social democracy?
64. See T. Cliff, 'Permanent revolution', *International Socialism* (first series), 12 (Spring 1963).
65. See Rosa Luxemburg's awareness of the dangers of generalizing from the Bolshevik experience, in *Rosa Luxemburg: Selected Political Writings* (Ed. R. Looker), Cape, London (1972), 250.
66. Lowy, *op. cit.*, 82.
67. See next chapter.
68. See Nigel Harris, *Of Bread and Guns*, Penguin, Harmondsworth (1983), Chapter 6 *passim*, on the limitations of this form of independent economic development.

9
Fighting Fascism

PROBLEMS AND ISSUES

The second major round in the Stalin-Trotsky conflict concerned how to fight German fascism, between 1930 and 1933. The issue rumbled on a little later in a slightly different form over the Comintern's 'Popular Front' strategy in France and Spain, between 1935 and 1939. In a historical sense Stalin's approach to the rise of fascism was deeply affected, first, by economic problems and changes within the Soviet Union itself, by the agrarian crisis and the beginnings of breakneck industrialization, creating a sense of vulnerability in the face of a potential British and/or French invasion. Second, after having defeated Trotsky, Stalin now entered into factional conflict with Bukharin, who had advocated gradual industrialization at home and building up links with left-wing social democrats abroad. Part of this struggle necessitated the undermining of Bukharin's support within the Comintern (hereafter, the CI).[1] Thus, the rise of fascism coincided with the elimination of any independent critical thinking within this organization.

In the light of these two considerations, an abrupt change of policy occurred at the sixth congress of the CI in August 1928. There was a 'left turn'. The congress announced that the conflict between world capitalism and the proletariat was going through its 'third period' since the Russian Revolution. The first period (1917-23) was characterized by a crisis in capitalism and proletarian offensive, followed by a second period (1924-8) of capitalism's 'partial stabilization' and the proletariat in defensive mode. Following Lenin's thesis in *Imperialism*, the report on 'communism and the international situation' postulated that the contradiction between the productive forces and the shortage of markets was 'inevitably giving rise to a series of imperialist wars; among the imperialist States themselves, wars of the imperialist States against the USSR, wars of national liberation against imperialism and imperialist intervention, and to gigantic class battles'.[2] Conditions were now ripe for turning an imperialist war against the Soviet Union into successful civil wars against the capitalist powers, given the strength of the Soviet Union and the CI. Hence, no doubt to galvanize support for industrialization and to minimize dissent, the world was presented as full of dangers (invasion of the Soviet Union) and opportunities (world revolution). As for fascism, a report of the tenth Executive Committee of the CI in July 1929 declared that growing imperialist contradictions and the intensifying class struggle meant that it was becoming the increasingly 'dominant method of bourgeois rule'.[3]

Yet whatever Stalin's motivations influencing his strategy against fascism, genuine problems were posed for Marxist theory and practice. First, the obvious question: what *was* fascism? How strong was it and what would its policies be, if it attained power? Second, given that the rise of fascism occurred during a world slump, what was the precise relationship between economic instability and workers' political consciousness? Third, and this was the most important question, what sort of political (and class) alliances should be established to combat fascism, since the German Communist Party (KPD) was a significant, if minority, party within the German working class?

MARX AND ENGELS

Although the Comintern had the opportunity to draw upon a rich vein of Marxist analysis of Italian fascism in the 1920s, ranging from the works of Gramsci and Klara Zetkin to Palmiro Toglatti,[4] the general view was that Italy was a special case, owing to its political and industrial backwardness, or that it was only distinctive insofar as it fell within the basic category of a military/authoritarian regime such as Pilsudski's in Poland. Although Trotsky did not rely on such writings, he nevertheless held that there were lessons to be learnt from the Italian experience. He also made use of Marx and Engels's ideas to analyse fascism. He wanted to differentiate clearly, in contrast to the CI, between the 1930–3 fundamentally non-parliamentary, executive-dominated governments of Brüning, von Papen and Schleicher and a Nazi regime. Here, he adopted Marx's analysis of the regime of Louis Napoleon (1852–70) in order to characterize the pre-Nazi system. Marx had described Louis Napoleon's as 'the only form of government possible at a time when the bourgeoisie had already lost, and the working class had not yet acquired, the faculty of ruling the nation'.[5] Louis Napoleon in this situation of class stalemate was able to acquire a good deal of 'relative' autonomy, even from the bourgeoisie, by balancing between the different classes in French society and playing them off against each other. Trotsky saw these pre-Nazi regimes as 'Bonapartist' or 'pre-Bonapartist'.[6] Hitler, however, once in power would not balance between anyone.

Marx and Engels's analysis of the petty bourgeoisie was also relevant to the debate, since this class provided bedrock support for fascism. They viewed this class as one of history's losers, of little political weight. It was an economically decaying class, whose individual members were 'being constantly hurled down into the proletariat by the action of competition, and as modern industry develops, they even see the moment approaching when they will completely disappear as an independent sector of modern society, to be replaced, in manufacture, agriculture and commerce, by overlookers, bailiffs and shopmen'.[7] The petty bourgeoisie's potential political trajectory was equivocal. It tended to be conservative insofar as it wanted to 'roll back the wheels of history'.[8] Or it could be revolutionary, if it accepted that it would form part of the proletariat in the future.[9] So a dilemma arose over how seriously fascism should be taken, if its support came predominantly from this class.

In terms of political and social alliances, which became one of the key issues in the debate, Marx and Engels, as indicated in Chapter 1, normally opposed anything that smacked of sectarianism in relation to other working class political parties and the working class generally.[10] More specifically, the question of party alignment was context-dependent, i.e. dependent upon the situation in which communists found themselves, either as a minority tendency within the working class or where the proletariat was not the majority class in society, and upon whether its 'immediate interests' coincided with other classes. The latter case arose in Germany in 1848, where the working class was in a minority, and the bourgeoisie had to overthrow feudalism. Marx proposed working-class support for the bourgeois demand for a 'single, indivisible democratic German republic'.[11] After the German bourgeoisie's capitulation in 1848, he called upon the revolutionary working-class party to cooperate with the petty bourgeoisie in the struggle for democracy, although it should oppose it when it sought to secure its 'own position' (i.e. against the big bourgeoisie).[12] Hence, as he later stated, he rejected the view that non-proletarian parties constituted 'one reactionary mass'. The bourgeoisie and the petty bourgeoisie could in certain situations and in a limited sense play a historically progressive role.[13]

Further, where the Communist Party did not have the overwhelming support of the proletariat in seeking 'the enforcement of the momentary interests of the working class' (e.g. the attainment of democracy), Marx recommended, for example, in 1848, cooperation with the French social democrats against the conservative and radical bourgeoisie. Yet, in order to 'safeguard the future' of the working-class movement, the party reserved the right of criticism and kept the 'property question' at the forefront of the movement.[14]

THE CONTEXT

The rise of Nazism between 1930 and 1933 was the culmination of a decade of economic and political convulsions which had dogged the Weimar Republic since its inception in 1919. The German economy had difficulty in recovering after the First World War, especially as a result of the Versailles Settlement, which encumbered it with heavy debts and reparations. Stratospheric inflation occurred in 1923, following the French occupation of the Rhineland on account of German non-payment of her debts. Economic stability was temporarily achieved between 1925 and 1928 as a result of United States aid, but the Wall Street crash of October 1929 immediately plunged Germany into deep recession. Within six months three million were unemployed, and by 1933 the figure had doubled. The social impact of all this was enormous. The inflation of 1923 had wiped out the savings of the middle class, driving it to anger, despair and desperation. And the economic nose-dive of 1929 had created a huge army of frustrated unemployed, demanding a drastic remedy to their plight.

The democratic political framework of the Weimar Republic was not built on firm foundations. Although strongly supported by the Social Democrats, it was opposed by the nationalist and revanchist right, embittered by defeat in the First World War and the harsh terms of the Versailles settlement, and by the communist left, who wanted a Soviet republic. Communists were enraged by the Social Democrats' crushing of various working-class uprisings, including the Bavarian Soviet Republic, between 1919 and 1920, in collaboration with the nationalist, paramilitary, Frei Korps. This repression also involved the murder of two well-known leaders of the Spartacist League, Rosa Luxemburg and Karl Liebnecht, in January 1919.

This intense left–right opposition to the republic manifested itself, first, in the so-called 'Kapp Putsch' of March 1920, which was defeated by a nationwide general strike. A year later this was followed by an unsuccessful KPD-organized uprising, the 'March Action'. In October 1923, as a result of inflation and industrial unrest, the KPD prepared for a revolution in highly favourable circumstances, but refused to trigger it off at the last moment. In November, Hitler led the abortive 'Beer Hall' putsch.

The next period of political instability arose after the Wall Street crash of 1929. The Grand Coalition Government, headed by the Social Democrat Hermann Müller, fell in March 1930, unable to agree on measures necessary to tackle the economic crisis. Hindenburg, the President, asked Brüning of the Catholic Centre Party to form a government. Unable to get majority Reichstag support, he called elections for September. These elections were the most significant in the Weimar's history. Although the KPD vote went up by 40 per cent compared with the 1928 electoral result, to four and a half million, the real shock was the rocketing Nazi vote, up in the same period by 800 per cent, from 810,000 to 6,407,600. Nevertheless, Brüning remained in office for the next two years, ruling mostly through presidential decrees, reducing wages and social security payments, and curtailing the rights of parliament and the press. The Social Democrats supported Brüning, as they did Hindenburg, as the 'lesser evil' to Hitler, fearing that a further election would bring the Nazis to power and hoping that the economic crisis would somehow evaporate. The KPD, for reasons explored below, regarded the Social Democrats as 'social fascists' and as the 'main enemy'.

Paramilitary violence returned to the agenda with a vengeance. The conservative nationalist Stalheim (SA) grew from 100,000 in 1932 to 400,000 in 1933. The Social Democrats had their own 'Reichsbanner' paramilitary organization, which they broadened out, in 1932, to include other bodies that they controlled to form an 'Iron Front' to defend the Republic. The Social Democrats felt confident that they had a strong defensive bulwark against the Nazis, especially because they controlled the Prussian government and its police force, which covered two-thirds of Germany, including Berlin. Indeed, this government was a primary Nazi target. In 1931 they used constitutional methods to trigger off a referendum of no confidence. It became known as the 'red referendum' as a result of the KPD siding with the Nazis.

Against this background of mounting violence, General Schleicher of the Reichswehr general staff assumed a greater role in German politics. He secured the dismissal of Brüning in May 1932 and the appointment of von Papen, who achieved one of the Nazis' important, intermediate objectives. As a result of the Prussian government's failure to prevent intense political rioting in June and July, which left 82 people dead, von Papen dismissed the government, albeit unconstitutionally. The moment of truth arrived. The Social Democrats, despite their much-vaunted commitment to legality, refused to mobilize their 'Iron Front', and the KPD call for a general strike went unheeded. The fate of the Weimar Republic was sealed. Although Schleicher became Chancellor in December 1932, big business eventually decided to replace him with Hitler in January 1933. Huge working-class demonstrations greeted Hitler's accession to power, yet the Social Democratic leadership maintained, in essence, that Hitler had come to power legally and that it would use the Iron Front only if Hitler acted unconstitutionally. Hitler, after his rapid integration of the SA and SS into the Reichswehr and the police, no longer felt constrained by the constitutional game. What followed was the physical annihilation of the German labour movement, its trade unions and its parties.

COMINTERN–KPD STRATEGY

As already indicated, the CI in 1929 held that the increased contradictions of capitalism would promote fascism. However, and this was deeply significant for the future course of German and world history, it argued that where social democratic parties were strong, such as in Germany and Britain (and were hostile towards the Soviet Union), fascism 'assumes the particular form of social fascism, which to an ever greater extent serves the bourgeoisie as an instrument for the paralysing of the activity of the masses in the struggle against the regime of fascist dictatorship'.[15] The intensification of the world capitalist crisis and the inevitable revolutionary upsurge necessitated a 'class against class' approach in Britain and Germany, where social democracy was 'chief support of capitalism'.[16] As such, social democrats crushed the working class by 'fascist methods'. For example, the Social Democratic police chief had bloodily suppressed a KPD-organized demonstration in Berlin in May 1929. Thus, the Social Democrats were 'social fascists'. The term was coined by Zinoviev in January 1924, with reference to the aborted German revolution of 1923.[17] It was quickly adopted by Stalin. In a passage much quoted by his supporters in the 'third period', he stated 'Social Democracy is objectively the moderate wing of fascism.' There was 'little ground for thinking that Social Democracy can achieve decisive successes in battles, or in governing the country, without the active support of the fighting organization of the bourgeoisie. These organizations do not negate, but supplement each other. They are not antipodes, they are twins.'[18] The 'social fascist' logic was for Stalinists obvious: if the political and economic situation was 'objectively' revolutionary, then the subjective factor of reformism, i.e. social democracy, became the major impediment, and had to be undermined at least by denunciation. Hence, throughout the rise of German fascism and beyond, the CI insisted that social democracy was the 'main enemy', regarded as 'the most active pacemaker in the development of the capitalist state towards fascism'.[19]

The CI drew a crucial strategic conclusion. As Ernst Thälmann, the KPD leader, stated in 1932, the fascists could only be fought if their 'moderate wing' was overthrown first.[20] Thus, in the face of the Nazi threat little official cooperation with the SPD was seriously sought, and even on the occasions that it was, such offers were rejected by the SDP, partly out of a deep distrust of KPD motives. Tactically, the KPD conducted a policy of a 'united front from below', which meant in effect an appeal to individual Social Democratic workers to join KPD-inspired campaigns. It also involved attempting to set up independent rank and file trade union organizations in opposition to the official – normally Social Democratic – leaderships.

The CI and the KPD clung steadfastly to the view that the SPD were a bigger threat than the Nazis, and that revolutionary crisis was deepening, as manifested in growing support for the KPD and the Nazis. The CI lived in a world of blind optimism. So although the Nazi vote increased astronomically in September 1930, the KPD congratulated themselves in increasing their number of Reichstag deputies from 54 to 77. In any case

Stalin saw in Hitler a German nationalist who would oppose French imperialism.[21] The KPD also drew strength from the increase in party membership, from 125,000 in the late 1920s to 360,000 in late 1932, although recruitment was mainly among the unemployed. The growth in Nazi support in this period, and indeed after Hitler's accession to power, was seen as merely the index of a ripening revolutionary situation, ushered in by the final crisis of capitalism.[22]

There were at least two reasons why the KPD did not take the Nazi threat seriously, apart from being obsessed by the 'social fascist' SPD. First, they regarded the governments of Brüning, von Papen and Schleicher as 'fascist dictatorships'. So Hitler was nothing qualitatively different. Second, they believed that support would melt away as soon as the masses perceived that he could not solve the economic crisis and was leading Germany into war, creating revolutionary opportunities.[23] Such a view stemmed not merely from the CI's economism, but also from its definition of fascism in terms of dictatorship, discounting the significance of its mass, petty bourgeois support. Rather, it was merely an agent of finance capital.[24] Not surprisingly, Remmele, leader of the KPD in the Reichstag, bragged in October 1931: 'We are not afraid of the fascists. They will shoot their bolt quicker than any other government.'[25] With this view of the Nazis and its misguided revolutionary optimism, the CI in December 1933 could still afford to castigate the SPD, after Hitler's rise to power and the crushing of the German labour movement, as the 'main social prop' of 'open fascist dictatorship'.[26]

TROTSKY'S CRITIQUE

Although Trotsky was in exile on the Turkish island of Prinkipo in this period and had only limited information, he was able to make a gruesomely accurate prognosis of fascism. In one of his earliest pieces on fascism, in September 1930, he commented that the 'underestimation of fascism by the present leadership of the Communist Party, may lead the revolution to a more severe crash for many years to come'.[27] A year later he told the German working class: 'Should fascism come to power, it will ride over your skulls and spines like a terrific tank. Your salvation lies in merciless struggle.'[28] In May 1932, he told an interviewer, 'The question of the fate of Germany is the question of the fate of Europe, of the Soviet Union and, in a considerable measure, the fate of all humanity for a long historical period.'[29]

All these dire predictions, Trotsky warned, would be fulfilled unless the whole basis of the Comintern strategy – its analysis of fascism and social democracy – was recast, so that the ranks of the German working class could be united to defeat fascism. Furthermore, the question of political leadership was more vital than ever. Trotsky challenged its root, 'third period', assumption that the 'radicalization of the masses' was a simple epiphenomenon of economic downturn. Such an assumption was unwarranted. The class struggle ebbed and flowed, 'depending upon complicated combinations of material and ideological conditions, national and international'.[30] In the present 'epoch', characterized by 'exceptionally sharp periodic fluctuations, by extraordinary abrupt turns in situation ... unusual obligations' were placed on the leadership 'in the matter of a correct orientation'.[31] The role of leadership was not to predict crises, wars and revolutions every day, but 'to prepare for wars and revolutions by soberly evaluating the circumstances and conditions that are *between* wars and revolutions'.[32] This required the ability to revise tactics in accord with objective and subjective changes in the class struggle. This was something that the Soviet bureaucracy, hidebound by 'centrism', and its subaltern parties in the capitalist West were unable to do.[33]

Not only did Trotsky have doubts about the capacity of the Comintern to lead a revolutionary struggle against fascism. He also declared that it misunderstood the nature of fascism, for such a form of government was no ordinary dictatorship. Drawing from the experience of Italian fascism, he noted that it was

> not merely a system of reprisals, of brute force, and of police terror. Fascism is a particular governmental system based upon the uprooting of all elements of proletarian democracy within bourgeois society. The task of fascism lies not only in destroying the Communist vanguard but in holding the entire class in a state of forced disunity. To this end the physical annihilation of the most revolutionary section of the workers does not suffice. It is also necessary to smash all independent and voluntary organisations, to demolish all the defensive bulwarks of the proletariat, and to uproot whatever has been achieved during three-quarters of a century by Social Democracy and the trade unions.[34]

From this observation Trotsky derived two crucial inferences, which brought him into sharp collision with the Comintern perspective, which was flawed by two 'category mistakes', thereby strategically disarming the working class. First, in dubbing the SPD 'social fascist' the KPD was unable to highlight the fundamental divergence between them and the Nazis. While finance capital might rely on either social democracy or fascism in different periods, the former, supported by the working class, stood for the defence of a 'parliamentary-bourgeois regime' and the latter, supported by the petty bourgeoisie, for its negation.[35] Finance capital, once it had decided to use the 'methods of civil war', enlisted, through fascism, the 'crazed petty bourgeoisie' as a 'battering ram' to annihilate workers' organizations.[36] Thus, the Social Democrats could not simply be seen as part of 'one reactionary mass' along with the Nazis.[37]

The second KPD 'category mistake', which no doubt contributed to its complacency, lay in characterizing the regimes of Brüning, von Papen and Schleicher as fascist. Hence, it was unable to pinpoint the unique nature – and threat – of Nazism. Such analysis could only confuse the working class: how could 'real' fascism be fought if it had already arrived? Trotsky categorized the pre-Hitler regimes as 'pre-Bonapartist' or 'Bonapartist', resting between the petty bourgeoisie and the proletariat.[38]

Trotsky argued that the KPD, owing to its 'social fascist' analysis which rendered the Social Democrats as the 'main enemy', bewildered and disarmed the working class in another sense. The KPD, by holding the impossibility of defeating fascism without first defeating social democracy, implied that fascism was inevitable.[39]

The only way in which fascism could be successfully resisted was by the KPD seeking a united front with the SPD. The arguments in support of this tactic were developed in the early 1920s by Lenin and Trotsky in their opposition to the 'ultra-leftist' Communist Parties, which had just joined the Comintern.[40] *Contra* the Comintern formulation, the united front did not mean a 'united front from below', grounded upon what Trotsky termed 'bureaucratic ultimatism', whereby workers about to participate in struggle were obliged to accept Communist Party leadership in advance.[41] Nor did it mean election agreements, parliamentary compromise or common platforms with reformist party or trade union leaders, which might limit the class struggle or restrict the opportunity for communists to criticize these leaders. The point was to 'march separately, but strike together! Agree only how to strike, whom to strike, and when to strike!'[42] Just as the Bolsheviks had united with the Mensheviks and Social Revolutionaries in August 1917 to defeat the Kornilov uprising to defend the Petrograd proletariat, so had factory defence organizations to be constructed by KPD and SPD workers against the fascists. Not only would such organizations serve to demoralize the fascists, they would intensify 'the differentiation within the Social Democracy'.[43] In particular, the reformist leaders' hold over the working class would be undermined. Communists through the united front confronted the 'reformist organizations before the eyes of the masses with the real problems of the class struggle. The policy of the united front hastens the revolutionary development of the class by revealing in the open that the common struggle is undermined not by the disruptive acts of the Communist Party but by the conscious sabotage of the leaders of the Social Democracy.'[44] Moreover, such factory defence committees had the potential to become organs of soviet democracy.[45] The crucial point, however, was that the appropriate revolutionary strategy consisted not primarily in denouncing the counter-revolutionary sins of social democracy, but in winning rank and file workers to the revolutionary cause by uniting with them in active class struggle.

In sum, Trotsky, unlike the Comintern, was alive to the specific properties of Nazism and the danger it posed to the German working class.

And while, like the Comintern, he saw the Social Democrats as a major obstacle to revolution, there was the key question of strategic priorities. Fascism and social democracy were not 'twins': their class bases of support were different, as were their functions for finance capital. Thus, ultimately, their interests stood in sharp opposition to each other. The job of communists was to make the social democratic rank and file aware of this and to win them over to a revolutionary position through united front activity against the Nazis.

TROTSKY'S CRITIQUE OF THE POPULAR FRONT

After Hitler's ascendency, Trotsky concluded that a Fourth International had to be built. Stalin's and the Comintern's role in this catastrophe for the German and international proletariat had been counter-revolutionary. He no longer relied on attempting to influence the Comintern policy through a left opposition. He continued to advocate the united front, although the Comintern underwent a 180-degree strategic reorientation, from the 'ultra-leftism' of 'class against class' to the class collaborationism of the popular front. This entailed cooperating not only with socialist organizations, but with bourgeois, anti-fascist parties. Stalin's volte-face was determined by foreign policy. He now saw Hitler as a greater threat than France and Britain, and therefore sought *rapprochement* with these two countries, leading, for instance, to a mutual assistance pact with France in 1935. And he was concerned to stop the spread of fascism. He must have in part taken his cue from a successful French general strike against an attempted fascist coup in February 1934, in which communists and socialists worked together. The change of line was announced at the seventh congress of the Comintern in July 1935. The 'self-satisfied sectarianism' of the previous period was rejected.[46] The congress called for a 'people's front' of communists, social democrats, peasants and the urban petty bourgeoisie.[47] Thus, it pressed for working-class unity and it aimed to win over potential fascist sympathisers.

The clearest examples of popular front policy in operation were in France and Spain, between 1936 and 1939. In both cases the working class was defeated in situations of revolutionary possibility. In France a popular front government came to power in May 1936 on an anti-fascist, social reform programme. It consisted of socialists and the liberal bourgeois radicals, supported by the communists (PCF). This raised huge expectations among the working class. In the next month widespread strikes and workplace occupations occurred to achieve primarily, but not exclusively, economic demands. While big gains were made through the Matignon Agreement in the same month, Thorez the PCF leader played a key role in dampening down militant activity. The popular front government, headed for the most part by the socialist Léon Blum, did very little to prevent the employers reversing workers' gains from this agreement. The PCF and the trade union confederation it controlled, the CGT, out of loyalty to a government ostensibly opposed to Germany and fascism, did not support any generalized resistance to the employers' offensive. And when, in November 1938, the by now right-wing-controlled popular front government proposed to restore the six-day working week and introduce other anti-working class measures, the CGT was in no position to organize effective resistance.

Trotsky, after the anti-fascist general strike of February 1934, maintained that 'the key to the situation is now in the united front'.[48] He called for workers' and peasants' defence committees, which could become embryonic soviets.[49] This was effectively the same type of united front he had advocated in Germany. And in June 1936, he maintained that the French revolution had 'begun' and felt that the need for soviets was even more pressing.[50] The choice lay between fascism and proletarian revolution. He argued that the 'people's front' was far too heterogeneous to become an effective force against fascism.[51] Moreover, it stood as an impediment in a 'revolutionary situation', subordinating workers to the bourgeoisie.

In Spain a popular front government came to power in February 1936. As in France its accession raised expectations, sparking off a rash of strikes, land occupations in the countryside and violence against the far right. In response, General Franco from Morocco with support from fifty garrisons on mainland Spain attempted a coup in July 1936. The government refused to supply arms to workers and peasants. Nevertheless, workers, led by the anarchist trade union federation, the CNT, and the independent Marxist POUM, which Trotsky sought to influence, successfully rose up and contained the rebellion, creating their own militias and committees to administer towns and regions. A situation of 'dual power' had arisen, most notably in Barcelona, but in a weaker form in Madrid. Stalin, not wanting to offend or worry France and Britain, supported the popular front government. During the next two years, the Spanish Communist Party and Stalin's agents played an instrumental part in crushing workers' and peasants' organizations. In doing so, they paved the way for Franco's victory. Such action was justified theoretically on the grounds that, socially, Spain was still emerging from its feudal past, and that only a 'bourgeois democratic revolution' could be on the agenda.[52]

Although Trotsky now clearly saw that the Comintern's position on Spain was dictated by Stalin's need to placate Britain and France, he had to demonstrate that it was strategically wrong-headed. Guided by his theory of permanent revolution, he rejected this 'stages' perspective of revolution in Spain. This merely replicated the Menshevik position. Fascism was a bourgeois, rather than a feudal, reaction. The most effective way to fight fascism was to bring about an agrarian revolution in the countryside. This necessitated a proletarian conquest of power because such a revolution could only be achieved in opposition to the bourgeoisie, since the landowners 'were intimately bound up with the commercial, industrial and banking bourgeoisie, and the bourgeois intelligentsia that depends on them'.[53] Moreover, a socialist programme, going beyond a bourgeois democratic revolution, would induce rank-and-file soldiers to join a people's militia and overthrow the officer corps, crucial to the defence of bourgeois interests.[54] Thus, as far as Trotsky was concerned, the popular front, by subordinating the working class and peasantry to the interests of the 'shadow' bourgeoisie (the real one had joined the fascist cause), could not fight fascism effectively. For this to occur, workers and peasants had to be fighting for their own emancipation.[55]

COMMENTARY

In assessing his critique of the popular front strategy, Trotsky correctly noted that the CI's strategy effectively contained working-class struggle, and that especially in the case of Spain it was determined by the needs of Soviet foreign policy. Here, indeed, the Soviet act of 'betrayal' was the sin of commission, rather than omission. Leftist opponents to the popular front line were often physically eliminated, undoubtedly weakening opposition forces to Franco. Whether a similar revolutionary situation existed in France is not quite so clear. The thrust of the workers' movement was more obviously economic in inspiration, and a spontaneous, dual-power scenario did not arise. Thus, the question remains as to whether workers in the advanced liberal capitalist economies of the West were susceptible, to use Gramsci's parlance, to moving from 'economic-corporate' consciousness to something far more hegemonic.

Moving to the issue of German fascism in the early 1930s, Trotsky was more aware of the true nature of fascism and alert to its dangers than the CI. Yet Stalin's and the CI's attitude towards the rise of Nazism cannot be wholly ascribed to domestic problems within the Soviet Union, fear of French/British invasion or the need to eliminate Bukharinite influence. The Comintern's change of policy in 1935 is testament to this. A genuine misunderstanding within the ranks of the Comintern also existed. First, it did not consider seriously the possibility that conclusions could be drawn from the Italian experience. This was seen somehow as an event unique to backward, peripheral societies, and not to advanced, 'democratic' ones. Second, the Comintern on the whole tended to equate any military/ authoritarian regime with fascism. Third, its dim view of social democracy as 'social fascist' was by no means new. It had used the term as early as 1924, prior to Stalin's ascendency, when describing social democracy's role in bringing about post-war capitalist stabilization in Germany, and in doing so it had cooperated with the right-wing paramilitary Frei Korps.

Fourth, the German SPD was responsible for expelling KPD members from trade unions and killing 25 May Day demonstrators in Berlin, in 1929. Fifth, the Grand Coalition government headed by the Social Democratic Herman Müller was antagonistic towards the Soviet Union. Indeed, from a Soviet point of view the capitalist West had been hostile towards it since 1917, whatever the political hue of their governments. Sixth, while the Comintern's optimism about the rapid demise of Hitler was simplistic, this in part derived from an economism found in Marxism and Marx himself. Unemployment throughout the advanced capitalist countries had reached record levels, and few predicted that Hitler would be able to bring about a dramatic revival of the German economy.

In the light of all these potential misunderstandings, Trotsky's prescience was an even greater achievement. Thus, he more readily detected fascism's anti-Soviet, anti-communist and warlike intentions. He also appreciated the strength that fascism gained from its mass, petty bourgeois base, and that it could be deployed by Hitler to prove his usefulness to big business, against the working class as a whole, including the SPD. Hence objective grounds existed for some form of SPD–KPD alliance.

However, even if his united front recommendations, 'from above and below' were in fact implemented by a KPD leadership, the difficulties in achieving cooperation need acknowledgement. The SPD leadership had a deep distrust of the KPD, and treated the occasional offer of cooperation with a good deal of cynicism, which would have been reinforced by the KPD's intense denunciations of 'social fascism' and its participation in the 'red referendum' in the summer of 1931. Moreover, it was antipathetic to the Soviet Union, which had suppressed democracy within its borders. Additionally, the leadership was committed to the very core of its being to legality and the Weimar Republic, which the KPD wished to undermine. The possibility of a successful united front from below would therefore depend largely upon the degree of loyalty rank-and-file SPD members had towards their leadership. A final obstacle to unity lay in a sociological fact: the overwhelming bulk of SPD members were relatively well-paid and unionized, while the KPD consisted largely of the unemployed. Nevertheless, although these problems existed, fascism's rise would have been far from inevitable if the KPD had not insisted upon making the SPD the 'main enemy'. A genuine, united front from 'below' was made doubly difficult if the SPD leadership was continuously denounced as 'social fascist'.

NOTES

1. D. Beetham, *Marxists in the Face of Fascism* (hereafter *MFF*), Manchester University Press, Manchester (1983), 20; F. Claudin, *The Communist Movement: from Comintern to Cominform*, Penguin, Harmondsworth (1975), 156.

2. R. V. Daniels, *A Documentary History of Communism*, Vol. 2, I. B. Taurus, London (1985), 84.
3. J. Degras (Ed.), *The Communist International, 1919-1943* (hereafter *CI*), Vol. 3, Frank Cass, London (1971), 44.
4. *MFF*, 82–148, *passim*.
5. Marx and Engels, *Selected Works*, Vol. 1, 'The civil war in France', 518.
6. See *MFF*, 36-7 for a critique of Trotsky's characterization of Bonapartism.
7. *CM*, 78. See also 62.
8. *CM*, 64.
9. *CM*, 65.
10. See page 8.
11. Quoted in D. Fernbach (Ed.), K. Marx, *The Revolutions of 1848*, Penguin, Harmondsworth (1973), 42.
12. 'Address to the Central Committee', March 1850, in Fernbach, *op. cit.*, 322.
13. 'Critique of the Gotha programme', Marx and Engels, *Selected Works*, Vol. 2, 26.
14. *CM*, 85, 86.
15. *CI*, 44.
16. *CI*, 47.
17. C. L. R. James, *World Revolution, 1917-1936*, Hyperion Press, Westport, CT (1973, first published 1937), 309.
18. *MFF*, 153-4.
19. Eleventh ECCI Plenum, April 1931, in *CI*, 159.
20. *CI*, 214.
21. E. H. Carr, *The Twilight of Comintern, 1930-1935*, Macmillan, London (1982), 27; *CI*, 296.,22.
    Carr, *op. cit.*, 29.
23. See, e.g. Report of ECCI Presidium, April 1933, *CI*, 262.
24. *CI*, 251.
25. Quoted in D. Hallas, *The Comintern*, Bookmarks, London (1985), 131.
26. *CI*, 297.
27. Trotsky, 'The turn in the Communist International and the German situation' in *The Struggle against Fascism in Germany* (hereafter *SAF*), Pathfinder, New York (1971), 61.
28. 'For a workers' united front against fascism' (December 1931), *SAF*, 141.
29. 'Interview with Montag Morgan', *SAF*, 264.
30. 'The "third period" of the Comintern's errors' (January 1930), *Writings of Leon Trotsky, 1930*, Pathfinder, New York (1975), 36.
31. *Ibid.*
32. *Ibid.*, 47.
33. *Ibid.*, 50-1.
34. 'What next? Vital questions for the German proletariat' (January 1932), *SAF*, 144; cf. 155.
35. *SAF*, 155.
36. *SAF*, 155.
37. *SAF*, 145.
38. 'The German puzzle' (August 1932), *SAF*, 268.

39. 'For a workers' united front against fascism', *SAF*, 135.
40. See, for example, L. Trotsky, 'On the united front' (March 1922), *The First Five Years of the Communist International, Vol. 2*, Monad Press, New York (1972), 92–3.
41. 'What next?', *SAF*, 165–6.
42. 'For a workers' united front against fascism', *SAF*, 139.
43. *Ibid.*, 141.
44. 'What next?', *SAF*, 182.
45. *Ibid.*, 195.
46. *CI*, 367.
47. *CI*, 364–5. See also G. Dimitrov, 'The working class against fascism', in *MFF*, 185.
48. L.Trotsky, *Whither France?* (1936), New Park Publications, London (1974), 33.
49. *Ibid.*, 155.
50. *Ibid.*, 136.
51. *Ibid.*, 118.
52. Hallas, *The Comintern*, 154.
53. L. Trotsky, 'The lessons of Spain: the last warning' (December 1937) in *The Spanish Revolution* (hereafter *SR*), Pathfinder Press, New York (1973), 307.
54. 'The lessons of Spain' (July 1936), *SR*, 235–7.
55. 'The lessons of Spain: the last warning', 309.

10

Soviet Union: Degenerated Workers' State or State Capitalist?

PROBLEMS AND ISSUES

For many Marxists the disintegration of the self-styled socialist states of Eastern Europe, including the former Soviet Union, which began in 1989, was profoundly significant. If these states were in some sense built upon a Marxist ideal, then this event represented a dramatic defeat. For other Marxists, if they were 'Marxist' in name only, then their eclipse could ultimately turn out for the good in the long run, increasing the possibilities of creating an authentic Marxist movement.

Even before 1989 Marxists saw the question of how to characterize the command economies of Eastern Europe as important. In the post-war period the western working class, whom they regarded as the key agency for communist advance, looked upon these repressive regimes with little sympathy. If they were truly Marxist, it would be hard to recruit these workers to the Marxist banner. Moreover, to describe these states in some sense as workers' states ran counter to Marx's idea that communism was inextricably bound up with the idea of workers' *self*-emancipation. If they were workers' states, then communism would seem to be less about workers' control over the state and economy, and more to do with state control and planning of production and distribution. Another vital implication of this question was whether during the Cold War these states should be supported against the West. If they were truly 'Marxist' then they should be supported. If not, then Marxists could remain neutral. The answer to this question of how to categorize these states also determined whether to support Third World regimes, such as China and Cuba, which to some extent modelled themselves on the Soviet Union.

Marxists before and after the Second World War have described the Soviet Union to a greater or lesser degree as either 'progressive' – as socialist (Stalin)[1] or as a 'degenerated workers' state' (Trotsky)[2] – or non-

progressive, as some form of non-capitalist class society (Djilas, Shachtman, Rizzi, Ticktin, Bahro)[3] or as state capitalist (Tony Cliff, C. L. R. James,
Raya Dunayevskaya, Charles Bettleheim).[4]

The debate over whether the Soviet Union and similar societies were
degenerated workers' states or state capitalist will be the focus of this
chapter. Of all the debates on the nature of these states, this has been the
most sustained.[5] Furthermore, the communist movement in its Eurocommunist phase during the 1970s, in wishing to create a critical if
friendly distance from the Soviet Union, implicitly embraced Trotsky's
analysis of the Soviet Union.[6] Ironically, this may suggest that Trotsky and
Stalin had greater affinities than is often supposed.

ORIGINS OF THE DEBATE

The origins of this debate lay within the Trotskyist movement in the late
1940s. World events challenged deeply held convictions. From 1945 the
Soviet Union expanded into East Europe and established a network of
communist regimes. This contradicted Trotsky's prediction in 1940 that
Stalin would be swept away by the Second World War, and his depiction of
Stalin as an essentially conservative force, as evidenced by his policy of
'socialism in one country'.[7] In 1946, in order to avoid confronting the
difficulty of whether Stalinism was a progressive force after all, Trotskyists
described the East European regimes as capitalist 'buffer' states, although
they were rapidly coming to look remarkably similar to the degenerated
workers' state of the Soviet Union.[8] This view became untenable after they
sided with Tito against Stalin in 1948. In taking Tito's side, they could
hardly be seen as supporting a capitalist 'buffer' state against a workers'
state, albeit a degenerated one. They saw Tito as heading a 'socialist
revolution'.[9]

By 1951 the Fourth International accepted the logic of its position on
Yugoslavia, and decided that the other states in East Europe were
'deformed workers' states'.[10] But this description raised more questions
than it answered. It implied that the Stalinist bureaucracy was a
progressive force in promoting workers' states, thereby undermining the
whole *raison d'être* of the Fourth International. It also contradicted Marx's
central claim that the transition from capitalism to communism was an
expression of working-class self-emancipation. The official Trotskyist
position implicitly conceded the possibility of workers' revolutions from
above, created principally by the Red Army (except in the case of
Yugoslavia), and that there could be a non-proletarian revolutionary force.

The leadership of the Fourth International, Pierre Frank, James Cannon,
Ernest Mandel and others, ignored the corrosive impact of this line of
reasoning. They reaffirmed Trotsky's position and concluded that the East
European states, including China, which had become communist in 1949,

were deformed workers' states. If, on the other hand, these states were not regarded as authentic workers' states, then the Soviet Union, with its similar economic, political and social structure, could not be a workers' state either. The question now became how best to characterize the Soviet Union and its satellite regimes. Tony Cliff, following in the footsteps of C. L. R. James and Raya Dunayevskaya (who formed the so-called 'Johnson–Forrest' Tendency), in response to these difficulties articulated the theory that the Soviet Union was 'bureaucratic state capitalist'. Although Marxists apart from James and Dunayevskaya, such as Kautsky and Bordiga, had described the Soviet Union as 'state capitalist', Cliff's *The Nature of Stalinist Russia* (1948), later expanded and retitled to become *State Capitalism in Russia*,[11] was the most comprehensive interpretation within this genre. The debate between orthodox Trotskyists, especially Ernst Mandel, and followers of Cliff has raged with a few lengthy pauses to this day.

MARX AND ENGELS ON TRANSITIONAL SOCIETIES

Both sides in the debate, in assessing whether Soviet society was moving in a communist direction could appeal to the authority of Marx and Engels, although their anti-utopianism made them naturally coy in spelling out the details of a post-revolutionary society. Nevertheless, they were clear about three things. First, such a society could not be reached unless there was an international revolution. Communism would be merely a 'local event' and 'each extension of intercourse [i.e. world trade] would abolish local communism'.[12] Second, under the dictatorship of the proletariat the state as a coercive force and its 'semi-autonomy' from the rest of society would begin to disappear. This was because the state would become increasingly subordinate to society through popular involvement in decision-making, administration and accountability.[13] Equally importantly, there would be less need for a coercive apparatus as society became increasingly classless and therefore conflict-free.[14] Third, the proletariat would 'use its political supremacy to wrest, by degrees all capital from the bourgeoisie', which entailed 'despotic inroads on the rights of property'.[15] Production would now be under the control of 'free and associated labour', planning in order to meet human needs.[16] This society, however, would still be 'stamped with the birthmarks of the old society from whose womb it emerges'.[17] Thus, given the continued existence of scarcity, distribution would be according to desert. Only with relative abundance would distribution be on a needs basis.

Soviet reality, however, did not fully match up to these basic notions. The state as an independent coercive force, standing over and above the workers and peasants, grew rather than receded. Nevertheless, Trotsky and his orthodox followers could still claim that the Soviet Union was in some sense progressive because private property had been eliminated and that some form of conscious planning had been introduced, overcoming the anarchy of capitalism. Yet Cliff and others could plausibly assert that the Soviet state itself hardly looked like a transitional one in a Marxist sense.

Both sides, however, made unusual moves in their argument. Orthodox Trotskyists held that the Soviet Union, without any semblance of workers' control over the state or economy, remained a workers' state. On the other side, Cliff and his followers maintained that capitalism could exist, despite the elimination of private ownership of the means of production.

SOVIET UNION AS DEGENERATED WORKERS' STATE: TROTSKY'S *REVOLUTION BETRAYED*

While *Revolution Betrayed*, first published in 1936, was not Trotsky's first or final word on the nature of Soviet Russia, it was by far his most comprehensive and systematic analysis of what had gone wrong in the Soviet Union and of its future trajectory.[18] The book's formulations became the site of sharp contestation between his erstwhile followers, such as Cliff, and his latter-day disciples, such as Ernest Mandel.

In *Revolution Betrayed* Trotsky sought to prove that although the Russian revolution had degenerated, its basic achievements had not been wiped out: 'The October Revolution has been betrayed by the ruling stratum, but not yet overthrown.'[19] He proudly defended its economic achievements, especially its economic growth between 1925 and 1935, when the capitalist West was in decline. This was one of the 'indubitable results of the October Revolution'.[20] Whatever else it may be, the Soviet Union remained a workers' state: 'The nationalization of the land, the means of industrial production, transport and exchange, together with the monopoly of foreign trade, constitute the basis of the Soviet social structure. Through these relations, established by the proletarian revolution, the nature of the Soviet Union as a proletarian state is for us basically defined.'[21]

Yet he admitted that it was not yet a socialist state owing to the continued existence of scarcity, which meant that the nationalized productive forces could not yet satisfy human needs.[22] Rather, it was a transitional society, a '*preparatory* regime *transitional* from capitalism to socialism'.[23] As such the regime exhibited a 'dual character': 'socialistic, insofar as it defends social property in the means of production; bourgeois, insofar as the distribution of life's goods is carried out with a capitalistic measure of value and all the consequences therefrom'.[24] This 'dual character' would persist until labour productivity was sufficient to overcome scarcity.

The crux of the problem facing the Soviet Union was the existence of intense scarcity. Building on what Marx had to say about the impossibility of communism under such conditions,[25] Trotsky argued that scarcity provided 'an indispensable theoretical key to the wholly concrete difficulties and sicknesses of the Soviet regime'.[26] In particular, the state bureaucracy, rather than disappearing according to Marxist theory, was getting ever larger and stronger. It derived its power from its role in the allocation of scarce consumption goods. In a famous passage he stated:

> The basis of bureaucratic rule is the poverty of society in the objects of consumption, with the resulting struggle of each against all ... the purchasers are compelled to stand in line. When the line is very long, it is necessary to appoint a policeman to keep order. Such is the starting point of the power of the bureaucracy. It 'knows' who is to get something and who has to wait.[27]

Trotsky also saw scarcity at the root of bureaucracy in a slightly different way. It generated social divisions: 'conflicts between city and country, between collectives and individual peasants, between different strata of the proletariat, between the whole toiling mass and the bureaucracy'.[28] And 'bureaucracy and social harmony were inversely proportional to each other'.[29] The bureaucracy, in mediating between all these social antagonisms, was able to accrue more power to itself: 'exploiting the social antagonisms, a bureaucracy has converted itself into an uncontrolled caste alien to socialism'.[30] It was thus a 'Bonapartist regime'.[31] Trotsky did, however, acknowledge that the bureaucracy had more specific, historical origins which lay in the early 1920s, after members of the demobilized Red Army assumed leading roles in many areas of Soviet society, within the context of masses who were 'culturally backward', a politically exhausted proletariat and the loss of many working-class leaders during the civil war. Moreover, the bureaucracy acquired more power as a result of its arbitrating role between the proletariat and the growing petty bourgeoisie during the New Economic Policy period (1921–8). The bureaucratic process was also reinforced by a series of important working-class defeats in the rest of the world during the 1920s.[32]

While Trotsky admitted that the regime had its imperfection, he strongly resisted the idea that 'finished social categories' could be applied to it.[33] It was a transitional society in a state of flux. It would be either pulled back towards capitalism or pushed forwards towards socialism. The revolution's fate rested on the proletariats of Russia and the world.[34]

More specifically he challenged the notion that the Soviet regime was 'state capitalist'. Such a term could be used to describe state intervention in capitalist economies designed to preserve existing property relations. It necessarily assumed a limited form. The total state expropriation of the means of production would be resisted by the capitalist class. Such an expropriation could only arise through a social revolution, as had occurred in the Soviet Union.[35] In addition, he rejected the idea that the bureaucracy was in some sense a state capitalist class:

> The bureaucracy has neither stocks nor bonds. It is recruited, supplemented and renewed in the manner of an administrative hierarchy, independently of any special property relations of its own. The individual bureaucrat cannot transmit to his heirs his rights in the exploitation of the state apparatus. The bureaucracy enjoys its privileges under the form of an abuse of power. It conceals its income; it pretends that as a special social group it does not even exist. Its appropriation of a vast share of the national income has the character of social parasitism.[36]

The absence of any legal justification of its privileges also denoted that the bureaucracy was not a ruling class. To constitute itself as such it would have to transform the existing socialized property relations, which defined the Soviet Union as a workers' state, into private legal relations.[37] Although it acquired an unusual degree of independence from the dominant class, i.e. the proletariat, its 'fear' of this class compelled it to 'defend state property as the source of its power and its income'.[38]

Thus, if the bureaucracy did manage to change property relations, it would mean that it would have to overthrow the working class through a social revolution. Since the bureaucracy was not a ruling class, then only a *political* and not a social revolution was necessary to purge the state, through the restoration of democracy to the soviets and trade unions and the granting of freedom to political parties.[39] Any economic reforms would take place within the existing planned framework. Conversely, a capitalist restoration required little democratization of the existing state, and would initiate a social revolution through the introduction of private ownership of the means of production.

Trotsky advanced a more general argument in favour of a political rather than a social revolution. Within bourgeois societies, political revolutions had occurred, leaving the economic foundations of society intact, as in France (1830 and 1848) and Russia (February 1917). Therefore, he argued, the overthrow of the 'Bonapartist caste' would have 'deep social consequences, but in itself it will be confined within the limits of political revolution'.[40]

TONY CLIFF: CRITIQUE AND THE STATE CAPITALIST ALTERNATIVE

Critique

Cliff challenged Trotsky's idea that a democratic political revolution would among other things merely involve a purge of the state apparatus, and therefore by implication that the bureaucracy was not a ruling class. He suggested that a close relationship existed between the *form* and *content* of a workers' state. A workers' state had *of necessity* to be democratic, because the working class, as a class, could not organize itself in any other way. In reality the Soviet state was a specialized coercive machine separate from society. Hence, if a bourgeoisie came to power it would be left essentially unchanged. The working class, on the other hand, would not merely purge the existing state apparatus, but would have to smash it in order to recast it in a democratic mould. Therefore Trotsky was wrong in citing the political revolutions in France (1830 and 1848) and Russia (February 1917) as analogous to the sort of revolution required in the Soviet Union. Here, there were changes in the form of government, but the form of state apparatus remained the same.[41]

The logic of political revolution was that even if the personnel of the state changed, the same class retained power. Trotsky therefore assumed that workers and bureaucrats were of the same class, and that no class struggle existed in the Soviet Union, which was precisely what Stalin argued![42]

Moreover, Trotsky, in wishing to avoid the uncomfortable conclusion that the bureaucracy was a ruling class, insisted that its power stemmed from its control over the means of distribution. Cliff saw this as a far too narrow account of the bureaucracy's power. It sundered the intimate connection between the realms of production and distribution, and ignored in an un-Marxist fashion the dependence of the latter upon the former. The bureaucracy controlled production relations as well as consumption relations. Indeed, it subordinated consumption to the requirements of production, and in so doing reproduced scarcity in the means of consumption. Cliff therefore suggested that the source of the bureaucracy's power was more its control over the means of production than its control over the means of consumption. Hence, it was a class.[43]

Trotsky also denied that the bureaucracy was a ruling class owing to its fear of the proletariat. This led it to defend socialized production relations, which defined the Soviet Union as a workers' state. Thus he put himself in the absurd position of claiming that the proletariat was sufficiently strong to prevent the bureaucracy from passing laws in favour of private property, yet unable to resist the harsh pattern of distribution imposed by the bureaucracy.[44]

The very notion that the absence of private property through state ownership of the means of production distinguished the Soviet Union as a workers' state was itself highly problematic. It involved a far too simplistic account of the relationship between legal relations and relations of production, with the former a mere reflection of the latter. Historically, similar types of exploitive production relations could coexist with different forms of ownership. For example, the peasantry in the Middle Ages was equally exploited whether it worked on non-privately owned church lands or on feudal estates. Moreover, Arab feudalism was based upon state property, with members of the ruling class having no individual property rights. Yet the Arab peasantry was exploited in a way similar to its European counterpart, although legal relations differed.[45]

Finally, the 'new democracies' of Eastern Europe severely tested Trotsky's definition of the Soviet Union. He would have had to admit that they too were workers' states because they possessed structures similar to the Soviet Union. Yet the East European revolutions, as revolutions from above, completely contradicted Marx's theory of proletarian revolution, which entailed the proletariat self-consciously emancipating itself. These states therefore had to be something other than workers' states.[46]

Cliff concluded that the central flaw in Trotsky's analysis was his assumption that private property was the fulcrum of the class struggle; that if the Soviet Union was isolated, capitalism in the form of private property would be restored. Thus, he was unable to contemplate seriously the possibility that the 'old capitalist class content' could take a 'new "socialist" form'.[47]

The bureaucratic state capitalist alternative

Cliff sought to show that the Soviet Union was not a transitional society and that a capitalist restoration had occurred, although the revolution had not returned to its point of departure. This restoration manifested itself in a novel capitalist formation, as 'bureaucratic state capitalism', in which the state bureaucracy constituted itself as a class, running the Soviet economy like a giant firm, 'USSR Ltd'.

Cliff held that the Soviet regime was indelibly etched with an essential hallmark of capitalism: the irrepressible imperative to accumulate the means of production. Consumption and the labour process were subordinated to the process of 'accumulation for accumulation's sake'.[48] The bureaucratic state capitalist 'counter-revolution' occurred in 1928 with the introduction of the first Five Year Plan. The bureaucracy was responding to the political setbacks abroad, such as the defeat of the Chinese communists by the Kuomintang in 1927, subsequent isolation and increased threats of invasion. The defence of the Soviet Union required a rapid build-up of the arms industry. This in turn necessitated the speedy development of heavy industry: hence the need for breakneck accumulation.[49]

The first Five Year Plan led to the loss of any remnants of workers' control over the labour process: the growth of one 'man' management, the emasculation of trade unions, the gradual elimination of collective agreements between management and workforce, the atomization of the working class through individual piece-work agreements, the use of Stakhanovite-influenced work norms, the subjection of women to heavy labour and the introduction of internal passports.[50] Moreover, in order to shift resources from consumption to 'capital investment' and defence, a turnover (or purchase) tax was introduced, the most important single source of state revenue.[51] Agriculture was collectivized in order to create large agricultural surpluses essential to industrialization.[52]

The bureaucracy, in 'owning' the state and thereby controlling the accumulation process, became the 'personification of capital in its purest form'.[53] Hence, in contrast to what Trotsky said, the significance of the bureaucracy stemmed from its role in the productive process, and not from its control over distribution or its parasitism as manifested in its material privileges. It was a class, not a caste.[54]

Cliff held that the Soviet Union resembled private capitalism in three crucial respects. First, he argued that the law of value – central to Marx's analysis of capitalism – operated in the Soviet Union. In brief, Marx had maintained that the law of value determined both the production and distribution of commodities within the capitalist mode of production. In an economy in which the division of labour operated and production was carried out by private producers, a system of exchange was necessary to coordinate these activities. In order for it to work, the commodities involved in this process had to possess a common, measurable characteristic, so that equivalents could be exchanged. For Marx, the only common measurable feature was the amount of 'abstract labour time'; that is, the amount of socially average labour time of an unskilled worker, embodied in a commodity. This determined its exchange value. Marx held that if the demand for a commodity rose then its price would exceed its value, which in turn would increase profits and investment of the firm producing the commodity. Similarly, the reverse process would occur if demand fell for the commodity. Thus, investment flowed from the less to the more profitable areas of an economy. Either way, because exchange takes place on a competitive basis, there is constant pressure upon capitalists to reduce the amount of abstract labour required to produce a given commodity. The principal means by which this is achieved is through increased investment in the means of production, which boosts productivity.[55]

In order to demonstrate that the law of value existed within the Soviet economy, Cliff conceded that price was not a regulator of production *within* the Soviet economy, that the law of value was 'partially negated'.[56] But he claimed, first, that the law of value was 'partially negated' in modern, private capitalism, either as a result of state intervention in the economy, regulating the flow of capital, or through monopolies undermining price competition.[57] More crucially, he argued that the law of value operated within the context of military competition with the West. Viewed

LIVERPOOL JOHN MOORES UNIVERSITY
LEARNING SERVICES

from this perspective, the Soviet Union could be seen as one large company, within which a planned division of labour operated, as within any capitalist firm. The planning of total labour time was determined by military competition; that is, competition in arms 'use values'. Such competition compelled the Soviet bureaucracy to subordinate the labour process to these dictates, entailing in effect a reduction of abstract labour times, etc.[58]

Second, Cliff suggested that the Soviet Union was *potentially* (he was writing before the gradual decline of the Soviet economy that began in the 1950s) subject to a crisis deriving from a problem found in private capitalism: the potential mismatch between the production of production goods and the production of consumption goods. However, he appeared uncertain about the precise way in which an economic crisis might manifest itself.[59]

There was a third explicit similarity with capitalism: the Soviet Union was an imperialist power, albeit closer to the Japanese than to the Western model prior to the Second World War. Thus, although Japan possessed little surplus capital, it industrialized its colonies, such as Manchuria, in order to catch up with the West. For a similar reason, the Soviet Union industrialized the Caucasus and Ukraine as part of its policy of general industrialization.[60] Furthermore, just as Japan looted China as part of a process of primitive accumulation, so the Soviet Union looted Eastern Europe.[61] The satellite states were also important to the Soviet economy. The lack of capital led to the wasteful use of labour power, and hence the need for fresh supplies of labour from Eastern Europe. Finally, apart from crushing nationalities as any imperialist power did, the Soviet Union behaved in a typically imperialist fashion in buying cheaply from Eastern Europe and selling dear, and using cheap labour from these satellite states.[62]

MANDEL'S CRITIQUE OF STATE CAPITALISM

The argument over the nature of the Soviet Union revived in the 1960s as various Trotskyist tendencies, in seeking to capitalize on student unrest and on various working-class upheavals in Europe and elsewhere, emphasized their ideological differences.[63] The debate now had implications for the characterization of other countries, such as China and Cuba, where statified production relations were in place.

Ernest Mandel, in his critique of state capitalism, aimed to do two things. First, he rejected the idea that Marx's analysis of capitalism could be applied to the Soviet Union. Second, he reasserted Trotsky's position, outlined in *Revolution Betrayed*, that the Soviet Union was a degenerated workers' state and therefore a society transitional between capitalism and communism. This formulation was held by most Trotskyist groups, apart from Cliff's International Socialists (which became the Socialist Workers' Party in 1977).

In the question of whether Marx's model of capitalism could be applied to the Soviet Union, a prior issue had to be decided: what were its most significant features? While Cliff insisted that the defining feature of capitalism was accumulation for accumulation's sake, Mandel wanted to put this process in a broader perspective. The *differentia specifica* of capitalism was that 'commodity production becomes generalized'.[64] This form of production expressed itself as universal competition between separate capitals, where each, in order to survive, was compelled to accumulate exchange values, because reinvestment was required in order to cut costs. The existence of money was central to the accumulation process, to further accumulation, to the purchase of more commodities in the form of the means of production and labour power.[65] Economic crises arose from a contradiction between the process of production and the realization of surplus value; that is, from the sale of the commodities produced. This was the so-called crisis of over-production, a crisis inherent in capitalism.[66] Finally, following Marx and partly agreeing with Cliff, Mandel held that resources under capitalism were allocated according to the law of value.

He maintained that this picture of capitalism did not fit the Soviet economy. Its principal impulse was not the accumulation of exchange values, but use values.[67] There was no flow of capital from less to more profitable areas, as would be expected if the law of value operated. No cyclical movements of investment, income and output, periodic crises or unemployment existed. If a tendency to crisis existed in the Soviet economy it was due to under-production rather than over-production. The law of value did not operate on an external basis as a result of the world market. The Soviet economy was involved in little international trade.[68] Moreover, Cliff and others had failed to demonstrate how arms competition carried out the same role as economic competition in ensuring that the law of value operated.[69] Further, workers were not exploited in a Marxist sense. Labour power was not sold through a market to employers as a commodity, essential for the augmentation of capital, and unemployment was not deliberately created to reduce the price of labour power.[70] Indeed, historically wages in the Soviet Union tended to fall when unemployment fell, and rise when unemployment rose, quite the opposite of wage fluctuation under capitalism.

Not only was class exploitation absent, the bureaucracy did not correspond to a capitalist class. It was under no compulsion to maximize output and optimize resource allocation, a consequence of market competition. Instead, the '*consumption desires* of the bureaucracy (like the consumption desires of pre-capitalist classes) *and not the need to maximise accumulation and output* are the motive force behind bureaucratic

LIVERPOOL JOHN MOORES UNIVERSITY
Aldham Roberts L.R.C.
TEL. 0151 231 3701/3634

management'.[71] Finally, closely following Trotsky, Mandel argued that the state apparatus could not be capitalist, because workers would resist a capitalist restoration, with its job losses, etc. The bureaucracy was therefore committed to defending a planned economy, and if a capitalist restoration was successful, the existing state would have to be 'replaced by a state apparatus of another type, geared to the defence of private property and "free enterprise"'.[72]

In defending Trotsky's analysis of the Soviet Union, he rejected the view that the first Five Year Plan heralded a social counter-revolution, the sole product of external pressure to increase arms production. Any workers' state would have to defend itself. It was not therefore capitalist.[73] Moreover, the plan was just as much the product of internal pressures. There was a need for 'accelerated industrialization', because growth had been too slow before 1928. Existing levels of production had failed to satisfy the consumption needs of the workers and poor peasants.[74] Industrialization was also crucial in preventing capitalist restoration: by increasing self-sufficiency, it reduced the pressure to increase ties with the world market. Additionally, the collectivization of agriculture also eliminated a potentially powerful restorationist force – the kulaks. Although the specific form of industrialization signalled the social and political defeat of the working class by the bureaucracy, it also represented a setback for the Russian and international bourgeoisies.[75] Furthermore, the type of industrialization was not forced upon the Soviet Union through the world market or military competition. Since the productive forces had been socialized, the working class did have a choice as to how to industrialize. For example, it could have assumed the form proposed by Trotsky, with lower investment coupled with higher wages and therefore higher productivity.[76]

Finally, while Mandel conceded that economic problems existed in the Soviet Union, they derived not from competitive relations with the rest of the world or from its 'capitalist' nature, but from its transitional status as a workers' state. So although the Soviet Union experienced rapid economic growth, often when the capitalist world stagnated, as in the 1930s, it suffered major contradictions between socialized production and a bourgeois mode of distribution, generated by scarcity. Put another way, there was a conflict between 'plan' and 'market', between production that is planned for and goods actually demanded.[77] This contradiction expressed itself in different ways: the existence of unsaleable stocks because prices were too high or quality poor,[78] and disproportional development between industry and agriculture, between the heavy goods and consumer goods sectors,[79] and between the purely accounting role of money in the former and its role as a real equivalent in the latter.[80] These contradictions were exacerbated by the move from extensive to more intensive or qualitative industrialization, requiring far more sophisticated products.[81] Finally, a contradiction arose between the plan and the personal interests of the bureaucracy, which led to waste, over-fulfilment of the plan and hoarding.[82]

IN DEFENCE OF STATE CAPITALISM

Defenders of the state capitalist thesis have sought to show that the Soviet Union and similarly statified economies operated *either* according to the laws of classical capitalism as depicted by Marx *or* according to the laws of modern capitalism.

They have suggested, using the theories of Hilferding, Bukharin and Lenin, that twentieth-century capitalism works differently from its nineteenth-century incarnation. First, Hilferding had asserted that monopolies had partially undermined the law of value because there was now no necessary correspondence between price and value. Second, Lenin and Bukharin in their different ways had noted that modern capitalist economies had been powerfully shaped by the need to wage war, arising from imperialist competition. Third, Bukharin in particular highlighted how the state and economy were merging in the most advanced countries, owing to both military conflict and economic competition between monopolies. The international order increasingly assumed the form of a generalized conflict between a series of state capitalist trusts.[83] The law of value became further modified in this process.

Building on these observations, Chris Harman and others restated the view that the Soviet Union, as part of a world economic and political system, was compelled on the pain of extinction to compete militarily with the West. This necessitated the rapid build-up of heavy industry. A state capitalist 'counter-revolution' had occurred in 1928 with the introduction of the first Five Year Plan. Stalin is quoted in support: 'We are fifty years behind the advanced countries. We must make good this [industrial] lag in ten years. Either we do it or they crush us.'[84] Hence, these exogenous factors determined the need for the millions of tons of iron and steel, rather than the consumption needs of the bureaucracy, as Mandel had argued.[85]

Harman agreed that capitalism consisted of 'competition on the basis of commodity production', but argued that military rather than economic competition with the West led to imposition of the law of value on the Soviet economy, however 'partially' negated.[86] Because arms and heavy goods producers in the West attempted to reduce labour costs, the Soviet Union in its bid to keep up had to follow suit. Thus, 'every concrete act of labour' in the Soviet Union was 'related to abstract labour on a world scale'.[87]

Insofar as the law of value was negated – that is, value not determining resource allocation through competition – this was merely reflecting a process that had been going on in the West during the twentieth century, albeit in a more exaggerated way. First, monopolies and cartels have arisen, as an expression of a long-run tendency towards the centralization and concentration of capital, whose internal planning mechanisms and outcomes are not determined by price competition in a direct sense.[88] Just as importantly, the role of the state has increased enormously in economic life, in both the West and the so-called Third World. In its most extreme form, during the First and Second World Wars, state involvement in the planned allocation of resources was in direct contradiction to private capitalist market relations. The major Western capitalist economies were in these periods remarkably similar to the Soviet economy.[89] Nevertheless, they remained capitalist: military competition forced comparisons in labour productivity between the contestants.[90]

Not only military survival required state intervention. Even in periods of relative peace, from the 1930s onwards the state intervened to secure the survival of national economies, preventing the law of value operating by subsidizing or nationalizing industries important to these economies that were failing to compete.[91] Before the Second World War the Japanese and German economies were both heavily under state control. After the Second World War, starting with the Chinese revolution in 1949, statized economies grew in the so-called Third World, in order to mobilize resources to facilitate capital accumulation, such as in Brazil and Mexico.[92]

However, although the Soviet economy bore striking similarities to modern capitalism, it also corresponded to its classic form. Apart from the overall compulsion to accumulate, it experienced periodic crises of over-production as a result of the over-accumulation of 'capital'. Competition with the West led to excessive levels of investment and bottlenecks in the economy, compelling the state to freeze investments in order to divert resources to other areas of the economy.[93] Yet Harman admitted that because bureaucratic directives rather than the market controlled the movement of resources, crises led to a cut in growth rates rather than 'a fall in industrial output, plant closures and sharp rises in unemployment'.[94] And he conceded that these crises 'did not express themselves exactly in accordance with Marx's model'.[95]

Second, state capitalist economies experienced something closely akin to long-term tendencies of the rate of profit to fall. There has been a gradual decline in the investment/output ratio, i.e. greater investment producing proportionately less output, which under private capitalism is expressed in the form of a declining rate of profit.[96]

EXPLAINING THE COLLAPSE OF 1989

An evaluation of both sides of the argument can be begun by examining their attempts to account for the collapse of the Eastern European and Soviet regimes which began in 1989.

Mandel, consistent with his Trotsky-inspired analysis, explained their demise ultimately in terms of bureaucratic deformation. True, in keeping with his previous position, there were many symptoms of the problem: 'too little central [democratic] planning and ... too little market',[97] dispropor-tionalities between heavy and light industry and subsequent waste,[98] and the difficulty in moving from 'extensive to intensive industrialisation'.[99] Yet the root cause lay with the behaviour of the bureaucracy, its 'conservative parasitism'.[100] It had lost its 'thirst' for sustaining high levels of productivity, because it 'had reached a satisfactory level of consump-tion'.[101] Its lack of dynamism was also explained in a slightly different, if potentially contradictory, way: its income was not determined by profitability, but by individual position in the hierarchy.[102] Thus, it had little incentive to be efficient. Whatever these problems, the process of democratization had confirmed Trotsky's view that the bureaucracy was not a ruling class. If the *nomenklatura* was a ruling class it would not readily have given up its power.[103]

On the whole there was little disagreement about the symptoms of the economic crisis. However, Harman saw the collapse of 1989 from a global perspective, as a result of states East and West being increasingly unable to suppress the symptoms of a deep-seated economic crisis.[104] Owing to the long-standing problems of over-accumulation, which created economic bottlenecks, the state capitalist economies became increasingly dependent on the international economy for both finance and markets. Firmly locked into the international economy, they then became subject to its fluctuations. From the 1970s onwards the rapid internationalization of the world economy, through the growth of international investment and increased international division of labour, meant that 'the state began to lose its ability to suppress the symptoms of crisis, to stop overaccumulation of capital ... giving rise to overproduction'.[105] The decline of the international economy meant that the state capitalist regimes' room for manoeuvre in trying to solve their economic problems became less. The introduction of the market, tied into the international economy, seemed to be the only option, however painful.

The move towards privatization and the market was a 'step sideways from one way of organising capitalist exploitation to another'.[106] Thus, in contrast to Mandel, who assumed that the *nomenklatura* could not be a class because it had given up power so easily, Harman asserted that it remained very much in the economic and political saddle, although certain changes in the economic and political structures had occurred.[107]

COMMENTARY

A strength of Mandel's account of the collapse of 1989 and after was that he focused on the specific nature of the economic problems of the Soviet

Union and Eastern Europe and how they arose from difficulties inherent in bureaucratic planning. Yet, because he put so much weight on the failings of the bureaucracy, he left the question of why the crisis happened when it did unanswered. This was the strength of the state capitalist position, which situated the Eastern European crisis within a global context and the growing international dependence of these economies. Such a perspective had the merit of explaining why this bureaucratically induced stagnation became significant at a specific time. More realistically domestic *and* international factors were brought into play. And this view closely reflected Marx's position, referred to earlier in the chapter, in acknowledging the insurmountable problems of an isolated workers' state in attempting to achieve socialism.

Another of Mandel's weaknesses, which again stemmed from his uncritical defence of Trotsky's workers' statist position, was his insistence that the bureaucracy would not bring about a capitalist restoration because it feared the working class. If the Soviet Union and the other regimes were genuine workers' states, strong working-class resistance to privatization and the market would have been expected. This has not occurred. The strength of the state capitalist view, that the Soviet Union was not a workers' state, is that it helps to explain why this did not happen.

More generally, the difficulty with Mandel's argument was that form tended to triumph over content. It assumed a progressive core to Stalinist regimes because nationalized property relations had replaced private ownership and planning had superseded market anarchy. The *actual* relations of production, in which workers were excluded from control over the production process, were largely ignored. So too was the *content* of economic planning, which was strongly influenced by the need to survive militaristically in a hostile capitalist world.

Nevertheless, Mandel's insistence that there was something distinctive about the Soviet and allied regimes suggests lines of criticism which can be developed against the state capitalist position.[108] For example, is arms competition strictly analogous to economic competition in imposing the law of value? Do strict comparisons of labour productivities in arms-related industries to those in the West necessarily have to be constantly made, given that the state can shift resources from other sectors of the economy to these industries? Do losers in military competition necessarily go bankrupt, or do they just go into a lower division? To what extent was military competition between the USSR and USA over-generalized in order to make it as universal as economic competition? What are we to make of the post-Cold War reductions of arms expenditure in the West and East? To what extent is arms competition as systemic as economic competition, especially given the importance of imponderable political factors in determining the rhythm of such competition? What is at least required is far more evidence to support the arms/economic competition analogy. Cliff's book, the bulk of it written in the 1940s and 1950s, was the last piece of serious empirical research to corroborate this perspective.

More broadly, we can ask: because there is a 'partial negation' of the law of value under modern capitalist conditions of monopoly, state control and state intervention, and because a 'partial negation' existed in the Soviet Union, must the latter therefore have been capitalist? Could we not argue that total state control of the economy *in certain circumstances* allows for a great deal of room for manoeuvre or *choice* as to whether the law of value can be to some degree negated or indeed followed? In terms of 'partially' negating the law of value, did not state control enable Soviet-style economies to promote relatively full employment, reasonable health and welfare services? Could not this type of control over the economy account for why the 'laws of motion' did not in fact correspond exactly to those in more obviously capitalist economies (which followers of Cliff admit)? Furthermore, if these laws of motion are different, did it also not mean that the dynamics of Soviet imperialism have to be perceived in a different way, as possibly not involving the same forms of compulsive and systemic exploitation? Finally, if the erstwhile Stalinist states were essentially capitalist, how do we explain the persistent antagonism of the West to them? True, capitalist states fought each other in two world wars, but their antagonism has not been so deep and persistent. Is there not a clear material and ideological basis to this conflict? Were not the 'state capitalist' states able to negate partially the law of value in important ways, which raised uncomfortable questions for the ruling classes of the West who wanted to resist improving the living conditions of their workers? And did not these statified economies deny the West easy access to their material resources? Was the Cold War explicable in terms of two forms of capitalist imperialism? All these questions arise from Cliff's and his followers' attempts to explain the structure and dynamics of these societies solely in terms of some form of capitalism.

Yet to admit that these states were in significant ways differerent from orthodox capitalist states does not mean agreeing with Trotsky's defencist position. These states could still be seen to be run by small and privileged ruling classes, compelled in many crucial respects to dance to the capitalist tune. Yet it could also be admitted that these ruling classes were able to negate partially the law of value in meaningful ways. However, as a consequence of the failure of a world socialist revolution to materialize, of growing dependence on the West and of global economic downturn, these states' power of 'negation' weakened, a process also replicated among Western states. Thus, although the state capitalist perspective may be overdrawn, it sharply highlights the limitations of the notion that islands of socialism are largely unaffected by existing in a sea of capitalism. Equally, unless the 'sea' can be changed they will be swamped by the inevitable tidal wave. Thus, the 'reforms' – the 'negations' of value – of these so-called state capitalist regimes possess a certain fragility.

NOTES

1. See e.g. J. V. Stalin, 'Marxism and linguistics' in C. Wright Mills (Ed.), *The Marxists*, Penguin, Harmondsworth (1962), 290–1.
2. L. Trotsky, 'The death agony of capitalism and the tasks of the Fourth International' (1938), Socialist Labour League, London (1972), 47.
3. M. Djilas, *The New Class*, Allen and Unwin, London (1957), 35; M. Shachtman, *The Bureaucratic Revolution*, Donald Press, New York (1962), 81; B. Rizzi, *The Bureaucratization of the World*, Tavistock, London (1985), 54; H. Ticktin, 'Towards a political economy of the USSR', *Critique*, 6 (1976), 17–44; R. Bahro, *The Alternative in Eastern Europe*, New Left Books, London (1978).
4. T. Cliff, *State Capitalism in Russia* (hereafter *SCR*), Pluto Press, London (1974); C. L. R. James, *State Capitalism and World Revolution*, Charles H. Kerr, Chicago (1985); R. Dunayevskaya, *Marxism and Freedom*, Twayne Publishers, New York (1958); C. Bettleheim, *Class Struggles in the USSR First Period: 1917–1923* and *Class Struggles in the USSR Second Period: 1923–1930*, Harvester, Hassocks (1976 and 1978). Earlier Marxist criticisms of the Russian revolution include Karl Kautsky, *The Dictatorship of the Proletariat*, National Labour Press, Manchester (1919); Rosa Luxemburg, *The Russian Revolution* (1922), University of Michigan Press, Ann Arbor, MI (1961); A. Pannekoek, *Lenin as Philosopher* (1938), Merlin Press, London (1975).
5. A rival theory that the Soviet Union was 'bureaucratic collectivist' (see Shachtman, *op. cit.*; Rizzi, *op. cit.*), that the bureaucracy collectively exploited the working class for their own material benefit, has also been held by some Trotskyists and ex-Trotskyists, but the theory never became as hotly debated.
6. E.g. D. Purdy, *The Soviet Union: State Capitalist or Socialist?*, Communist Party, London (1975); S. Carrillo, *Eurocommunism and the State*, Lawrence and Wishart, London (1977), Chapter 6, *passim*.
7. A. Callinicos, *Trotskyism*, Open University Press, Milton Keynes (1990), 21.
8. *Ibid.*, 28–31.
9. D. Hallas, 'Fourth International in decline', *International Socialism*, 60 (July 1973), 21.
10. Callinicos, *op. cit.*, 32.
11. An enlarged version of the original text was published as *Russia: a Marxist Analysis* in 1964.
12. K. Marx and F. Engels, *The German Ideology* (hereafter *GI*), Progress Publishers, Moscow (1968), 47.
13. K. Marx, 'The civil war in France', in *The First International and After* (Ed. D. Fernbach), Penguin Books, Harmondsworth (1974), 209–10.
14. Quoted in D. McLellan, *The Thought of Karl Marx*, Macmillan, London (1980), 219.
15. K. Marx and F. Engels, *The Communist Manifesto* (Ed. F. L. Bender), Norton, New York (1988), 74.
16. Marx, 'The civil war in France', 213.

17. K. Marx, 'Critique of the Gotha programme', quoted in McLellan, *op. cit.*, 250.
18. E.g. 'Problems of the development of the USSR', *Writings of Leon Trotsky, 1930-1*, Pathfinder Press, New York (1973); 'The class nature of the Soviet state', *Writings of Leon Trotsky, 1933-34*, Pathfinder Press, New York (1972); 'The USSR in war' in L. Trotsky, *In Defence of Marxism*, New Park Publications, London (1966). For extended analysis of *Revolution Betrayed*, see D. W. Lovell, *Trotsky's Analysis of Soviet Bureaucratisation*, Croom Helm, London (1985), Chapter 4; J. Molyneux, *Leon Trotsky's Theory of Revolution*, Harvester, Brighton (1981), Chapter 4; B. Knei-Paz, *The Social and Political Thought of Leon Trotsky*, Clarendon, Oxford (1978), Chapter 10; P. Anderson, 'Trotsky's interpretation of Stalin', *New Left Review*, 139 (May/June 1983), 49-58; C. L. R. James, 'Trotsky's "Revolution Betrayed"', *International Socialism*, 16 (Spring 1964), 25-9.
19. L. Trotsky, *Revolution Betrayed* (hereafter *RB*), New Park Publications, London (1967), 252.
20. *RB*, 7.
21. *RB*, 248.
22. *RB*, 61-2.
23. *RB*, 47, Trotsky's emphasis.
24. *RB*, 54.
25. *GI*, 47.
26. *RB*, 56.
27. *RB*, 112.
28. *RB*, 62.
29. *RB*, 52.
30. *RB*, 255.
31. *RB*, 278.
32. *RB, 89-90*.
33. *RB*, 254.
34. *RB*, 255.
35. *RB*, 246-8.
36. *RB*, 249-50.
37. *RB*, 248-9.
38. *RB*, 249.
39. *RB*, 252.
40. *RB*, 288.
41. T. Cliff, *SCR*, 268-70.
42. *SCR*, 278.
43. *SCR*, 276.
44. *SCR*, 281.
45. *SCR*, 270-5.
46. *SCR*, 283-5.
47. *SCR*, 287.
48. *SCR*, 130.
49. *SCR*, 46.
50. *SCR*, Chapter 1 *passim*.
51. *SCR*, 55.

52. *SCR*, 50.
53. *SCR*, 169.
54. *SCR*, 167.
55. See e.g. K. Marx, *Capital, Vol. 1*, Penguin, Harmondsworth, Chapters 1 and 25, *passim*.
56. *SCR*, 161, 202–9.
57. *SCR*, 160.
58. *SCR*, 211–12.
59. *SCR*, 230–2.
60. *SCR*, 240.
61. *SCR*, 241.
62. *SCR*, 243.
63. Maoists were also a significant Marxist tendency in Continental Europe, and C. Bettleheim's critique of the Soviet Union (see above) was written from this perspective.
64. E. Mandel, 'The mystifications of state capitalism' (hereafter *MSC*), *International*, 1, 2 (Sept/Oct 1970), 2; E. Mandel, 'A theory which has not stood the test of facts' (hereafter *TWF*), *International Socialism*, 49 (Winter 1990), 44.
65. *MSC*, 3.
66. *TWF*, 44.
67. E. Mandel, *The Inconsistencies of State Capitalism* (hereafter *ISC*), International Marxist Group, London (1969) 10.
68. *TWF*, 46; *MSC*, 9.
69. *MSC*, 9.
70. *MSC*, 12.
71. *ISC*, 14; cf. *MSC*, 13, *TWF*, 56. Mandel's emphasis.
72. *ISC*, 16.
73. *MSC*, 8.
74. *MSC*, 14.
75. *MSC*, 14.
76. *MSC*, 15.
77. E. Mandel, *Marxist Economic Theory* (hereafter *MET*), Vol. 2, Merlin Press, London (1968), 565–72; cf. *MSC*, 11, *ISC*, 16, *TWF*, 47.
78. *MET*, 571.
79. *MET*, 573.
80. *MET*, 593.
81. *MET*, 573.
82. *MET*, 575.
83. See Chapter 4.
84. C. Harman, 'The inconsistencies of Ernest Mandel' (hereafter *IEM*), *International Socialism* (old series), 41, (Dec/Jan 1969), 38.
85. *IEM*, 38.
86. *IEM*, 37.
87. *IEM*, 38.
88. C. Harman, 'Criticism which does not withstand the test of logic' (hereafter *CTL*), *International Socialism* (new series), 49 (Winter 1990), 66–8.
89. A. Callinicos, 'Rhetoric which cannot conceal a bankrupt theory: a reply to

Ernest Mandel' (hereafter *RBT*), *International Socialism* (new series), 57 (Winter 1992), 151.

90. C. Harman 'From Trotskyism to state capitalism', *International Socialism* (new series), 47 (Summer 1990), 152.

91. D. Howl, 'The law of value and the USSR' (hereafter *LVU*), *International Socialism* (new series), 49 (Winter 1990), 94.

92. C. Harman, 'Poland: the crisis of state capitalism, part 1' (hereafter *PCSC*), *International Socialism* (old series), 93 (Nov/Dec 1976), 27.

93. *TWF*, 70-1; *PCSC*, 27.

94. *PCSC*, 27.

95. *TWF*, 71; see also *LVU*, 90, 106; Callinicos, 'Wage labour and state capitalism', *International Socialism* (new series), 12 (Spring 1981), 117.

96. *PCSC*, 28; *LVU*, 106-7.

97. *TWF*, 48.

98. *TWF*, 50.

99. Mandel, 'The impasse of schematic dogmatism' (hereafter *ISD*), *International Socialism* (new series), 56 (Autumn 1992), 145.

100. *ISD*, 146.

101. *TWF*, 57.

102. *TWF*, 58.

103. *TWF*, 45.

104. *CTL*, 65.

105. *CTL*, 78.

106. *CTL*, 83.

107. *CTL*, 82.

108. P. Beilharz, *Trotsky, Trotskyism and the Transition to Socialism*, Croom Helm, London (1987), 108-9, raises this point in a slightly different fashion.

11
Marxism and Third World Revolution

PROBLEMS AND ISSUES

Revolutions and conflicts in the so-called 'Third World' did much to ignite European and North American radicalism in the late 1960s.[1] While the working classes, with the notable exceptions of the French and Italian, seemed to be relatively dormant in the advanced capitalist countries, the peasantry, along with the intelligentsias, of Asia, Africa and Latin America were making revolutions, or creating societies, in the name of socialism. From Asia came the inspiration of Mao's Cultural Revolution in 1966 in China and Ho Chi Min's Vietcong resistance to the Americans in Vietnam; from Africa the socialist and emancipatory visions of Nyerere of Tanzania, Nkrumah of Ghana, Cabral of Guinea-Bissau and Franz Fanon of Algeria; and from Latin America the Cuban Revolution of Fidel Castro and Che Guevara.

While Maoism was a potent force among the European Left, especially among communists disillusioned with the Soviet Union, more strategic controversies were generated by the Cuban Revolution of 1959 and its aftermath. The revolution, after it had become officially 'Marxist-Leninist' in the spring of 1961, put socialism on Latin America's immediate political agenda. Some Marxists, in hoping to promote the cause of both Cuba and socialism in Latin America, argued, first, that socialism was *necessary* because Western or 'metropolitan' capitalism had systematically under-developed Latin America and the Third World generally. It exploited their 'dependent' position, thereby throwing them into reverse economic gear. The Third World had become *the* site of capitalism's major contradictions. Workers in the metropolitan countries, living off the surpluses produced by the peoples of the periphery, no longer had the desire to overthrow capitalism.[2] Material improvement could only come for these peoples if they broke from the world capitalist system. Andre Gundar Frank was the most notable popularizer of this perspective.[3] Second, Marxists such as Régis Debray held that socialism in Latin America was *possible* if the guerilla methods that brought about the successful Cuban revolution were followed. Frank and Debray were in their different ways the major intellectual champions of the Cuban revolution in the West. Indeed, Frank's political and economic analysis could be said to complement Debray's political conclusions.[4] And both in their own ways implicitly or explicitly questioned, at a theoretical level, orthodox Marxist assumptions about the nature of modern imperialism and capitalism, as well as the relation between the revolutionary party and the working class.

At a political level Frank and Debray, inspired by the socialist and/or violent nature of the Cuban Revolution, challenged the prevailing communist strategic orthodoxy, which had been unchanged since the sixth and seventh congresses of Comintern of 1928 and 1935. This orthodoxy sought to advance democratic, anti-imperialist and anti-feudal revolutions in backward colonial and semi-colonial countries. It implied a two-stage theory of revolution: the first bourgeois, the second proletarian, when economic and political conditions had matured. The initial stage necessitated a popular front strategy, an alliance between the proletariat, national and petty bourgeoisies and the peasantry. All this implied that the context of struggle should be legal and parliamentary, a position reinforced from the mid-1950s when the Soviet Union began to follow a policy of peaceful coexistence with the West.[5] In terms of economic development, the purpose of such an alliance in combating imperialism and destroying feudalism in the countryside was to unblock the path to industrialization.[6]

This chapter will consider, first, the debates surrounding Frank's thesis on underdevelopment, second, the more explicitly Marxist counter-critique of Bill Warren and, third, Debray's strategic theory and its critics.

FRANK: CAPITALISM AND UNDERDEVELOPMENT

Frank, in his widely influential and much discussed *Capitalism and Underdevelopment in Latin America*, first published in 1967, aimed to underpin theoretically the Cuban strategy for revolution in Latin America, as outlined in the Second Declaration of Havana of February 1962.[7] Its message was simple: Latin American bourgeoisies were incapable of playing a historically progressive role in spearheading a democratic, anti-imperialist revolution. They were 'too paralyzed by fear of social revolution and frightened by the cry of the exploited masses'.[8] A two-stage revolution was impossible. Revolutions in Latin America henceforth had to be socialist.

The early 1960s was a formative period in Frank's intellectual development, when as a Chicago-trained orthodox economist, he went to work and live in Chile. He quickly came to realize that conventional economic wisdom, which saw the international division of labour and the law of comparative advantage as universally beneficial, was inappropriate for the Third World. Although in a number of crucial respects he differed from the ideas of the United Nations' Economic Commission of Latin America (ECLA), they nevertheless provided an important context to his thinking. The ECLA, established in the late 1940s under the chairmanship of Raul Prebisch, rejected the law of comparative advantage, because the terms of trade generally moved against raw material exporters. The 'core', industrialized countries were always the winners, and the 'peripheral', raw material-producing countries the losers. It therefore advocated policies of import-substituting industrialization (ISI), through either autarky or regional trade groupings.[9]

Frank was more overtly influenced by the work of Paul Baran, especially *The Political Economy of Growth*, first published in 1957.[10] From Baran he drew his key idea: the peripheral, or 'satellite', regions were systematically underdeveloped by the core, or 'metropolitan', regions through the transfer of economic surpluses, which could have been used to increase domestic investment and consumption. Post-war decolonization had made little difference to this process.

Frank's thesis

Frank set out to prove that the historical role of the national bourgeoisies of Latin America was played out: 'National capitalism and the national bourgeoisie do not and cannot offer any way out of underdevelopment in Latin America ... The historical mission and role of the bourgeoisie ... [are] finished'.[11] This was for two reasons. First, capitalism produced underdevelopment in peripheral areas, which included the whole of Latin America. Second, contrary to the communist view that a backward feudal sector existed, requiring modernization by a bourgeoisie, Latin America had been capitalist since the sixteenth century.

Frank argued, generalizing from the historical experience of Chile and Brazil, that the Latin American bourgeoisie's incapacity to develop productive forces was congenital, because it inhabited the outer region of world capitalism. The metropolitan economies of Northern Europe and the United States sucked out the investible surplus from these areas.

He explained this process as a result of capitalism's three 'internal contradictions', which he applied to the history of Chile. The first was expropriation of the surplus by the few from the many. He invoked the metaphor of a chain:

> It is this exploitative relation which in chain-like fashion extends the capitalist link between the capitalist world and national metropolises to the regional centres (part of whose surplus they appropriate), and from these to local centres, and so on to large landowners or merchants who expropriate surplus from small peasants or tenants, and sometimes even from these latter to landless labourers exploited by them in turn. At

each step along the way, the relatively few capitalists above exercise monopoly power over the many below, expropriating some or all of their economic surplus and, to the extent that they are not expropriated in turn by still fewer above them, appropriating it for their own use. Thus at each point, the international, national, and local capitalist system generates economic development for the few and underdevelopment for the many.[12]

The surplus retained was not invested but spent on consumer imports.[13]

This few/many contradiction he explained by a second contradiction: the process of the centralization of capital as depicted by Marx, which polarized the world economy into metropolitan centres and peripheral satellites. The former were able to use their monopoly position to extract the surplus from the latter, in a zero-sum game. Thus, the core became economically developed and the periphery underdeveloped. 'Economic development and underdevelopment are opposite faces of the same coin.'[14] This metropolitan–satellite relationship was replicated within the periphery itself, between town and countryside. The essential corollary of this – and here Frank was close to the ECLA thesis – was that the weaker the metropolitan–satellite links the greater the possibility of economic development in the periphery, as occurred during world wars or recessions.[15]

The third major contradiction consisted of 'continuity in change'. Whatever the changes in the economic form of the core–periphery relationship, whether commercial, industrial or financial, the actual content, i.e. surplus extraction, remained the same. From this contradiction he deduced that economic development through the reform of these relations was impossible. It could only be achieved through socialist revolution against the local bourgeoisie, separating periphery from core.[16] The bourgeoisie could not make this break. He argued with reference to the Brazilian bourgeoisie that it was 'hemmed in by the structure and the development of the capitalist system and by its old and new monopolistic instruments of property, trade loans, investment, technology and the rest'.[17] Equally importantly its anti-imperialism was muted by 'its economic and political contradiction vis-à-vis the people whom it exploits at home and vis-à-vis stronger bourgeoisies at home and abroad which exploit the same people and also exploit the national bourgeoisie itself'.[18]

There was a second reason why the bourgeoisies of Latin America possessed no progressive *raison d'être*. Against the standpoint of communists and orthodox economists such as Arthur Lewis, Frank argued that the idea of dual economies – advanced in cities and archaic and feudal in the countryside – was false. Thus, the notion that the role of the bourgeoisie was to modernize 'feudal' agriculture made no sense. He maintained that the various parts of the Brazilian economy could not be differentiated, because all sectors were enmeshed in exchange relations, as either satellites or mini-metropolises, which were in turn satellites of larger metropolises.[19] The totality of these relations he deemed capitalist. He did not define capitalism in Marxian terms of property relations, i.e. the private ownership and control of the means of production. Rather, it was constituted by market relations, whose impetus derived from the quest for profit. On the basis of this definition, Frank claimed that Latin America had been capitalist from the sixteenth century onwards, when trading relations with Europe began. These relations covered the whole of the Latin American economy, however the labour process was organized.[20] 'Cash nexus' rather than feudal relations 'ruled Latin America from the very beginning'.[21] More specifically, Brazilian agriculture had for centuries been market orientated, meeting direct foreign demand or local demand generated by foreign demand. Frank also provided statistics to show, first, that the economy could not be said to be dual, because landowners were often merchants, and, second, that a fluidity of owner–worker relations in Brazilian agriculture existed, i.e. peasants worked on their own plots *or* for the local lord, depending on the movements of the market.[22]

The breaking up of the large landed estates, as proposed by the Communist Party, would not solve the problem of surplus appropriation. This would leave the 'commercial monopoly organization' of Brazilian agriculture, which was locked into the world capitalist system, untouched. Indeed, land reform would strengthen the financial and commercial monopolies, as small farmers would be in a weaker position against them than large landowners.[23]

Frank concluded that the 'role of promoting historical progress' in Latin America and 'elsewhere' had now 'fallen to the masses of the people alone'.[24] And crucially, because the local and national bourgeoisies were essentially *comprador* bourgeoisies, totally dependent on, and allies with, foreign imperialism, they were, as he stated elsewhere, the 'immediate class enemy'. 'Popular mobilisation' against them produced 'a stronger confrontation with the principal imperialist enemy than does direct anti-imperialist mobilisation'.[25] If successful, such struggles would enable Latin American nations to create socialism by resisting the grip of the world capitalist system and its economically retarding tendencies.

Frank's critics

While many of Frank's critics agreed with his rejection of the dualistic account of the Latin American economy, they questioned the validity of the rest of his thesis.[26] They regarded it as conceptually, methodologically and empirically flawed. And they objected to his political conclusions.

First, there were the conceptual difficulties. His argument was tautological, i.e. its conclusions were already logically contained within the premise. So Frank defined underdevelopment as lack of *self*-sustained growth, and thereby concluded that growth occurred if core–periphery ties were weakened. He could empirically illustrate this proposition, but not prove it by considering counterfactual examples, owing to his form of reasoning. Such a definition also led him into self-contradiction: the notion of economic development as self-sustained growth ran counter to his second proposition that economic growth of the core occurred as a result of the underdevelopment of the periphery. Another problem was that his position was teleological: he explained underdevelopment in terms of what the economic surplus could have been *potentially* used for, but his did not account for the process of underdevelopment itself.[27] In addition, Frank viewed the terms 'dependency' and 'underdevelopment' as identical. In reality, dependency *and* development were possible. Foreign investment did not have to be seen as a 'simple zero-sum game of exploitation'.[28]

Second, methodological problems seriously vitiated attempts at concrete analysis. The initial framing of the question posed difficulties. Frank set out to prove that development was not possible. Thus he was unable to explore what was actually happening in Latin America.[29] Just as crucial, his formal class model was highly deterministic and abstract, and seen by him as applicable to the whole of the periphery, past and present.[30] Although he gave greater emphasis to class analysis in his later work, class structures remained epiphenomena of the global capitalist system, with little allowance made for national differences or changes through struggles. Moreover, his account of class behaviour was deterministic. He assumed that only an industrial bourgeoisie would want industrialization. Yet many Third World states after the Second World War attempted to industrialize through protectionism and state investment, although industrial capital itself was politically weak.[31]

Another impediment to concreteness stemmed from his model of exploitation. His explanation of surplus transfers from periphery to core as a result of monopoly was over-simplified. Brewer noted that Frank failed to differentiate between different types of monopoly, especially between mercantile, grounded on control of markets, and modern, multinational ones, based upon production.[32] Importantly, different types of monopoly could have different effects on economic development. Mercantile monopolies could easily hinder development by creaming off profits from the pre-capitalist productive sector, whereas with modern corporate monopolies investment decisions were not mediated by groups with separate and conflicting interests.[33]

The core–periphery model of exploitation also generated methodological confusion, because there was no differentiation between geographical and economic hierarchies of exploitation. Frank assumed that they coincided.[34] Although Frank may have described the mercantile model accurately, multinationals were different, with only one link in the chain, and the investable surplus going to wherever profits were highest globally, irrespective of whether areas were 'core' or peripheral.

This methodological imprecision was not helped by his market-plus-profit definition of capitalism, which made distinguishing between different modes of production difficult.[35] Thus, he minimized the significance of production relations in his understanding of peripheral societies. Laclau suggested that feudal production relations existed in Latin America; that is, forced labour based upon feudal obligations. Indeed, feudalism and capitalism could stand in symbiotic relationship to one another. The expansion of capitalism and the demand for primary products in Europe from the sixteenth century onwards led to the re-feudalization of Eastern Europe.[36] By the same token, Frank's exclusion of production relations in his definition of capitalism meant that different types of dependence could not be analysed, generated by, for example, the changing pattern of foreign investment in Latin America, from raw materials to industrial production.[37]

Robert Brenner explored the implications of the absence of production relations in Frank's definition of capitalism for the understanding of underdevelopment, especially the impact of class structure on these relations. Underdevelopment had less to do with surplus transfers and far more to do with the 'class structured character of profit opportunities'.[38] Brenner argued that the productivity of labour was the key to economic development. Forced labour systems, such as those based upon feudalism, hindered labour productivity by discouraging fixed capital investment. They restricted domestic demand, necessary for building up local industry, and encouraged the option of increasing 'absolute surplus value', i.e. getting 'direct labourers' to work longer or harder for the same or less subsistence, rather than the introduction of labour-saving techniques, which increased 'relative surplus value'. 'Free' wage labour, on the other hand, promoted domestic demand and capital investment.

Brenner also noted that class relations were crucial to an understanding of which societies would develop and which would not. Frank assumed that underdevelopment would automatically occur through incorporation into the world market. Yet Britain's Mid-Atlantic colonies, especially Pennsylvania, experienced general and long-term prosperity through the export of wheat, while Eastern Europe did not. These colonies' class structure consisted of smallholding farmers, while in Eastern Europe there were large landowners with production organized on feudal lines.[39]

Brenner, therefore, defended an orthodox Marxist position, stressing the importance of class relations and endogenous factors in causing under-development. Others, while attempting to remain within the Marxist framework, advanced a more complex, balanced and nuanced methodo-logy, involving the interplay of a number of factors to account for concrete differences between undeveloped economies. Cardoso and Faletto in

Dependency and Development in Latin America,[40] although they did not directly challenge Frank, put forward such a perspective. They were interested in how internal and external factors intersected to produce specific, differentiated forms of dependency. Thus, they had to discover

> what forms of exploitation there are, to what degree industrialisation and capital accumulation in the periphery had advanced, how local economies relate to the international market and so forth; and this as the result not only of the abstract 'logic of capital accumulation', but also of particular relationships and struggles between social classes and groups at the international as well as at the local level.[41]

The weight of bureaucracies, the role of armies, forms of state and ideologies underlying social movements also had to be taken into account. This approach would help to explain why, although the external economic environment could be uniform, different states responded to it differently, and why multinational companies behaved differently from state to state.[42]

Frank's methodological weaknesses in his thesis led to empirical weaknesses. It could not tolerate counterfactual evidence to underdevelopment. As we shall see in the next section, Bill Warren offered a sharply contrasting description of Third World development. His perspective coincided with Cardoso's in demonstrating that foreign investment was moving away from agriculture and raw materials into manufacturing in Latin America, Africa and Asia.[43] The distinguishing feature of this new trend in manufacturing investment was that it took place under the auspices of joint venture enterprises consisting of the local state, private national capital and foreign monopoly capital. Individual case studies of certain areas also proved that peripheral development was possible.[44]

Moreover, his argument that less dependency meant more growth could be refuted. The NICs (newly industrializing countries), such as Taiwan, South Korea and Brazil, were developing in the 1950s and 1960s, long before the economic crisis hit the advanced capitalist countries in the 1970s. Furthermore, in the case of South Korea and Taiwan, *contra* Frank, capitalist land reform in the 1950s laid the basis for later industrialization.[45] What was also factually questionable was his conclusion that self-sufficiency was good for growth. Economies that had opted for export-led growth had consistently out-performed those which had attempted to move towards self-sufficiency.[46]

Finally, some Marxists have questioned the political implications of Frank's underdevelopment hypothesis. Its logic was not socialism, but autarky. If international capitalism, by incorporating the Third World into the world market, caused underdevelopment, then some form of self-sufficient growth was entailed. Frank, however, failed to demonstrate that socialism was necessarily the solution, rather than autarky.[47] His position, in emphasizing the importance of independent national economic development, was strategically flawed. It was essentially 'ideological' or propagandistic, justifying socialism on the grounds of economic superiority to capitalism, which underdeveloped the periphery. Thus, Frank's arguments 'centre on why [socialism] is necessary, not on whether it is immediately possible'.[48] In effect, Frank offered a critique of capitalism, based upon an idealized notion of self-sustaining growth within a nation-state. A 'scientific' approach would entail the question of whether socialism was a realistic proposition, supported by an analysis of existing class struggles and the relationship between national and international capital.

Additionally, Frank's identification of national economic development with socialism was dubious. First, if economic development did occur under capitalism, then in a sense the case for socialism fell.[49] Second, if this definition of socialism were accepted, then it was clearly not part of the Marxist project of workers' self-emancipation.[50] Indeed, a programme of national economic development would subordinate the working class to this objective.[51] No surprisingly, some critics associated Frank's vision of socialism with Soviet practice.[52] One of the problems with this practice, which entailed a socialism-in-one-country perspective, was its under-emphasis of the connection between the development of national productive forces and the international capitalist division of labour. It therefore obscured the importance of external pressures and internal political degeneration arising from this dependency.[53] By the same token it downplayed the need for, and potential of, uniting workers of the core and the periphery, within a global strategy to overthrow capitalism.

Frank's response to his critics

Frank, in repudiating these criticisms, did not deal with them comprehensively. For example, he avoided dealing with the methodological problems of defining capitalism, abstraction, over-generalization and he failed to account for different forms of dependency. He acknowledged that he may have not communicated adequately to his readers the importance of internal class formation in explaining underdevelopment, and sought to make amends in *Lumpenbourgeoisie: Lumpendevelopment*.[54] Nevertheless, theoretically he added little to his previous position. He did not attempt to examine different forms of dependency arising from varying class structures. He focused exclusively on the bourgeoisies, which were dependent through and through: 'precisely because dependence is indivisible [it] makes the bourgeoisie dependent'.[55] Latin American bourgeoisies were merely epiphenomena of the world capitalist system.

> When a change in the forms of dependence alters the economic and class structure, changes in turn are produced in the policy of the dominant bourgeoisie, and these changes, with few partial exceptions, ... strengthen still further the same ties of economic dependence which

gave rise to these policies and which consequently serve to deepen still further the development of underdevelopment in Latin America.[56]

He thus ruled out, for instance, any possibility of the local state in combating international capital in any way. Naturally, to have made any significant concessions to his critics on this score would have thrown into question his revolutionary socialist strategy of independence from the world capitalist system.

Frank did address the question of the NICs. He held that they were exceptional. They were either the product of an adjustment in the international division of labour or the result of United States' geopolitical strategy. For other Third World countries to imitate the policies of export-led growth was economically and ecologically impossible, owing to the limitations of global demand and resources.[57]

The only significant concession was that he now allowed for regional variations stemming from different modes of production, effectively endorsing Laclau's point. 'Within the world-system there are different modes ... of production. Today pre-capitalist relations of production are still very prevalent in many parts of the world, combined with capitalist wage-labor relations of production.'[58] Formerly, he had assumed that different production relations meant 'dualism'. Now he recognized that they could be interconnected. This concession could, however, be viewed as endangering his strategic position. Pre-capitalist and capitalist sectors do not necessarily have a symbiotic relationship. Labour productivity could be held back in the former sector, thereby opening up the possibility that the bourgeoisie could after all undertake a 'modernizing' role.

Commentary

Frank did more than anyone else in the 1960s to register capitalism's inability to develop consistently the productive forces throughout the world, even if he exaggerated his case. At least he underlined the existence of dependency, and the impact that imperialism could have on Third World economies. Furthermore, the virtue of his approach was its holism, stressing, albeit imperfectly, the interconnectedness of the world economic system. He did not examine Third World economies as isolated entities.

Nevertheless, criticisms that his thesis was over-generalized, too abstract, deterministic and endogenously oriented cannot be discounted. Moreover, it was politically flawed. His all-or-nothing stance, putting socialism on the immediate agenda, did little to show how the day-to-day struggles of workers and peasants could be related to this project. Finally, the explicitly world-system approach of his later period, focusing on the global accumulation of capital and its extremely powerful political and economic effects on the periphery, called into question the efficacy of his socialism-in-one-country prescription. He gave little consideration to the need to build up an international movement against international capital.

WARREN'S COUNTER-THESIS

Bill Warren, in his provocative article, 'Imperialism and capitalist industrialisation', articulated a thesis that was the direct opposite of Frank's.[59] The object of his criticism was not only Frank, but also the traditional communist anti-imperialist strategy and the dependency school in general. He sought to rescue the Third World proletariat from what he saw as the embrace of bourgeois nationalism, and save it for socialism. These two trends of thought, he maintained, consolidated the bourgeoisie's ideological control. His 'class' perspective, he claimed, entailed a reaffirmation of Marx's image of capitalism in *The Communist Manifesto, Capital* and elsewhere, as, globally, a materially and culturally dynamic and progressive, if contradictory, force. We will consider Warren's position mainly insofar as it impinges on Frank's underdevelopment thesis.

Paradoxically, Warren adopted a view similar to Frank's in calling for a struggle against the bourgeoisie in the Third World. Thereafter, he contradicted Frank at virtually every turn. Where Frank was pessimistic about Third World development, he was optimistic; where Frank saw nothing but dependency and underdevelopment as metropolitan capitalism expanded, he saw Third World economies becoming increasingly powerful and independent; where Frank saw major obstacles to development as exogenously induced and insurmountable without 'delinking', he saw them as endogenous and surmountable within the existing world capitalist system; where Frank saw centre–periphery relations as a fixed, asymmetrical chasm, he viewed such differences as progressively disappearing; where Frank saw imperialism as integral to capitalism and as evil and parasitic, he saw it as an entity, separate yet connected to capitalism, and as a culturally and materially progressive force, destined to disappear under its own volition; where Frank saw foreign investment as a channel through which the surplus was drained out in the form of profits, he saw it (to mix a metaphor!) as industrial seed corn; where Frank held dependency to be a game with only one winner, he maintained that both players could benefit, if in unequal amounts; finally, whereas Frank argued that political independence in the Third World was rendered meaningless by neo-colonialism, he suggested that it was vital to economic development.

Warren's alternative vision of Third World development challenged a number of dependency theory's premises, including Frank's. He rejected its assumptions: that dependency always exists under capitalism, and could not be viewed as a declining phenomenon; that centre–periphery relations are a 'one-way street', in which the latter could not affect the former, and by the same token multinational companies were always seen as exerting power over the periphery, and never the converse; that the centre automatically foreclosed the developmental options of the satellites; that dependency was inherently incapable of developing the productive forces and generating possibilities for autonomous industrialization; that indigenous elites were automatically controlled by the metropolises and could not be equal partners; and finally that autonomous development was more rapid than dependent development.[60]

His substantive position aimed to demonstrate how these assumptions could be falsified. Although he conceded that development had occurred unevenly in the Third World, overall the evidence pointed to a far more optimistic vision. This could be shown in a number of ways. First, figures revealed that growth rates in Third World manufacturing in the 1960s were higher than in the advanced capitalist world, and, more specifically against Frank, that many less-developed countries (LDCs) experienced sustained manufacturing growth between 1951 and 1969, when there was no war in the metropolitan countries or protectionism, i.e. no core-periphery separation.[61] Moreover, the gap between the periphery and the centre in terms of the proportion of manufactures within the gross domestic product was diminishing, so that by the early 1960s it was half that of the advanced capitalist countries.[62] Indeed, for Mexico, Argentina, Chile and Iran the proportion was equal to many advanced countries. In 1970, 25 per cent of export from ex-colonies consisted of manufactures.[63]

Second, the productive forces were clearly developing in the Third World, as displayed by rising growth rates per capita in the post-war period, and were often higher than those in developed economies when they began industrializing, benefiting from the 'advantages of back-wardness in market opportunities and technological development'.[64] Third, he admitted that economic inequality had possibly grown in these states, but argued that this was a condition for economic growth, advantageous to the poor in the long run.[65] Fourth, he indicated that a growth of marginalization, of an unemployed or under-employed under-class, had not occurred. Employment had increased, as had the number of wage workers.[66] Finally, material welfare – nutrition, health and housing – had improved in the 1960s, as attested to by population growth.[67]

Warren also looked at the question of autonomous industrialization. He maintained that it *was* occurring in the Third World, as exemplified by the diversification of trade, either geographically or in terms of commodities produced.[68] It had occurred especially in heavy industry.[69] There was additionally an increased potential for technological development arising from technological imports and rising educational standards.[70] And the growth of home markets was facilitating industrial development.[71] Furthermore, he saw the 'domestication' of foreign enterprises as a long-term trend, and held that in the 1960s most capital formation, for instance in Latin America, came from local sources, or reinvested earnings, rather than from foreign investment.[72] However, he admitted that the latter was vital in building up manufacturing sectors for export-led growth, as in Latin America, South Korea and Taiwan.[73] Indeed, the 'domestication' of ownership of foreign enterprises was a long-term trend.[74] Autonomous development was reflected in other ways: African states in particular had strengthened their position against multinational companies by playing them off against each other, and generally the Third World's growing economic power and independence were reflected by less indebtedness, as a result of its improved balance of trade in the 1970s, even before the rise of oil prices.[75] In any case, he argued, perhaps in a contradictory fashion, that the countries that were most 'dependent' in terms of foreign investment and trade were the richer ones.[76]

Warren offered two explanations for Third World industrialization, which flew in the face of the Frankian perspective. First, he contended that political independence yielded great developmental benefits. It enabled the ex-colonies to use the state to diversify, control and expropriate foreign firms, bargain with multinational companies to increase local financing, shareholding and personnel, transfer modern technology, restructure their economies to meet local needs and exploit East–West rivalries.[77] There were also popular pressures for industrialization in the post-independence situation. What obstacles existed to industrialization were internally generated, especially stemming from the lack of development of capitalist agriculture.[78]

In the second place, he held that foreign investment was crucial in generating export-led growth. Although he admitted the possibility of an outward drain, he argued that foreign investment was deemed by these states to be valuable in introducing advanced technology and systems of organization.[79]

He concluded that international trade and investment had a positive virtue in promoting Third World economic development, and that the prospects for further industrialization were 'quite good'.[80] He also inferred, in contrast to Frank, that economic development could occur without a powerful indigenous bourgeoisie. Often external forces 'compelled' industrialization, although the social forces that brought it about were often semi-feudal, bureaucratic or military elites, or merely petty bourgeois. He also deduced that industrialization, in making the Third World economically stronger, would eventually lead to the elimination of imperialism as a 'system of economic inequality'.[81] 'Imperialism was declining as capitalism was growing.'[82] Thus, centre–periphery relations would disappear.

He drew an important strategic implication: either imperialism would disappear or it would have a benign influence. Therefore, the working classes of the Third World should not allow themselves to be enlisted under the anti-imperialist banner, concealing their differences of interest with their bourgeoisies.[83]

Warren's critics

Critics took strong exception to Warren's vision of a progressive, modernizing imperialism, destined to roll over into benign retirement, once it had scattered its seeds of capitalist industrialization over the planet, a process supposedly facilitated by political independence. First, apart from noting that he did not have a clearly developed theory of imperialism and capitalism, they took him to task for his over-generalized approach.[84] He treated the Third World as a 'uniform category', both past and present.[85] For example, he assumed that colonialism brought about industrialization. Yet this was not evident in Portuguese colonies.[86] Furthermore, not all the Third World experienced colonization, and many countries had different agrarian structures.[87] Crucially, he deduced too much from his statistics, in assuming that the whole of the Third World would develop. This was not so in sub-Saharan Africa, where per capita incomes had fallen.[88] Indeed, his figures for manufacturing growth were based on only 29 Third World countries, which were the fastest growing.[89] He lumped together NICs, LDCs, OPEC states and those with no raw materials.[90]

This lack of differentiation also applied to his notion of industrialization. He assumed that it was the same in both the Third World and the advanced capitalist countries, when at best development was dependent in form, as with the NICs,[91] and was generally confined to assembly plant production.[92] On a more technical note, he failed to distinguish between the different ways in which a rising gross national product (GNP) per capita could be interpreted as a ratio between gross market product and total population. This ratio may measure not only the growth of labour productivity, as Warren assumed, but also the development of a market economy: an increase in monetary values, although not necessarily an increase in physical output.[93] Moreover, industrial growth was possible without overall economic growth.[94]

Critics also challenged his assertion that Third World economies were undergoing independent self-sustained industrialization and were catching up the advanced countries. Growth itself was hardly self-sustaining. Warren ignored the slumps.[95] Two years after his death, for example, the Brazilian economy crashed in 1980.[96] Furthermore, there was little evidence of independent technological development.[97] Industrialization was limited to a small number of countries, merely reflecting a restructuring of the international division of labour, and creating a greater economic differentiation among the Third World countries themselves. Only a few of the industrializing countries were able to avoid assembly plant/processed food industrialization, such as Hong Kong and Brazil, and with the latter this was achieved through export subsidies, which generated a great deal of foreign indebtedness. Indeed, although there was a growth in Third World manufacturing exports in the 1960s, the multinational companies were responsible for much of it, and the overwhelming bulk of exports still remained in raw materials, foodstuffs and fuels.[98]

That the Third World was catching up industrially, that a redistribution of industrial power was occurring, could also be doubted. There was only a 1 per cent difference in manufacturing growth rates, and the growth of the industrial sector relative to other parts of Third World economies could be accounted for by the low productivity in the non-manufacturing sectors, while in the metropolitan economies non-manufacturing sectors, such as agriculture, were already highly mechanized, and there were large, skilled, low productivity, service sectors.[99] Moreover, other statistics could be used to demonstrate that, relative to the advanced countries, growth rates in the Third World were stagnating.[100]

Critics rejected other evidence of autonomous industrialization. The multinational had not necessarily been tamed, as Warren asserted. Joint ventures could be viewed as a form of co-option.[101] And his argument that Third World economies were becoming financially independent was unconvincing. Most of the developed areas of the Third World, such as Brazil, were having the greatest difficulty in repaying their loans. Future debt crises for the Third World were predicted, as was an increased trade gap between this and the 'First' World.[102]

In addition they queried part of his explanation for industrial development, supposedly aided by political independence and the product of popular pressures. Rather, the opposite was true. Industrial growth had been most significant in countries that were least politically independent – for example, Brazil, Zaire and Indonesia – and where the regimes were extremely repressive.[103]

Critics also wondered whether his position had any warrant in Marxist theory. Warren relied heavily on Marx's seemingly progressive view of British colonialism in India, and even here did not fully appreciate that he saw British rule as consisting of progress *and* plunder. Further, Marx in his later writings was far less sanguine about economic progress, stressing how Britain was 'bleeding' India, hardly a recipe for developing the productive forces,[104] and arguing that independence was crucial to Ireland if further economic progress was to be made.[105] While Marx may have applauded the civilizing effects of British rule in India and elsewhere, he nevertheless supported anti-imperialist revolts.[106] Warren therefore effectively ignored the dialectical complexities of Marx's writings on imperialism.

Finally, the political implications of his productivist account of Marxism, where the development of the productive forces took priority over other values central to Marxism, especially equality, were challenged. In effect, he rejected anti-capitalist struggles, because he saw inequality and marginalization as functional to capitalism. By the same token, he rejected anti-imperialist struggles, thereby adopting a Eurocentric stance.[107]

In sum, his critics insisted that significant industrialization in the Third World was the exception rather than the rule. Generally, the possibilities of industrial expansion were limited, for instance, by the lack of natural resources or internal markets, and dependency was exacerbated by debt problems.[108] Hence, the global inequalities manifested in core–periphery relations were in capitalism's very lifeblood.

Commentary

The virtue of Warren's position *vis-à-vis* Frank is that he pointed out the obvious: the forces of production were developing in the Third World through capitalist industrialization. He thereby undermined Frank's static, core–periphery model of underdevelopment. Nevertheless, he exaggerated in attempting to prove Frank and communist Marxists wrong. He assumed that equalization of industrial strength between the Third World and the advanced capitalist economies would occur. His position would have been far more balanced, and therefore considerably strengthened, if he had seriously acknowledged that capitalism necessarily develops unevenly in its overall rhythms and specific geographical and sectoral dynamics. Unevenness is both an effect and a prerequisite of capitalist development. It is the product of capitalist competition, as well as a condition for that competition.

His exaggeration was at a cost in Marxist terms, both theoretically and politically. Theoretically, it entailed the portrayal of imperialism in a benevolent light, developing the world's productive forces and then retiring gracefully once its capitalist siblings had grown up. This glossed over the conflictual side of capitalist imperialism, which in the past has often attempted to prevent local elites from 'statizing' certain sectors of their economies in order to bring about more rapid development. Indeed, in stressing the economic benefits consequent upon political independence, he depicted the state as possessing a high degree of autonomy, separated from the pressures and constraints of local power blocs and international capital, acting singly or in combination.

Politically, his attempt to rescue the Third World proletariat from the clutches of local bourgeoisies by debunking anti-imperialist struggles was problematic. In enthusiastically demonstrating capitalism's dynamism in the Third World, he understated its contradictions. In downplaying its oppressive and exploitative character, he had little left upon which to build a working class, anti-capitalist strategy. Indeed, his causal separation of imperialism from capitalism, implied in the notion of an advancing capitalism and a declining imperialism, meant that he could not contemplate the combination of an anti-imperialist with an anti-capitalist strategy. Thus, although he apparently had intended to construct a Marxist strategy for the Third World proletariat, its precise delineation is hard to guess.[109]

General comments

Frank's and Warren's positions can be seen as the two sides of the capitalist coin. Dependency and underdevelopment, in the sense of economic decline, do exist in the Third World. So does industrial growth. In other words, capitalism develops unevenly. And quite possibly in the future, as capital becomes increasingly mobile, it will become difficult to associate underdevelopment and development as unalterably tied to certain geographical regions. While both theories could be said to have their strengths and weaknesses as accounts of economic development in the Third World, their strategic value is questionable. Both were locked into propagandistic parameters. Frank made a case for revolutionary socialism by saying that imperialism, in collusion with indigenous bourgeoisies, underdeveloped the Third World. Warren insisted that capitalism was extremely dynamic in this region. Neither provided the methodological tools for, or offered, a concrete analysis upon which to build a socialist movement.

RÉGIS DEBRAY AND *REVOLUTION IN THE REVOLUTION?*

In a sense, the strategic vacuum in Frank's and Warren's work was filled by a young French Marxist, Régis Debray, who proposed a veritable 'revolution in the revolution'. In wishing to further the Cuban cause, he argued that its model of revolution could be exported to the rest of Latin America. He upset the communist orthodoxy of the two-stage revolution, as already outlined, by suggesting that a socialist revolution in Latin America, as Cuba had demonstrated, was an immediate possibility. More significantly, in holding that a rural guerilla vanguard could create the political preconditions for revolution, he reversed the traditional notion of Marxist political–military causality. This had all sorts of implications for Marxist assumptions upon which Latin American Communist Parties had built their strategies: the traditional conception of a Marxist political vanguard, both its organization and its relationship to the 'masses', and the role of the working class in the revolutionary process, class alliances and the importance of theory.

The context

Régis Debray's *Revolution in the Revolution?*, published in January 1967, was a contribution to Cuba's attempt to promote a Latin America-wide revolution.[110] Fidel Castro, the Cuban leader, formed an organization – the

Organization of Latin American Solidarity (OLAS) – to support the ongoing armed struggle in Latin America, including Che Guevara's campaign in Bolivia, which ended with his death in October 1967. Its founding conference was held in July and August in Havana. The Cubans desperately needed to overcome their political and economic isolation in Latin America, resulting from the United States' hostility to their revolution. They were not helped by their supposed patron, the Soviet Union, which had its own diplomatic agenda in seeking *rapprochement* with the United States, thereby encouraging Latin American Communist Parties to undertake a strategy of peaceful transition to socialism. Thus, it only gave half-hearted support to guerilla struggles in the 1960s in Venezuela, Colombia and Guatemala. Moreover, the leaderships of the local parties were often old and committed to popular front strategies as followed in the 1930s.[111] If they undertook guerilla warfare, it stemmed from the need to pacify a youthful rank-and-file, influenced by the Cuban strategic model, or to avoid outflanking by Maoist and Trotskyist parties on their left. They saw this form of struggle as a tactic to increase their influence within the 'official' political life of these countries, rather than as a strategy for revolutionary transformation.

The Cubans also had to contend with Maoists and Trotskyists, who had their own political, military and strategic agendas. They were critical of the Cubans, either because of their relationship with the Soviet Union or because of the type of guerilla tactics they proposed. Trotskyists in particular played a significant part in the guerilla movements of Guatemala, Peru and Brazil in the mid-1960s. And the Maoists, who were not as influential in these movements, offered their own style of guerilla struggle, based on the Chinese model. Thus, the Cuban leaders, in promoting their brand of guerilla technique, had a double task. They had to demonstrate that Trotskyist and Maoist models were ill-conceived and, more importantly, given their influence, they had to indicate the shortcomings in the communists' conduct of, and attitude towards, guerilla warfare as an optional extra.

Within this context Régis Debray, who took up a chair in the history of philosophy at the University of Havana in January 1966, and who later was imprisoned by the Bolivian authorities between 1967 and 1970, because of his association with Che Guevara's guerilla activities in that country, was extremely useful as a propagandist to the Cuban leadership. Apart from his known sympathies for the Cuban revolution, his intellectual qualities and his understanding of Marxism – he had been a pupil of Louis Althusser – he also had an intimate knowledge of Latin American guerilla movements.[112] *Revolution in the Revolution?*, reiterating many of the themes of Fidel Castro's speeches in 1967 and of the OLAS conference, was intended as a call to arms.[113] It demanded that Communist Parties abandon their essential reformism and that Marxists in general discard their obsession with theoretical issues and commit themselves to the practice of guerilla warfare. Fidel Castro and the Guatemalan revolutionary Orlando Fernandez were Debray's collaborators.

This work, even more than his earlier writings, bore the heavy imprint of the lessons that Che Guevara and Fidel Castro had drawn from the Cuban revolution – all of which ran counter to the 'Marxist-Leninist' theory and practice of the Latin American Communist Parties.[114] Reflecting on the Cuban revolution, Guevara had observed: first, that 'popular forces can win a war against the army'; second, that 'it is not necessary to wait until all conditions for making a revolution exist; insurrection can create them'; and, third, that 'in underdeveloped America, the countryside is the basic area for armed fighting'.[115]

Not only was *Revolution in the Revolution?* a theoretical echo of these conclusions, it elaborated the revolutionary nostrums proposed by Fidel Castro in various speeches of that year, contained in his attack on Latin American Communist Parties, especially the Venezuelan (PCV), which had withdrawn from guerilla activity in favour of peaceful popular frontism in 1965. Such parties underestimated the importance of the peasantry and the guerilla movement. He also criticized the notion that guerilla struggles could be directed from the city and that guerillas could be used as political tools. He advocated an alternative perspective: 'Armed struggle' was 'the immediate and fundamental task of the revolutionary movement', which constituted the 'embryo of liberation armies';[116] the military and political commands had to be united; miliary action was as important as propaganda, and practice came before theory.

Revolution in the Revolution?

Revolution in the Revolution?, as a call to arms, aimed to persuade young militants to give up party-building and revolutionary activity in the cities, and to pick up a gun and take to the hills. Debray started with the concrete question: 'How to overthrow the power of the capitalist state? In other words, how to break its backbone, the army, continuously reinforced by North American military missions?'[117] For Latin America, the Cuban model of revolution provided the answer. It lay in the creation of a '*mobile strategic force*', or *foco*, the product of guerilla warfare in 'suitably chosen rural zones'. Such a force would constitute the nucleus of a people's army and of a future socialist state.[118] The *foco* consisted of a small group of mobile guerillas, who, in taking on the regular army in the initial stages by essentially hit-and-run tactics, aimed to build up the support of the local population and recruit more members. When it reached a certain size it would split, thereby creating another *foco*. Eventually, they would merge, forming a revolutionary army. The *foco* would assume political as well as military functions.

In presenting this solution Debray rejected the 'imported' Trotskyist and Maoist models of guerilla warfare. He opposed the Trotskyist strategy of 'armed self-defence' as practised or called for in Bolivia, Columbia, Guatemala and Peru. It was incapable of achieving political power. In essence, it entailed 'armed spontaneity', denying the need for an armed unit 'organically separate' from the civilian population. Committed to localized, and not 'total', struggle, it offered, unlike the mobile armed unit, no 'choice of site of combat, no benefits of mobility, manoeuvre or surprise'.[119] Mobility was particularly important in order to reduce the possibilities of betrayal, intentional or unwitting, by the local peasantry.[120] And being militarily static, it was vulnerable to army attack at a time of the enemy's own choosing, economic blockade, shortage of military supplies and aerial bombardment. Unable to go on the offensive, it could not expose the class nature of the regime, whether democratic or oligarchical, and become a pole of attraction for the whole country. Finally, such a strategy meant that a regular army could not be defeated. This required military professionalism and sufficient military hardware, which 'armed spontaneity' did not provide.[121]

Second, he maintained that the strategy of 'armed propaganda', as practised by Chinese and Vietnamese communists, where local populations were won over by the guerillas through propaganda work, was unsuitable in Latin American conditions. In China and Vietnam, owing to high population density in rural areas and the foreign nature of the enemy, propagandists could be 'like fish in water'.[122] By contrast, in Latin America the population was sparse in the countryside, and outsiders were looked upon with distrust. Moreover, in Latin America armed propaganda *preceding* military action rendered the *foco* vulnerable to, for example, enemy infiltration.[123] Far more effective was the propaganda of arms: 'The destruction of a troop transport truck or the public execution of a police torturer is more effective propaganda for the local population than a hundred speeches.'[124] Armed propaganda, important in establishing a support base, was only appropriate behind guerilla lines, where the local population was safe from enemy attack. Thus, 'armed propaganda has more to do with the internal than with the external guerilla front'.[125]

Third, consistent with this method of constructing a guerilla base, he criticized the efforts of Luis de la Puente in Peru in 1965, who, possibly under Maoist influence, built one at the initial stage of his campaign. It had worked in China and Vietnam, where there was extensive territory, a high-density rural population, common borders with a friendly country, the absence of airborne enemy troops and few enemy forces.[126] These conditions were absent in Latin America, where mobility was an imperative to avoid betrayal by the local population, enemy infiltration and attack. During the Cuban revolution, as already indicated, bases were only created after *focos* had been well established. In the Sierra Maestra they 'grew from the outside in, from the periphery towards the centre'.[127] Hence, in the first stages of the struggle 'the base of support is the guerilla fighter's knapsack'.[128]

Debray was nevertheless more concerned to demonstrate how the Cuban model of revolution revealed the inadequacy of the Latin American Communist Parties' organization and strategy. His proposed 'revolution in the revolution' focused upon the nature, organization, training and development of the vanguard and its relationship to the 'masses'. He argued, following the Cuban example, that the *rural*, guerilla *foco* had to be *the* vanguard. The theatre of war had to be rural, not merely because the forces of repression were greater in the towns, but also because combat on this terrain produced better fighters: 'The mountain proletarianizes the bourgeois and peasant elements, and the city can bourgeoisify the proletarians.'[129] Indeed, such combat, by its very nature, required young, rather than old, men who would eventually form the basis of a new, more revolutionary leadership.[130]

Equally importantly, the *foco* should not be subordinated to an 'external' political party, based in the city and accustomed to operating in peacetime conditions.[131] Otherwise it would be open to various dangers: the guerilla commanders going to the city for consultations with the party leadership, rendering them vulnerable to assassination; demoralization arising from dependence on the 'bourgeois' party, insensitive to the guerillas' practical needs; the leadership formulating a military strategy, with little direct knowledge of such matters and usually with electoral considerations uppermost.[132] Dangers would be even more acute if military activities were subordinated to an inter-class popular front with different agendas.[133] Crucially, it was the 'small motor' of the *foco* that 'sets the "big motor" of the masses in motion and precipitates the formation of a [political] front, as the victories won by the small motor increase'.[134]

A division of the military and political functions within the vanguard, each with its different priorities – in particular the latter's preoccupation with legal activity – led to a lack of coordination between both, as well as between armed actions in town and country.[135] Overall coordination to implement a general strategic plan necessitated the fusion of both functions, as occurred in the Cuban Revolution under Fidel Castro. Thus, crucially, the leadership had to be based in the countryside, and not in the town, where it was conservative, unadaptable and vulnerable to repression.[136]

More significantly, within this fusion, military leadership took precedence over political. Given the need for the violent overthrow of the state, politicians were unsuited to lead armed struggle, yet guerillas were able to develop political skills by leading armed struggles and administering liberated zones.[137] Learning from experience was superior to learning from political training schools. And in Cuba guerilla leaders proved to be the most politically resolute, in a socialist sense, after the revolution.[138]

Here Debray produced his most startling conclusion: the issue was not the party versus military organization. The fundamental lesson of the Cuban revolution was: in the initial stages, a party was unnecessary. Later on, the *foco* would *become* the party. Thus, the 'staggering novelty' of the revolution was that the *foco* constituted the vanguard party in embryo.[139] Reversing the normal Marxist strategic sequence from the political to the military, because in Latin America this had led to an avoidance of armed struggle, he held that the *foco* became the people's army, and the people's army became the party.[140] In the combination of military and political functions with the *foco* itself, a genuine unity of Marxist theory and revolutionary practice was achieved. Debray seemed to imply that this avoided the degeneration of Marxist theory and practice into reformism, which occurred when they were separated.

This intermeshing of functions also compelled guerilla leaders to realize that they could not develop militarily, unless they did so politically, especially in the latter stages of the campaign when a generalized urban insurrection was required.[141] In this part of the Cuban revolutionary process, radio broadcasts had been vital in establishing the Rebel Army as the political vanguard.[142] Furthermore, the *foco* was able to become the political vanguard because it personified a worker–peasant alliance, 'whose interests are those of socialism', actually integrating workers and peasants (as well as intellectuals) in struggle.[143] Thus, in contrast to the orthodox communist conception, where class alliances were achieved through popular front activity, it formed within the guerilla struggle itself. The *foco*'s other political advantage lay in its capacity to overcome political factionalism. Such differences were overridden by the practical needs of armed struggle.[144]

In sum, Debray, in seeking to generalize the Cuban revolutionary experience, rejected communist strategic thought. No longer were the party and the popular front, based on a stages theory of revolution, central. No longer was guerilla activity a mere adjunct. Because the struggle for socialism, which entailed the destruction of the existing state apparatus, was an immediate priority agenda, the armed, rural *foco* now became the vanguard.

Debray's critics

Debray's critics made few concessions to his argument. They doubted whether there was a ready Latin American market for the consumption of the Cuban revolutionary model; they questioned his prioritization of the military over the political in the relationship between the vanguard and masses, and his rejection of the need for a party; finally, they were sceptical about whether his account of the relationship between theory and practice was Marxist.

That the Cuban model could be exported, critics held, rested upon a number of question-begging assumptions. First, he presupposed that an analysis of objective conditions in Latin America, in order to assess the possibility of revolution, had become redundant.[145] This was either because he assumed that the *foco* was sustainable independently of historical conditions,[146] or because conditions were similar to those in Cuba before the revolution.[147] If he had carried out such an analysis, he would have discovered three things. First, Cuba's social structure was atypical compared to the rest of Latin America. The latter, unlike Cuba, had undergone rapid urbanization in recent years.[148] This had crucial implications for the choice of the terrain of combat, because especially in Brazil and Argentina the towns had much more economic and political weight than the countryside, and there the status quo could coexist indefinitely with rural insurrection.[149] And the rural population lived in semi-feudal conditions, whereas in Cuba it consisted largely of wage workers in the sugar and tobacco industries. Furthermore, unlike many other Latin American states, Cuba had a strong anti-imperialist political tradition. Additionally, there was a good deal of linguistic and cultural homogeneity.[150] Second, an analysis of Latin America would have shown that political, economic, social and geographic conditions were different between each state. Thus, there could be no uniform strategy.[151] Third, an investigation of the preconditions would have highlighted the uniqueness of the Cuban Revolution. It was the product of an unrepeatable situation: the failure of the United States in initially assessing its significance, especially because Fidel Castro was not a communist until after the revolution.[152] The United States was unlikely to be caught napping again.[153]

The revolution could not be exported on the basis of Debray's *foco* theory, because he had misunderstood the dynamics of the Cuban Revolution. In particular, he underestimated the importance of urban organization in the process: 'there were organized forces that directed men and material to the mountains and to the streets, in the cities, towns, sugar *centrales* and universities. The Student Directorate, the July 26th Movement and militant trade unionists provided massive urban support for that revolutionary struggle.'[154] Both in towns and in the country in the Oriente province, people were already familiar with revolutionary movements.[155] In addition, the Cuban Communist Party (the Popular Socialist Party, PSP) was important in creating the objective conditions for the revolution through its involvement in anti-imperialist struggles.[156]

The second major area of criticism concentrated on his conception of the relationship between the armed vanguard and the 'masses' and his rejection of the need for a party. First, the relationship was 'undialectical' and therefore elitist.[157] Second, the *foco* could not be seen as a fully formed self-sufficient entity. In the preparatory phase, the twin dangers of putschism, where the *foco* substitutes itself for the masses, or spontaneism, where the masses would supposedly join the guerilla vanguard spontaneously, had to be avoided. A political/organizational relationship had to be established, enabling the vanguard to be firmly implanted in 'objectively revolutionary classes'.[158] Lack of attention to the initial phase had led to two disastrous attempts to form *focos* in Brazil in 1969.[159] Further, the policy of deliberate isolation from the peasantry to avoid betrayal was an important reason for the failure of Che Guevara's campaign in Bolivia in 1967.[160]

Connected with his underestimation of the need for a political relationship was his mistaken assumption that peasants would be automatically won over to the *foco* through military action. By themselves, 'weapons are dumb'. An appreciation of the concrete conditions of the class struggle within the strategic area, and the way in which weapons were used, was critical.[161] Armed struggle by itself did not necessarily induce revolutionary consciousness.[162] Indeed, Debray failed to analyse the failure of campaigns in Latin America in the mid-1960s that had relied on the 'propaganda of arms'.[163] As a consequence of the need to build up political support, guerillas had to be politically trained or experienced, as Fidel Castro and Che Guevara were before the Cuban Revolution.[164]

Even more crucially, a political party was a necessity. Here again Cuba was the exception. Elsewhere the masses would have to be organized in urban areas, and that required a party.[165] This was especially so in the transition to socialism, when political argument was just as important as force, and a need arose to create political institutions and mass participation in the running of society.[166] Indeed, the Cuban leadership after the 1959 revolution acknowledged the importance of the party in this transition.[167]

A number of critics noted that Debray, in dispensing with the party, relied on a confusing argument. His rejection of the party on principle was based upon false generalization derived from the policies and behaviour of Communist parties. They were reformist, so all political parties were reformist.[168] He wrongly ascribed their reformism to their urban base, rather than the fact that they were instruments of Soviet foreign policy.[169] There was another pitfall in his form of argument, related not just to the question of the party, but also to his failure to analyse the relationship between concrete conditions and the appropriate forms of organization and strategy: 'There is no need to choose between the party and the guerilla, between the city and the countryside, between military and political struggle. The problem is to decide on the forms in which these elements must be combined in the overall process of revolutionary struggle.'[170]

The third area of criticism centred on the question of whether Debray was advocating a *Marxist* strategy at all, whatever his explicit intentions. Thus, he was ahistorical: the guerillas existed in nature, independently of historical conditions.[171] Class analysis was also absent in *Revolution in the Revolution?* Town and country were perceived by Debray as the significant determinants of political positions, rather than class.[172] More substantively, in viewing students, intellectuals and peasants as the main source of social change, he marginalized the working class in the revolutionary process, thereby challenging one of Marxism's central tenets.[173] He underemphasized its importance, along with that of the urban population in general, not only in the Cuban revolution of 1959, but also in other Latin American revolutions, such as those in Venezuela (1958), Bolivia (1952) and the Dominican Republic (1965). Further, urban populations could often be more militant than rural ones.[174]

Just as seriously, he rejected the need for theory, thereby sundering the theory/practice nexus at the heart of Marxism. He had replaced the force of political argument, whose basis lay in theory, with the argument of force, of physical confrontation, which would spontaneously activate the masses.[175] Moreover, the Cuban Revolution could not be used as an example of not needing theory, because it had not been initially socialist. It happened to evolve in that direction. It was unique in this sense. Revolutionaries in Latin America were confronted with a different situation, requiring a theoretical compass.[176] For example, reformism was more entrenched in Latin America, and the peasantry was not 'virgin', but would have to be won over politically.[177]

Self-criticism

Régis Debray began retreating from his *foco* theory while in a Bolivian prison. He now saw it as 'utopian'.[178] Nevertheless, he claimed, albeit weakly, that Cuba was a 'model' of revolution for the rest of Latin America. He also maintained that his critics had misunderstood him. Yes, he had omitted to discuss Latin American economic structures, but the purpose of the book was different, expressing the 'urgency of immediate practice at any price'.[179] Second, he had not excluded discussion of political questions: in circumstances where armed struggle was ongoing, the political could be 'expressed mainly in a military form'.[180] Third, he was not concerned with the question of whether conditions were ripe for armed struggle, but with what happened where they were.[181]

A much fuller repudiation of his *foco* formulation appeared in his aptly entitled *A Critique of Arms*, first published in 1974.[182] It was a work of damning self-criticism. In it, he performed one of the greatest theoretical somersaults in the history of Marxism. He recognized that *Revolution in the Revolution?* was a 'book of a moment', when 'armed revolution' was 'uppermost';[183] that '*foquismo*' was a product of the retreat of the 'popular movement' in Latin America;[184] that it reflected the 'politicist' culture of the Latin American left, which ignored the importance of economic conditions. Now was the time to take stock, after the numerous defeats of Latin American guerilla movements in the 1960s, which remorselessly exposed the defects of the *foco* theory. His new points of reference became the classical Marxism of Marx and a non-Stalinist interpretation of Lenin's views on the relationship between party and class.[185] This meant emphasizing the importance of concrete political, social and economic analysis, of a 'dialectical' more flexible, approach to strategic and tactical questions, of the unity of theory and practice, of democratic party organization, of the role of the working class in the revolutionary process and, finally, of the organic connection between the vanguard and class.

He acknowledged that he had committed a 'basic error' in *Revolution in the Revolution?* He had

> passed quickly over the (politico-economic) premises to get straight to the conclusions: it presented the result (a guerrilla force in action, linked closely with the people and becoming the nation's vanguard) without any cause, a specific military product without the (economic, social and political) conditions that produced it.... The subjective was totally disconnected from the objective; the guidelines for aware and organized revolutionary action were isolated from the laws of the class struggle and its development; military *art* from political *science*.[186]

Thus, he had failed to analyse the conditions for successful guerilla warfare. In other words, strategy was *condition-dependent*.

In following through the implications of this fundamental flaw he in effect conceded that most of his critics had been correct. He now realized that an examination of objective conditions in its different forms would have revealed that the Cuban strategy for revolution could not be simply exported to Latin America. He had learnt to his 'cost that any political line that is not based on an analysis of what is really happening in a specific national context is not merely useless, but positively dangerous'. Hence, militants ought to make sociological and economic studies of specific Latin American societies in order to adapt their strategy to local conditions, in order to see whether they were conducive to popular violence.[187] He also admitted that he had had a 'grossly simplified image of the Cuban revolution'.[188] For example, he now recognized the pivotal importance of the urbanized and proletarianized province of Oriente in supporting Castro in the revolution.[189]

Equally significantly, he now regarded the Cuban Revolution as exceptional. Unique conditions had enabled it to become socialist. As it was the last country in Latin America to overthrow imperialism, its bourgeois state form was immature, meaning that its institutions had engendered little sense of legality and therefore little popular support.[190]

Further, the ruling class was not ideologically hegemonic,[191] Cuba possessed a politically mature workers' movement[192] and the rural population had developed strong fighting traditions.[193] Finally, the revolution would not have succeeded if the bourgeois state had not been destroyed and if it had been explicitly socialist from the outset, given the likely opposition of the United States. It moved in this direction when the programme for land reform after 1959 brought it into direct conflict with American imperialism, which compelled Castro to nationalize American companies in 1960.[194]

His failure to recognize that strategy was condition-dependent led him to revise his previous account of the vanguard–mass relationship, with its insistence on *foco* mobility, the exclusive importance of armed struggle, self-sufficiency of the 'knapsack' and independence from a mass base. A successful 'peoples' war' had been fought in Cuba. An unsuccessful 'vanguard war', based upon the *foco* strategy, had been fought in Latin America. The masses had to be directly involved in struggle, which meant that the vanguard had to be firmly implanted within it, rather than being external to it.[195] Otherwise the danger of elitist, 'revolutionary alienation' from the masses existed.[196] Just as crucially, without a mass base, the *foco* could not survive, because it required new members and the replenishing of supplies:[197] 'the *raison d'être* of the *foco* becomes simply armed survival'.[198] He attributed the failures of Che Guevara in Bolivia and the guerilla campaigns in Peru, Venezuela and Colombia in the 1960s to the absence of a base of support among the masses.[199] He summed up the situation in Latin America epigrammatically, as 'the crisis of the revolutionary rearguards', which was 'social, political and logistical'.[200] This was *the* strategic problem.[201] In particular, for the vanguard to fuse with the masses, a proper preparatory phase was required, which necessitated a class analysis of terrain of combat. From this a political programme could be formulated, combining, for example, the short-term goals of the peasantry with the long-term goals of the guerilla movement.[202]

Equally vitally, he realized that the countryside was not in Latin America the central site of struggle. It was either deserted, or, unlike in China and Vietnam, of little significance to the economic and political life of the country. Hence, guerilla combat could not be confined to rural areas.[203] In addition, he now maintained that *focos* could not be built politically through purely military confrontations:

> since there is no national organization that can handle the repercussions, no explanatory political campaign either before or after the event and no visible connection with concrete struggles of the people taking place simultaneously in the towns, factories and colleges, there is nothing to capture and extend the fleeting echoes of such small acts of harassment.[204]

This narrowly militaristic approach was now viewed as symptomatic of a larger failure of perspective. All the questions of strategy and the nature of the vanguard had to be seen dialectically. 'Dialectic is the oxygen of history and those who ignore it can only shrivel and die.'[205] His *foco* theory had 'resulted in dissociating the military struggle from the political, the underground from the legal, the action of the vanguard from the mass movement, strategy from tactics, hills from towns, the advanced sectors of the populace from the more backward'.[206] *Foquismo* saw these different elements as juxtaposed absolutes, not as interrelated, capable of being united by establishing 'intermediate links'. It had rejected 'the necessary instruments and mechanisms of organization: "no Party", no "minimum programme", few if any intermediate cadres, no half-way forms of association for those who, though they cannot actually become guerrillas, could and would like to get involved in some kind of militant action'.[207]

In keeping with this dialectical approach, he now no longer maintained that the *foco* could substitute itself for the party. 'The real problem is not: Party versus guerrilla force, but: what sort of Party? how is it formed? what is its relationships with the mass of the people?'[208] It had to be adaptable, 'able to switch from one form of struggle to another', depending on the situation in which it found itself.[209] Debray held that his *foco* theory had been modelled on Lenin's *What Is to Be Done?*, with revolutionary consciousness external to the working class. He now recognized that the later Lenin had a much more dialectical, organic, view of party and class.[210] Now the small guerilla motor had to be 'directly coupled to the large class motor',[211] and much more tied to the working class.[212] Again, consistent with his dialectical perspective, he rejected the notion that a party could be run on militaristic lines. Rather, there had to be internal democracy, enabling deep debate over issues, in order to avoid splits, to be more adaptable to changing situations and to bring the party closer to the class struggle.[213]

In his final volte-face, he now stressed the importance of theory and theoretical training.[214] 'Practical experience and theoretical research' were vital in considering the appropriate strategy.[215]

Commentary

From a theoretical point of view Debray had now adopted a far more formally correct Marxist position, after having read the classics of Marxism: virtually all aspects of a Marxist strategy were given their due place within a dialectical framework. He now adopted a far less prescriptive position, based on technique and subjective commitment to the revolutionary cause. The choice of strategy now became condition-dependent, and therefore more open-ended and flexible. One implication of his change of stance was that *Revolution in the Revolution?* could be viewed essentially as a non-Marxist document although he claimed that his *foco* theory had been modelled on Lenin's *What Is to Be Done?*[216] There was little visible dialectical undergirding, little acknowledgement that the techniques of guerilla warfare he advocated were influenced, for example, by class analysis. Finally, given that his strategy was condition-dependent, it is hard to know whether in the end his position was an advance on communist orthodoxy, which at least in part was determined by the existence of bourgeois democracy. For he now admitted that 'Revolutionary violence cannot win against a broadly liberal republic in which universal suffrage and normal political life serve to canalize and deflect the energy of the masses.'[217] Indeed, Guevara, his erstwhile mentor, had made a similar point in 1960.[218] Perhaps this new emphasis on circumstances influenced Debray's decision to join the French Socialist Party in the mid-1970s.

GENERAL CONCLUSION

What is striking about these two debates that emerged from the Cuban revolution is that their trajectory pointed to a return to a more formally Marxist framework. Warren more obviously than Frank wanted to revitalize what he perceived to be Marx's attitude towards imperialism, albeit in an undialectical, one-sided way. This mean that he did not allow for the possibility of uneven capitalist development on a global scale, and did not consider the development of a combined anti-imperialist and anti-capitalist strategy. Debray definitely moved in a dialectical direction after *Revolution in the Revolution?* His advocacy of the *foco* with its emphasis on technique and leadership was replaced by a Marxist reaffirmation of the importance of the party, politically and militarily flexible, democratic, organically and dialectically linked to the working class.

NOTES

1. The term 'Third World' derives from the notion that the advanced capitalist countries are the 'First World', the so-called socialist states the 'Second World' and the economically underdeveloped countries the 'Third World'.
2. See, for example, A. Emmanuel, *Unequal Exchange: A Study of the Imperialism of Trade*, New Left Books, London (1972).
3. Frank claimed that he was not a Marxist: e.g. his *World Accumulation*, Macmillan, London (1978), 363, and *Critique and Anti-critique*, Macmillan, London (1984), 26. However, he was deeply inspired by Paul Baran, an avowed Marxist. And he strongly supported the Cuban revolution, which became officially 'Marxist'.
4. T. Halperin-Donghi, ' "Dependency theory" and Latin American historiography', *Latin American Research Review*, 17, 11 (1982), 117.

5. D. C. Hodges, *The Latin American Revolution*, William Morrow, New York (1974), 46-7.
6. I. Roxborough, *Theories of Underdevelopment*, Macmillan, London (1979), 33-4.
7. A. G. Frank, *Capitalism and Underdevelopment in Latin America* (hereafter *CULA*), Monthly Review Press, New York (1967).
8. M. Kenner and J. Petras, *Fidel Castro Speaks*, Penguin Books, Harmondsworth (1969), 163; D. Booth, 'Andre Gundar Frank: an introduction and apprecia-tion' in I. Oxaal, A. Barnett and D. Booth (Eds), *Beyond the Sociology of Development*, Routledge and Kegan Paul, London (1975), 65-6.
9. Booth, *ibid.*, 52-62.
10. P. Baran, *The Political Economy of Growth*, Monthly Review Press, New York (1957).
11. *CULA*, xv-xvi.
12. *CULA*, 7-8, see also 20.
13. *CULA*, 42.
14. *CULA*, 9.
15. *CULA*, 11-12, 149.
16. *CULA*, 13.
17. *CULA*, 215.
18. *Ibid.*
19. *CULA*, 148-50.
20. *CULA*, 20-3.
21. *CULA*, 24.
22. *CULA*, 270.
23. *CULA*, 277.
24. *CULA*, xvi.
25. 'Who is the immediate enemy?' in J. D. Cockcroft, A. G. Frank and D. L. Johnson (Eds), *Dependence and Underdevelopment: Latin America's Political Economy*, Anchor Books, New York (1972), 425.
26. E. Laclau, 'Feudalism and capitalism in Latin America', *New Left Review*, 67, (May/June 1971), 22; J. Larrain, *Theories of Development*, Polity Press, Cambridge (1989), 129; G. Palma, 'Dependency: a formal theory of under-development or a methodology for the analysis of concrete situations of underdevelopment?', *World Development*, 6 (1978), 900.
27. Larrain, *op. cit.*, 188-9.
28. F. H. Cardoso, 'Dependency and development in Latin America', *New Left Review*, 74 (July/August 1972), 89.
29. A. Phillips, 'The concept of "Development"', *Review of African Political Economy*, 8 (Jan/Apr 1977), 19.
30. Larrain, *op. cit.*, 125. See also Palma, *op. cit.*, 903-4.
31. A. Brewer, *Marxist Theories of Imperialism: a Critical Survey*, 2nd edn, Routledge, London (1990), 175.
32. *Ibid.*, 165-6. See also Booth, *op.cit.*, 73.
33. Brewer, *op. cit.*, 169.
34. *Ibid.*, 166; Booth, *op. cit.*, 79.
35. Laclau, *op. cit.*, 24-5.
36. *Ibid.*, 31.

37. *Ibid.*, 37.
38. R. Brenner, 'The origins of capitalist development: a critique of neo-Smithian Marxism', *New Left Review*, 104 (July/August 1977), 85.
39. *Ibid.*, 85 and 89-90.
40. F. H. Cardoso and Faletto, *Dependency and Development in Latin America*, University of California Press, Berkeley (1979).
41. *Ibid.*, xvi-xvii.
42. *Ibid.*, 186.
43. Cardoso, *op. cit.*, 88.
44. E.g. C. Leys, 'Capital accumulation, class formation and dependency – the significance of the Kenyan case' in R. Miliband and J. Saville (Eds), *Socialist Register, 1978*, Merlin Press, London, 241-66.
45. Larrain, *op. cit.*, 132.
46. M. C. Howard and J. E. King, *A History of Marxian Economics, Vol. 2*, Macmillan, Basingstoke (1992), 216.
47. Brenner, *op. cit.*, 91.
48. Phillips, *op. cit.*, 20, See also C. Leys, 'Underdevelopment and dependency: critical notes' in P. Limqueco and B. McFarlane (Eds), *Neo-Marxist Theories of Development*, Croom Helm, London (1983), 36-43.
49. Phillips, *op. cit.*, 21.
50. Bill Warren, *Imperialism: Pioneer of Capitalism* (hereafter *IPC*), Verso, London (1980), 105-9. See also H. Gulalp, 'Frank and Wallerstein revisited: a contribution to Brenner's critique', in Limqueco and McFarlane, *op. cit.*, 133.
51. *IPC*, 171; see also J. Banaji, 'Gundar Frank in retreat?' in Limqueco and McFarlane, *op. cit.*, 109.
52. Howard and King, *op. cit.*, 176.
53. Brenner, *op. cit.*, 92.
54. A. G. Frank, *Lumpenbourgeoisie: Lumpendevelopment*, Monthly Review Press, New York (1972), 1-2.
55. *Ibid.*, 4.
56. *Ibid.*, 4-5.
57. Frank, *Critique and Anti-critique*, 214-17.
58. 'Crisis and transformation and dependency in the world-system' in R. H. Chilcote and D. L. Johnson (Eds), *Theories of Development: Mode of Production or Dependency?*, Sage, Beverly Hills (1983), 182; see also his *World Accumulation*, 240-1.
59. B. Warren, 'Imperialism and capitalist industrialisation' (hereafter *ICI*), *New Left Review*, 81 (Sept/Oct 1973); later developed into *Imperialism: Pioneer of Capitalism* (hereafter *IPC*), Verso, London (1980), published two years after his death in 1978.
60. *IPC*, 162-70.
61. *ICI*, 5-6.
62. *ICI*, 7; *IPC*, 244.
63. *IPC*, 171.
64. *IPC*, 190-4.
65. *IPC*, 211.
66. *IPC*, 212.

67. *IPC*, 235.
68. *IPC*, 170.
69. *IPC*, 182; *ICI*, 17.
70. *IPC*, 180; *ICI*, 30.
71. *ICI*, 17.
72. *ICI*, 18, 28.
73. *ICI*, 26.
74. *ICI*, 28.
75. *IPC*, 179, 183.
76. *IPC*, 184.
77. *ICI*, 12; *IPC*, 173.
78. *IPC*, 177, 235.
79. *ICI*, 39; *IPC*, 175.
80. *ICI*, 3.
81. *ICI*, 40.
82. *IPC*, 10.
83. *ICI*, 44.
84. P. McMichael, J. Petras and R. Rhodes, 'Imperialism and the contradictions of development' (hereafter *ICD*), *New Left Review*, 85 (May/June 1974), 85.
85. A. Ahmad, 'Imperialism and progress' in Chilcote and Johnson, *op. cit.*, 40.
86. Ahmad, *op. cit.*, 41.
87. *Ibid.*, 40 and 50.
88. Brewer, *op. cit.*, 283.
89. *ICD*, 87 and 95.
90. A. Lipietz, 'Marx or Rostow?', *New Left Review*, 132 (March/April 1982), 52.
91. *Ibid.*, 51.
92. *ICD*, 86.
93. Lipietz, *op. cit.*, 53.
94. *ICD*, 87.
95. *ICD*, 87; Ahmad, *op. cit.*, 45.
96. Lipietz, *op. cit.*, 53.
97. *ICD*, 90; Ahmad, *op. cit.*, 45.
98. *ICD*, 91 and 92.
99. *ICD*, 87-8.
100. *ICD*, 99.
101. *ICD*, 90.
102. *ICD*, 102; Lipietz, *op. cit.*, 52.
103. *ICD*, 89-90.
104. Ahmad, *op. cit.*, 52.
105. Howard and King, *op. cit.*, 217.
106. Ahmad, *op. cit.*, 51.
107. Lipietz, *op. cit.*, 56-8.
108. *ICD*, 104.
109. *IPC*, xi.
110. H. Ramm, *The Marxism of Régis Debray: between Lenin and Guevara* (hereafter *MRD*), The Regents Press of Kansas, Lawrence, KS (1978), 39.
111. *MRD*, 44.

112. He had published two articles on the guerilla movement in Latin America, later appearing in English as, 'Latin America: the long march', *New Left Review*, 33 (Sept/Oct 1965), 17–58, and 'Problems of revolutionary strategy in Latin America', *New Left Review*, 45, (Sept/Oct 1967), 13–41.

113. *MRB*, 56–60. R. Debray, *Revolution in the Revolution?* (hereafter *RR*), Penguin, Harmondsworth (1967).

114. L. Huberman and P. M. Sweezy (Eds), *Régis Debray and the Latin American Revolution* (hereafter *RDLAR*), Monthly Review Press, New York (1969), 9. Although in 'Latin America: the long march' (p. 27) he had cautioned against too hasty an imitation of the Cuban revolution, and remarked that the *foco* was not appropriate unless one 'finds a point of insertion within maturing contradictions' (p. 30).

115. Ernesto Che Guevara, *Guerilla Warfare*, Monthly Review Press, New York (1961), 1.

116. W. Pomeroy (Ed.), *Guerrilla Warfare and Marxism,* International Publishers, New York (1968), 293–4.

117. *RR*, 25.

118. *RR*, 25.

119. *RR*, 29.

120. *RR*, 43–4.

121. *RR*, 35.

122. *RR*, 49.

123. *RR*, 56.

124. *RR*, 53.

125. *RR*, 56.

126. *RR*, 60.

127. *RR*, 63.

128. *RR*, 64.

129. *RR*, 75.

130. *RR*, 100–1.

131. *RR*, 65, 120.

132. *RR*, 65–71.

133. *RR*, 85.

134. *RR*, 83.

135. *RR*, 72–3.

136. *RR*, 72.

137. *RR*, 89, 110–11.

138. *RR*, 109–10.

139. *RR*, 105, 115.

140. *RR*, 120.

141. *RR*, 106–7.

142. *RR*, 108.

143. *RR*, 108–9.

144. *RR*, 123–6.

145. W. A. Williams, 'Debray: black power and student power', in *RDLAR*, 84.

146. L. Althusser, 'Letter from Louis Althusser', in R. Debray, *Critique of Arms* (hereafter *CA*), Vol. 1, Penguin, Harmondsworth (1977), 262; P. Worsley,

'Revolutionary theory: Guevara and Debray' in *RDLAR*, 132.

147. E. Ahmed, 'Radical but wrong', in *RDLAR*, 75.
148. J. Woddis, *New Theories of Revolution*, Lawrence and Wishart, London (1972).
149. C. Silva, 'The errors of the foco theory', in *RDLAR*, 24.
150. Woddis, *op. cit.*, 231-3.
151. *Ibid.*, 180, 250-60; Worsley, *op. cit.*, 135.
152. Silva, *op. cit.*, 24; Woddis, *op. cit.*, 217.
153. D. McKelvey, 'Régis Debray: historical truths and historical aberrations' in *RDLAR*, 92; Worsley, *op. cit.*, 130; Woddis, *op. cit.*, 237.
154. J. Petras, 'Debray: revolutionary or elitist?' in *RDLAR*, 111; *MRB*, 96-7.
155. W. Pomeroy, 'Questions on the Debray thesis' in *RDLAR*, 36.
156. Woddis, *op. cit.*, 195.
157. Petras, *RDLAR*, 108.
158. J. Quartim, 'Régis Debray and the Brazilian Revolution', *New Left Review*, 59 (Jan/Feb 1970), 71.
159. J. Quartim, *Dictatorship and Armed Struggle in Brazil*, New Left Books, London (1971), 151-4.
160. *MRB*, 88.
161. Quartim, *op. cit.* (1970), 63.
162. Silva, *RDLAR* 18; Petras, *RDLAR*, 111.
163. Huberman and Sweezy, *RDLAR*, 7; Silva, *RDLAR*, 25; Worsley, *RDLAR*, 135.
164. Pomeroy, *RDLAR*, 38; Silva, *RDLAR*, 18, 30.
165. Silva, *RDLAR*, 19; Quartim, *op. cit.* (1970), 78.
166. Silva, *RDLAR*, 21; Ahmed, *RDLAR*, 82; McKelvey, *RDLAR*, 94.
167. J. Bosch, 'An anti-communist manifesto' in *RDLAR*, 97.
168. Silva, *RDLAR*, 22; Petras, *RDLAR*, 109; Quartim, *op. cit.* (1970), 69.
169. Quartim, *op. cit.* (1970), 78.
170. Quartim, *op. cit.* (1971), 197.
171. Althusser, *op. cit.*, 263.
172. *Ibid.*, 264.
173. Woddis, *op. cit.*, 274.
174. Petras, *RDLAR*, 112-13.
175. Silva, *RDLAR*, 23; Woddis, *op. cit.*, 267-9.
176. Silva, *RDLAR*, 24.
177. S. Torres and J. Aronde, 'Debray and the Cuban experience' in *RDLAR*, 61.
178. 'Reply to my critics' in R. Debray, *Strategy for Revolution* (Ed. R. Blackburn), Cape, London (1970), 237.
179. *Ibid.*, 234.
180. *Ibid.*, 235.
181. *Ibid.*
182. *CA*. He also wrote *Revolution on Trial*, Volume 2 of *A Critique of Arms*, Penguin, Harmondsworth (1978), which was a factual, rather than a theoretical, account of the failure of Latin American guerilla movements in the 1960s.
183. *CA*, 225.
184. *CA*, 238.
185. See Chapter 6.

186. *CA*, 232–3.
187. *CA*, 33, 156.
188. *CA*, 107.
189. *CA*, 128.
190. *CA*, 60–1.
191. *CA*, 62.
192. *CA*, 64.
193. *CA*, 62.
194. *CA*, 69–72.
195. *CA*, 118.
196. *CA*, 193.
197. *CA*, 123, 134.
198. *CA*, 137.
199. *CA*, 145–51.
200. *CA*, 155.
201. *CA*, 116.
202. *CA*, 187–8.
203. *CA*, 125–6, 140.
204. *CA*, 154.
205. *CA*, 109.
206. *CA*, 107.
207. *CA*, 108.
208. *CA*, 172.
209. *CA*, 219.
210. *CA*, 168.
211. *CA*, 191.
212. *CA*, 206.
213. *CA*, 201–14.
214. *CA*, 206.
215. *CA*, 183, 189.
216. *CA*, 159. See also Ramm, *MRB*, 184–6.
217. *Revolution on Trial*, 119.
218. C. Guevara, *Guerilla Warfare* (1960), reprinted with introduction by B. Loveman and T. Davies, Jr, Manchester University Press, Manchester (1986), 48.

12
Eurocommunism: the Democratic Road to Socialism

PROBLEMS AND ISSUES

This chapter takes up the issue debated between Lenin and Kautsky, as outlined in Chapter 7. The key question concerned the role of parliament in the transition to socialism. While, arguably, in practice Western Communist Parties had endorsed the parliamentary road to socialism since the popular front period in the 1930s, they had not spelt out the theoretical consequences for their Marxist-Leninist ideology until the 1970s. In a sense Kautsky's ghost had returned to haunt these parties, although Eurocommunists preferred to seek legitimation in the works of the Italian Marxist and martyr, Antonio Gramsci, rather than in Lenin's old adversary. The problem of ideological reorientation was symptomatic of a deeper difficulty for Marxist politics: how to formulate a revolutionary strategy in the West when liberal, parliamentary democracy played such a key role in political life.

The neologism 'Eurocommunism' was coined by a Yugoslav journalist in 1975 to mark the new ideological and strategic turn of the three so-called 'Mediterranean' Communist Parties – the Italian, French and Spanish. Leaders of these parties, after an initial reluctance, because it smacked of disloyalty towards the Soviet Union, came to accept the term.[1] Some other Communist Party leaderships, such as the British and Japanese, also endorsed this self-description, if reluctantly. Other parties, such as the Portuguese, preferred to remain 'Marxist-Leninist'.

The key features of Eurocommunism were, first, the seeking of some form of power-sharing in government, reversing what had effectively been a minority oppositional stance. To this end, the French Communist Party (PCF) entered into a 'union of the left' – a joint election programme – with the Socialist Party in 1972. More dramatically, the Italian (PCI) and Spanish (PCE) Communist Parties proposed to collaborate with right-wing parties.[2] The second and more significant characteristic, partly determined by the first, because electoral considerations became paramount, was that these parties in varying degrees overtly cut many of their ties with the Soviet Union. They made explicit criticisms of the Soviet politico-economic system, jettisoned Marxism-Leninism, the code-name for Stalinist ideology, and emphatically embraced the liberal democratic political framework. Third, consonant with their anti-Stalinism, these parties gestured towards greater internal democracy and abandoned 'vanguardist' notions, which supposedly had totalitarian implications.[3]

This chapter will examine the theoretical positions articulated by Eurocommunists to justify this new strategic and ideological orientation as well as the criticisms advanced by those generally to their left. This will entail a consideration of: first, the most famous Eurocommunist text by Santiago Carrillo, *'Eurocommunism' and the State*; second, Nicos Poulantzas's rejection of the Leninist dual-power scenario of revolution; and, third, the use of Gramsci's work by Eurocommunists to legitimate their position. Finally, criticisms of Eurocommunist practice will be briefly registered.

THE CONTEXT

Put at its simplest, Eurocommunism can be interpreted as the penultimate phase of the dialectic of disintegration of Soviet communism as a powerful, monolithic, world movement. The final collapse came between 1989 and 1991, with the demise of the Eastern European and Soviet regimes. The *raison d'être* of Communist Parties after the victory of Stalin and his 'socialism in one country' policy over Trotsky in the mid-1920s had been the defence of the Soviet Union. As such, their main function was to act as Soviet ambassadors and to implement the imperatives of its foreign policy, whether it consisted of a cooperative or an antagonistic posture towards the Western powers.

The strength of the relationship between the Soviet Union and its satellite parties was determined by a number of factors. First was the extent to which the Soviet Union required them for its defence. This began to diminish in the post-war period as a result of the Eastern European countries coming under Soviet control and China becoming communist in 1949. Equally importantly, it acquired nuclear weapons in the 1950s, enabling it to maintain a 'balance of terror' with the United States. Moreover, after the Cuban missile crisis of 1962, the Soviet Union adopted a far more conciliatory attitude towards the United States so that it was even less reliant on international communist support.

The second factor was the degree to which the Soviet Union could mobilize the idealism of rank and file members of these parties. Arguably, the ideological power of the Soviet Union was greater in the so-called 'Third World', at least until the Sino-Soviet split in the early 1960s, where democratic traditions were virtually non-existent. It provided a model of economic development which could meet the basic material needs of the various populations. In the West, however, with its relatively developed democratic culture and higher living standards, the Soviet model was potentially far less attractive. While the Soviet Union had gained enormous prestige during the Second World War in the West owing to its success in helping to crush fascism and Nazism, its own use of force against its own or contiguous populations was much harder to defend. Thus, its treatment of dissidents, which became highly publicized in the West in the 1960s, brought into sharp focus the question of civil liberties. Even more importantly, the official criticisms of Stalin by Khrushchev, General Secretary of the Soviet Communist Party, in 1956, coupled with the invasion of Hungary in the same year, and later of Czechoslovakia in 1968, raised enormous doubts among many Western communists about whether the Soviet model was a desirable alternative to Western liberal capitalism.

Nevertheless, the crucial effect of this distancing process, which became so manifest in the early 1970s, was that defence of the Soviet Union was no longer the prime determinant of the Western parties' strategy and tactics. So, for instance, the Italian Communist Party supported NATO and the EEC, and the PCF the French nuclear deterrent. They could now give their essentially electoral orientation, originating in the early 1950s, full rein.[4]

Electability and office now became the name of the game. They had to make themselves more obviously acceptable to the Americans and local ruling elites as well as the electorate. Here the junking of 'Marxism-Leninism', with its totalitarian overtones, was vital. Yet some ideological replacement was essential in order to sustain the support of the party faithfully for this new strategic departure. The principal Eurocommunist leaders – Marchais in France, Carrillo in Spain and Berlinguer in Italy – pursued what they termed a 'third road' between Stalinism and social democracy. However, they had in effect adopted a 'fourth' road because they ruled out the classic Marxist strategy of potentially violent, yet democratic, revolution based on class struggle, which they had subsumed under Marxism-Leninism.

The growing radicalization of the electorates of France and Italy in the late 1960s and early 1970s provided the more immediate background to the rise of Eurocommunism. This held out the promise of an increase in the political strength of the PCF and the PCI, such that other parties could not govern without their cooperation, as senior partner with the French Socialist Party, and probably as a junior partner with the Italian Christian Democrats. As for the PCE, it hoped to become a respectable part of Spanish political life after the death of Franco in 1975, heralding the return of some form of constitutional democracy. Indeed, the PCI and PCE, both of whom had experienced fascist rule, after the overthrow of the constitutionally elected socialist government of Allende in Chile in September 1973 were sharply reminded of the possibility of some form of authoritarian takeover if the economic and political situation became too chaotic. Thus, both parties sought to woo the middle classes, especially because these countries were experiencing heavy inflation following the large increases in oil prices. Given their influence in the trade unions, these parties realized that they could avoid the possibility of repression or marginalization by being useful to political and economic elites. They hoped to sell wage restraint to the unions in which they were influential, with the promise of increased investment, jobs and various economic and social reforms.

However, the objective of power-sharing through cooperation with other parties backfired in the late 1970s. The famous 'historic compromise' with the ruling Christian Democrats, proposed by Berlinguer, General Secretary of the PCI, in 1973, came unstuck in 1977 after revolts by youth, women and the unemployed against the lack of social reform or jobs. The PCI called for wage restraint and increased law and order. PCI membership dropped significantly and pressure from the party rank-and-file led it to abandon the compromise.[5] In the elections of 1979 the PCI vote fell by 4 per cent, with increasing support for the parties to the left of the PCI. It had failed to live up to its own slogan: 'party of struggle and of government'. The PCF – effectively the most Stalinist of the three parties – in 1972 had aspired to office through collaborating with the socialists on a common programme. It pulled out in 1977 when it realized that its electoral support would be sufficient only for it to become the junior partner in a socialist-dominated government. As for the PCE, it collaborated with the centre-right UCD (Unión del Centro Democrático) between 1977 and 1979. It agreed to the Moncloa Pacts, which meant supporting economic austerity in return for constitutional and fiscal reforms. As a consequence, the membership haemorrhaged. The UCD dropped the PCE in 1979 prior to the March elections. In these and the elections of 1982 the PCE lost out to its much larger socialist rival. Indeed, in the 1980s the main beneficiaries of the swing to the left in Italy, France and Spain were the socialists, all of whom managed to form governments in that decade.

SANTIAGO CARRILLO: DEMOCRATIZING THE CAPITALIST STATE

Carrillo's *'Eurocommunism' and the State*, published in 1976, was the most accessible and comprehensive statement of the Eurocommunist position. Carrillo, General Secretary of the Spanish Communist Party, was indebted to Gramsci and the French Marxist philosopher Louis Althusser, both of whom stressed the importance of the ideological 'cement' needed either to hold society together or to maintain class rule. He wrote this book after the death of General Franco, who had ruled Spain for over thirty years, but before political parties had become legalized. He wanted to demonstrate, first, that the PCE was no longer wedded to the Soviet model of revolution, which implied the need for violence and a vanguard party, and, second, that it was committed to the pluralism and constitutionalism of Western liberal democracy. He insisted that an indissoluble tie existed between democracy and socialism.[6] In presenting his arguments Carrillo hoped that the PCE could play an influential part in post-Francoist politics, by cooperating with other parties and broadening its social base beyond the working class.

Carrillo's prime objection to the Soviet model of the state and revolution was its irrelevance in contemporary political and social conditions, which were quite unlike those of Russia in 1917. The successful use of violence was no longer possible or necessary. Contemporary European states were strong, in contrast to the Russian state in 1917, which was disintegrating as a result of war, a situation unlikely to arise in Europe owing to the nuclear stalemate.[7] Equally, a *dictatorship* of the proletariat was not necessary, because unlike in Russia in 1917 the proletariat was no longer in a minority, having to use force against other classes.[8]

Neither was the model of the Soviet state, where 'the bureaucratic stratum, at its various levels, wields excessive and almost uncontrolled political power', apposite.[9] Owing to its isolation after 1917 it became highly bureaucratic and militarized. The imperatives of defence and economic development had ridden roughshod over workers' democracy.[10] Modern conditions for socialism in the West were quite different: the productive forces were highly developed, so that consumption no longer had to be subordinated to 'primitive accumulation', consisting of a drastic restriction of consumption in favour of production, and necessitating a highly authoritarian state. Further, if socialist states emerged in Europe, they would no longer be isolated, because they would get support from Eastern Europe and Asia. US intervention would also be easier to resist if, as was possible, owing to the internationalization of capital, the industrially advanced European countries became socialist at the same time.[11]

Carrillo not only distanced himself from the Soviet experience. He reconnoitred the strategic terrain of Western Europe in order to attain his socialist objective. Accordingly, he analysed the economic and political structures and the interrelation between both, the opportunities to change them and the social and political forces that could bring this about.

He noted that the modern state possessed three important character-istics conducive to socialism. It was under the control of the monopoly fraction of the bourgeoisie.[12] As a result, it stood in contradiction to the rest of society – workers, farmers, traders and professional groups – which would therefore want to democratize it. Second, it was closely connected to the economy. The productive forces had become more socialized. Owing to the growing cost of technological innovation, investment was increasingly state, rather than privately, financed.[13] Third, echoing Gramsci and

Althusser, modern capitalist power no longer rested primarily on state coercion, but on 'ideological state apparatuses' – the church, education, the media, the legal system and the ideology of democracy.[14]

Opportunities had arisen for a democratic, constitutional non-violent transition to socialism, stemming from crises or contradictions both inside and outside the modern state. They possessed the potential to propel the 'people' into struggle, democratizing the state in the process. Contradictions outside the state were, first, between the enormously developed forces of production – including nuclear energy and a highly trained workforce – which would lay the foundations for socialism on the one hand, and the capitalist relations on the other, which stymied their further development. Moreover, resources could easily be transferred, with appropriate policies, from arms expenditure to economic development and the overcoming of world hunger.[15] The second contradiction was between the internationalization and socialization of the productive forces, which had regionalized national economies (e.g. the EEC) and had brought state and industry closer together, on the one hand, and the private appropriation of profit on the other. Third, a contradiction arose between the needs of the population met by the welfare state and the monopolies' quest for profit, which cut into such forms of social distribution.[16] Fourth, a contradiction had developed between the oligarchic minority and the rest of society, especially professional people who were becoming proletarianized. The last contradiction was between monopoly capital and the former oil- and raw material-producing colonies, which was generating a pressure to democratize international relations.[17]

He expected these manifold contradictions in one way or another to exacerbate contradictions within the ideological state apparatuses (hereafter ISAs), undermining the monopolies' hegemony over them. For example, anti-capitalist movements had developed within churches in Spain, Italy and Latin America. In higher education, expansion of numbers had eroded the elite status of students, and had brought them closer to the working class. Moreover, the family was no longer reproducing traditional social relations, as a consequence of women's liberation and intergenerational conflicts. The legal system was increasingly questioned by those working within it, and the political system, as an ideological apparatus, was in a state of flux. Support was moving away from traditional conservative and social democratic parties which buttressed the system and towards the far more critical, left parties. He also suggested, if a little unclearly, that a crisis had arisen in the media.[18]

Carrillo advocated counter-hegemonic struggles within the ISAs, turning them against their original purpose, the legitimation of capitalism. This could not be the work of one party – indeed, he recognized that the Communist Party was not the only representative of the working class[19] but merely one component of the 'revolutionary and progressive forces' that 'increasingly identify themselves with democracy'.[20] Out of these forces a 'new historic bloc' of 'labour and culture', i.e. the working class plus those working within the ISAs, could be created.

Through transformation of the ISAs, he hoped that the coercive and administrative apparatuses of the state could be democratized.[21] While he did not suggest how this could be done concretely, he cited the activities of the French students in May 1968, which to some extent demobilized the forces of law and order. The administrative apparatus of the state was also open to change, consequent upon the growth of unionization among civil servants. Moreover, they were resisting becoming tools of monopoly capital.

However, a vital element in the democratization of the coercive machine, if only by implication, lay in the policies of a left-wing government. It should aim at winning over the military from the 'monopolist oligarchic State' through, among other things, the 'democratic transformation of the military mentality'. Soldiers should serve the people rather than monopoly capital, which stemmed from their blind commitment to the existing social order. They had to see themselves as skilled technicians, whose principal purpose was the protection of national territory when attacked.[22]

The object of this democratization was not merely to undermine the resistance of monopoly capitalists. It was also to ensure that the economy was democratically planned, in both public and private spheres and from above and below, especially in the spheres of foodstuffs, energy, education, health and urban life. The upshot of Carrillo's argument was that socialism could be achieved through the democratization of the existing state, through an alliance of 'labour and culture', which would avoid civil war and the possibility of a fascist-style right-wing reaction.

Carrillo's position rejected

This section will examine the theoretical responses of those to the left of Carrillo, who either directly criticized his views or attacked the general position of which he was merely one, if the most important, exponent. Thus, Carrillo is partly taken here to be *representative* of the general Eurocommunist strategic perspective.[23]

Chris Harman offered the most explicit rebuttal of Carrillo. First, he questioned whether the ISAs could be turned against the bourgeoisie. Overall, he argued, they were far too hierarchical and controlled by small minorities, loyal to the ruling class, to be subverted from the base. Only individual sections of the ISAs from time to time could escape such domination.[24] Moreover, for the left to control the media, it would have to take it over physically, and to do this the courts and the repressive arm of the state would have to be neutralized. Indeed, the notion that the armed forces could be transformed into pro-socialist organizations was highly dubious given the strength of the ideological control that the ruling class had over them. Rather, in a revolutionary situation, splits within the armed forces were likely, with different sections adopting different positions. In these circumstances, the left had to win as much support as possible from the armed forces, so that they could disarm those backing the bourgeoisie. Civil war was thus inevitable, precisely because part of the armed forces was bound to remain loyal to the ruling class.[25]

Second, he challenged Carrillo's assumption that socialism could be achieved through a left-wing parliamentary majority. For example, the mere fact that the left Popular Front had a majority government in Spain in 1936 did not prevent Franco's military uprising. Just as crucially, a parliamentary strategy demobilized the worker's movement. Electoral politics, based on the representative principle, by very definition hindered workers' *self*-activities. Moreover, owing to the rhythm of elections, the ruling class had time to organize against workers during a period of social upheaval.[26]

Henri Weber also challenged the Eurocommunist parliamentary perspective, of which Carrillo's could be taken as typical, because it effectively legitimated class rule. Rather like Kautsky, Eurocommunists had an 'abstract' view of democracy and therefore failed to see how it performed this ideological role.[27] A distinction had to be made between people's democratic freedoms, which served this function, and the institutions of the bourgeois democratic state. Universal suffrage, in particular, owing to its atomizing propensities, undermined working-class capacities for self-activity, and in effect kept them away from state institutions. Hence, limits existed to the extent to which the bourgeois state could be democratized, and any attempt to advance the democratic rights and freedoms necessary for socialist production relations would soon 'run up' against these institutions.

More concretely, adopting Poulantzas's arguments in *State, Power and Socialism*, while not agreeing with his conclusions, he maintained that transforming the state from within was impossible. First, subordinate classes within the state had only a marginal presence, especially where the exercise of bourgeois power was extremely important (e.g. the army, top civil servants, judiciary and mass media). Second, even if the masses were to win formal power, the bourgeoisie could move its power base elsewhere, and restore its domination in a new form. Third, there were limits to the politicization of state employees, especially since they were likely to want to maintain their positions and function in relation to the masses. Finally, the attempt to democratize the existing state was difficult in the light of the decline of bourgeois representative democracy and the growth of 'authoritarian statism'.[28]

Carl Boggs presented a critique of the Eurocommunist strategy from a different angle, in terms of its implicit outcomes. The type of democratization through the existing state, proposed by Carrillo and others, was ultimately unsustainable, because they were strongly committed to the project of 'rationalization' as a solution to the economic and political crises of Italy and Spain. The state became the 'primary locus of political initiative'.[29] This project was very much part of the twentieth-century communist tradition, which has prevailed over the other, democratic, Marxist impulse. The process of rationalization, associated with industrialization, consisted of 'the expansion of productive efficiency and administrative control through the progressive adoption of new scientific, technological, and organisational methods'. It fulfilled three objectives: 'accumulation, domination and legitimation'.[30] And it spawned a state bureaucracy, ideologically grounded upon notions of scientific and technological expertise.

Crucially, this disempowered the masses, for these rationalizing bureaucracies not merely accepted, but exalted, the division of labour. Marx's overall aim to surmount this division thus became obscured.[31] Although Eurocommunists wished to democratize the process, rationalization was inherently antithetical to democracy. So, for example, the rationalizing project of the Eurocommunists gave a critical role to the new middle classes, and was likely to conflict with working-class democracy, which would erode the authority relations that this strategy implied.[32] Indeed, Communist support for austerity policies in Italy and Spain, which stemmed in part from this commitment to rationalization, had already brought these parties into conflict with workers. In sum, the Eurocommunist vision, as expounded by Carrillo and others, placed obstacles in front of a workers' self-emancipatory movement, the logic of which was the elimination of the division of labour. Such a strategy would necessitate a prefigurative socialist politics, standing in sharp contrast to the elitist, bureaucratic vision of rationalization, which at best involved the transformation of the *existing* bourgeois state.

Commentary

Carrillo can be evaluated on the basis of the means and ends he proposed. In advocating a non-violent, parliamentary strategy for socialism he assumed that the state was at least potentially not class specific, an organization not necessarily shaped by, or inherently designed to serve, the interests of the dominant class, namely the bourgeoisie. Therefore, it could be turned against this class. In other words, the superstructure could be detached from its socio-economic class base. Although this is a complex question, the historical record, so far, has amply demonstrated that attempts to achieve socialism, involving the wholesale change of property relations, by parliamentary methods have never succeeded. Where attempts have been made, as in Chile in 1973, the bourgeoisie resorts to extra-parliamentary methods to resist. And where such changes in production relations have occurred, they have been the result of civil war, as in the Soviet Union in 1917, or in many so-called Third World countries. Moreover, even milder attempts at reform in a socialist direction can cause economic dislocation, as in Britain in 1964, when a Labour Government under Harold Wilson came to office, and in France after François Mitterand came to power in 1980. This suggests that there are clear limitations as to what a socialist parliamentary majority can achieve, however 'autonomous' it is, given the economic and military power of capital. In reality politics and economics, state and society, are deeply interconnected. 'Society' in particular can have an enormous impact on the shape and operation of the state, as is revealed in times of intense class conflict, causing different forms of authoritarianism, whether overt as with fascism or more covert as in liberal democracies (as, for example, under Margaret Thatcher from 1979 onwards). The contours of the state and its policies can be profoundly affected by issues of distribution, not merely who gets what, but also who decides who is to get what.

Moreover, dangers exist in ruling out, except in defence against reaction, the possibility of a violent strategy in advance. This means not only that the socialist movement would be ideologically 'disarmed', but also that the coercive arm of the state would be more confident in defeating this movement if violence were to erupt, knowing that the leadership would be attempting to avoid the use of force.

Concerning his proposed end of 'rationalization', which, as Boggs suggests, failed to eliminate the division of labour, he may be at fault in strictly Marxist terms. Nevertheless, the question of how this division can be reduced, or eliminated, is complicated by the potentially conflicting satisfaction of needs in consumption and production. And even a reduction of the impact of the division of labour could take time, given the likely priority of consumption over job satisfaction. While Carrillo neglected this question, the abolition of the division of labour, even in a revolutionary situation, would be unlikely to be at the top of the proletariat's agenda. However, insofar as the division of labour referred to political and economic decision-making, changes would be inevitable.

ABANDONING THE DUAL-POWER PERSPECTIVE: POULANTZAS

Another aspect of the Eurocommunists' laying of Stalin's ghost was their rejection of the 1917 dual-power scenario, enshrined in the slogan of 'dictatorship of the proletariat', a term officially erased from the French party programme in 1976. They strongly believed that this strategy made Stalinism inevitable. Nicos Poulantzas in *State, Power and Socialism*,[33] with this decision very much in mind, articulated the most sophisticated rebuttal of the dual-power approach.[34]

Poulantzas held to Marx's vision of a stateless society. He envisaged a 'tending towards' a 'withering away of the state'. He opposed what he regarded as the statism of social democracy, as well as the statism inscribed in the dual-power strategy. With social democracy or dual power the state always ended up the winner.[35] Stalinism could not be attributed solely to the post-revolutionary conditions that existed in the post-1917 Soviet Union. He argued that the Soviet model consisting of decentralized workers' councils necessarily created some form of centralization. Who better to do the job than the Communist Party? And if direct democracy did not engender this 'statist despotism', it led to the 'dictatorship of experts'.[36]

The dual-power perspective was not in fact anti-state, but assumed a 'parallel state'; that is, a proletarian state paralleling a bourgeois state. This implied the need for: first, a 'frontal struggle' against the state, the existence of a 'big day' of confrontation, rather than the possibility of a lengthy transition period, in which the masses intervened within the state itself; and, second, the destruction of the old state in favour of a new state.

Today, these assumptions no longer held. The modern state was not isolated from the masses: 'their struggles constantly traverse the State'.[37] In any case, the state was not a 'thing' to be possessed. It was a 'condensation of a particular class relationship of forces'.[38] Because of this, contradictions emerged within the state itself. A shift in the relationship of forces within the state – parliament, ideological state and coercive apparatuses – was required, entailing a series of 'real breaks'.

> In the democratic road to socialism, a long process of taking power essentially consists in the spreading, development, re-inforcement, co-ordination and direction of these diffuse centres of resistance, which the masses always possess within state networks, in such a way that they become the real centres of power on the strategic terrain of the State.[39]

This involved extra-state struggles, which would intensify its internal contradictions, even within the coercive apparatuses, as occurred in Portugal in 1974. Such struggles were important not merely because of their effect on the state. They also provided the basis for the development of rank-and-file democracy, an expression of rank-and-file autonomy, *vis-à-vis* the state.[40]

Yet rather than consider rank-and-file democracy as a dual-power alternative to representative democracy, he called for an 'organic' relationship between 'citizens' committees and universal suffrage assemblies that will themselves have been transformed as a function of the relationship'.[41] He hoped that through such a transformation the state would wither away, as a bureaucratic, coercive body separate from society, although he did not advance any concrete suggestions about how this could occur. He acknowledged the threat from the forces of reaction, but this was preferable to the risks of Stalinism that flowed from the dual-power strategy.[42]

Poulantzas's critics

Responses to Poulantzas's version of the socialist transition were characterized: first, by a reaffirmation of the 'class struggle' perspective that lay at the heart of the dual-power scenario, its dynamics and its interrelation with the state within the process of revolution; second, by a questioning of the feasibility of fusing representative and direct democracy; third, by a rejection of his notion that Stalinism is inherent in direct democracy.

Viewed from class struggle assumptions, while 'ruptures' in the state could be admitted during a revolution, one critic argued that they were likely to occur at its periphery, rather than its core – army, police, higher echelons of the civil service, judiciary and mass media. Being part of the ruling class, it would 'polarize' to the right in the event of a revolutionary upheaval; hence 'the need to deal with it once and for all'.[43] This was the lesson of the Chilean coup of September 1973. Moreover, a critical problem emerged if a final showdown was to be avoided, for this allowed the bourgeoisie to regroup.[44] What Poulantzas was proposing – a series of ruptures in the state by a left government supported by the masses, but which avoided an ultimate power contestation – was quite tricky. It was likely to lead to a restriction on the self-activity of the masses, which would weaken their resistance against a ruling class counter-offensive.[45] The belief that a left government could attack bourgeois interests, constitutionally and peacefully, without a bourgeois reaction that employed extra-parliamentary methods – economic, political and physical – effectively disarmed workers.[46]

Thus, the danger of counter-revolution in revolutionary situations rendered as overwhelming the need to bring about the rapid disintegration of the state. To facilitate this process, an alternative pole of attraction in the form of workers' committees and other types of popular self-organization had to be established, so that former personnel of the bourgeois state could be won over.[47] Another problem with the precarious equilibrium of Poulantzas's scenario was that he assumed that the bourgeois state was too strong to be directly confronted, yet sufficiently weak to permit his proposed democratic road.[48]

Second, critics contended that his proposed integration of representative democracy, especially in its bourgeois form, with direct democracy was problematic. They noted the vagueness of his proposals.[49] And historically parliamentary and direct democracy have stood in direct opposition to each other, as, for example, in the Spanish Republican

Government's suppression of workers' and peasants' forms of self-organization.[50] Further, the restriction of mass workers' movements by parliamentary socialist governments occurred on numerous occasions, as, for instance, in Chile in 1970–3, and France in 1936.

Third, critics have rebutted Poulantzas's suggestion that direct democracy inevitably leads to some sort of Stalinism, irrespective of historical conditions. They rejected his presumption that workers' councils *necessarily* disallowed a plurality of parties. They existed in the Paris Commune of 1872, and in Spain in 1936–7.[51] In addition, his assumption that *only* representative institutions could protect individual rights was questionable. 'Codified' procedures, concerning secret ballots and the right of recall, could be drawn up for institutions built on the principles of direct democracy. And direct democracy, rooted in 'real communities', was likely to be far more representative than bourgeois democracy.[52]

Commentary

There are at least three questions arising from Poulantzas's rejection of the dual-power scenario and his advocacy of a combined direct and representative democracy. The first is, how realistic is it? In a sense, Poulantzas suffers from the same 'abstract' assumptions of Carrillo, in suggesting that different forms of democracy can be totally decanted of their class content. Historically, this has not been so, whether in Russia in 1917, Germany in 1918, Spain in 1936, and so on. In a revolutionary situation different classes have tended to group behind the different democratic institutions when the issue of popular sovereignty has arisen. Apart from the direct use of force, the likelihood would be for the bourgeoisie to support parliament, since it has traditionally never made drastic inroads into private property, and perhaps more importantly, given its voting procedures, is less under popular control than direct forms of democracy.

Second, notwithstanding the vagueness of his proposal for uniting citizens' committees with universal suffrage assemblies, the dynamics of this 'organic' relation between both are unclear. Put another way: what is the specific context of his suggestion? Does it refer to the period during or after the revolution, or both? Certainly, if it pertained to the revolutionary process itself, a danger would arise if direct and representative democratic institutions became rival power centres. To whom should workers give their allegiance?

Third, Poulantzas, in rejecting the dual-power scenario, like Carrillo assumed that the dictatorship of the proletariat led to Stalinist totalitarianism, or to the dictatorship of experts. As to whether this latter outcome was inevitable is questionable. It would depend on the degree of organization, technical and political competence of the rank-and-file. As to the former outcome, which presupposes that Stalinism could not be solely attributable to historical circumstances, it may of course be true. Yet to assume that the employment of unconstitutional violence inevitably engenders totalitarianism is equally dubious, for this suggests that *only* through constitutional change can totalitarianism be avoided. However, conditions which do not entail this consequence can be imagined: widespread support for the revolution with little opposition, a politically active population with strong democratic traditions, little international pressure on the revolution and a plurality of parties involved in the revolutionary process. Not all these conditions may necessarily exist. What would then be required is an analysis of which ones were absent, and the likely effects that this would have. Thus, rather than rejecting outright the use of force, as Poulantzas does, preferring the risk of reaction to the even bigger risk of Stalinism, one could consider the possibilities of an unconstitutional, non-totalitarian revolution.

GRAMSCI: EUROCOMMUNISM'S PATRON SAINT?

Eurocommunists, in fully accepting the rules of parliamentary democracy and in laying the ghost of 1917, have relied heavily on the Italian Marxist, Antonio Gramsci, as a source of inspiration and legitimation. His writings were chosen for a number of reasons. The success of the PCI's theory and practice was a major influence on the Eurocommunist movement, and Gramsci's historical stature within the party, as leader, martyr and theoretician, was enormous. His veneration was enhanced by the long-standing leader Palmiro Togliatti, who made continual references to him in support of his 'Italian' strategy for socialism. Second, communists wanting to distance themselves from the Soviet experience – its revolution, subsequent regime and Marxism-Leninism – were naturally predisposed to adopt an indigenous European, as opposed to a Russian, thinker.[53] Above all, Gramsci seemed to articulate an orientation, either implicitly or explicitly, which could be used to justify a peaceful, pluralistic parliamentary strategy.

Eurocommunists did not embrace Gramsci's writings comprehensively. Rather, they relied on various descriptions of Russia and Western Europe and theoretical insights found in *The Prison Notebooks*.[54] They endorsed his contrasting of the political terrains of Russia in 1917 and West Europe:

> In Russia the state was everything, civil society was primordial and gelatinous; in the West, there was a proper relation between state and civil society, and when the state trembled a sturdy structure of civil society was at once revealed. The state was only an outer ditch, behind which there stood a powerful system of fortresses and earthworks: more or less numerous from one state to the next, it goes without saying – but

this precisely necessitated an accurate reconnaissance of each individual country.[55]

By 'civil society' Gramsci normally meant private, non-state organizations, such as the church, political parties, educational institutions, trade unions and mass media, all of which ideologically 'normalized' capitalist society.

From this quotation they drew a number of crucial strategic inferences. The first was political and social conditions were different between 'East' and 'West'.[56] In the 'West' capitalist domination rested primarily on consent, generated in 'civil society', in contrast to Russia, where the state had been the locus of control. In the 'West', therefore, the successful overthrow of the capitalist class required a 'war of position' within civil society to undermine its ideological control, its 'hegemony', of the 'subaltern classes'. Thus, a frontal assault on the state, a 'war of manoeuvre', would not be effective in the 'West'. This necessitated a long-term strategy to win the battle of ideas. Gramsci maintained that Western Europe had been objectively ripe for socialism for the past fifty years. The key obstacle to socialism was thus ideological.

Second, this battle was perceived by Eurocommunists as a struggle for the minds of 'the nation'. The proletariat had to win 'national' leadership, entailing class alliances and attendant 'sacrifices' in favour of other classes, if it was to become genuinely 'hegemonic' in embodying the common or 'universal' interest.[57] They did not specify precisely who the 'nation' was, although the monopoly capitalists would presumably be excluded, and hence there seemed to be few class limits to hegemony.[58] Hegemony was therefore inherently pluralistic.[59] They also held that the winning over of the 'nation' was something constructive, rather than destructive. The working class had to outdo the capitalists – demonstrating its capacities as a new ruling class – in creating a framework for economic development.[60]

Third, they used Gramsci's writings in support of their rejection of the dual-power strategy, which implied a break in the state. They adopted what they interpreted as Gramsci's strategy against fascism, which hinged upon the restoration of bourgeois democracy. Togliatti, General Secretary of the PCI from 1927 to 1964, regarded as one of the founders of Eurocommunism, was apparently inspired by Gramsci when developing between 1944 and 1947 a theory of 'progressive' democracy, or democracy of a 'new type'. It consisted of the working class gaining a parliamentary majority to obtain social and economic reforms.[61] In addition, Eurocommunists embraced what they deemed his 'anti-economistic' critique of orthodox (i.e. Second International) Marxism. The superstructure, especially the state, was regarded as semi-detached from its economic/ class base. It was no longer merely an instrument or 'thing' in the hands of the economically dominant class, but shaped by class conflict. They quoted Gramsci:

the dominant group is coordinated concretely with the general interests of the subordinate groups, and the life of the state is conceived of as a continuous process of formation and superseding of unstable equilibria (on the judicial plane) between the interests of the fundamental group and those of the subordinate groups – equilibria in which the interests of the dominant group prevail, but only up to a certain point, i.e. stopping short of narrowly corporate economic interests.[62]

Therefore, a crude distinction between 'bourgeois' and 'proletarian' democracy could not be sustained, since universalistic elements were already present within the existing state, expressed in terms of a complex compromise between governors and governed. What the state did was therefore dependent upon the balance of class forces acting upon it.[63]

The critics

Critics argued that this interpretation of Gramsci, as potentially a parliamentary gradualist, was profoundly mistaken. Underlying much of their unease with this perspective was that it decontextualized Gramsci's thought, especially his rejection of 'third period' Stalinism (discussed in Chapter 9), and ignored what he took for granted, namely the Marxist theory of history, in which the class struggle in all its ramifications played a central part.

First, they held that the Eurocommunists misread his East–West distinction, implying that the 'war of position' was the *only* type of strategy suitable for the West. In essence, they contended that Gramsci did not separate the war of position from the war of movement. Rather, a 'dialectical' relationship existed between both.[64] The war of position was dictated by immediate circumstances: the failure of the Russian revolution to spread to the West, after the war of manoeuvre strategy had been tried until 1921, and more specifically, after the defeat of the Italian working class by the fascists in 1922. Thus, a war of position, particularly the construction of a worker–peasant alliance, was essential before a war of manoeuvre was possible. That a war of manoeuvre was indispensable was evidenced by Gramsci's remark that 'every political struggle always has a military substratum'.[65] When the bourgeoisie lost ideological control, it would increasingly rely on the use of force.[66] Hence, the war of position was 'preparatory' to an inevitable war of manoeuvre, as a revolutionary situation emerged.[67]

Second, critics questioned whether the concept of hegemony could be viewed outside the context of class struggle. They argued that the whole object of hegemony was to win over allies in order to dominate the class enemy, and especially for the Italian working class to obtain the backing of the southern peasantry so as to defeat the bourgeoisie. Hegemony was the path to proletarian dictatorship.[68] And insofar as the concept of hegemony also contained within it a coercive element,[69] state power was necessary to the full realization of hegemony.[70] Moreover, hegemony had to be perceived within the framework of a united front strategy that would undermine the non-revolutionary influences on both workers and peasants. Such a strategy involved uniting workers on specific issues in order to expose reformist leaders who were unwilling to struggle.[71] These critics also stressed that the actual ideological content of working-class hegemony was Marxism itself, albeit a 'living' dialectical Marxism built on the actual lives and struggles of workers, because it contained genuinely universalistic properties.[72] Further, in contrast to the Eurocommunist's pluralistic interpretation, which admitted compromises with other ideologies, Marxism was a 'total', self-sufficient world view.[73] Marxism was in addition uncompromising in the sense that Gramsci saw the dialectic as deeply negative, implicitly destructive of any 'constructive', reformist strategies.[74]

Third, the notion that Gramsci broke with the dual-power perspective, wholeheartedly advocating parliamentary democracy, could not be sustained. Against the view that Gramsci's strategy against fascism could be construed as evidence that he had rejected dual power, Eurocommunism's critics indicate that reports on his views while in prison suggest that his call for the restitution of bourgeois democracy was a purely intermediate, instrumental demand. Bourgeois democracy, once achieved, would create the basis for the next step in the transition to the dictatorship of the proletariat, enabling communists to increase support for their ideas among the masses.[75] Only within this context could Gramsci's endorsement of an alliance with the lower middle class and peasantry be conceived. Such an alliance was still to be under working-class leadership, and no contemporary extrapolation, suggesting that it could include an equal partnership of capitalists and workers, could be legitimately inferred.[76]

As to whether Gramsci departed from the view that the bourgeois state was a 'thing' that had to be 'smashed', critics asserted that he was an orthodox Leninist. Hence, he conceived the 1919–20 Council movement in Turin as a replication of the Russian Soviets in forming the basis of a proletarian dictatorship. And there was little to suggest in his later writings that he repudiated this view, that he broke with Third International orthodoxy.[77] Further, Gramsci in the *Lyons Theses* of 1926 showed nothing but contempt for parliament, with an armed insurrection leading to a proletarian dictatorship very much in mind.[78] Additionally, in political discussions while in prison Gramsci is reported to have advocated a party of a 'military type' in combating the state.[79]

Finally, on the issue of Gramsci's anti-economism, which supposedly detached base from superstructure, permitting an inter-class view of the state, critics argue that Eurocommunists were drawing the wrong inference. Rather, he was merely attempting to indicate that super-structural, especially ideological, struggles were important, because ideas tended to lag behind developments in the economic base. Indeed, he saw base and superstructure as ultimately coinciding in a proletarian revolution, when ideology became a 'material force'.[80]

In sum, critics of the Eurocommunist appropriation of Gramsci reasserted his Leninist pedigree – his commitment to class struggle and his insistence upon analysing concrete conditions required to advance this struggle.

Commentary

That there has been conflict over Gramsci's political and intellectual legacy is not surprising. Commentators often bring in their own ideological baggage – conscious or unconscious – when interpreting a thinker, especially when the political stakes are high. Yet Gramsci himself, as Perry Anderson indicates, was partly, if inadvertently, to blame: the *Prison Notebooks* contained crucial ambiguities, leaving him open to reformist interpretation. Nevertheless, these ambiguities to some extent stemmed from prison censorship, which prevented him from writing a full-blooded Marxist text, in contrast to his pre-prison writings. Second, the *Prison Notebooks* were merely notebooks, his private musings, reflecting his intellectual and political preoccupations, and not intended for public persuasion.

However, as Anderson suggests, a lack of clarity did exist over the relationship between force and consent. This was exacerbated by his importation of the term 'hegemony' from the Russian context, where it referred to proletarian hegemony over a non-antagonistic class, the peasantry. Gramsci, in applying this notion of consensus to the bourgeoisie in relation to the proletariat in the West – two antagonistic classes – made it appear as though bourgeois rule rested heavily on it. This position was reinforced by the idea that consent was lodged in civil society, which was pre-eminent over the state in the West.[81] Thus, he opened up the possibility of an essentially ideological, conflict-free strategy. Further, he tended to assimilate bourgeois and proletarian revolutions, which implied that the proletariat, following the bourgeois example, ought to develop cultural hegemony before making a revolution. Such a conflation arose because he failed to integrate his analysis of consent with Third International axioms about the use of force.[82] However, in one sense Gramsci did intentionally integrate both revolutions, giving rise to a potential division between Eurocommunists and revolutionary Marxists. As a result of the failure of two 'passive' revolutions (i.e. the Risorgimento and fascism) to unite Italy, because they were revolutions from above, the task now fell to the working class. It had to instigate a 'national-popular' revolution, constituted by uniting the northern proletariat with the southern peasantry. Eurocommunists take this to mean that 'national-popular' struggles do not have to be necessarily class rooted.[83] Those to the left construe this as a 'plea for social revolution'.[84] Nevertheless, Gramsci could be more properly interpreted as wanting the proletariat to undertake the double and inseparable tasks of national unification and socialist revolution.

Yet if Gramsci may have been guilty of ambiguity, the Eurocommunists can be charged with failing to make explicit that they were engaged in a double activity: first, building upon a number of theoretical insights and descriptive statements; second, using his writings to justify current communist strategy and tactics, especially the historic compromise. To develop some of Gramsci's ideas in a certain political or theoretical direction is a perfectly legitimate activity, which can be evaluated openly, according to the normal criteria of political effectiveness, theoretical coherence and empirical veracity. Confusion, however, arises if this process is then identified with the 'real' Gramsci, who wanted to adapt the Soviet model of revolution to Western European, especially Italian, conditions in a way that avoided the parliamentary embrace.

EUROCOMMUNIST PRACTICE AND ITS CRITICS

Both sympathetic and unsympathetic critics have indicated the difficulties in attempting to be a party of power, i.e. electorally acceptable to ruling elites, and also to be radical. The contradictions in this policy were particularly evident in the historic compromise, particularly in 1977, when the PCI sided with the forces of law and order against those revolting against the austerity policies of the Christian Democrat Andreotti Government and the lack of social reform. This upset the party rank-and-file. To please big business and the working class simultaneously was a tall order.[85]

There was, moreover, the problem of proposing reforms in a situation of economic crisis: either the reforms could be rejected by the Christian Democrats on the ground of expense, or they could be accepted, thereby having a destabilizing effect.[86] Third, an alliance with the Christian Democrats – a party that had always opposed reform – was bound to be fraught with difficulty.[87] The Christian Democrats were ideologically opposed to significant change, and in any case were far too reliant on the so-called 'clientele' system to support measures to overcome corruption and parasitism, even if they wished to. Moreover, the PCI would inevitably frighten middle-class Christian Democrat supporters, however moderate it became, and the party leadership was not averse to playing the anti-communist card in order to maintain internal cohesion.[88] The French party had also experienced the alliance problem with the Socialist Party. It faced the dilemma of choosing allies and therefore moderating its policies, or being a party of radical reform.[89]

A *class* alliance, i.e. an anti-monopoly alliance, was also dubious. Not only *were* monopolies capitalism in its present phase of development, but small capitalists would not oppose monopoly capital because they were often dependent upon it.[90]

Finally, a problem has arisen because, having discarded the Soviet experience in its totality, and in becoming more obviously social democratic, Eurocommunists face the difficulty of competing with 'home grown' social democratic parties. Why should voters not go for the real article, rather than the recent converts?[91]

Commentary

Eurocommunists, in seeking office through political alliances, were bound to be engaged in a tricky business. In the cases of the PCF's alliance with the Socialist Party and the PCI's alliance with the Christian Democrats, the partners seemed to gain more than the communists. Presumably in the case of the union of the left in France, voters in moving leftwards saw the socialists as more trustworthy or less radical. As for the historic compromise, it could be interpreted as highly beneficial to the Christian Democrats and the employers, because the PCI attempted to curb social conflict and became weakened in the process, owing to the internal divisions that this caused. There were obvious limits to any 'social contract' of wage restraint in return for social reform when the capitalist economy is doing badly. The employers are engaged in a 'zero-sum' game of winners and losers, i.e. wage restraint meant larger profits, with no necessary guarantee of larger investment or social reform through higher taxes. The PCI, on the other hand, was playing a 'non-zero-sum game', hoping that both workers and employers could benefit through cooperating. Similarly, the PCE was the loser in its alliance with the UCD. It lost much of its influence in the trade union movement, and caused disgruntlement among the party rank-and-file. All this illustrates the problems created by a relatively radical working-class party attempting to become a party of government through alliances. It has to develop a political formula that pleases many constituencies, many with deeply conflicting interests: ruling elites, the United States, the partner in the alliance and the trade unions, as well as the party rank-and-file.

GENERAL COMMENTS

Although critics of Eurocommunism may have generally got the better of the arguments, this does not mean that they necessarily offered a superior alternative. While they may have been closer to Marx's analysis of capitalism, class struggle and his vision of history, there is still the dilemma so graphically indicated by Bernstein. What is unique about Marxism is that it is a theory of socialism rooted in the movement of history. What happens if theory and movement refuse to coincide? Two options seem to be available: either follow the Bernsteinian temptation of immersion in a 'reformist' reality at the risk of dispensing with theory, or remain theoretically pure, waiting for 'the day', which may or may not come in the lifetime of an individual Marxist. The powder may be dry, but rather small in quantity. Thus, the problem becomes how to strike a balance between these two positions, so as to fight effectively within and against capitalism, building and sustaining a mass movement, without 'selling out'.

NOTES

1. H. T. Willets, 'The USSR and Eurocommunism' in R. Kindersley (Ed.), *In Search of Eurocommunism*, Macmillan, London (1981), 1.
2. This feature, however, was not completely novel. For example, the Italian CP had cooperated in government with the Christian Democrats between 1945 and 1947.
3. There was a fourth characteristic: 'left' Eurocommunists wanted to ally themselves with the 'new social movements', concerned with issues of sexual equality, ecology and peace, that had emerged from the revolts of the 1960s. This will be given some attention in Chapter 14.
4. Although Western European Communist Parties got involved in electoral politics in the 1930s in the 'popular front' period from 1935, their position was more tactical than strategic in the sense that they upheld Lenin's distinction between 'bourgeois' and 'proletarian' democracy, as outlined in *The State and Revolution* and elsewhere.
5. S. Hellman, 'Italian communism in crisis' in R. Miliband, L. Panitch and J. Saville (Eds), *Socialist Register, 1988*, Merlin Press, London, 258.
6. S. Carrillo, *'Eurocommunism' and the State* (hereafter *ES*), Lawrence and Wishart, London (1977), 40.
7. *ES*, 50.
8. *ES*, 149–53.
9. *ES*, 164.
10. *ES*, 163–6.
11. *ES*, 105–6.
12. *ES*, 24.
13. *ES*, 20–1.
14. *ES*, 20 and 40.
15. *ES*, 46.
16. *ES*, 47.
17. *ES*, 47–8.
18. *ES*, 34–48.
19. *ES*, 100.
20. *ES*, 44.

21. *ES*, 52.
22. *ES*, 66.
23. The Soviet ideologists responded angrily to Carrillo's criticisms of the Soviet system, thereby playing into the hands of imperialism, but they did not offer a sustained theoretical critique. P. Preston, 'The PCE's long road to democracy, 1954-77' in Kindersley, *op. cit.*, 37-8; E. Mandel, *From Stalinism to Eurocommunism*, New Left Books, London (1978), 87-99.
24. C. Harman, 'Eurocommunism, the state and revolution', *International Socialism* (old series), 101 (September 1977), 12.
25. *Ibid.*, 12-13.
26. *Ibid.*, 13.
27. H. Weber, 'Eurocommunism, socialism and democracy', *New Left Review*, 110 (1978), 8.
28. *Ibid.*, 10.
29. C. Boggs, 'The democratic road: new departures and old problems' in C. Boggs and D. Plotke (Eds), *The Politics of Eurocommunism*, South End Press, Boston (1980), 456.
30. *Ibid.*, 445.
31. *Ibid.*, 447. See also R. Miliband, 'Constitutionalism and revolution: some notes on Eurocommunism' in R. Miliband and J. Saville (Eds), *Socialist Register, 1978*, Merlin Press, London, 166-7.
32. *Ibid.*, 464.
33. N. Poulantzas, *State, Power and Socialism* (hereafter *SPS*), New Left Books, London (1978).
34. See also other rejections contained in E. Balibar, *On the Dictatorship of the Proletariat*, New Left Books, London (1977), 157-92; *ES*, 149-60.
35. *SPS*, 264.
36. *SPS*, 256.
37. *SPS*, 257.
38. *SPS*, 257.
39. *SPS*, 258.
40. *SPS*, 259.
41. *SPS*, 262.
42. *SPS*, 265.
43. H. Weber in interview with Poulantzas, in 'The state and the transition to socialism', *Socialist Review*, 38 (April 1978), 18.
44. Mandel, *op. cit.*, 175.
45. Bob Jessop, *Nicos Poulantzas: Marxist Theory and Political Strategy*, Macmillan, Basingstoke (1985), 307. See also Mandel, *op. cit.*, 175-6.
46. Weber, *op. cit.*, 28.
47. Mandel, *op. cit.*, 176.
48. C. Barker, 'A "new" reformism? A critique of the political theory of Nicos Poulantzas', *International Socialism* (new series), 4 (Spring 1979), 101.
49. *Ibid.*, 99; Jessop, *op. cit.*, 299.
50. Barker, *op. cit.*, 104-5.
51. *Ibid.*, 102.
52. Weber, *op. cit.*, 25.

53. Ironically, Karl Kautsky's writings were far more suited to justifying the Eurocommunist stance, but had to be ruled out because he was anathema to the Stalinists in the party, who were all too familiar with Lenin's rubbishing of his ideas. Cynically, it could be said that the Eurocommunists were therefore compelled to reinvent the 'centrist' (i.e. a position between reform and revolution) wheel.

54. They were written between 1929 and 1935, while Gramsci was imprisoned by the Italian fascist government. They were first published in Britain as *Selections from the Prison Notebooks of Antonio Gramsci* (Ed. Q. Hoare and G. W. Smith), Lawrence and Wishart, London (1971) (hereafter *PN*).

55. *PN*, 238. See R. Simon, *Gramsci's Political Thought*, Lawrence and Wishart, London (1982), 28; G. Vacca, 'The "Eurocommunist" perspective: the contribution of the Italian Communist Party' in R. Kindersley, *op. cit.*, 125; J. Hoffman, *The Gramscian Challenge*, Basil Blackwell, Oxford (1984), 125.

56. R. Simon, 'Gramsci's concept of hegemony', *Marxism Today*, 21 (March), 86.

57. *Ibid.*; G. Napolitano, *The Italian Road to Socialism*, interview with Eric Hobsbawm, Journeyman Press, London (1977), 111-12.

58. E.g. Simon, *Gramsci's Political Thought*, 23 and 43.

59. *Ibid.* 62-4.

60. Napolitano, *op. cit.*, 46-7.

61. Vacca in Kindersley, *op. cit.*, 131.

62. *Ibid.*, 120.

63. Simon, *Gramsci's Political Thought*, 67.

64. Hoffman, *The Gramscian Challenge*, 150.

65. Quoted in J. Femia, *Gramsci's Political Thought*, Clarendon Press, Oxford (1987), 206. See also C. Harman, 'Gramsci versus Eurocommunism', *International Socialism* (old series), 99 (June 1977), 12.

66. Femia, *op. cit.*, 207.

67. Mandel, *op. cit.*, 201-2; M. Salvadori, 'Gramsci and the PCI: two conceptions of hegemony' in C. Mouffe (Ed.), *Gramsci and Marxist Theory*, Routledge and Kegan Paul, London (1979), 244.

68. Salvadori, *op. cit.*, 248-9; P. Gibbon, 'Gramsci, Eurocommunism and the Comintern', *Economy and Society*, 12 (1983), 341; P. Anderson, 'The antinomies of Antonio Gramsci', *New Left Review*, 100 (Nov. 1976 to Jan. 1977), 45.

69. See Anderson, *op. cit.*, 31.

70. Gibbon, *op. cit.*, 336.

71. *Ibid.*, 361; Harman, *op. cit.*, 12.

72. Gibbon, *op. cit.*, 376; Salvadori, *op. cit.*, 250.

73. Salvadori, *op. cit.*, 249.

74. Femia, *op. cit.*, 211.

75. Salvadori, *op. cit.*, 253; Femia, *op. cit.*, 210.

76. Femia, *op. cit.*, 210.

77. Salvadori, *op. cit.*, 242.

78. *Ibid.*, 248-9; Gibbon, *op. cit.*, 341; Anderson, *op. cit.*, 45.

79. Femia, *op. cit.*, 207.

80. Gibbon, *op. cit.*, 346-7; Harman, *op. cit.*, Part 2, 12.

81. Anderson, *op. cit.*, 44–6 and 70.
82. *Ibid.*, 69.
83. Simon, *Gramsci's Political Thought*, 43 and 45.
84. Tom Nairn, 'Antonu Su Gobbu', in Anne Showstack Sassoon (Ed.), *Approaches to Gramsci*, Writers and Readers, London (1982), 175.
85. G. Russo, 'Il compresso storico: the Italian Communist Party from 1968 to 1978' in P. F. della Torre, E. Mortimer and J. Story (Eds), *Eurocommunism: Myth or Reality?* Penguin, Harmondsworth (1979), 94–101; E. Shaw, 'The Italian historical compromise: a new pathway to power?' *Political Quarterly*, 49, 4 (1978), 421–3.
86. S. Tarrow, 'Historic compromise or bourgeois majority? Eurocommunism in Italy, 1976–9' in H. Machin (Ed.), *National Communism in Western Europe: A Third Way for Socialism*, Methuen, London (1983), 141.
87. J. Barkin, 'Italian communism at the crossroads' in Boggs and Plotke, *op. cit.*, 65; Tarrow, *op. cit.*, 148.
88. Shaw, *op. cit.*, 421–2.
89. G. Ross, 'The PCF and the end of the Bolshevik dream' in Boggs and Plotke, *op. cit.*, 39.
90. P. Richards, 'The strategy of the Italian Communist Party', *International Bulletin of the Socialist Workers' Party*, 6 (February 1978), 9. See also Bill Warren, 'The programme of the CPGB – a critique', *New Left Review*, 63 (Sept/ Oct 1970), 29.
91. T. Potter, 'The death of Eurocommunism', *International Socialism* (new series), 13 (Summer 1981), 12.

13
Marxism and Women's Oppression

PROBLEMS AND ISSUES

The rise of the women's movement in the United States and Britain in the late 1960s and early 1970s raised critical questions for Marxist theory and practice. The fundamental objective of this movement was the redefinition of the role of women in society and their personal relationships with men. It sought to overturn the commonly held conception of women as mothers and home-makers, men as 'bread-winners'. Rather, women were entitled to the same treatment as men, in rewards and opportunities, in the workplace and in the wider society, particularly in education and politics. Not only did the movement challenge the prevailing view of what constituted women's 'labour' in the home and outside it. It also aimed to give women control over their own bodies, in the areas of reproduction and sexuality. This raised issues of child-care, contraception, abortion and heterosexuality. The aspirations of this movement explicitly called into question male attitudes and assumptions about women.

More than this, the objective of the movement was the re-casting of the very meaning, the very stuff of politics. Although its methods of political struggle could be conventional – demonstrations, lobbying, propaganda – its organization took a novel turn in the form of consciousness raising groups, especially in the early 1970s. Members of these groups endeavoured to find out what they really felt and wanted. In doing so, they confronted male power inside and outside the home. Thus, they undermined the conventional political boundary between the public and the private. The 'personal' was 'political'. And the 'political' was male power. Although these groups did not last long in Britain, they had an important impact in setting the terms of feminist discourse.

The language of feminism in this period was most forcefully expressed in two books, Kate Millett's *Sexual Politics*[1] and Shulamith Firestone's *Dialectic of Sex*.[2] Millett argued that the form sexual activity took between men and women was political: it was symbolic of a universal system of male domination and women's subordination, which she termed 'patriarchy'. Firestone retold the Marxist historical narrative with sex rather than class as the primary contradiction in society. Women's subordination stemmed from the 'biological' facts of child-bearing and rearing.

How were Marxists to intervene in such a movement? Some offered a knee-jerk rejection: it was a 'bourgeois' diversion from the class struggle. Others, while acknowledging the existence of women's oppression, were more polite, if non-committal: a problem that could be sorted out after 'the revolution'. For those who perceived it as a phenomenon to be taken seriously, there were questions about the extent to which women's demands should be supported, and whether their struggles should be autonomous from the class struggle. This question was addressed by Juliet Mitchell in her pioneering article 'Women: the longest revolution'.[3] An important corollary of this was whether women should form separate groupings within Marxist organizations. These questions became more pressing during the 1970s as many women in left-wing organizations in the United States and Britain became disillusioned with the way in which 'women's' issues were handled by the predominantly male leaderships.[4]

At bottom, Marxists had to demonstrate that capital and not men oppressed women. 'We should ask the feminist questions, but try to come up with some Marxist answers.'[5] The answers found that Marx and Engels's analysis of women's oppression was inadequate. We have already noted, in Chapter 1, that they offered a simple diagnosis and remedy to the problem of women's oppression in *The Communist Manifesto*. They were particularly concerned with how the institutions of private property and the family distorted sexual relations between men and women. They made the 'bourgeois' see his wife as a 'mere instrument of production' (in producing heirs) and pursue sexual relationships outside marriage, often involving prostitution. Thus, a *de facto* 'community of women' existed.[6] They implied that the destruction of private property would lead to true sexual freedom, or, using Engels's term, 'sex love' between men and women.

Engels, however, took a far more considered view of women's oppression in his later work, *The Origins of the Family, Private Property and the State*, published in 1884. He regarded the organization of the production of people as equally important as the production of the means of existence in explaining the historical dynamic.[7] Yet, rather than exploring the historical impact of the social system surrounding human reproduction, he focused more narrowly: he viewed women's oppression as an epiphenomenon of the development of the forces and relations of production. As a result of the sexual division of labour, men became responsible for producing food. When greater surpluses were created through increased productivity (and slavery), male power over women increased and also gave rise to monogamy. Men, in wanting to pass their property on to their children, had to know who their children were. The 'mother right', whereby property was transferred through women, was overthrown. This constituted the 'world historical defeat of the female sex'.[8] The woman became 'the slave of his [the man's] lust and a mere instrument for the production of children'.[9] She was also subject to 'domestic slavery'.[10]

In the modern world, Engels argued, the solution to women's oppression was at hand. The proletarian woman was well on the way to emancipation. 'Sex love' – what today we would call 'serial monogamy' – was possible. The proletariat had no property to pass on to the next generation. So inheritance, and therefore monogamy, was not an issue. Equally importantly, women were going into 'public industry', enabling them to achieve some financial independence from the husband, thereby abolishing the 'monogamous family as the economic unity of society'.[11] The legal creation of equal rights between men and women would facilitate this process. It would foreground the need for real social equality. However, the freedom of 'all' women could only occur when the means of production became 'common property' and 'private housekeeping is transformed into a social industry. The care and education of the children become a public affair.'[12]

Subsequent Marxist thinkers, such as August Babel, Clara Zetkin, Lenin and Trotsky, although they deepened Engels's analysis of women's oppression and stressed the importance of the struggle for equal rights, by and large worked within his framework. Only the Bolshevik Alexandra Kollantai differed radically. She disagreed with Engels's concept of sex love. She emphasized the dangers of its exclusivity under communism.[13]

Contemporary Marxists subjected Engels's account of women's oppression to critical scrutiny. They challenged the historical accuracy of his account, his confusion of the matriarchal with the matrilineal, his supposition that the proletarian family was radically different from the bourgeois, his assumption that the sexual division of labour was natural and that women would be paid the same as men in industry. He also ignored the oppression of women arising from their 'double shift' as domestic and as wage labourers.[14]

Engels offered little help to Marxists responding to the women's liberation movement in two crucial areas. First, in holding that the proletarian family was disappearing under capitalism through women being drawn into 'public labour', he was unable to analyse why the family persisted, its economic importance to capitalism and the significance of women's domestic labour within it. Second, in explaining patriarchy solely in terms of private property, Engels could not account for its universality, its existence in different societies. His account of patriarchy excluded psychological, cultural and, to some extent, biological factors. In both these areas – domestic labour and patriarchy – Marxists were most divided.

THE DOMESTIC LABOUR DEBATE

The first and most significant theoretical and political response to the women's liberation movement in the late 1960s gave rise to what became known as the 'domestic labour debate'. It signalled an attempt by Marxists, first, to prove the relevance of Marxism to this movement by demonstrating that the roots of women's oppression lay within capitalism. It shaped the family by creating a sexual division of labour. Men became wage workers outside the home, and women became unpaid domestic labourers within it. Margret Benston, in a path-breaking article in 1969, argued that the cause of women's inferior status *vis-à-vis* men, lay in their different relation to the means of production. 'The woman, denied an active place in the market, has little control over the conditions that govern her life. Her economic dependence is reflected in emotional dependence, passivity, and other "typical" female personality traits.'[15] The woman worked outside the money economy, and her labour was therefore 'valueless'. Thus, capitalism, not men, was the main enemy. Thus, ultimately, women had the same 'objective' interest in overthrowing capitalism as working-class men. Second, some Marxists intended to show that an analysis of domestic labour pointed to a distinctive political strategy, especially encapsulated in the 'wages for housework' campaign in the early 1970s. Indeed, this campaign more than anything else initiated the various exchanges between Marxists over the nature of housework.

Before we examine the differences in this debate, the areas of general consensus among the protagonists need acknowledgement. They agreed that the object of domestic labour in an economic sense consisted of the production and reproduction of labour power: that it involved renewing the energies of the wage worker (i.e. the man) so that wage labour could be performed the next day, and the replacing of the existing generation of wage labourers with a new one; that it entailed in the first instance the production of use values; that it was intrinsically oppressive, monotonous, lonely, unfulfilling; that it was devalued because it was unpaid; that when women undertook both domestic and wage labour they were doubly oppressed (they still had to perform domestic labour when they returned home from work, and at work they were not merely exploited in common with male workers, they were oppressed because in comparison with their male counterparts they were unequally paid, and did not have the same job opportunities); that the family performed important ideological functions in socializing the future labour force to an acceptance of capitalist norms; and finally that the sexual division of labour had to be overcome. That was the case for socialism.

Divisions emerged, however, over, first, the precise way in which capitalism benefited from domestic labour. Different applications of Marxist economic categories yielded different results, with, for some participants in the debate, different political implications. Specifically, the points at issue were whether domestic labour created surplus value, i.e. whether it was productive in a Marxian sense, or merely value, or no value at all, and whether it reduced the value of labour power, because capitalists would otherwise have had to pay for the services required to maintain domestic labour. Second, disagreement focused on whether domestic labour was a mode of production, and the allied question of whether women were a separate class from men. Third, argument arose over the extent to which domestic labour could be socialized under capitalism.

As in the case of many debates between Marxists, Marx's own utterances on the subject helped little. All he said explicitly on the subject of domestic labour was that 'The maintenance and reproduction of the working class [are] ... a necessary condition to the reproduction of capital. But the capitalist may safely leave its fulfilment to the labourer's instincts of self-preservation and of propagation.'[16] He ignored women and their domestic toil in two senses. The 'labourer', in reality usually the man, was seen as propagating and preserving himself, and this process did not entail domestic labour.

Domestic labour equals exploitation? Wages for housework

The thesis that women were exploited through their domestic labour was first advanced by Mariarosa Dalla Costa in 1972.[17] Her argument was straightforward: domestic labour was 'an essential function in the production of surplus value'.[18] Capital, in creating family structures, had freed men from the function of reproducing labour power, so that they were free for exploitation in the labour process. Women's exploitation was hidden because they were not paid a wage for their domestic activities, i.e. they performed unpaid labour. Women were also 'productive' in the sense that they acted as safety valves for the 'social tensions' caused by capitalism.[19] They were outlets for all the oppressions suffered by men in the world outside the home. Women, owing to their exploitation by capital, thus had a shared interest with working-class men in its overthrow.

Interestingly, Dalla Costa explicitly rejected one political conclusion that could be drawn from her analysis, namely that women should demand wages for housework. Such a demand would 'further entrench the condition of the institutionalized slavery which is produced with the condition of housework'.[20] Rather, women had to reject root and branch the slavery of domestic labour by getting out of the house, and to 'destroy the role of the housewife'.[21] They should solidarize with other women, instead of accepting privatized domestic labour. However, Selma James a year later, basing her analysis on Dalla Costa's work, urged that domestic labour should be paid for. Acknowledging that in reality women would not be able to refuse domestic duties, and that trade unions did not take women's issues seriously, she proposed the slogan of 'wages for housework'.[22]

Criticisms

Few critics held that Dalla Costa's analysis of domestic labour and the demand of wages for housework had much to commend them. The notion that domestic labour could be productive fell outside the Marxist framework. Marx had always identified productive labour with surplus-value producing labour, which directly augmented the capitalist's profits.[23] Her failure to understand the precise nature of surplus value led to a basic error. She mistakenly assumed that labour which was necessary was therefore productive. However, within Marxist categories unproductive, i.e. non-profit-making labour, such as supervisory labour, was also necessary to capitalist production.[24] Put another way, she confused the usefulness of labour with its social form. Domestic labour was definitely useful, creating use-values, but its social form was not productive in the sense that it created surplus value.[25]

As for the demand for wages for housework, critics argued that it was strategically flawed. Even if the notion that domestic labour created surplus value was accepted, women within the home did not have the same collective potential to overthrow capitalism as industrial workers. Their labour was atomized rather than concentrated and it did not occupy a central strategic position within the capitalist economy.[26] There was the further question of whether the demand was practical. The cost of paying women on the basis of effort and hours put into domestic labour could not be afforded by capitalist society.[27] It was not practical in another sense: argument could easily arise over who should pay the wage – the husband, the boss or the state.[28] And who should be paid? Should single, childless, female workers be included, for example?[29] There were also difficulties in measuring the work undertaken in order to calculate the size of the wage.[30] Further, the demand was undesirable in terms of its political effects. It reinforced the sexual division of labour, with all its oppressiveness,[31] legitimated 'privatized domestic labour'[32] and did not undermine the notion that there was something inherently feminine about domestic labour.[33] Additionally, in paying a wage the capitalist state would be brought further into people's lives.[34] Finally, it implicitly endorsed the continued existence of capitalist ownership of the means of production.[35]

Commentary

Dalla Costa's view that women are exploited in a Marxist sense is not persuasive, not merely because no exchange takes place between women and capitalists which increases the latter's profits. She failed to demonstrate that women through domestic labour create exchange values greater than the value of their labour power. She could of course have argued that women are exploited in a non-capitalist sense in that they undertake surplus labour on behalf of non-working members of the household. Moreover, she did not make a clear distinction between conditions necessary for exploitation and the process of exploitation itself. The actual production of labour power could be seen as falling within the former category rather than the latter, given the lack of proof that women are exploited in a capitalist sense through their domestic labour.

As for the wages for housework demand, most criticisms of it are hard to rebut. Nevertheless, as a Marxist 'transitional demand' (i.e. a demand that could in effect only be realized under socialism) it did have the effect of highlighting the existence of housewives' unpaid labour and its importance to the capitalist economy. Equally, it sought to address the problems of women who had no alternative to being housewives for at least a period of their lives.

Domestic labour creates value?

Wally Seccombe attempted to apply Marxist categories to domestic labour in a far more rigorous fashion than Dalla Costa. In particular, he wanted to demonstrate that the Marxian law of value explicitly, if tangentially, could be used to explain the domestic labour process. Briefly put, and as indicated in Chapter 10 (p. 129), the law of value posits that all commodities exchange according to the amount of 'socially necessary', or the average amount of 'abstract' (i.e. unskilled, homogenized), labour time embodied in them. The distribution of labour within capitalist society is regulated by the 'law of value'. Thus, through the exchange process, i.e. the market, more labour and investment would go to firms and industries where the labour times required to produce commodities were below average. As for the value of labour power itself, sold by the worker to the capitalist, it too was determined by the amount of socially necessary labour time needed in its production and reproduction, namely the time involved in producing the worker's means of subsistence and 'his' replacement. Hence, the wage the worker received was equivalent to the cost of the production and reproduction of 'his' labour power.

Seccombe suggested that domestic labour was explicable within this value schema. He agreed with Dalla Costa that domestic labour produces labour power, but did not regard the housewife as exploited. She, in producing labour power, did not have a 'direct relation' with capital.[36] And as such she did not exchange her labour with capital to create surplus value. He classified domestic labour as 'unproductive' in the Marxist sense. It was paid for from the 'revenue' of capital, in the form of the male worker's wages.[37] This 'exchange' was hidden, because the wage appeared to be for the labour power of the wage labourer. In reality, the wage also paid for the labour that reproduced the labour power of the entire family –

wife, husband and children.[38] Thus, the wage was divided into two parts – to sustain the male worker and his substitute and the domestic worker and her substitute. Domestic labour could be measured in value terms as that which reproduces the housewife's labour on a generational and daily basis, i.e. it was equivalent to the costs of its own production and reproduction.[39]

If the ultimate economic purpose of domestic labour was the production and reproduction of labour power, its precise activity consisted of transforming commodities purchased with the wage into consumable objects to regenerate and reproduce labour power. The housewife either 'transfers or creates value'.[40] Her labour created value in the sense that it became 'part of the congealed mass of past labour embodied in labour power. The value she creates was realized as one part of the value labour power achieved as a commodity when sold.'[41] Yet she was part of the metamorphosis of value – the transfer of value – which occurs within the household. The means of subsistence are bought with a wage. Her labour renders them consumable for herself and the rest of the family, producing or reproducing labour power in the process. The value of her labour is equivalent to her cost of subsistence, which she of course consumes. Thus, 'overall' within the household, 'value is neither created nor destroyed', but merely transferred.[42]

The fact that domestic labour was privatized labour and not directly socially mediated through the market (i.e. there was no market for a housewife's domestic services) was irrelevant, Seccombe argued. The housewife's labour was realized as abstract labour, when the labour power of the husband enters the market, as with simple commodity production. Yet, although domestic labour was essential to capitalism, the latter had no interest in its socialization or in improving its efficiency, because it was beyond the 'exercise of the law of value'.[43]

Seccombe concluded that women's oppression within the family had material roots. The need to produce and reproduce labour power created a psychology of self-denial, reinforced by the male control over the wage packet. For the woman to rebel against this situation would be to the immediate detriment of her husband and children.[44] Nevertheless, the more women became involved in work outside the home, the greater the possibility for conflicts over the domestic division of labour to assume a 'progressive' character (presumably greater possibilities of resolution and therefore a greater possibility of class unity between the sexes). Among the most important demands, however, that women could make as housewives were for the socialization of housework and price watch committees.

Critics
Various criticisms were made of Seccombe's attempt to incorporate domestic labour within the law of value. First, his concentration upon domestic labour was too narrow. Consequently, he had an inadequate

understanding of women's oppression under capitalism, and, therefore, of the forces that would lead to the abolition of domestic labour. Rather, women's oppression and the growth of the women's liberation movement had to be viewed as stemming from their *dual* labour, as both domestic *and* wage workers.[45] Second, critics doubted whether Seccombe had correctly used Marx's categories. For example, if the labour theory of value was applied consistently, it would mean that labour power would be sold below its value, because the wage would not merely cover the means of subsistence, but also the value created by domestic labour.[46] Critics also queried whether domestic labour could be classified as unproductive, since Marx clearly indicated that both productive and unproductive labour entailed acts of exchange. No such exchange occurred between husband and wife. Other factors – such as emotional and cultural – explain the husband's support of the wife.[47] Seccombe's assumption that an equal exchange occurred between husband and wife, whereby the wife received from the husband's pay packet a value equal to the services she provided, was debatable. Ideological pressures, rather than the inducement of exchange, were more important factors in getting them to service their husbands.[48]

Further, critics had difficulty with the proposition that domestic labour simultaneously created value yet was outside the law of value.[49] Rather, they maintained that domestic labour took place outside the law of value, and was neither productive nor unproductive in a Marxist sense. They held that it was concrete labour, which produced use values for individual consumption by workers and their offspring. Since no exchange occurred, such labour could not assume a value form, as abstract labour.[50] They all argued in different ways that these concrete, private labours in the absence of a market could not be compared, and in the absence of competition were not regulated in terms of the type of tasks, their intensity and duration. Thus, the labour of housewives was not analogous to that of petty commodity producers, as Seccombe had argued, because there existed no market, imposing the law of value through comparisons of labour times.[51] Indeed, one could not talk about concrete labours being 'realized', thereby creating value, in the way Seccombe suggested. Value, the product of abstract labour, was created before exchange occurred, in the production process itself. Domestic labour, in producing the commodity labour power, was not compelled to become abstract, measurable labour.[52] Thus, domestic labour was 'not value creating' because it was 'not subject to the law of value'.[53] One consequence, if it was value-creating labour, would be that virtually anything could be included in this process, such as eating and sleeping, since these activities also served to regenerate labour power.[54] Such an implication arose in Seccombe's argument because he had conflated the reproduction of labour power with the reproduction of the living individual.[55]

That domestic labour could not be subsumed under commodity

production – the process whereby concrete labour was transformed into abstract labour – was demonstrated in a number of ways. Fluctuations in the price of labour power did not have a significant effect on the performance of domestic labour: it had to be performed whether the wage earner was laid off or not, or whether women were drawn into the labour force during periods of rapid capital accumulation.[56] Put another way, from the perspective of the capitalist, whether the wife of the male worker prepared TV or gourmet meals was irrelevant, because this labour did not affect surplus value extraction.[57] If domestic labour was not subject to the law of value, then neither could it be measured. Therefore, Seccombe's attempt to compute the value of a women's domestic labour as equal to her means of subsistence was fatally flawed.[58]

The upshot of this critique was that domestic labour could not be regarded as an integral, quantifiable part of the value process in working on the means of subsistence. It was nevertheless 'one of the external conditions of existence' in the reproduction of the capitalist mode of production, and as such merely transferred rather than created value.[59]

Commentary

Seccombe conceded to his critics that he had paid insufficient attention to women's dual labour inside and outside the household.[60] Nevertheless, he insisted that domestic labour created value, even if it did not produce directly for the market, on the grounds that most work under capitalism consisted of the production of use values, 'far removed – in terms of time, space and product form – from the finished commodity exchanged on the market'.[61] Yet this left the crucial question of which concrete labour was to count as value creating, and which was not, unanswered. Seccombe also endeavoured to show how the law of value determined the domestic labour time necessary to produce the commodity labour power. He argued that housework would intensify and take longer if wages fell: there would be more shopping for cheaper goods, more cooking from scratch, etc.[62] However, the opposite scenario could be the outcome: with less cash the housewife may spend less time shopping and less time cooking, because fewer foods may be available to her. Finally, he sought to show how increases in the productivity of domestic labour had an effect on the law of value by making more women available for work.[63] Yet to prove his point he would have had to demonstrate that the male wage would necessarily fall, owing to a reduction in the labour time taken to maintain his subsistence.

In sum, Seccombe was unable to demonstrate convincingly the extent of the exchange-value significance of domestic labour and how it could be measured in value terms. He failed to show how domestic labour was systematically affected by, or systematically impacted upon, the law of value, unlike other forms of commodity production. It was not necessarily value-driven nor did it drive value.

Domestic labour: a mode of production?

The question remained, then, for those who maintained that domestic labour lay outside the law of value, of how it should be categorized as a form of production.[64] Seccombe, when he wished to stress the difference between wage and domestic labour, argued that it was analogous to petty commodity production, where direct producers sold the products of their labour on the market, rather than their labour power.[65] This position was rejected on the grounds that domestic labour did not directly produce the commodity labour power, but use values, for immediate consumption within the family, thereby merely contributing to the production and reproduction of labour power.[66] John Harrison made the most serious Marxist attempt at classification. Unlike with petty commodity production, there was little specialization of housework and crucially the product, use values, did not directly enter into exchange.[67] Rather, it was a 'client mode of production', which was 'created or co-opted by the dominant [capitalist] mode to fulfil certain functions'.[68] It was a form of production, dependent upon capitalism through the male wage. Although he claimed that it did not directly produce the commodity labour power, capitalism benefited because it was unpaid labour, which included a surplus element after the housewife's costs of subsistence had been deducted. This surplus was transferred to capital through the payment of wages below their value.[69] Consequently, although hypothetically capitalism could take over this domestic function, through launderettes, brothels, etc., it generally had an interest in not doing so. Harrison was prepared to accept a crucial political implication: insofar as they laboured within a different mode of production, women were in a different class from male workers.[70] If women also undertook wage labour, then it merely meant that they were members of two classes, just like people who derive an income from stocks and shares and also perform wage labour.

Criticisms

Three principal objections were levelled against Harrison's thesis. First, critics doubted whether a 'client mode of production' was meaningful. It could not satisfy the formal conceptual requirements of a mode of production. A fundamental desideratum is its universalizability, so that it could become 'hegemonic' within a social formation. Dependent upon capitalism, it lacked its own productive base to produce its own means of production, to reproduce itself and to become the economic and social foundation.[71] An implication of domestic labour as a 'client mode of production' dependent upon capitalism, which Harrison did not deal with, was that he assumed, rather than proved, that the latter was dominant in this relationship.[72]

Second, Harrison's argument that capitalism gained from women's surplus domestic labour was unconvincing. The transfer of the surplus to the capitalist sector could not be conceptualized, since domestic labour was not subject to the law of value and was therefore not commensurable with wage labour.[73] By the same token, if domestic labour was non-capitalist, how could it appear in the capitalist sector as additional value? Moreover, if domestic labour subsidized capitalism through a reduction in the value of labour power, it would be in the latter's interest to keep women at home. Yet the cost of labour power is often lowest where domestic labour is minimal, such as among single and immigrant workers.[74]

Third, the political implications of his thesis were unacceptable. Treating women as a class was problematic. It obscured women's relationship with capitalism. True, all women were oppressed, but in explaining the precise nature and extent of that oppression class had a decisive role. For example, working-class women were likely to be more 'exploited' in domestic and wage work, to be more subject to sexual abuse and to have less reproductive freedom than middle- and upper-class women.[75] Further, women were not subject to the same structural situation as the working class. They were not compelled to marry, have children and perform housework in the same sense that workers were compelled to undertake wage labour.[76]

Commentary

In attempting to show how capitalism benefited from this 'client mode of production', Harrison encountered the same difficulty as Seccombe in assuming that domestic labour created value. Yet underlining the specificity of domestic labour, contrasting it with wage labour, by viewing it as a mode of production, was also problematic. True, he could claim that his notion of a 'client mode of production' was not intended as a full-blown mode of production in a conceptual sense – that was why it was a 'client' mode. Thus, it did not have to possess a self-sustaining, reproductive, dynamic of its own, capable of becoming 'hegemonic'. However, we are still left with the problem that if it is dependent upon capitalism, the reverse is also held to be true, because capital has to purchase labour power external to itself, from this 'client' mode. So it too is not capable of self-reproduction, and could not therefore be theoretically constituted as a mode of production. A way round this problem is to see a mode of production as consisting of the production of use values as well as the 'production' of people. Capitalism requires both forms of production in order to be self-sustaining. Thus, domestic labour and wage labour are equally integral to its self-reproduction.[77]

The socialization of housework under capitalism?

Another question that arose concerning the relationship between domestic labour and capital was whether the former could be socialized under capitalism, through its tasks being undertaken either by the market or by the state. Clearly, if they could, then the argument for socialism as the solution to the problem of domestic labour would be less compelling. Both Seccombe and Harrison argued that there was nothing in principle preventing capitalism from socializing housework: 'There is no reason, at the level of the laws of motion of capitalist mode of production, why the principle of launderettes could not be extended to capitalist creches, and if you like brothels.'[78]

This position has been faulted on logical and empirical grounds. That domestic labour could be socialized under capitalism was a logical impossibility: it would subvert its own production relations by producing a living labourer that was the private property of capital. Workers would no longer be 'free' to sell their labour power to whomever they chose.[79] Moreover, an 'absolute' limit to socialization existed. Privatized, domestic labour would still have to be performed after work in the socialized domestic labour sector had been finished every day.[80]

Then there were practical difficulties. For capitalism to provide universal pre-school, especially 24-hour, child-care was too costly.[81] Moreover, to release all women for wage work, when insufficient possibilities for such employment existed, was pointless.[82] Finally, capitalism had little desire to socialize domestic labour. It benefited from the flexibility engendered by domestic labour: women were an important reserve army of potential wage labour, required as and when necessary, according to the rhythms of capital accumulation.[83]

Commentary

The socialization of domestic work is theoretically *conceivable* under capitalism. True, labourers if they were produced by capitalist baby farms would no longer be 'free'. Yet it was and is possible for capitalism and slavery to coexist. And as for there existing an 'absolute' limit to the working day, socialized domestic shift work is possible. However, intuitively there seem good practical reasons why capitalism has no interest in fully socializing domestic labour. First, it is unlikely that the cost of releasing women totally from domestic labour, especially child-care, would be outweighed by the gains in surplus value from wage employment. Second, capitalism clearly benefits from the potential and real twofold nature of women's labour, especially as a reserve army. And finally, the ideological advantages to capital of socializing future new generations of workers by privatized domestic labour cannot be discounted.

General commentary

The attempts by Dalla Costa and Seccombe to locate domestic labour in some way within the labour theory of value, and by Harrison to view it as a mode of production, must be regarded as unsuccessful applications of Marxist economic categories. Yet, as indicated at the beginning of the chapter, there were clear areas of agreement and, where the different participants in these debates did agree, certain insights into the material roots of women's oppression are evident. In particular, put in its starkest and perhaps most exaggerated form, insofar as women performed unpaid labour on a full-time basis and men performed waged work outside the home, women's work was undervalued and they were financially dependent on men. The coexistence of these types of labour is accounted for by the sexual division of labour. Capitalism broke down the household as a productive unit, separating domestic labour from 'productive' wage labour. Although this sexual division of labour is marginally overcome when women undertake wage labour, they often become involved in a 'double shift'. Domestic work thereby becomes more stressful, and women are simultaneously disadvantaged in competing with men in the labour market.

However, what the debate failed to explain was the gender specificity of much domestic labour, why it is performed mainly by women rather than men.[84] Here, patriarchal ideology and the existence of human reproduction within a capitalist context are important considerations. Such a shortcoming can be attributable to an overemphasis on the 'economic'. This meant that various issues were generally left unexplored: of men benefiting from women's domestic labour, and sharing more equally domestic labour under capitalism.[85] Indeed, the question of whether privatized, domestic labour was necessarily functional to capitalism was not explored.[86] Further, the exclusive focus on the 'economic' assumes that women's oppression would automatically disappear in a socialist society.

Finally, the political implications arising from the debate were not always clear. We have already noted that the demand for 'wages for housework' need not necessarily be appropriate even if the proposition that women as domestic labourers produced surplus value was accepted. Equally, to endorse the notion that capitalism benefited from domestic labour through the creation of surplus value or value, or by involuntarily subsidizing male subsistence, did not necessarily indicate a political disagreement with those who rejected such an analysis: women, as domestic labourers, still had an interest in overthrowing capitalism, because their labour still had an 'alienating' character, stemming from a genderized division of labour created by capitalism. Indeterminate political conclusions can also be drawn from perceiving domestic labour as a 'client mode of production', where women, as domestic labourers, formed a separate class. The grounds for, and the objectives of, an alliance with working-class men against capitalism are not obvious. Nevertheless, the basis of a female/working-class anti-capitalist alliance is more readily apparent if, first, the material source of oppression is seen to lie in the capitalist-created sexual division of labour, and, second, capitalism could not significantly socialize domestic labour. However, all this ignores not only the possibility that men may materially benefit from women's domestic labour, but also the non-economic elements that contribute to women's oppression, both inside and outside the home, such as compulsory heterosexuality, male violence and sexual harassment. Nevertheless, whatever the deficiencies in the debate, Marxists were at least attempting to uncover the material roots of a fundamental site of women's oppression.

MARXISM AND FEMINISM: WHAT KIND OF MARRIAGE?

Some Marxists, in part influenced by the patriarchal theories of radical feminists, held at least implicitly that traditional Marxist categories of analysis, as exemplified in the domestic labour debate, were inherently unable to explain the full essence of women's oppression. They lacked gender specificity. The domestic labour debate itself was symptomatic of this weakness. Reflecting upon this debate, Wally Seccombe noted that, 'while the overall labour burden of the household was amenable to Marxist explanation, its unequal allocation between spouses was not'.[87] One response to this general problems was to develop a Marxist–feminist synthesis, which became known as 'dual systems' theory.

Heidi Hartmann was its most famous exponent.[88] In an influential and widely discussed article, 'The unhappy marriage of Marxism and feminism: towards a more progressive union',[89] she suggested that the marriage was indeed an unhappy one. Marxism was the dominant partner, and in effect, as with all bad marriages, a state of 'denial' had set in. Marxism could not acknowledge that the distribution of labour in society, with its hierarchy of differences of intrinsic and extrinsic rewards, had anything to do fundamentally with male power or patriarchy.[90] Yet, she was also aware that for any successful marriage to occur, the concept of patriarchy itself needed some refinement. She sought to avoid common criticisms made against it; for example, that it smacked of biological determinism, or that it lacked specificity because it was too static, ahistorical and universalistic.[91] So she did not want a concept of patriarchy which led to a form of feminism that was 'blind to history and insufficiently materialist'.[92] Accordingly, she defined patriarchy as: 'a set of social relations between men, which have a material base, and which, though hierarchical, establish or create interdependence and solidarity among men that enable them to dominate women'.[93] Marxism, she thought, would enable the material bases of patriarchy to be understood. On the other hand, Marxism by itself could not fully explain patriarchy, because its categories were 'sex blind'. Women's oppression thus had to be explained in terms of both capitalism and patriarchy, two separate but interlinked systems, which symbiotically adapted to each other.

Nevertheless, rather than concentrating on feminism's failings, she focused on Marxism's. It had not explored the differences between men's and women's experiences of capitalism, and how and why women were oppressed as women. They were disadvantaged in the labour market, and crucially their domestic labour benefited men as well as capital. Men, at least in the short term, 'have a higher standard of living than women in terms of luxury consumption, leisure time, and personalized services', ensuring that they have a material interest in women's continued oppression.[94] Although Marxism convincingly analysed the structure and development of capitalism, it did not effectively explain the gendered nature of the tasks and attendant benefits within the working class. A theory of patriarchy filled this explanatory gap.

Patriarchy was, however, not merely ideological. It possessed a material base, which lay in men's control over women's labour power, denying them access to economically productive resources and restricting their sexuality. Women experienced 'patriarchal capitalism' in the form of 'heterosexual marriage (and consequent homophobia), female child rearing and housework, women's economic dependence on men (enforced by arrangements in the labour market), the state, and numerous institutions based on social relations among men – clubs, sports, unions, professions, universities, churches, corporations, and armies'.[95]

Women were oppressed by a partnership between patriarchy and capitalism. Although a tension could exist between male capitalists and workers over the use of female labour – for domestic and wage labour – cooperation by both in the nineteenth century led to the creation of the family wage through protective legislation, which excluded women from certain jobs and industries, and job segregation according to sex. Men benefited from the absence of female competition for jobs, women's unpaid domestic labour and their economic dependency. Further, women's domestic responsibilities undermined their competitive strength in the labour market. In keeping women in the home, capital gained through the reproduction of a healthier labour force.[96] Even in modern times, although more women participated in the labour force, the family wage, Hartmann argued, still constituted the basis of the sexual division of labour. Moreover, this division of labour often replicated itself in the job market, with women undertaking tasks of cooking, cleaning and caring.[97] And the wage differential perpetuated the patriarchal family by compelling the woman's financial dependence on the man.

The partnership of patriarchy and capital also expressed itself

ideologically. Capitalist values assumed a patriarchal form. 'Male' characteristics of competitiveness, rationality and domination were exalted, and
'female' characteristics of irrationality and emotionality were denigrated.
By the same token, women's labour, whether inside or outside the home,
was undervalued. It was needs, rather than market, oriented.[98]

Finally, she argued that the male left could not be relied upon to take up
feminist struggles seriously. Women therefore needed to set up their own
organizations, while at the same time aligning themselves with other
groups fighting for socialism. Furthermore, women's contribution to the
struggle for socialism required greater recognition. The sexual division of
labour meant that they understood better than men the nature and value of
human interdependence and need, and hence the ends of socialism.

Hartmann's critics

Hartmann's thesis was subjected to wide criticism, ranging from radical
feminists, who called for an instant divorce between Marxism and
feminism,[99] to those concerned with other forms of oppression, who
insisted that the marriage would be impoverished without the inclusion of
racial or sexual oppression,[100] and to those seeking a deeper understanding of this marriage.[101] Marxist critics, on the other hand, denied the
need for a marriage in the first place. Marxism would be marrying a non-
existent partner. Although gender oppression existed, it was not a
manifestation of patriarchy, but capitalism. Their defence of Marxism
took two forms. They either reasserted the classic position: capitalism was
the problem, not men. Or they argued for the reformulation of Marxist
categories of historical materialism. Either way they insisted upon a single
explanation for women's oppression, thereby denying the *necessity* for an
autonomous women's movement and the potential split between the
women's movement and the struggle for socialism.

Lindsey German, in reaffirming capitalism's responsibility for oppressing women, rejected Hartmann's thesis *in toto*. First, she maintained that
the emergence of the family wage and protective legislation in the
nineteenth century was not the result of an inter-class male conspiracy.
Rather, these two phenomena could be explained by the capitalists'
reaction to the high rate of infant mortality and the need for a more
efficient reproduction of the labour force, qualitatively and quantitatively,
coupled with the desire of working-class men and women for better living
standards for themselves and their children.[102] Moreover, skilled male
workers' collusion with capital to exclude women from certain trades was
not directed only against women, but also against the children of unskilled
and immigrant workers. In addition, Hartmann's interpretation could not
account for women's exclusion from industries where trade unions were
weak.

Second, she queried Hartmann's argument that the family wage was to men's advantage, and that for this reason they did not fight for wage equality between men and women. However, male workers after the defeat of Chartism in the mid-nineteenth century were in no position to struggle for anything. Just as importantly, given the absence of contraception, periodic pregnancies and the dangers of childbirth, to both the mother and the child, the working class of both sexes wanted to exclude women from the workforce.[103]

Third, she could not agree with Hartmann that men unilaterally benefited from women's domestic labour. Making comparisons between (women's) domestic labour and (men's) wage labour in terms of drudgery, intensity and meaninglessness was difficult, resting on subjective estimations.[104] Again, comparing leisure times was problematic owing to qualitative differences. Although men might have more leisure than women, it was more rigidly defined. The real disadvantage that women suffered from, as domestic labourers, was not exploitation by men, but atomization and therefore a collective inability to change their conditions of existence.

Fourth, she countered Hartmann's view that men conspired together to control women's wage labour in terms of unequal pay and job segregation. The fact that women have their working life disrupted by childbirth and child-care offered a better explanation for this phenomenon.[105] She also could not endorse the 'women as reserve army' hypothesis as evidence of male control over women's labour. The 1930s slump in Germany and the United States witnessed an increase in women's employment.

Fifth, she challenged Hartmann's assumption that because capitalism and patriarchy were two separate but interlocking systems, the former adapted to the pre-existing patriarchal family. It implied in some sense that the family was unchanging. She argued that it was part of capitalism's superstructure and would inevitably be transformed by the emergence of a socialist economic base and the socialization of housework and child-care.[106] Furthermore, capitalism had wrought large changes in the family during and after the industrial revolution, with women at first pulled into the factory labour force and then pushed out when the question of biological reproduction became paramount. And after the Second World War improved contraception and the increase in female employment changed women's attitude towards marriage, with it no longer being seen as a lifetime commitment. Nevertheless, although increases in divorces, re-marriages and single parent families have occurred, capitalism still requires the family as a cheap way of reproducing the labour force through women's unpaid labour, and as an institution perpetuating conservative ideas.

German concluded that Marxism was not 'sex-blind'. The reason why women filled certain 'empty places' was obvious. It stemmed from their 'individual responsibility for reproduction, which in turn structures the whole of [their] lives'.[107]

Iris Young, in 'Beyond the unhappy marriage: a critique of dual systems theory',[108] attempting to save Marxism from the grips of Hartmann's dual-systems thesis and to defend it against the charge of gender blindness, suggested that a 'feminist historical materialism' could be formulated, centring on the concept of the 'gender division of labour'.[109] She came to this position because she was not satisfied with Hartmann's attempt to maintain the separation of patriarchy from the system of social relations of production.[110] Hartmann had admitted that the division of labour reinforced both patriarchy and capitalism and that, in a 'thoroughly patriarchal capitalist society', isolating patriarchy was difficult. Indeed, Young deduced, if patriarchy and capitalism appeared in identical social and economic structures, they would seem to belong to one, rather than two, systems.

A unitary theory could be developed in which 'gender differentiation' was a 'core attribute' of material social relations. Although class analysis may be 'sex-blind', a notion of gender-divided labour would overcome this problem. Crucially, the gender division of labour manifested itself under capitalism through a female reserve army, which has been used to keep male wages low. Pre-existing patriarchal ideology and the necessity for women to be near small children 'operated to make sex the most natural criterion by which to divide the workforce'.[111] In order to create this reserve army, women's economic activity had to be marginalized. Capitalism for the first time in human history pushed women into the periphery of economic activity. Protective legislation and the family wage, in order to achieve this, were therefore effects of the capitalist, gender division of labour, rather than male conspiracy. This female reserve army was 'an essential and fundamental characteristic of capitalism'.[112]

Two qualifications to her position ought to be noted. First, she attempted to avoid the charge of reductionism. The gender division of labour should be seen as a part of the situation of women, but not the 'only part'.[113] Second, in claiming that capitalism necessarily marginalized women in the labour force, she was not implying that their non-marginalization was logically inconceivable. Rather, this marginalization was 'the only historical possibility', given the 'initial gender differentiation and a pre-existing sexist ideology'.[114]

The unitary alternative

Lise Vogel in the same volume of essays criticizing Hartmann's work argued that Marxism did not necessarily have to be 'sex-blind' and that its economism could be transcended not through synthesis with patriarchal theory, but by an expansion of Marxist categories.[115] In particular, the mode of reproduction could be reworked.[116] In other words, a unitary Marxist theory was possible.

Vogel sought to demonstrate this in *Marxism and the Oppression of Women: toward a Unitary Theory*.[117] She rejected Young's attempt to retain the primacy of Marx's categories though the development of the concept of the 'gender division of labour'. Gender divisions by themselves did not automatically entail oppression of men by women. They occurred with the emergence of class society.[118] Women in the biological sense that they produced babies could not avoid playing a key part in 'generational replacement'. Specifically, in capitalist society this meant that they were primarily responsible for the reproduction of labour power, working within a 'domestic' sphere, while men performed 'surplus labour' for the capitalist and created the means of subsistence for themselves and their spouses. What lay at the root of their oppression was their 'differential role in the reproduction of labour power'. This 'differential role' meant that male workers, through wage labour, provided the women with the means of subsistence during pregnancy and lactation. 'The ruling class, in order to stabilize the reproduction of labor power as well as to keep the amount of necessary labor at acceptable levels, encourages male supremacy within the exploited class.'[119]

Vogel, however, noted that a contradiction could arise for the ruling class between wanting to maximize surplus labour, which could involve increased demand for women as wage labourers, and seeking to make generational replacement as efficient as possible by keeping women in the home. This caused struggles between working-class men and women against capital over the protection of the family, and also over women's participation in the labour force.[120]

She drew the political conclusion that women ought to widen the struggle for democratic rights as a result of the contradiction between formal political equality arising from the sphere of 'circulation', i.e. where labour is bought and sold, and real inequality stemming from their differential place within capitalist social reproduction. Struggles in this direction were indeed occurring, with women demanding 'equality within the household, freedom of sexual choice and the right to bear or not bear children'.[121] In the realm of paid work women were demanding equal pay for similar work. Such demands contained a revolutionary socialist potential, involving the reorganization of society, in order to 'draw women into public production' and to reduce and redistribute domestic labour through making it 'an integral component of social production in communist society'.[122]

In seeking to create a single framework based on historical materialism, in order to understand women's oppression, Vogel made two important provisos. First, she acknowledged that men could derive 'immediate advantages' from their supremacy over women in the home.[123] Second, she recognized that the highly institutionalized demarcation between wage and domestic labour within the context of male supremacy created 'the basis for a series of powerful ideological structures, which develop a forceful life of their own'.[124] In other words, there was no requirement for the tight anchoring of the ideological 'superstructure' of patriarchy to the economic 'base'.

Commentary

How convincing were the arguments of Hartmann's Marxist critics? German's rebuttal was far from conclusive. On the question of the origins of the family wage and protective legislation in nineteenth-century Britain, even if we accept that both working-class men and women wanted these things, thereby refuting the male conspiracy theory, we are still left with an outcome which entailed women's economic dependence on men. As for her point that skilled trade unionists excluded not only women from certain trades, but also children of the unskilled and immigrants, all this proves is that they were not only sexist, but also xenophobic and elitist. And although, as German states, women were not in areas of employment where trade unions were weak, there may have been other reasons for or means of excluding them, such as the family wage, or pressure from men within the family itself or arising from the tasks of child-care.

She was on stronger ground in noting against Hartmann the complexity of the question as to whether men benefited from women's domestic labour. When domestic and wage labour are compared, like is not being compared with like. Even if labour times could be compared, questions of intensity, danger and intrinsic meaning have to be considered. Again, her criticism of Hartmann's view that unequal pay and segregation in the job market are a product of patriarchy also has strength, emphasizing childbirth and child-rearing as important explanatory factors. Nevertheless, that men can benefit from job segregation cannot be easily explained away. German also correctly indicated the empirical falsity of the 'women as industrial reserve army' hypothesis. Intuitively, there would appear to be little reason why women should not be employed by capital on a permanent basis. Their wages are lower than men's and they can be employed just as easily in boom or recession.[125]

Finally, her rejection of Hartmann's suggestion that capitalism adapts to patriarchy has plausibility. Rather, capitalism has undermined it when deemed necessary, as in the early days of the Industrial Revolution, or today when women are often employed in preference to men. Or capital has supported patriarchy; for instance, in order to divide the workforce, or when the priority is to keep women in the home as unpaid domestic labourers cheaply reproducing the workforce. However, asserting that Hartmann assumes the family as an unchanging phenomenon is questionable, since, as already noted, she specifically criticized feminist analysis for being 'blind to history and insufficiently materialist'.[126] Patriarchy, she stated, was not 'a universal, unchanging phenomenon'.[127] Moreover, German's argument that the family is part of the superstructure, yet benefits capital through the cheap reproduction of labour, implying that it is also part of the economic base, is somewhat contradictory.

Young's critique of Hartmann was also not wholly convincing. Her point that patriarchy and capitalism were analytically inseparable, belonging to 'one system, not two', does not fully take into account the possibility of conflict between capitalism and patriarchy, which Hartmann acknowledged. This is most obviously manifest when working-class men want to keep women in the home in circumstances where the demand for female labour is high. Her attempt to make the concept of the gender division of labour a key category in historical materialism was not successful, as Vogel argued. It may be part of a necessary explanation of women's oppression, but not sufficient, because gender divisions by themselves do not automatically create gender hierarchies of power.

Further, the qualifications she made in seeking to interpret the gender division of labour as a 'core attribute' in the understanding of capitalist patriarchy weakened her case. She conceded that women's marginalization in the labour force as a reserve army, as a manifestation of the gender division of labour under capitalism, was the 'only historical possibility', rather than the only 'logical' possibility. This raised questions as to the extent to which gender-divided labour can be viewed as a 'core attribute' of capitalism. And we have already noted that the 'women as reserve army' concept was problematic. She also admitted that the gender division of labour, although it should always be part of the explanation of women's oppression, was 'almost never the *only* part'.[128] Because she did not specify the relationship between these two parts, there could easily be room for two systems rather than one.

Finally, did Lise Vogel provide a persuasive alternative to Hartmann, in ruling out the possibility of two systems? She demonstrated that working-class women through their role in the reproduction of labour power had a material interest in socialism, but not that working-class men had no material interest in oppressing women. Indeed, as already indicated, she agreed that men could have 'immediate advantages' derived from their supremacy in the home. Equally, she allowed that the ideological structures of male supremacy could 'develop a forceful life of their own'. This independence could easily be expressed in patriarchal forms, of language, knowledge, pornography, sexual harassment and male violence, all of which would seem to undermine the notion of a 'unitary' theory.[129]

GENERAL COMMENTARY

While Marxist critics of Hartmann may not have been able to offer a totally convincing alternative, they nevertheless demonstrated that Marxism was not inherently 'sex-blind'. Rather than working within the 'sex-blind' categories used by Marx to understand capitalism, they expanded the categories of historical materialism, as initially suggested, but not developed, by Engels. They explored the implications of human reproduction: how it both affected and was affected by capitalism. Yet even if a 'feminist' historical materialism can be created, that it would be able to explain *all* forms of oppression is dubious. This is not to ignore the possibility that capitalism will exploit gender differences, whatever their origins.

Perhaps because of the potential limitations of such a historical materialism, Sylvia Walby has attempted to resurrect the dual-systems perspective in *Theorising Patriarchy*.[130] Although she maintained that Hartmann had underestimated the tension between patriarchy and capitalism, particularly over the use of female labour, and had failed to specify and include all the different structures of patriarchy, she argued that a dual-systems approach was recoverable.[131] Sensitive to the pitfalls of essentialism, she theorized patriarchy at different levels of abstraction, the most abstract of which was as a 'system of social relations'. This system was 'in articulation with capitalism' (and with racism), yet was not 'homologous in internal structure' with it.[132] At lower, more concrete levels, patriarchy manifested itself in six 'relatively autonomous' but interacting structures: mode of production, paid work, the state, male violence, sexuality and cultural institutions. Within this dual-systems approach, capitalism's most significant, contemporary impact on patriarchy has been in the movement from private to public patriarchy. Building on 'first-wave feminism', which brought political citizenship, women through increased paid employment are now more independent of individual men, but are still dominated by public patriarchal structures, in both work and the wider political arena.[133]

However, even her solution to the problem posed by dual-systems analysis has been found wanting. Ben Fine has argued that Walby, in trying to retain this approach, moved into a methodological minefield. She had difficulties in manoeuvring between different levels of abstraction. For example, after identifying women's oppression, she explained it as part of the more abstract concept of patriarchy, or conversely, in her description of patriarchy in detail, within one of the six structures, the general concept of patriarchy disappeared.[134] Inconsistency also arose over the relationship between causal relations between the higher and lower levels; for instance, between patriarchy at the former and the sexual division of labour at the latter. Moreover, the concept of patriarchy itself faced methodological difficulties. Although different forms of oppression by individual males can be identified and related to the general concept of patriarchy, the exact origins and changes in social structure that led to this situation still need explanation.[135]

Other problems can be added to this list. In emphasizing the patriarchy side of the patriarchy–capitalism couplet in her analysis of women's oppression, she does not consider the possibility of capitalism having an active presence in explaining the context of male violence and sexuality, and the formation of gender identities, in terms of male alienation, powerlessness, commodification of women, genderized division of labour, etc. Further, while she sees capitalism as significant in the move from private to public patriarchy, the question remains as to how capitalism precisely relates to this form of patriarchy. To what extent is the relationship a symbiotic one? Or, consistent with her critique of Hartmann, is it potentially antagonistic?

These problems underline two related difficulties that are perhaps inherent in the dual-systems analysis. The first has to do with the concept of patriarchy. It contains an ambiguity: it is both a descriptive category and an explanation. It is descriptive shorthand for male power over women, yet it also purports to explain this power in terms of 'male' properties. The problem is whether the concept retains at the most abstract, generic level its universality both descriptively and causally. If fact and explanation are analytically separated in order to historicize the phenomenon and avoid essentialism, especially biological determinism (with universality retained in a categorical sense of male domination), then the methodological problems of causality need unravelling. The arenas of male domination have to be clearly indicated, as Walby does with her six 'structures'. Then, crucially, different types of male behaviour need to be distinguished within these different arenas: for example, first, male intentions, which assume a collective force in some explicit or implicit 'conspiratorial' sense; second, individual male intentions that derive from a situation of having to deal with existing social, economic and political structures, which bring them into conflict with women (but possibly also with other men); third, male-dominated structures, which have the *effect*, but not necessarily the *intention*, of oppressing women.

Linked to the question of male intentionality and behaviour is whether men benefit from oppressing women. This is usually defined in terms of whether this oppression is in male interests. Here again the answer may depend upon which arena is under discussion. Equally importantly, the meaning of the term 'interests' needs elaboration. It can refer to material or emotional, long- or short-term, 'real' or perceived interests. And interests may be fixed or static. Are they to be conceived as part of a 'zero-sum' or 'non-zero-sum' game with women? And to add to the complication, an interpretation of such interests will be conditional upon how 'male' human nature is perceived, and whether men are 'interest'-driven, or develop a set of interests in opposition to women, owing to the situation in which they find themselves.

Thus women's counter-strategies, within the patriarchal paradigm, will in part be determined, first, by the arena in which male oppression takes place, second, by conceptions of male intentionality and, third, related to this, by which notions of interest are adopted.

The second and connected difficulty in dual-systems analysis arises from the assumption that patriarchy, like capitalism, is a 'system'. Although Walby asserted that patriarchy was not 'homologous in internal structure with capitalism', she still assumed that it could be subjected to the same type of analysis as capitalism, entailing different levels of abstraction, thereby laying herself open to Fine's methodological objections, grounded upon Marx's analysis and theoretical representation of the capitalist mode of production. Clearly, there are and have been forms of male organization that implicitly or explicitly oppress women. But the question is whether such forms have a strength and collective 'interest' similar to capitalism, with its powerful internal logic of accumulation, in preserving or changing human relationships. Do they possess the same necessity as capitalism to survive and grow? Perhaps capitalism and patriarchy do not have to be regarded as containing comparable causal properties if the basic definitions of both are constantly borne in mind. Capitalism is a mode of production; patriarchy refers to a mode of domination, of men over women. Patriarchy can accordingly be viewed as a historical, generic category identifying asymmetrical power relations, but like the term 'imperialism' it can assume different forms in different epochs, thereby allowing the question of explanation to remain analytically separate.

Certain areas are more obviously open to economic explanation than others in a non-reductionist sense. For instance, changing patterns of domestic labour with women perceiving themselves not merely as home-makers can in part be explained by women's greater participation in paid labour, male unemployment, commodification of food preparation and labour-saving devices in the home. Moreover, women's greater sexual freedom and greater unwillingness to remain imprisoned in an unfulfilling marriage are to some extent premised upon their greater economic independence, stemming from increased involvement in paid labour (as well as improved contraception). Economic factors can be regarded at least as predisposing, if not precipitating, ones. Yet explanations of gender identities, sexuality, male violence, rape and 'malestream' knowledge and language clearly involve other forms of analysis: psychological, social and cultural. What this means is that certain forms of women's oppression are more independent of capitalism than others, and are therefore more amenable to change without the abolition of capitalism. Yet, while capitalism may not necessarily cause certain forms of oppression in a direct sense, its abolition may be part of the solution. The current focus by feminists on less obviously materially generated forms of oppression may have more to do with pessimism about the possibilities of wholesale societal change, overcoming the oppressive implications of women's responsibility for human reproduction under capitalism, than with the inadequacies of Marxism.

NOTES

1. Doubleday, New York (1971).
2. Morrow, New York (1970).
3. *New Left Review*, 40 (Nov/Dec 1966), 11–37.
4. See especially S. Rowbotham, L. Segal and H. Wainwright, *Beyond the Fragments*, Newcastle and London (1979).
5. J. Mitchell, *Women's Estate*, Penguin, Harmondsworth (1971), 99.
6. K. Marx, *The Communist Manifesto*, 72.
7. F. Engels, *The Origins of the Family, Private Property and the State* (1884), Penguin, Harmondsworth (1985), 36.
8. *Ibid.*, 85–7.
9. *Ibid.*, 87.
10. *Ibid.*, 105.
11. *Ibid.*, 105.
12. *Ibid.*, 107.
13. V. Bryson, *Feminist Political Theory*, Macmillan, Basingstoke (1992), 138–9.
14. R. Delmar, 'Looking again at Engels' "Origins of the family, private property and the state"' in J. Mitchell and A. Oakley (Eds), *The Rights and Wrongs of Women*, Penguin, Harmondsworth (1976); M. Barrett, 'Feminism' in T. Bottomore (Ed.), *A Dictionary of Marxist Thought*, Blackwell, Oxford, 1991, 187; V. Beechey, *Unequal Work*, Verso, London (1987), 55. See also J. Sayers, M. Evans and N. Redclift (Eds), *Engels Revisited*, Tavistock, London (1987).
15. M. Benston, 'The political economy of women's liberation', in E. Malos (Ed.), *The Politics of Housework*, Allison and Busby, London (1980), 125.
16. K. Marx, *Capital, Vol. 1*, Progress Publishers, Moscow (1965), 572.
17. M. Dalla Costa, 'Women and the subversion of the community', *Radical America*, 6 (1972), 67–102.
18. *Ibid.*, 79.
19. *Ibid.*, 89.
20. *Ibid.*, 82.
21. *Ibid.*, 84.
22. S. James, 'Women, the unions and work, or … what is not to be done', *Radical America*, 7, 4–5 (1973), 68.
23. See e.g. N. Holmstrom, ' "Women's work", the family and capitalism', *Science and Society*, 45 (1981), 188; T. Fee, 'Domestic labour: an analysis of housework and its relation to the production process', *Review of Radical Political Economy*, 8, 1 (1976), 2–4.
24. Holmstrom, *op. cit.*, 189.

25. I. Gerstein, 'Domestic work and capitalism', *Radical America*, 7 (July/Oct 1973) 112.
26. Holmstrom, *op. cit.*, 199.
27. Malos, *op. cit.*, 33.
28. L. Vogel, 'The earthly family', *Radical America*, 7 (July/Oct 1976), 41.
29. C. Freeman, in Malos, *op. cit.*, 170.
30. Malos, in Malos, *op. cit.*, 34-5.
31. Holmstrom, *op. cit.*, 199; Malos, in Malos, *op. cit.*, 33.
32. P. Smith, 'Domestic labour and Marx's theory of value' in A. Kuhn and A. M. Wolpe (Eds), *Feminism and Materialism*, Routledge and Kegan Paul, London (1978), 209.
33. Freeman, *op. cit.*, 169.
34. Holmstrom, *op. cit.*, 199.
35. Malos, in Malos, *op. cit.*, 30.
36. W. Seccombe, 'The housewife and her labour under capitalism', *New Left Review*, 83 (Jan/Feb 1973), 7.
37. *Ibid.*, 11.
38. *Ibid.*, 12.
39. *Ibid.*, 10.
40. *Ibid.*, 10.
41. *Ibid.*, 9.
42. W. Seccombe, 'Domestic labour: reply to critics', *New Left Review*, 94 (Nov/Dec 1975), 89.
43. *Ibid.*, 17.
44. *Ibid.*, 21.
45. M. Coulson, B. Magas and H. Wainwright, ' "The housewife and her labour under capitalism" - a critique', *New Left Review*, 89 (Jan/Feb 1975), 60-1.
46. Smith, *op. cit.*, 202.
47. T. Fee, 'Domestic labour: an analysis of housework and its relation to the production process', *Review of Radical Political Economy*, 8, 1 (1976), 5; O. Adamson, C. Brown, J. Harrison and J. Price, 'Women's oppression under capitalism', *Revolutionary Communist*, 5 (1976), 12.
48. J. Gardiner, 'Women's domestic labour', *New Left Review*, 89 (Jan/Feb 1975), 51.
49. Coulson *et al.*, *op. cit.*, 59; Adamson *et al.*, *op. cit.*, 11.
50. *Ibid.*; Coulson *et al.*, *op. cit.*, 62; Smith, *op. cit.*, 204; J. Harrison, 'The political economy of housework', *Bulletin of the Conference of Economists* (Winter 1973), 38.
51. Gardiner, *op. cit.*, 48. See also B. Fine, *Women's Employment and the Capitalist Family*, Routledge, London (1992), 177-8.
52. Adamson *et al.*, *op. cit.*, 11; Smith, *op. cit.*, 206.
53. S. Himmelweit and S. Mohun, 'Domestic labour and capital', *Cambridge Journal of Economics*, 1 (1977), 27. See also L. Briskin, 'Domestic labour: a methodological discussion' in B. Fox (Ed.), *Hidden in the Household*, The Women's Press, Toronto (1980), 159.
54. Adamson *et al.*, *op. cit.*, 11; Smith, *op. cit.*, 212.
55. Himmelweit and Mohun, *op. cit.*, 23.
56. Smith, *op. cit.*, 204-6.

57. Holmstrom, *op. cit.*, 192.
58. Smith, *op. cit.*, 209-10; Himmelweit and Mohun, *op. cit.*, 27-8.
59. Smith, *op. cit.*, 211; see also Adamson *et al.*, *op. cit.*, 9.
60. Seccombe, 'Domestic labour: reply to critics', 83.
61. *Ibid.*, 87.
62. *Ibid.*, 88-9.
63. *Ibid.*, 93.
64. Benston had viewed it as a 'pre-capitalist', pre-market, pre-industrialized type of labour. Benston, *op. cit.*, 121.
65. Seccombe, 'The housewife and her labour under capitalism', 9.
66. Holmstrom, *op. cit.*, 193; Coulson *et al.*, *op. cit.*, 2.
67. Harrison, *op. cit.*, 38.
68. *Ibid.*, 40.
69. *Ibid.*, 43. See also Gardiner, *op. cit.*, 54; Holmstrom, *op. cit.*, 187.
70. Harrison, *op. cit.*, 50.
71. M. Molyneux, 'Beyond the housework debate', *New Left Review*, 116 (July/August 1979), 17. See also Holmstrom, *op. cit.*, 206; S. Himmelweit, *Dictionary of Marxist Thought*, 158.
72. Himmelweit and Mohun, *op. cit.*, 21.
73. Molyneux, *op. cit.*, 8; Himmelweit and Mohun, *op. cit.*, 25; J. Gardiner, S. Himmelweit and M. Mackintosh, 'Women's domestic labour' in Malos, *op. cit.*, 208.
74. Molyneux, *op. cit.*, 10.
75. Holmstrom, *op. cit.*, 208-9.
76. Fox, *op. cit.*, 17.
77. Himmelweit and Mohun, *op. cit.*, 21.
78. Harrison, *op. cit.*, 51. See also Seccombe, 'The housewife and her labour under capitalism', 17.
79. Himmelweit and Mohun, *op. cit.*, 25.
80. Adamson *et al.*, *op. cit.*, 9.
81. Gardiner *et al.*, *op. cit.*, 213.
82. Molyneux, *op. cit.*, 26.
83. Coulson *et al.*, *op. cit.*, 65-7.
84. Bryson, *op. cit.*, 239.
85. *Ibid.*
86. M. Barrett, *Women's Oppression Today*, revised edition, Verso, London (1988), 172-80.
87. 'Reflections on the domestic labour debate and prospects for Marxist feminist synthesis' in R. Hamilton and M. Barrett (Eds), *The Politics of Diversity*, Verso, London (1986), 191.
88. See also A. Ferguson, *Blood and the Root*, Pandora Press, London (1989); Z. Eisenstein, 'Developing a theory of capitalist patriarchy' in Z. Eisenstein (Ed.), *Capitalist Patriarchy and the Case for Socialist Feminism*, Monthly Review Press, New York (1977), 5-40; J. Mitchell, *Women: the Longest Revolution*, Virago, London (1984).
89. H. Hartmann, 'The unhappy marriage of Marxism and feminism: towards a more progressive union' (hereafter *UMMF*), *Capital and Class*, 8 (Summer 1979), 1-33.

90. Originally this term had referred to the notion of rule by the father of both younger men and women within kinship relations, but by the 1960s it was used to describe male domination over women in either an individual or a structural sense.

91. See, for example, S. Rowbotham, 'The trouble with "patriarchy"' in M. Evans (Ed.), *The Woman Question*, Fontana, London (1982), 74–8.

92. *UMMF*, 2.

93. *UMMF*, 11.

94. *UMMF*, 6.

95. *UMMF*, 14.

96. *UMMF*, 19.

97. *UMMF*, 21.

98. *UMMF*, 22.

99. C. Erlich, 'The unhappy marriage of Marxism and feminism: can it be saved?' in L. Sargent (Ed.), *Women and Revolution*, Black Rose Books, Montreal (1981).

100. G. Joseph, 'The incompatible menage à trois: Marxism, feminism and racism' in Sargent, *op. cit.*

101. A. Ferguson and N. Folbre, 'The unhappy marriage of patriarchy and capitalism' in Sargent, *op. cit.*

102. L. German, 'Theories of patriarchy' (hereafter *TP*), *International Socialism* (new series), 12 (Spring 1981), 37. See also J. Humphries, 'The working class family, women's liberation, and class struggle: the case of nineteenth century British history', *Review of Radical Political Economics*, 9, 3 (1977), 25–41; see M. Barrett's critique of her argument in Barrett, *op. cit.*, 215.

103. *TP*, 39. See also J. Brenner and M. Ramas, 'Rethinking women's oppression', *New Left Review*, 144 (March/April 1984), 53.

104. *TP*, 40.

105. *TP*, 41.

106. *TP*, 43.

107. *TP*, 47.

108. I. Young, 'Beyond the unhappy marriage: a critique of dual systems theory', in Sargent, *op. cit.* (hereafter *BUM*).

109. *BUM*, 52.

110. *BUM*, 47.

111. *BUM*, 58.

112. *BUM*, 58.

113. *BUM*, 55.

114. *BUM*, 62.

115. L. Vogel, 'Marxism and feminism: unhappy marriage, trial or something else?', in Sargent, *op. cit.*, 197–8.

116. *Ibid.*, 209. Alison Jagger in *Feminist Politics and Human Nature* also accords reproduction an important explanatory role.

117. L. Vogel, *Marxism and the Oppression of Women: toward a Unitary Theory*, Pluto Press, London (1983) (hereafter *MOW*).

118. *MOW*, 147.

119. *MOW*, 147.

LIVERPOOL JOHN MOORES UNIVERSITY
LEARNING SERVICES

120. *MOW*, 150.
121. *MOW*, 167.
122. *MOW*, 175.
123. *MOW*, 147.
124. *MOW*, 154.
125. B. Fine, *Women's Employment and the Capitalist Family* (hereafter WECF), Routledge, London (1992), 68.
126. *UMMF*, 1–2.
127. *UMMF*, 13.
128. *BUM*, 56.
129. Valerie Bryson, in *Feminist Political Theory*, 246–7, also offers other criticisms of Vogel: her unproven assumption that the sexual division of labour in non-classless societies was non-oppressive for women and her static concept of women's role in social reproduction, which excluded questions of women's sexuality, changes in contraceptive and reproductive knowledge.
130. S. Walby, *Theorising Patriarchy* (hereafter *Th.P*), Blackwell, Oxford (1990).
131. *Th.P*, 7, 41. See 40 for an outline of other criticisms. Michele Barrett, in *Women's Oppression Today*, attempts to avoid the dual systems approach by reworking historical materialism, stressing its ideological components. For a criticism, see Brenner and Ramas, *op. cit.*, and her defence, 'Rethinking women's oppression; a reply to Brenner and Ramas', *New Left Review*, 146 (July/August 1984), 123–8.
132. *Th.P*, 20.
133. *Th.P*, 184–5.
134. *WECF*, 40.
135. *WECF*, 42.

14
Farewell to the Working Class? The New Revisionism

PROBLEMS AND ISSUES

From the late 1970s to the mid-1980s, many Marxists – both those in academia and those more closely involved with political activity – challenged a core assumption of the Marxist project: the working class's potential capacity and interest in creating a socialist society. These 'new revisionist' Marxists suggested either that the working class was becoming sociologically or politically marginalized under conditions of advanced capitalism, or that collectively it had no fundamental socialist intent. Andre Gorz's polemical *tour de force, Farewell to the Working Class,*[1] first published in 1980, in totally writing off the working class as a revolutionary agent, captured the spirit of disillusion of these times. Yet, for the most part, controversy within the Marxist camp centred on other works dealing with the *extent* to which the proletariat should be accorded its privileged revolutionary status.

This re-evaluation of the proletariat's historical role was prompted by the confluence of a number of factors. First, working-class militancy in Western Europe and the United States had generally subsided in comparison with the heady days of the late 1960s and early 1970s. And in Britain the Labour Party, the party 'of' the working class, suffered heavy electoral defeats in 1979, 1983 and 1987. Second, in Britain and the United States strong right-wing governments, determined to wage class war, had been elected, and the working classes in these countries (with the exception of the British miners in 1984–5) did little to resist. Third, there appeared on the horizon 'new social movements', concerned with ethnic, gender, sexual, ecological and peace issues, which in some sense could be viewed as a radical alternative to the working class. Fourth, significant changes in the social structures of advanced capitalist countries had occurred, which seemed to confirm the need for a revision of Marxism. As a result of technological changes and de-industrialization, the traditional, manual working class in manufacturing declined, while white collar workers in service industries and state employment expanded, creating a 'new middle class'.

Fifth, the debate about the working class in its more explicitly political inflection arose within the communist movement, which since its inception in 1917 had been preoccupied with the question of class alliances. From the 1950s onwards, the British Communist Party had pursued an anti-monopoly alliance strategy, consisting of workers, who played a key part, and the petty bourgeoisie (shopkeepers, small farmers, etc.). However, in the light of the social trends already indicated, elements within the Communist Party sought to reduce the working class's strategic importance. The link between the working class and socialism was further eroded within the communist movement elsewhere. Mao Tse-Tung's successful peasant revolution in China in 1949 implied that peasants could be as much an agency for socialism as workers. Maoism had an important influence in France in the late 1960s, and was theoretically important because it suggested that class positions could be determined by ideology and not necessarily by relations of production.

Finally, an intellectual trend developed within this movement, partly influenced by Maoism, and initiated by the French structuralist Marxist Louis Althusser and by those who interpreted Gramsci in a particular way, which called into question the overriding importance of economic and social explanation within Marxist theory. They maintained that political and ideological – i.e. 'superstructural' – factors were as significant. They rejected the economic determinism contained in certain forms of Marxism, whereby the economic 'base' determined the political and ideological 'superstructure'. They argued that the latter had a 'relative' autonomy. This meant that politics and ideology could be to some extent detached from their economic and class moorings. Thus, the socialist constituency could be now unequivocally much wider than the working class, and political discourse no longer had to be constrained by class interest.

The move to 'de-throne' the working class could indeed be viewed as a 'new revisionism'.[2] Although this new brand of Marxism was not identical to Bernstein's revisionism, there were at least three significant parallels: first, an insistence that the working class had to align itself with sections of the middle classes or the 'petty bourgeoisie'; second, that the working class should no longer be seen as *the* hegemonic force in the socialist project; and third, a looser form of the base–superstructure relationship was required in order to make the struggle for socialism less class-based.

The 'new revisionists' focused on one of two areas. The first was the social terrain of modern capitalism. They concluded either that the working class was contracting (Poulantzas) or that it was declining in its 'classic' form (Hobsbawm). Or, second, they pursued a more theoretical gambit, which challenged the determinism implied in the base–super-structure relations and therefore the working class's pre-eminent role in the struggle for socialism (Laclau and Mouffe).

MARX'S LEGACY

Marx's own writings indicated that even for him these two areas were problematic. While he did not entertain the idea that the working class was contracting, unlike his prognostications in *The Communist Manifesto*, he recognized, as indicated in Chapter 1, towards the end of his life that the middle class was growing in Britain. He acknowledged 'the continual increase in numbers of the middle classes ... situated midway between the workers on the one side and the capitalists and the landowners on the other side'.[3] If the middle class was expanding relatively to other classes, making the structure of society look more diamond-shaped and less pyramidal, then two questions arise. Will the proletariat ultimately have sufficient social weight to create a communist society? And, if not, then should it not enter into some sort of alliance with this middle class to improve its conditions of existence?

The other problem that Marx bequeathed to his successors was that implicitly his account of the relationship between 'social being' and 'consciousness', between his objective definition of class and his subjective account of class consciousness (i.e. a sense of class identity and specific class goals and interests), was complicated. In the *Poverty of Philosophy*, he made a famous distinction between the working class 'in itself' and 'for itself': 'Economic conditions had in the first place transformed the mass of the people into workers ... this mass is ... not yet a class for itself. In the struggle ... this mass unites and forms itself into a class for itself.'[4] The in-itself–for-itself relation was therefore mediated by class struggle, whose form and intensity could not be predetermined. There was no automatic 'fit' between the objective class position of a worker and his or her state of class awareness.

CLASS BOUNDARIES IN MODERN CAPITALISM: NICOS POULANTZAS

The Greek Marxist, Nicos Poulantzas, played an important theoretical role in the Eurocommunist movement in the late 1960s and early 1970s. In *Classes in Contemporary Capitalism* he sought to analyse the strategic significance of the 'new wage earning groupings', such as 'commercial and bank employees, office and service workers, etc.', in short, all those who are commonly referred to as 'white collar' or 'tertiary sector' workers, which he termed the 'new petty bourgeoisie'.[5] Poulantzas was primarily concerned with the strategic orientation of the French Communist Party.

Historically, it had failed to construct a worker–peasant alliance. The peasantry had aligned with the French right. However, the peasantry was a declining social force at a time when a 'new petty bourgeoisie' was emerging. The French Communist Party had a golden opportunity to construct an alliance with this new class, as well as to draw in sections of the old petty bourgeoisie, such as artisans and shopkeepers. Hitherto, the party had mistakenly assumed that the 'new petty bourgeoisie' would automatically align itself with the proletariat.[6] He argued to the contrary, that the party had to devise an explicit strategy to win it over to the working class. The only way that it would 'polarize' towards the working class was by it 'being *represented* by the class struggle organisations of the working class themselves'.[7] Representation should not be based on concessions, but on a developing working-class hegemony through struggles. Hegemony was created by the 'establishment of objectives which can transform these allies in the course of the uninterrupted struggle and its stages, account being taken of their specific class determination and the specific polarization that affects them'.[8] He admitted that he did not know how such an alliance would be constructed in practice. He was merely intending to 'locate the problem'.[9]

He was convinced that a problem existed, because not all wage workers could be automatically assimilated to the working class. 'Although every worker is a wage-earner, every wage earner is certainly not a worker.'[10] In order to distinguish who was a 'real' worker, he reinterpreted Marx's theory of class, and his distinction between production and non-productive workers. He defined productive labour in the capitalist mode of production as 'labour that produces surplus value while directly reproducing the material elements that serve as the substratum of the relation of exploitation: labour that is directly involved in material production by producing use values that increase material wealth'.[11] Therefore, wage earners in commerce, banks, advertising agencies and service industries were not productive workers, because they either belonged to the 'sphere of circulation' of commodities, or did not produce surplus value, merely assisting its realization.[12]

Poulantzas also excluded engineers and technicians, although they were directly involved in material production and the creation of surplus value. This entailed a reformulation of Marx's explanation of class. The 'structural determination' of class, Poulantzas argued, was not exclusively economic. In class societies production relations could not be conceived in a purely technical or neutral way, because they involved relations of exploitation, which necessarily entailed relations of power and domination. Thus, political and ideological relations were built into production relations, especially in the reproduction of social classes. He asserted that the social division of labour, implicit in these political and ideological relations, 'dominates the technical division of labour'.[13] Thus, while managers and supervisors had an obvious political function,[14] engineers and technicians, whatever their technical skills, also performed a primary ideological role within the social division of labour. His position rested on an explicit distinction between mental and manual labour. All mental labour had an ideological function within production. Thus, engineers and technicians were not significant owing to their expertise, but because they legitimated workers' subordination to capital. Their supposed monopoly of knowledge made workers feel that they could not run production themselves.[15]

Employing the productive–unproductive labour and the mental–manual labour distinctions, and assigning to managers and supervisors an essentially political role within production relations, E. O. Wright has calculated that the working class would be about 20 per cent of the United States labour force, and the new petty bourgeoisie 70 per cent.[16]

Nevertheless, Poulantzas held that this new petty bourgeoisie was potentially open to an alliance with the working class against monopoly capitalism. He made a distinction between the 'structural determination of class' and a 'class position' adopted by classes in certain circumstances or 'conjunctures'. For example, the late-nineteenth-century 'labour aristocracy' could take up a class position identical to the bourgeoisie, yet still remain structurally determined as workers. By the same token, production technicians' class position could result in their supporting workers on strike, although they were structurally determined as part of the new petty bourgeoisie.[17]

He further claimed that although the old and new petty bourgeoisies related to the means of production in different ways, they were still members of the same class because they adopted similar *ideological* positions, namely

> petty bourgeois individualism; attraction to the status quo and fear of revolution, the myth of 'social advancement' and aspirations to bourgeois status; belief in the 'neutral State' above classes; political instability and a tendency to support 'strong States' and Bonapartist regimes; revolts taking the form of 'petty bourgeois' jacqueries.[18]

Wright's critique

Erik Olin Wright formulated the best-known critique of Poulantzas's minimalist definition of the working class.[19] He offered two main objections. First, he held that the productive–unproductive labour distinction was untenable. Such a distinction, as construed by Poulantzas, had little warrant in Marx or reality. Marx explicitly rejected the notion that only workers who created surplus value through the production of material objects were productive. Service workers who yielded surplus value were equally productive, precisely because they contributed 'towards the self-valorization of capital'.[20] Moreover, the same worker could be both productive and non-productive. For example, the task of packaging could simultaneously be seen as productive insofar as it contributed to the use value of a commodity, and as unproductive insofar as it was part of the realization of the costs of production through advertising.[21] Most importantly, this distinction could not serve as the basis of a *class* distinction, for it implied that productive and unproductive workers had different economic interests. While there may be differences of short-term interest, neither group had a long-term interest in perpetuating a system of capitalist exploitation. Whether workers are productive or unproductive, employers will attempt to pay them as little as possible for as much work as possible, and will deny them control over the labour process.[22]

Second, Poulantzas, in making political and ideological criteria as important as economic criteria in defining class, was led into difficulty. When categorizing supervisors, technicians and engineers, he admitted that they performed productive labour, i.e. they contributed to material production, yet he asserted that their political and ideological role in the social division of labour was more important on the basis of his mental–manual labour distinction. Productive labour here, therefore, was merely a technical category. This contradicted his (and Marx's) earlier economic definition of productive labour, where it was constituted by the 'dominant capitalist relation of exploitation'.[23] Indeed, why the mental–manual division was chosen as a class boundary, rather than viewed merely as a division within the working class, was not clear.

The use of ideological criteria to define class was also problematic in his attempt to view the old and new petty bourgeoisie as members of the same class. Apart from embracing different forms of individualist ideology (e.g. individual advancement through the bureaucracy versus being your own boss), they had clear differences of interest. For instance, the new petty bourgeoisie was dependent on monopoly capital, while the old petty bourgeoisie was threatened by it, and equally they had differences of interest on the question of state expenditure.[24]

Commentary

Perhaps the importance of Poulantzas's analysis lies not in the analysis itself, but in the way it prompted Marxists to undertake a serious investigation of the class structure of modern capitalism.[25] His attempt to draw the line between the working class and the 'new petty bourgeoisie' was fatally flawed. Wright's critique was much closer to Marx and reality. First, as already indicated, Marx did not think that productive labour only consisted of material commodity production. It included other forms of labour which directly contributed to the accumulation of capital. Moreover, while Marx may have seen workers in the sphere of 'circulation', e.g. commerce, as non-productive, in all likelihood he still saw them as workers, because they performed 'unpaid' labour, with employers attempting to gain as much surplus value made in the 'productive' sector as possible.[26] Thus, productive and unproductive workers had a common interest in abolishing exploitation. In addition, there is a difficulty in conceiving how manual workers in the 'non-productive' sector would view their work experience as any different from those in the 'productive' sector. They would be subject to similar pay, conditions, insecurity of employment and loss of job control. As for white-collar workers, Marx explicitly maintained that managers, engineers and technologists were productive, as part of the 'collective worker' that emerged through an ever-increasing division of labour.[27]

A further problem arises from Poulantzas's ideological conception of class determination in his discussion of the old and new petty bourgeoisie. No longer does 'social being' determine consciousness and no longer is class defined in terms of the relations of ownership or non-ownership to the means of production.

While Poulantzas's delimitation of class may have been unsatisfactory, the problem of defining the 'new middle class' has remained for Marxists, with few agreed solutions.[28] Yet, empirically, to categorize lower-level white collar workers, who have no control over their labour and experience job insecurity and poor wages, as non-members of the working class is intuitively questionable.

THE FORWARD MARCH OF LABOUR HALTED?

Another debate that sprang out of the Western communist movement, in Britain in the 1980s, also challenged the strategic centrality of the working class, in stressing the necessity of some sort of cross-class political alliance. Such an alliance was seen as particularly urgent in the light of the Tories' resounding electoral successes in the 1979 and 1983 elections and its virulently anti-working class policies, under Margaret Thatcher.[29] The well-known Marxist historian Eric Hobsbawm initiated the debate in a lecture entitled 'The forward march of labour halted?', delivered in 1978.[30] His thesis was that the British labour movement in its 'classic' form began to decline from approximately 1951, the year in which the famously reforming 1945–51 Labour Government was ousted from office. By 'classic' Hobsbawm meant a labour movement that was white, male, manual, predominantly in manufacturing, culturally distinct, relatively non-segmented, class conscious and Labour voting. Many of these characteristics began to disappear from 1951 onwards.

Crucially, although the wage-earning population had risen, the proportion of manual workers, as a result of technological change, had fallen from 75 to 50 per cent between 1911 and 1976. By the latter date, 45 per cent of the occupied population were non-manual. Employment in the public sector had also dramatically expanded to 30 per cent of the workforce. Moreover, the growth of female employment had been enormous, with 50 per cent of married women now working. The workforce had also changed ethnically, due to immigration, with an attendant growth in racism. The improvements in living standards and the growth of consumerism had undermined the common lifestyle of the working class. The post-1951 period had in addition witnessed the development of sectionalism, with different groups of workers antagonizing each other. For example, they employed sanctions that affected the 'public', i.e. other workers, aimed not at the employer but designed to influence the political will of the government. This fragmentation partly arose because these trade union struggles were primarily 'economistic', over wages, rather than political. Another division in the working class was that the poor had become relatively worse off.

Significantly, a decline in class consciousness had occurred. Hobsbawm used various indices to demonstrate this point. First, trade union membership had stagnated, standing at 46 per cent of the labour force in the 1970s, only a little higher than in 1948, and falling behind many other industrial countries. Second, the Labour vote had fallen substantially, both relatively and absolutely. In 1951 the party had obtained 49 per cent of all votes cast and in 1974 under 40 per cent, although the vote had been 48 per cent in 1966. In the elections of this period it never came within a million of its peak vote of 14 million in 1951. Hobsbawm distanced himself from a sociologically deterministic account of the decline of the Labour vote. Although there were great possibilities for the labour movement to resume the 'forward march' in the 1960s, workers lost faith in the party because of its inadequate leadership in this period. However, elsewhere he strongly correlated Labour's decline with the decline of the manual working class.[31] New white collar trade unionists were far less likely to support the Labour Party on a purely class basis. Third, the number of socialist activists had declined since the 1950s. He did, however, acknowledge that there had been the development in the 1960s of a radicalized, non-manual, ex-student, white collar and professional stratum, which formed a 'new' labour aristocracy. Finally, in support of his hypothesis about a decline in class consciousness, he later noted that workers were far less inclined to look to Eastern Europe for inspiration and were unenthusiastic about nationalization.[32]

Subsequently, Hobsbawm maintained that Labour's defeat in the elections of 1979, 1983 and 1987 merely confirmed his original thesis. In 1979 Labour's share of the vote was at its lowest since 1931. In absolute terms it had fallen from 14 million votes in 1951 to 11.5 million in 1979, and for the first time since 1923 Labour's electorate was smaller than the number of trade unionists affiliated to the TUC. Moreover, in 1979, a third of trade unionists voted Tory.[33] He observed in the 1983 elections that while the Labour vote was larger than that of any other party among the unskilled, semi-skilled, unemployed and trade unionists, it did not have majority support in any of these groups, and had lost support among all these groups since 1979.[34] As for the 1987 election, he noted that almost 50 per cent of Conservative support came from the working class, that two-thirds of skilled and 50 per cent of unskilled and semi-skilled workers voted for parties other than Labour, and that only 50 per cent of the unemployed voted Labour.[35] Thus, traditional working-class conscious-ness, as expressed in support for the Labour Party, had sharply declined, primarily as a result of the decline of the industrial proletariat.

These pessimistic observations served to reinforce Hobsbawm's general strategic point: the Labour Party had to broaden its electoral appeal. It could no longer rely on its traditional working-class constituency if it was serious about seeking office and replacing the Thatcher Government. The Labour Party had to become a 'people's party', and seek alliances to form a 'broad progressive front' that included blue and white collar workers, intellectuals and possibly left-of-centre middle-class supporters of the Social Democratic Party (SDP).[36] Labour had to appeal 'not only to working people, but [to] all who need ... a fairer and better world'. The future of Labour and the 'advance of socialism depends on mobilizing people who remember the date of the Beatles' break-up and not the date of the Saltley pickets'.[37] Labour could learn something from the successful 'neo-socialist' parties of France and Spain, as well as from the Italian Communist Party, which had been able to maintain its electoral strength. All these parties had turned away from narrow class issues.

Nevertheless, although he advocated a 'broad alliance' strategy, he claimed that this was not antithetical to 'class politics'. He was merely opposed to the sectarian 'class against class' policy of Comintern in the early 1930s, which had enabled Hitler to come to power. The key point, if only by implication, was that a broad alliance strategy was in the working classes' *interest*. Historically, the proletariat constituted a majority of the population in only a few countries. Lenin in 1917, for example, had to form an alliance with the peasantry in order to bring about a successful revolution. The strategy was effective in defeating Hitler, essential to the socialist revolutions in Eastern Europe after 1945, and in producing the radicalization that led to the Labour victory of 1945. Thus, 'to judge by results, it was by a long way the most effective strategy Communists have ever discovered in countries such as ours'.[38] Today, in Britain, 'we can no longer rely on an absolute majority [of the proletariat] to sweep a Labour government in single-handed'.[39] Hence, if Labour wanted to regain office, it had to ally itself with non-proletarian parties and social forces.

Hobsbawm's critics

His critics assessed his arguments in two broad areas. They examined the evidence that he had marshalled to support his case, and they questioned his proposed broad alliance strategy.

Many critics doubted whether on empirical grounds a secular political and economic decline in the working class had occurred since 1951. For example, the strength of the shop stewards' movement had grown enormously in the post-war period.[40] In addition, although there had been an important shift away from traditional manual jobs, the unionization of women had grown dramatically, reflecting the growth in female employment,[41] and union density had increased between 1967 and 1978.[42] Indeed, although the manual working class was smaller, it was a long way from disappearing. It still constituted half the labour force.[43] Manual workers were also more exploited or oppressed than other workers, experiencing more unemployment, fewer holidays and sickness benefits, with little possibility of individual social advancement. Culturally they were different from the rest of the population; for example, in choice of newspaper.[44]

Evidence could also be produced to show that sectionalism was declining: shop steward combine committees had developed,[45] trade unions had amalgamated[46] and trade unions in the public sector often had support for their struggles.[47] Anyway, sectionalism had always been a feature of the working-class movement.[48] Furthermore, 1970–4 was a notable period of working-class struggle in terms of militancy and solidarity, which culminated in the miners effectively bringing down the Tory Government in 1974.[49]

Moreover, many of the workers' struggles in the 1960s and 1970s, although they were about wages, could not be interpreted in a simple 'economistic' sense, because the state through directly interfering in collective bargaining had in effect made these struggles political.[50] Indeed, Hobsbawm had a narrow idea of the 'political', focusing exclusively on the parliamentary process, and thereby ignoring extra-parliamentary struggles in the 1960s and 1970s, which involved campaigns about disarmament, the war in Vietnam, trade union legislation and fascism. Even in electoral terms, although the 1983 election was an exceptionally bad year for Labour, once foremen and technicians were excluded from the manual working class, the party obtained 51 per cent of skilled and 48 per cent of semi- and unskilled workers' votes.[51] What Hobsbawm also tended to underplay was the Labour Party's alienation of traditional supporters when in office in the 1960s and 1970s.[52]

On a final empirical note, Hobsbawm, in later extending a similar diagnosis to the European movement, also ran into difficulty.[53] First, although a downturn started in the late 1970s, generally the period from the mid-1960s to the early 1980s was one of major working-class advance in terms of collective bargaining strength and the expansion of the welfare state, all in contrast to Hobsbawm's notion that the downturn began in the early 1950s.[54] Secondly, socialist parties had achieved significant election victories in the early 1980s, in France, Greece, Spain and Australia.[55]

The alliance strategy was the second major contested area of the Hobsbawm thesis. Insofar as he tended to suggest that class issues and those raised by new social movements were somehow antithetical, he was wrong to do so. The trade union movement had not been hostile to the peace movement,[56] and the women's movement, for example, had to acknowledge the full extent to which capitalism was responsible for increasing their oppression.[57] Although multiple forms of oppression existed, where the individual or group was located in the class structure could make a great difference as to the extent of their oppression.[58] Moreover, oppressed groups, such as women, could be united with men in the class struggle, as occurred during the 1984–5 miners' strike.[59] And insofar as capitalism contributed massively to oppression, the question arises as to whether there is any other class, other than the working class, which has the power and a basic interest in overthrowing capitalism.[60]

Just as crucially, the notion of the broad democratic alliance was problematic. It led to a dilution of radical policies and a hostility towards the left. It was also impracticable. A formula for uniting people of deeply differing opinions – as, say, between Labour and SDP supporters – was 'a perfect recipe for flabbiness and indecision in opposition, and ineffectiveness and failure in government'.[61] Furthermore, the broad democratic alliance in Hobsbawm's hands was the direct descendant of the anti-fascist 'popular front' strategy launched by Georgi Dimitrov, General Secretary of Comintern, in 1935. Historically, such fronts between workers' and bourgeois parties, which entailed a 'self-limiting formula' by the former parties, had not benefited the working class. Previously, they had contributed to the defeat of the Chinese working class in 1925–7, and the 1936 popular front government in France had pursued anti-working class policies. After the Second World War, Communist Parties in Western Europe had collaborated with their respective bourgeoisie in impeding social change.[62] Critics to the left of Hobsbawm outside the British Communist Party offered an alternative strategy not based upon class compromise, but centred upon workers' self-activity, attempting to unite them in struggle, whatever their different forms of oppression, occupation, status, etc.[63]

Commentary

Since the debate started in 1978, Hobsbawm could argue that events have strengthened his case. The number of manual workers in manufacturing, le union membership (especially as a result of unemployment), Labour Party membership (as well as a change in its composition from manual to white-collar workers) and the number of socialist activists had all declined. Nevertheless, the debate between Hobsbawm and his left-wing critics outside the Communist Party was really about different conceptions of the socialist project. Hobsbawm advocated the transformation of capitalism into socialism through parliament – socialism from above – whereas his left-wing critics, keeping to Marx's vision of socialism as consisting of workers' self-emancipation – socialism from below – stressed the importance of class struggle in both uniting workers and generating class consciousness. Hence, they had different notions of the 'political'. Hobsbawm viewed it almost exclusively in electoral terms, his critics more in the form of extra-parliamentary struggles, of which there were many in the late 1960s and early 1970s. Thus, they tended to use different indices of class consciousness. Hence, although the 'classic' labour movement may have declined, his critics argued that it had far from disappeared, was in the process of being reconstituted as capitalism changed and would become a 'class-for-itself' in struggle. Thus, rather than being seen as characterized by long-term decline, the labour movement could be perceived in terms of the ebb and flow of class struggle, of which 1970–4 would be regarded as a high point.

As a result of these differing fields of strategic vision, Hobsbawm's commitment to a parliamentary socialism meant that he assumed that his alliance strategy was relatively unproblematic, and although he held that Labour's performances in office might have had something to do with its decline, he did not pursue this point in any detail. Indeed, he ignored an exploration of the well-known contradiction of the Labour Party as a party *of* the working class, but not *for* the working class when in office, which would call into question his strategic assumptions.[64] Nevertheless, the assumption that whichever party is in office has a negligible impact on the balance of class forces is highly dubious in the light of the militantly anti-working class policies of the Tory governments since 1979.

LACLAU AND MOUFFE: WORKING CLASS DETHRONED

While Hobsbawm and Poulantzas played down the social and political significance of the working class in order to emphasize the need for the working class to ally itself with other classes, Laclau and Mouffe in *Hegemony and Socialist Strategy: towards a Radical Democratic Politics*[65] virtually eliminated workers *qua* workers from the political script altogether. In what they saw as a dialogue with, rather than a complete rejection of, Marxist theory, they proposed a complete rewriting of this script, with different actors and a different ending.[66] The new actors were the 'new social movements', involved in struggles over peace, ethnicity, sexual identity and gender. The new ending was the further development of 'radical and plural democracy', a process that began with the French Revolution of 1789, through a deepening and expansion of 'liberal-democratic' ideology.[67] They saw socialism as a 'moment internal to the democratic revolution'.[68] It was merely part of a larger struggle against oppressive, unequal power relations, and the relationship between the working class and socialism, if it existed, was contingent rather than necessary.[69]

For Laclau and Mouffe, too many problems existed in Marxist theory to support the notion of a historic goal of socialism in which the working class played a pre-eminent part. They argued that at the heart of the 'crisis of socialism' (i.e. Marxism) lay a growing mismatch between theory and reality. Marxism's theoretical shortcomings were exposed because they rested

> upon the ontological centrality of the working class, upon the role of Revolution, with a capital 'r', as the founding moment in the transition from the one type of society to another, and upon the illusory prospects of a perfectly unitary and homogenous collective that will render pointless the moment of politics.[70]

The working class had failed to live up to Marxism's expectations. Strongly influenced by the French post-structuralists, especially Michel Foucault and Jacques Derrida, Laclau and Mouffe sought to 'deconstruct' Marxism, thereby demonstrating that the 'privileging' of the proletariat was unsustainable.

That Marxist theory was fatally flawed from the start only gradually emerged as a result of its need for constant revision in order to keep a grip on reality. What was Laclau and Mouffe's version of Marxism? It told a simple story. Human history was a conflict between productive forces and production relations, which *necessarily* engendered new modes of production. Capitalism would inevitably be replaced by a socialist or communist mode of production through a revolution, made by the proletariat, whose common identity had been 'fixed' by the capitalist production relations and who wanted to overturn these relations because they were hindering the further development of the productive forces. Thus, the proletariat had an 'objective' interest in socialism and the potential ideological homogeneity to act as a class in the overthrow of capital. This narrative was guilty of many untenable 'isms'. First, it stood condemned by 'essentialism' and 'monism'. It gave a single explanation of, and meaning to, history, as moving inevitably towards communism, stemming from a simple conflict within the sphere of production. In highlighting the importance of economics it was thereby 'economistic' and 'reductionist' because it explained politics and ideology in terms of economic calculation. Such a reductionism in addition implied that society was 'transparent' rather than 'opaque' and 'complex'. Furthermore, by reducing individual identities to class identities Marxism was vitiated by 'classism'. The inevitability of communism was also rooted in historical necessity or determinism, which meant that Marxism was weakened by 'a priorism', entailed in the prediction of a proletarian revolution. Because of the workers' historic mission, their 'subject positions' were therefore 'fixed'. Thus, Marxism was a 'closed' system, which could not adequately account for the historically contingent fact that on the whole the working class had been either unwilling or unable to make a revolution.

The net result of Marxism's ontological and epistemological privileging of the proletariat *vis-à-vis* the 'masses' (e.g. the petty bourgeoisie and peasantry) was that it led necessarily, in a differentiated society such as post-revolutionary Russia, to authoritarianism.[71] Marxism could not adequately account for, and relate to, other forms of differentiation, such as fragmentation within the working class, 'popular' anti-fascist struggles in the inter-war period, anti-colonial revolutions in the Third World and contemporary new social movements. The latter movements were the product of the emergence of consumer capitalism and the welfare state, which had generated struggles for new rights in consumption and welfare.[72] In attempting to come to terms with these 'contingent' phenomena Marxism resorted to 'dualism', which suggested that departures from the 'normal' historical process were irrelevant or temporary. Working-class unity would occur at some point in the future.[73] All paths effectively led back to the monist logic of necessity.[74]

The reason for this theoretical failure lay in Marxism's ontologically primitive understanding of the formation of human identity. Every identity was 'precarious', manifesting itself as a 'continuous movement of differences'.[75] Laclau and Mouffe held that this 'precariousness' and 'unfixity' arose because individual identities were inherently relational; that is, they stemmed from a recognition of differences with other individuals. These differences were themselves unstable, presumably because perceptions (of self and the world), subjective desires and dispositions could never be taken as constant. Hence, there existed an 'irresoluble interiority/exteriority tension'.[76] The 'field of identities' never manages 'to be fully fixed'.[77] This meant that all social relations were contingent and open to constant negotiation, between what they termed 'floating signifiers'.

That the proletariat had failed to carry out its historic mission was therefore not surprising, especially in 'modern times'. There had occurred crucial changes in the forms of production and consumption, causing the 'reproduction of the different social areas' to take place 'in permanently changing conditions which constantly require the construction of new systems of differences'.[78] Their examination of the history of Marxism revealed that:

far from a rationalist game in which social agents, perfectly constituted around interests, wage a struggle defined by transparent parameters, we have seen the difficulties of the working class in constituting itself as a historical subject, the dispersion and fragmentation of its positionalities, the emergence of forms of social and political reaggregation – 'historical bloc', 'collective will', 'masses', 'popular sectors' – which define new objects and new logics of their conformation.[79]

Historically, the working class had failed to transform itself as a class-in-itself in the economic sphere to a class-for-itself in the political realm. Instead, it had concentrated on the reform of 'relations in production'.[80]

Nevertheless, they suggested that Marxism did try to come to terms with these 'contingent' developments and formulated a potentially fruitful concept – hegemony. This allowed the working class to adopt, albeit temporarily, a 'subject position', or an identity, different from its own. Thus, in late-nineteenth-century Russia, Plekhanov's response to the inability of the bourgeoisie to create a bourgeois revolution was to propose the 'hegemony of the proletariat'; that is, the proletariat undertaking the historic tasks of the bourgeoisie. Yet such a change of 'subject position' was merely 'external' to the Russian working class. Once proletarian revolutions had occurred in the West, it could return to its normal subject position and directly pursue its own interests.[81]

Lenin also developed the theory of hegemony, conceiving of it as a form of proletarian leadership in a class alliance with the peasantry. Hegemony was again 'external' to the working class, especially as the leadership 'represented' its interests. This resulted in authoritarianism, because the leadership 'substituted' itself for the working class. However, such a conception possessed a democratic potential because the political tasks of both the 'masses' (i.e. peasants) and the proletariat coexisted 'at the same historical conjuncture', thus encountering 'a plurality of antagonisms and points of rupture', which implied a more complex idea of social struggles.[82]

Laclau and Mouffe held that Gramsci's notion of hegemony was better than Lenin's. He incorporated into the concept an element of populist, non-class identity. He called for 'moral and intellectual' leadership, generating ideas and values 'shared by a number of sectors'. This created a 'collective will', which enabled 'certain subject positions' to 'traverse a number of class sectors'.[83] Crucially, this implied that the working class would lose its class identity. Nevertheless, Gramsci's concept was limited. It was still anchored in a strategy of class alliances, and it privileged the working class, which was identified as the ultimate, unifying hegemonic subject.[84]

Laclau and Mouffe, accordingly, sought to construct a theory of hegemony which was non-class based, non-authoritarian and democratic. Democratic hegemony could not be built upon a notion of representation, which was inherently authoritarian. Rather, it consisted of 'articulatory practices', which modified the identities of those participating. The totality of these practices constituted a 'discursive formation'. The differential positions within this formation were 'moments', and were contrasted with 'elements', which were differences not discursively articulated. What occurs through discourse is a transformation of pre-discursive elements into moments, i.e. identities discursively constructed. This process of discursive formation is open-ended, because the nature of the differences between the elements could not be determined in an *a priori* fashion, given their relational character and the 'irresoluble interiority/exteriority tension'.[85] Thus, although meaning and identity could be partially fixed in 'privileged discursive points', as 'nodal points', they were open to continual subversion. Concretely, this subversion was manifested in the growth of the new social movements, through a process of 'emergence', where a subject in a condition of subordination comes to realize that it is oppressive and 'articulates' this fact, thereby creating a new site of 'antagonism' and appropriate forms of political organization.

This is where democratic hegemony came in. Only through the medium of democracy could these identities emerge, allowing for all struggles against oppression to be 'equivalent' to each other, with none privileged. Given the 'radically open character of the social', the experience of democracy 'should consist of the recognition of the multiplicity of social logics along with the necessity of their articulation', which should be 'constantly re-created and re-negotiated'.[86] Laclau and Mouffe proposed a 'democratic revolution', consisting of the 'multiplication of spaces and ... institutional diversification', which allowed for a genuinely anti-authoritarian form of hegemony to arise through some form of unifying discourse developed by oppressed groups.[87] Such a revolution would enable diverse oppressed groups through the political construction of the 'social' to overcome their specific forms of domination, and would allow for new types of struggle against inequality to arise in an open-ended process.

Criticisms

Whilst diverse criticisms have been made of Laclau and Mouffe's work, the primary focus will be on their rejection of the working class as *the* agent of socialism and their proposed strategy based upon democracy and a developing hegemony of new social movements.[88]

Ellen Meiksins Wood has challenged their critique of the Marxist historical plot, the working class automatically uniting in a moment of revolutionary 'chiliasm' to overthrow the capitalists, who at some stage will be unable to develop the productive forces. This scenario, they argued, rested on the assumption that the economy was a primary and autonomous sphere, operating on the basis of neutral or natural self-regulating, endogenous laws, which constituted social agents.[89] The neutrality of the economic realm was underpinned by the notion that labour power was a commodity like any other. On the contrary, it was not a commodity like any other, because it consisted of human beings 'capable of social practices'.[90] For this reason the productive sphere became a site of capitalist domination and workers' resistance; that is, of 'political' contestation. The development of the productive forces was powerfully shaped by this conflict. Thus, the economic realm was neither autonomous, because it was intensely political, nor subject to 'natural' deterministic laws, owing to workers' struggles.

Wood responded to this interpretation by maintaining that it was merely a 're-statement' of a central feature of Marx's analysis of the capitalist labour process as depicted in *Capital*, where living labour was subjected to the imperatives of commodity production and the creation of surplus value. The resulting contradiction lay at the heart of class antagonisms within capitalist society. The forms of domination and resistance were both political and social within the economic sphere, and were also 'organically' connected to external political and social spheres.[91] Hence, Marx did not make crude divisions between these different spheres. Nor did he conceive of the 'economic' in a simplistic manner.

Wood also criticized their argument against the Marxist conception of the relationship between the working class and socialism, that working-class unity and its socialist impulse were a 'simple effect of capitalist development'. They concluded that if such unity and the socialist goal could not be achieved without 'external intervention' from the realms of ideology and politics, then its own economistic premises were undermined. Moreover, if the working class required political education from an external agent, and was unable to create its own identity, unity and socialist objectives, then it was like any other class or group whose interests had to be 'discursively constructed'. As a result the working class could not be said to have an 'objective interest' in socialism. It thereby lost its privileged status. Wood suggested that this implied that workers' material interests were generated through 'discursive construction' and not through a process of exploitation. The ultimate inference was that 'a caveman is as likely to become a socialist as is a proletarian – provided only that he comes within hailing distance of the appropriate discourse'.[92]

She denied their root assumption that all social identities were 'discursively constructed'. This, in effect, undermined any notion of historical and social process. The way in which they viewed Marx's theory of history meant that

> where there is no simple, absolute, mechanical, unilinear, and non-contradictory determination, there is no determinacy, no relationship,

no causality at all. There are no historical conditions, connections, limits, possibilities. There are only arbitrary juxtapositions, 'conjunctures', and contingencies. If anything holds the discrete and isolated fragments of reality together, it is only the logic of discourse.[93]

This brings us to the second major area of criticism, of their proposed strategy. Most critics have stressed Laclau and Mouffe's voluntarism and philosophical idealism grounded in their discourse analysis.[94] The world of social, economic and political relations, which shape and provide the content of such discourse, is only erratically referred to. The general lack of acknowledgement of what we may term 'extra-discursive conditions' had profound strategic implications. Thus, Geras and Mouzelis argued that because Laclau and Mouffe were unwilling to explain the conditions for why certain 'articulatory practices' do and did predominate over others, they are unable to provide any theoretical means of assessing whether some of these practices are more central than others in 'hegemonizing' a political space.[95] Nothing, then, can be said in advance about the relative importance of subject positions in a strategy of socialist transformation. Strategic privileging does not, *contra* Laclau and Mouffe, necessarily entail essentialism, for it can involve an analysis of institutions and structures within capitalism which can recognize systematic differences. They are in effect saying that 'anything goes', with all social movements equally capable of playing a hegemonic role, whether a workers' or a sexual liberation movement.[96]

Further, they offered no account of the 'conditions of possibility' for the development of hegemony, where there was enough stability in discursive construction for relations of subordination to be converted into relations of oppression and then into political organization. Yet at the same time there must be sufficient fluidity for these oppressed groups to form part of a chain of democratic equivalents, and, through articulatory practice, to change their identities to become part of an expanding hegemony without losing sight of the component group's original demands.[97]

Their inability to prioritize any hegemonic forces in advance stemmed not only from their failure to consider adequately the extra-discursive dimension, but also from their avoidance of normative questions, derived from their commitment to the politics of identity, the 'logic of equivalence' and attendant relativism. While they saw themselves as 'progressive', their position forbade them to identify which groups might be progressive. To do so would be to fall into the trap of unwittingly committing themselves to the potentially universalistic discourse of human nature, 'objective interests' and justice.[98]

Another consequence of underemphasizing or ignoring extra-discursive conditions was that they defined the 'political' as 'the practice of creating, reproducing and transforming social relations'.[99] Thus, all social relations were political ('the personal is political'), which meant that they saw the boundaries between the political and the social as totally unfixed and political spaces as undifferentiated. As a consequence, actual social and political institutions which concretely embodied power relations and the question of how they were to be analysed and transformed were deemed unimportant.[100]

Specifically, their neglect of the extra-discursive realm created crucial weaknesses in their discussion of democracy. They did not provide any clear idea of the procedures and institutional forms it should take.[101] Equally significantly, Wood indicated, they did not consider how democratic discourse itself was shaped by class interest. There is nothing inherently egalitarian about democracy, especially in its liberal form, which Laclau and Mouffe sought to 'widen and deepen'. Liberal democracy glossed over capitalist relations of subordination and exploitation, and subverted the original Greek meaning of democracy as rule by the poor, by restricting the scope of popular power. Hence, a potential conflict arose over the meaning of democracy itself owing to antagonistic class interests. Liberal and socialist discourses on democracy 'have their roots in anterior social relations'.[102] Therefore, socialism could not be viewed merely as part of a democratic revolution, because ultimately socialist and liberal visions of democracy were different.

Commentary

Laclau and Mouffe's work contains a number of positive qualities. They attempt to address problems that Marxists have either ignored or not satisfactorily addressed. In particular, they highlight the difficulties surrounding the process of how the working class transforms itself from a class-in-itself into a class-for-itself, especially within the context of changes in the nature of work and consumption generated by modern capitalism. Second, they explore a theoretical area where Marxism has been notoriously weak. In focusing on the macro-socio-historical level it has, especially in its deterministic form, largely ignored the question of how personal and group identities are formed. And third, they are very much alive to the totalitarian dangers inherent at least in certain forms of Marxism.

Nevertheless, their critics make some telling points. First, Laclau and Mouffe constructed an incorrect and highly simplified – indeed, Cold War – model of Marxism. Second, in reducing the meaning of the world to discursive construction and people to 'floating signifiers' for fear of 'essentialism', they were unable to consider 'objective', extra-discursive factors that can have a decisive impact on this process, and on formulating a political strategy. Their reluctance to privilege any social agent as a result of identity politics and their fear of advocating anything potentially authoritarian could be attributable to a confusion about the notion of 'privileging' itself. They see the privileging of the working class as possessing a compelling, authoritarian logic: the interests of the working class are privileged in relation to other classes, the working class is 'represented' by the party, the leadership of the party substitutes itself for the working class. However, there is no reason why in principle privileging has to go down this slippery slope. There can be a strategic privileging of the working class owing to its potential power in overthrowing capitalism, and there is no reason why oppressed groups, who often may be members of the working class, cannot be authentically represented in such a movement. Nor is there any reason in principle why a political party has to substitute itself for the working class. What seems to be missing in Laclau and Mouffe's analysis, because they see discourse in a self-contained way, is the interplay of ideas and circumstances, or of discourse and extra-discursive conditions. Hence, Stalinism ought in part to be explained by the post-revolutionary conditions that existed in the Soviet Union, rather than be simplistically ascribed to the privileging of the working class, the product of Marxist 'essentialism'.

In order to avoid any taint of authoritarianism, they have presented a highly abstract theory with little 'practico-normative' content.[103] However, they could be seen as equally guilty of certain forms of essentialism, in their categorical anti-essentialism, in their insistence that all struggles against oppression are 'equivalent' and in their championing of liberal democracy.

Yet, although many of Laclau and Mouffe's arguments and solutions to the problems that face Marxists may not have been satisfactory, they raise in a very clear fashion questions of personal identity and forms of political representation that they have to address if Marxists want to claim that their discourse is *the* discourse of human emancipation.

GENERAL COMMENTS

The fundamental question of this chapter has been whether the working class should be written off as the key social agent in the struggle for socialism, whether we should say farewell to the working class. As we have seen, 'farewell' can be taken to have different senses. For Poulantzas it meant that it was literally becoming a diminishing part of the workforce. This proposition, as we have seen, is hard to accept. Globally, there would appear to be a growing working class, and in Europe and North America it has undergone a significant re-composition. Hobsbawm bade farewell to the classic labour movement, which had been the fundamental source of the labour vote. His response, a widening of Labour's electoral appeal to other classes, may of course enable the party to become a party of government again. However, such a government would probably be even more impotent in bringing about socialism, at least from a Marxist perspective, than previous Labour governments. Laclau and Mouffe, in concentrating on new social movements, said very little about what sort of role workers as workers should have in the struggle for socialism, which they saw as a 'moment' in the democratic revolution. Indeed, their emphasis on the 'equivalence' of all struggles against oppression and their unwillingness to incorporate these movements within a broader socialist movement, possibly to avoid accusations of authoritarianism, meant that in effect they were silent on the issue of an appropriate socialist strategy. Further, they did not discuss how the struggles of the new social movements could be integrated into the struggle for socialism.

In a more general sense, on the question of bidding farewell to the working class as a potentially unified political force or as a force wanting socialism, the jury is still out, if only because historical prediction is notoriously difficult. Few predicted the collapse of the Eastern European regimes in 1989. Historically, the working class has been involved in waves of struggle, experiencing clear moments of unity, such as in Russia in 1917, subsequently in various parts of Europe until the mid-1920s, again in Europe after the Second World War and from 1968 until the mid-1970s. There have also been massive working-class struggles in Brazil, South Korea and South Africa.

However, the working class ideologically has tended towards reform rather than revolution. Yet in considering its revolutionary potential something crucial has to be noted. Those who wish to bid it farewell in a revolutionary sense usually focus solely on the working class itself, and not on the way in which the capitalist class can exercise an extraordinary influence upon it, through physical repression and ideological control, or by creating divisions within it. Thus, the possibility of a revolutionary turn in the working class in the future cannot be categorically ruled out, if a deep, multi-faceted capitalist crisis occurred at all levels, economic, social, political and ideological, so that the capitalist class had neither the physical nor the moral resources to continue its rule.

NOTES

1. Andre Gorz, *Farewell to the Working Class*, Pluto Press, London (1982). For a critique, see R. Hyman, 'Andre Gorz and his disappearing proletariat' in R. Miliband and J. Saville (Eds), *Socialist Register, 1983*, Merlin Press, London.
2. A term first used by John Westergaard in the 'Class of '84', *New Socialist*, 15, (Jan/Feb 1984), and taken up by Ralph Miliband in his article, 'New revisionism in Britain', *New Left Review*, 150 (March/April 1985), 5–26, in his discussion of the politics of communist intellectuals writing for *Marxism Today*.
3. K. Marx, *Theories of Surplus Value, Vol. 3*, Lawrence and Wishart, London

(1969), 573. Marx also soon after *The Communist Manifesto* acknowledged the class complexities of existing social formations, although until this crucial modification, as we have noted, he believed that capitalist development would simplify them. See A. Cottrell, *Social Classes in Marxist Theory*, Routledge and Kegan Paul, London (1984), Chapter 1.

4. K. Marx, *The Poverty of Philosophy*, Progress Publishers, Moscow (1955), 150. See also *CM*, 63 and 67.
5. N. Poulantzas, *Classes in Contemporary Capitalism* (hereafter *CCC*), New Left Books, London (1975).
6. N. Poulantzas, 'On social classes', *New Left Review*, 78 (March/April 1973), 34.
7. *CCC*, 334-5.
8. *CCC*, 335.
9. *CCC*, 335.
10. *CCC*, 20. Cf. 'On social classes', 30.
11. *CCC*, 216, Poulantzas's emphasis.
12. 'On social classes', 31.
13. *CCC*, 21.
14. 'On social classes', 31.
15. *Ibid.*, 35.
16. E. O. Wright, 'Class boundaries in advanced capitalist societies', *New Left Review*, 98 (July/August 1976) (hereafter *CBACS*).
17. *CCC*, 15.
18. 'On social classes', 37-8, cf. *CCC*, 291-9.
19. *CBACS*. See also P. M. Wood, 'Productive and unproductive labor and Marx's theory of class', *Review of Radical Political Economics*, 13, 3 (1981), 32-42; E. Mandel, *From Stalinism to Eurocommunism*, New Left Books, London (1978), 209-10; E. M. Wood, *The Retreat from Class*, Verso, London (1986), Chapter 3 *passim*.
20. K. Marx, *Capital, Vol. 1*, Penguin, Harmondsworth (1976), 644.
21. *CBACS*, 15.
22. *CBACS*, 16.
23. *CBACS*, 19.
24. *CBACS*, 24.
25. E.g. G. Carchedi, *On the Economic Identification of Social Classes*, Routledge and Kegan Paul, London (1977); E. O. Wright, *Class, Crisis and the State*, New Left Books, London (1978); Cottrell, *op. cit.*
26. K. Marx, *Capital, Vol. 3*, Penguin, Harmondsworth (1981), 407.
27. Marx, *Capital, Vol. 1*, 1039-40.
28. See E. O. Wright, *Class, Crisis and the State* and *The Debate on Classes*, Verso, London (1989); A. Callinicos and C. Harman (Eds), *The Changing Working Class*, Bookmarks, London (1987); Carchedi, *op. cit.*; B. and J. Ehrenreich, 'The professional-managerial class' in P. Walker (Ed.), *Between Labour and Capital*, Harvester, Hassocks (1979).
29. Also note S. Hall's thesis on Thatcher's 'authoritarian populism', justifying such alliances, in e.g. S. Hall *et al.*, *Policing the Crisis*, Macmillan, London (1978).
30. M. Jacques and F. Mulhern (Eds), *The Forward March of Labour Halted?*,

(hereafter *FMLH*), Verso, London (1981).
31. *FMLH*, 176.
32. *FMLH*, 177.
33. *FMLH*, 169.
34. E. Hobsbawm, *Politics for a Rational Left*, Verso, London (1989), 63.
35. E. Hobsbawm, 'Farewell to the classic labour movement?' *New Left Review*, 173 (Jan/Feb 1989), 73.
36. *FMLH*, 179-80.
37. *FMLH*, 181.
38. Hobsbawm, *Politics for a Rational Left*, 93.
39. *Ibid.*
40. K. Gill in *FMLH*, 23.
41. Gill, *FMLH*, 23; R. Harrison in *FMLH*, 55; S. Jefferys in *FMLH*, 103-4.
42. Jeffreys, *FMLH*, 104.
43. C. Harman, 'The working class after the recession', in Callinicos and Harman, *op. cit.*, 59. See also R. Miliband, 'The new revisionism in Britain', *op. cit.*, 9. Even less so on a global scale: see P. Kellogg, 'Goodbye to the working class?', *International Socialism* (second series), 36 (Autumn 1987), 105-11.
44. Harman, *op. cit.*, 60-2.
45. H. Wainwright in *FMLH*, 129.
46. Harrison, *FMLH*, 56.
47. Wainwright, *FMLH*, 130.
48. Harrison, *FMLH*, 55-6.
49. Gill, *FMLH*, 21; K. Halpin in *FMLH*, 36; Harrison, *FMLH*, 55. See also A. Callinicos, 'The politics of "Marxism Today"', *International Socialism* (second series), 29 (Summer 1985), 146-7.
50. Gill, *FMLH*, 21; Harrison, *FMLH*, 57.
51. C. Harman, 'How the working class votes' in Callinicos and Harman, *op. cit.*, 84.
52. B. Fine *et al.*, *Class Politics: an Answer to Its Critics*, Leftover Pamphlets, London (1984), 33; Callinicos, *op. cit.*, 146.
53. 'The state of the left in Western Europe', *Marxism Today* (October 1982).
54. Callinicos, *op. cit.*, 145.
55. *Ibid.*
56. Fine, *op. cit.*, 29.
57. *Ibid.*, 44.
58. Miliband, *op. cit.*, 10.
59. *Ibid.*, 10-11.
60. *Ibid.*, 12-13.
61. *Ibid.*, 21.
62. Callinicos, *op. cit.*, 156-7.
63. E.g. Miliband, *op. cit.*, 10-11.
64. See the explorations in the works of R. Miliband, *Parliamentary Socialism*, Merlin, London (1961); L. Panitch, *Social Democracy and Industrial Militancy*, Cambridge University Press, Cambridge (1976); D. Coates, *Labour in Power?* Longmans, London (1980).
65. E. Laclau and C. Mouffe, *Hegemony and Socialist Strategy: towards a Radical Democratic Politics* (hereafter *HSS*), Verso, London (1985).

66. They claim that their book is both '*post*-Marxist' and 'post-*Marxist*', HSS, 4.
67. *HSS*, 176.
68. *HSS*, 156.
69. *HSS*, 84.
70. *HSS*, 2.
71. *HSS*, 56–7.
72. *HSS*, 161–2.
73. *HSS*, 151.
74. *HSS*, 47–8.
75. *HSS*, 122.
76. *HSS*, 111.
77. *HSS*, 111.
78. *HSS*, 138.
79. *HSS*, 104–5.
80. *HSS*, 157.
81. *HSS*, 54.
82. *HSS*, 55–6.
83. *HSS*, 66.
84. *HSS*, 66, 69 and 76.
85. *HSS*, 111–13.
86. *HSS*, 188.
87. *HSS*, 189.
88. See Norman Geras, *Discourses of Extremity* (hereafter *DE*), Verso, London (1990) for a comprehensive rejection of their style of argument, ontology and epistemology.
89. *HSS*, 77–80.
90. *HSS*, 78.
91. E. M. Wood, *The Retreat from Class* (hereafter *RFC*), 59.
92. *RFC*, 61. See also *DE*, 76–7, 118.
93. *RFC*, 62.
94. E.g. M. Rustin, 'Absolute voluntarism: critique of a post-Marxist concept of hegemony', *New German Critique*, 43 (Winter 1988), 147–73; *DE*, 98–102.
95. *DE*, 108–9; N. Mouzelis, 'Marxism or post-Marxism?', *New Left Review*, 167 (Jan/Feb 1988), 115–16.
96. Mouzelis, *ibid*.
97. P. Osborne, *Socialism and the Limits of Liberalism*, Verso, London (1991), 217–18.
98. *DE*, 110–11.
99. *HSS* 153.
100. Mouzelis, *op. cit.*, 119; Osborne, *op. cit.*, 220.
101. *DE*, 116–17.
102. *RFC*, 68–9.
103. *DE*, 110.

15
Has Marxist Politics a Future?

In this book the political debates have been treated either implicitly or explicitly as a continuation of a discussion of the various arguments set out in *The Communist Manifesto*. Controversy arose because an unpredictable reality constantly broke out of the theoretical template established in the *Manifesto*. The question now firmly placed on the historical agenda is whether this passionate debate, neatly spanning a century from the founding of the Second International in 1889 to the fall of the Berlin Wall in 1989, will fall silent. Will there be no more chapters to write on the history of Marxist politics, because 'history' itself has arrived at its ultimate destination in the form of liberal capitalism? Is Marxism not merely hugely overdrawn but a bankrupt political force in the modern world, destined to continue 'only in the academic playgrounds of the West'?[1] Have the collapse of the self-styled Marxist regimes of Eastern Europe, the persistent failure of the Western working class to carry out its revolutionary role according to the Marxist script, the rise of new social movements that owe little to Marxism and the postmodernist onslaught against all 'grand narratives' rendered the current crisis of Marxism terminal?

Obviously any speculation on this question has to be made in a muted register. Historical prediction is notoriously difficult, as confirmed by the unforeseen historical circumstances prompting the debates in the foregoing chapters. Or take the politics of the post-war period: few in the mid-1980s would have foretold the rapid demise of the totalitarian regimes of Eastern Europe. Similarly, few in the 1960s would have predicted the ascendency of right-wing neo-liberalism in the United States and Britain in the 1980s, when at the time it was confined to a lunatic fringe. Indeed, this demonstrates just how rapidly marginal ideologies can fill political vacuums in periods of social, economic and political instability. Thus, just as prediction is problematic, historical possibilities cannot be eliminated either. Moreover, the difficulty of foretelling the future of ideologies is compounded by the fact that no necessary relation exists between an ideology and its institutional embodiment. For example, the British Liberal Party as a hegemonic force collapsed during the First World War. Yet liberalism as an ideology in its 'new' liberal form continued, arguably, in the Labour Party, and in its 'old' liberal configuration was reincarnated in the 1980s Tory Party. In a slightly different way, the relationship between Marx's original vision and the movements he spawned could be conceived as problematic, with, to put the matter crudely, the bureaucratic, reformist Marxism of the Second International, the bureaucratic, Soviet-centred Marxism of the Third and the messianic, internationalist Marxism of the Fourth.

RESPONSES TO THE CRISIS OF MARXISM

Before we look at this question directly, various responses to the crisis of Marxism will be examined. Marxists have had to react to 'end of history' triumphalism, associated with the fall of communism in Eastern Europe, and demonstrate Marxism's continued relevance as a political creed; this collapse also compelled them to reflect upon the meaning of the Soviet 'experiment'; they have considered socialist alternatives to centralized planning (an intellectual project started long before the collapse); in addition, various strategic possibilities have been contemplated; finally, they have meditated upon various theoretical revisions. Their responses to the postmodernist critique will be omitted here. This issue has in part been dealt with in Chapter 14 and sustained and plausible defences of Marxism[2] and counter-critiques of postmodernism have been mounted.[3] And, interestingly, one of the leading lights in the postmodernist firmament, Jacques Derrida, has proclaimed his wish to be associated with a 'certain spirit of Marxism', namely its capacity to criticize itself and the 'multiple logics of capital'.[4]

The end of history?

Marxists have had to reply to the 'end of history' hypothesis advanced most notably by Francis Fukuyama in *The End of History and the Last Man*.[5] His central proposition was straightforward: liberal democratic capitalism marked the institutional end-point of human economic and political progress. Historically, no rational alternative existed: 'there could be no further progress in the development of the underlying principles and institutions, because all the really big questions had been settled'.[6] Democratic capitalism satisfied two of the most fundamental human needs, celebrated in Western political philosophy from Plato onwards. The first was the desire for individual recognition, originally conceived by Plato as *thymos*, part of the human soul that demanded justice, and later developed by Hegel. Humans were essentially social beings, who could get a sense of their own self-worth only through recognition by others. Liberal democracy, unlike previous political organizations, was built on a system of universal individual rights. The second need, corresponding to the 'appetitive' element of the human soul as depicted by Plato, was the demand for material satisfaction. Capitalism was the product of human reason applied to nature, the application of science and technology, involving a sophisticated division of labour. There was no conceivably more productive economic system. Capitalism also encouraged liberal democracy, because economic development required an educated work-force, which demanded democratic rights.[7]

Communist regimes failed on both counts: their totalitarian political structures could not provide individual recognition;[8] their centrally planned economies were unable to compete in the new, highly complex and dynamic 'post-industrial' international environment.[9] Fukuyama admitted that liberal democracies were 'plagued by a host of problems like unemployment, pollution, drugs, crime and the like', but stated that nevertheless they satisfied 'the most fundamental human longing', the desire for recognition.[10]

Marxists rebutting his thesis have done so on four levels. First, they questioned the empirical plausibility of his argument. He had not demonstrated that capitalism could bring about universal prosperity.[11] Whatever the internal obstacles within the accumulation process itself, there were also contingent factors: ecological limits to consumption levels[12] and the barriers of the nation-state to the bringing about of international economic equality.[13] Furthermore, there was little evidence that the satisfaction of *thymos* existed even in the liberal democratic epicentre. Only 50 per cent of US voters participated in elections.[14] Moreover, the supposed correlation between the spread of capitalist prosperity and democracy was unfounded, as capitalist development in Asia demonstrated.[15] And if authoritarian capitalist states consistently outperformed liberal democratic ones economically, then there was little reason to assume any automatic correlation.[16] Indeed, Fukuyama exaggerated the global expansion of liberal democracy. Only 24 out of 180 independent states could claim to be liberal democratic.[17] Addition-ally, the human problems highlighted by Hegel – war, poverty and lack of community – were still all too evident.[18]

At a second level, Marxist critics of Fukuyama highlighted what they regarded as his conceptual weaknesses. In viewing science (the product of the desire to satisfy material needs) and the desire for recognition as the twin forces in history, he was philosophically idealist. He ignored the dynamic generated by the collective political action classes, nations and states.[19] The same could be said for his view of human nature, which along with his notion of *thymos* was ahistorical. He was thus unable to see how specific, historically shaped meanings had an ideological function in serving the interests of various ruling classes.[20] Moreover, in stressing the hubristic elements in human nature, Fukuyama offered a decidedly masculine perspective.[21]

Third, the critics maintained that his position was incoherent. He did not acknowledge the potential instability of the relationship between capitalism and liberal democracy. Elected majority socialist parties intent on changing capitalism soon experience the disappearance of parliamentary democracy, as occurred in Chile in 1973.[22] More conceptually, a tension existed between the individualism fostered by capitalism and the moral requirements of democracy which demanded ethical reflection on social choices.[23] Fukuyama admitted that liberal contractualism and capitalism could undermine the sense of community essential to satisfying the desire for recognition.[24] This pointed to a deeper tension between the desire for material satisfaction and the desire for recognition. He acknowledged the success of the authoritarian Asian capitalist economies in relation to the democratic capitalist ones. Thus, the 'appetitive' part of the human soul was hard to reconcile with *thymos*.[25] Finally, he did not entertain the logical possibility that the desire for recognition could lead to radical egalitarian demands.[26]

This brings us to the fourth area of criticism: his failure to address seriously the possibility of a socialist alternative to liberal capitalism. Institutionally, he ignored the case for socialist democracy, i.e. a mixed economy with significant elements of economic planning and social ownership, involving a strong state, held in check through democratic accountability and a well-developed 'civil society'.[27] Wrongly, he assumed that the sources of socialism had evaporated. Preconditions for international socialism were being created through increased global interdependence arising from the development of multinational corporations. And although the global industrial workforce was a diminishing proportion of the global population, the proportion of wage earners had increased. Further, corporate planning had increased, as had equality as a 'legal claim and customary norm'.[28] Finally, socialist theory was in the process of revision, recognizing, for example, the need for some form of market, albeit a socialized one, a more accountable form of democracy and a broadened appeal to include not merely the proletariat but also other wage earners.[29]

The fall of communism

Some Marxists have claimed that the collapse of the Soviet Union and its satellite states had little to do with Marxism, because they were not truly Marxist. The demise marked the 'end of an experiment, socialism in one zone, which had nothing to do with the Marxism of Marx'.[30] Or it was the death of 'really inexisting socialism'.[31] Or it signified 'a step sideways from one form of capitalism to another, from the state capitalism of the early

20th century to the multinational capitalism of our *fin de siècle*.[32] The Soviet-styled regimes had little in common with Marx's vision of proletarian self-emancipation.[33] Or these regimes were characterized as class regimes, which were neither capitalist nor socialist.[34]

Such Marxists also held that a Marxist explanation could be deployed to understand the débâcle. The Soviet Union could be seen as quickly ceasing to be socialist after its inception in 1917, as a result of its isolation and material scarcity.[35] The Soviet system of bureaucratic planning could be viewed as a fetter holding back the productive forces as demand became more heterogeneous.[36] Or the Soviet Union was perceived as being unable to adapt to the increased globalization of capital since the 1970s, which rendered states less able to control their internal economies.[37] These Marxists thus claimed that the failure of these regimes signalled not the death of Marxism, but its liberation from Stalinism.[38]

However, other Marxists insisted that the Soviet experience could not be so easily discarded. The Soviet state had been run by people who thought they were Marxists, and it implemented some key aspects of a Marxist political programme, i.e. public ownership and popular welfare and employment measures. The practice of the regime also revealed 'blindspots' in Marxist thought; for example, the 'rule of law, or the rights of the individual, or the need for checks and balances in political structures, or the abolition of commodity–money relations'.[39] In addition, Leninism had to be re-evaluated.[40]

Marxism's continuing relevance

Marxists have insisted that their case for socialism is still as relevant as ever, as an explanation of capitalism's problems, which cannot be 'reformed' away, thereby proving the need for an alternative political, economic and social system. Problems include: the economic difficulties within the former Soviet bloc now that it is firmly locked into the international capitalist system; Third World austerity programmes stemming from international indebtedness; famines; ecological limits to growth and international economic inequality; international migration.[41] Further, the increased movements of international capital were generating problems of global dimensions.[42] Finally, the ending of the Cold War had ushered in a new era of global political instability, a 'back to the future' of before 1914, of multipolar inter-state conflict.[43] This manifested itself in nationalist rivalries in Eastern Europe, Greater Russian nationalism, German expansionism and various conflicts in the Middle East. Hence, the stark choice of socialism or barbarism clearly presented itself.[44] All this pointed to the need for an international socialist movement and organization capable of dealing with such problems.

Economic and political alternatives to capitalism

For some Marxists the Soviet 'experiment' was an object lesson in 'what is not to be done'. They agreed that centralized planning on a command basis became increasingly inefficient. In contemplating an alternative economic system, they defined themselves in relation to Alec Nove's ground-breaking work, *The Economics of Feasible Socialism*.[45] As a result of his analysis of the Soviet economy he came to the conclusion that effective, detailed central planning was impossible, owing to the inherent lack of total knowledge and foresight entailed in such a process. He proposed a dual economy. There was to be a state sector concerned with some state planning, which related to major investments and the need to avoid duplication and waste. This sector would also be responsible for the administration of natural monopolies, the restriction of income differentials, the control of inflation, the regulation of unemployment and the administration of social services. The other sector would consist of cooperatives and small capitalist firms, which would survive through making profits, having to bear the costs of their own mistakes.

Marxists have responded to Nove in a number of ways. Some have rejected his views outright. In doing so, they have pointed out the waste and inefficiency of the market[46] and the existence of much planning under capitalism within large firms.[47] They have additionally rejected market socialism on moral grounds as promoting inequality and sustaining the motives of greed and fear.[48] Furthermore, it lacked the transformatory potential to develop people's sense of social responsibility and was unable to eliminate alienation.[49] Differences of opinion clearly emerged over the role of the market in a socialist society. Some saw it as having either a minimal role[50] or a temporary one in the transition to socialism.[51] They emphasized the virtues of democratic planning by self-managing enterprises, which have inputs from consumers and other interest groups.[52] The notion of democratic planning has been most comprehensively dealt with by Pat Devine in *Democracy and Democratic Planning*.[53] It is based upon the principle of 'negotiated coordination', and rests on a distinction between market exchange and market forces.[54] Others, however, have stressed the importance of the market as a planning tool, rather than as the decisive regulator of output and consumption. The market would be 'socialized' through 'price and wage commissions', using information technology and involving various interest groups. A public sector would exist, accountable to a 'regulator of public enterprises'.[55]

As for alternative socialist political systems, all agreed that a socialist society had to be more democratic than either liberal capitalism or the former communist regimes. Some, such as Callinicos, have championed the model of Soviet democracy celebrated in Lenin's *The State and Revolution*. This form of socialist democracy, based upon the workplace, was superior to formal, liberal democracy. The key to preventing degeneration was the existence of a large working class and a revolution of international dimensions.[56] Anderson, arguing against this position, has warned against 'too close an imaginative adherence to the paradigm of the October Revolution, made against the husk of a feudal monarchy, and too distant a theoretical concern with the contours of a capitalist democracy the Bolsheviks never had to confront'.[57] And Miliband remarked that, historically, Soviets have not proved a viable alternative to bourgeois democracy. The idea of council communism has had only marginal support among the Western European working class, and in Eastern Europe since 1989 and in Latin America there has been the spread of liberal democracy.[58] A fundamental consideration could not be ignored: 'habit and tradition, deeply encrusted beliefs and ancient prejudices, inherited patterns of thought and behaviour' formed part of a 'stubborn reality, with a remarkable capacity to endure'.[59] Thus, socialists had to participate in electoral struggles, while simultaneously exposing the limitations of parliamentary democracy.[60] Socialist democracy represented 'both an *extension* of capitalist democracy and a *transcendence* of it'.[61]

Agency and strategy

The current crisis of Marxism has been associated with the crisis of human agency, or the 'crisis of the identification of the revolutionary subject'; that is, the inability of the proletariat to play its historical part.[62] Some commentators have suggested that the working class could behave as traditionally conceived by Marxists in the semi-peripheral areas of world capitalism, such as South Korea, South Africa, Brazil, Mexico and Poland.[63] And class movements in the Third World have been viewed as playing a key strategic role.[64] The feminist and green 'New Left' in Finland, Norway, Denmark, Spain, Turkey and the Netherlands and working-class opposition to capitalist restructuring in Eastern Europe have also been cited as significant.[65]

In their search for socialist agency some Marxists, apart from those within the communist tradition discussed in Chapter 14, have argued that alliances are crucial. Adam Przeworski has argued that, in electoral terms, working-class parties, because the proletariat usually constitutes a minority of the electorate, have had to woo allies from other classes at the risk of watering down their socialist programme.[66] Lawrence Wilde has advocated a uniting of 'old' labour movements and 'new' social movements through 'pluralist negotiation' against global capitalism.[67] Erik Olin Wright has suggested that an analysis of the conditions and the devising of a strategy are necessary in order to unite the middle class and the underclass around the working class in the struggle for socialism.[68]

And Goran Therborn has proposed the building of a movement through alliances on the basis of 'life politics', a programme concerned with the environment and human rights in the broadest senses of the term.[69]

Strategic rethinking has also entailed questioning the validity of the distinction between reform and revolution, and the preference for the latter over the former, within Marxism. First, reformist themes existed in Marx's own writing; for example, with reference to factory legislation in *Capital*.[70] Second, a tension existed in Marx's writings between evolutionary and revolutionary transformation. He acknowledged that capitalism had taken centuries to develop, yet assumed that it would quickly disappear. If capitalism's longevity was unpredictable, then reforms could play a useful part in laying the basis for a future socialist society. For example, the reform of state education could help to prepare workers culturally for industrial democracy.[71] Finally, preferences for either reform or revolution should not be held as strategic dogmas. They depended upon the situation in which mass movements found themselves, and whether institutions could accede to their demands. If they could not, the choice had to be revolution, but if they could, then reforms could be viewed as beneficial in promoting societal change by, for instance, transforming workers' perceptions of themselves and promoting class awareness and new sets of demands.[72]

Revising Marxism

The major theoretical element that some Marxists have sought to amend has been the teleological assumption that history has a 'purpose', inevitably culminating in the overthrow of capitalism and the establishment of communism, as described in *The Communist Manifesto* or *Capital*. Marxism had to be liberated from its 'teleological shackles'.[73] History had to be interpreted in a less deterministic, more open-ended fashion, even seen in Marx as the 'activity of men in pursuit of their ends'.[74]

A number of implications followed from this rejection of teleology. First, historical presuppositions had to be made in terms of possibilities – albeit allowing for 'directionality' – rather than a single and necessary trajectory.[75] Second, Marx's simplifying assumptions concerning social development (as in *The Communist Manifesto* but not in *Capital*) had to be abandoned, and the recognition of social complexity embraced.[76]

However, the main reason for jettisoning this teleological perspective was the working class's failure to fulfil its historical mission. This necessitated broadening socialism's appeal, beyond the boundaries of the working class. One such form was campaigning around the demand for free time, which capitalism is unable to provide in any meaningful or universal sense.[77] This could be associated with a '*socialist* ethic', involving the 'creation of formal and substantive conditions that expand the arena wherein individuals can freely determine their lives and make their choices responsibly'.[78] This implied a 'new logic of accumulation', so that everyone was treated as a self-determining end, rather than as an alienated means to capital accumulation. Another option lay in developing an ethic, embracing a 'radical-democratic universalisation of interests' from a 'normative point of view', through raising issues that do not merely affect minorities, such as nuclear power, urban decay and poverty and global ecological problems.[79] Any socialist ethic had to be grounded upon a naturalistic theory of human nature.[80]

Another approach to the theoretical and political crisis of Marxism has been to make the opposite move: the 'true' Marxism of Marx needed to be restated, not revised. Theoretically, Marx's materialist dialectic could be deployed in order to carry out his unfinished programme, which was becoming increasingly realizable. Capitalism's contradictions were only now being fully played out on the scale of the world market.[81] Or the epistemological status of Marxism as an inherently practice-orientated theory had to be reaffirmed, and was essentially 'open', because it had to accept the inherently provisional and historically limited nature of the conclusions derived from practice, situated in a specific time and place.[82]

Commentary

Some of the issues raised by various reactions to the crisis of Marxism will be dealt with in the next section. The strength of Fukuyama's 'end of history' argument lies in its statement of the obvious: however critical Western Marxists may have been of the Soviet Union, in the popular imagination the failure of communism signifies the failure of Marxism. And, second, at this historical moment no clear, viable and realistic socialist alternative to liberal democratic capitalism has presented itself. Capitalism has turned out the historical winner. The weakness of the thesis, apart from its various tensions, and conceptual and empirical shortcomings, is that it suffers from the defects of Hegelian idealism, which assumed that history consisted of the conflict of ideas in which the more rational won. However, this ignores the whole process leading to the perversion of the Marxist ideal in the Soviet Union and elsewhere. As a result of capitalism's political resilience and material strength, the Soviet Union, isolated and economically backward, could only survive by discarding its most fundamental principle, grounded on demonstrably rational premises: proletarian self-emancipation. Second, is liberal capitalism rational? Can it 'truly' satisfy the twin needs of material contentment and the desire for recognition (discounting the possibility of boredom suggested by Fukuyama)?[83] As noted in Chapter 1, Marx's starting point was his 'immanent' critique of liberalism and capitalism: what was promised could not be delivered. Limits existed to capitalism's expansion, and liberalism could only offer the 'political' emancipation of abstract citizenship and not the 'human' emancipation of a socialized humanity, arguably absolutely fundamental in meeting the desire for recognition. Thus, Marx's case was that these two needs would be better satisfied in a socialist society. The problems in liberal democratic society referred to by Fukuyama – unemployment, drugs, crime, etc. – could be seen as symptomatic of its underlying irrationality, rather than as contingent phenomena.

As for what the fall of communism means for Marxism, the question of what type of regime 'fell' has already been examined in Chapter 10. Arguably, these regimes were neither capitalist or socialist – not capitalist owing to the lack of commodified production, and not socialist because an identifiable class had a monopoly of economic and political power. Yet clearly the imperatives of the international political and economic environment were major factors in shaping domestic economic, social and political processes. Whether the collapse can be explained in Marxist terms does not necessarily add grist to the Marxist mill. A difficulty exists in distinguishing such an explanation from non-Marxist ones, focusing on the failure of such regimes to compete economically with the West. And the view that few lessons can be learnt from the débâcle is questionable. The former communist regimes exposed certain lacunae in Marx's original thought in connection with individual rights and centralized economic planning. Moreover, the question of whether Lenin can be fully absolved from Stalinism, whatever his personal hopes and inclinations may have been, does require careful treatment. This will be considered in more detail in the next section.

To insist upon the relevance of Marxism to the modern world after communism's collapse is a perfectly reasonable position for Marxists to adopt, given the demonstrable inability of capitalism in dealing with war, poverty, famine, 'ecocide' and the like. Yet the real difficulty lies in being able to offer a convincing practical economic and political alternative to liberal capitalism. Which of the post-capitalist economic structures would prove the most viable yet satisfy socialist values is at least in part an empirical question, to be decided by those working within such structures as they developed, involving a whole host of potentially competing preferences: from job satisfaction and ecologically 'sound' production to maximization of output, from the maximization of democratic participation to the right to be apathetic and from the global to the internal distribution of resources on the basis of some notion of justice, to mention just a few. Thus, to be categorical on the 'plan versus market' debate is difficult. Nevertheless, the process of thinking about such structures is far from 'utopian' and helps to demonstrate the potential relevance of Marxism in the sense that some form of initiative, deriving from a 'plan', would be crucial if capitalism fell into deep and protracted crisis. Indeed,

Lenin in 1917 found himself having rapidly to provide a political blueprint, *The State and Revolution*, relying heavily on quotations from Marx and Engels, rather than on his own sustained thinking.

Here we come to the question of political alternatives, the Soviet model based upon a dual-power scenario, as proposed by Callinicos, or a parliamentary model, as commended by Miliband, that undergoes various democratic mutations. What tend to get omitted in debates on these alternatives are two crucial analytic distinctions: first, between the process of revolutionary transition and the desired end-state; second, between the form and content of socio-political power. Thus, in a revolutionary situation the issue of dual power might arise, but the best future form of state may require some modified form of parliamentary system, based on a distinction between legislature and executive and geographical and individual forms of representation, but with a 'producer' input and far greater executive accountability than at present. A Soviet system, based upon workplace representation, could easily fail to represent adequately all non-workplace interests and may not have a mechanism to mediate between differences of interest between workplaces, especially between larger and smaller, and between workplaces and the rest of 'society'. In other words, a parliamentary form of political decision-making and representation does not necessarily have to be bound up with minority class power, as tends to occur under capitalism. The question of form and content can be put another way: what if, by differences in the timing of the elections in Russia in 1917, the Bolsheviks had had a majority in the constituent assembly and a minority in the Soviets? Would the latter have been disbanded in January 1918, because their form was 'bourgeois'? Moreover, a revolutionary strategy is determined by circumstances. A future revolutionary situation cannot be 'read off' from October 1917. A whole series of complex parliamentary and extra-parliamentary man-oeuvres may be required, and even this scenario begs the question relating to the degree of resistance that a capitalist class might put up against a powerful working class which had widespread support in society and within the state apparatus. However, as indicated in Chapter 12, the dual-power scenario of October 1917 should not be ruled out either.

The problem of transition is made more complex because the economic and political alternatives considered have to be related to the social forces likely to achieve these ends. For example, women concerned with reproductive issues may not be too enthusiastic about a system of democracy mainly based upon workplace representation. And if a socialist movement was more united in its anti-capitalism than in its working-class identity, then quite possibly complex, 'pluralistic' forms of representation would be needed. This question of social agency and the reform–revolution dichotomy will be more fully explored in the next section.

Again, the question of theoretical revision has to be linked to the problem of agency. Once the notion of teleology, and its simple grounding in working-class self-interest, is abandoned and the issue of human volition more fully embraced, the scope for moral argument becomes greater. Yet while the anger and unity derived from such argument may be important, so is the role of interests in understanding political action. But the universalization of such interests in some normative fashion, as argued by Habermas, in relation, say, to ecology, may be harder than it appears at first sight. Even on ecological issues differences of interest and/or values could arise in a world without capitalists, between those who wanted growth and those who wished to preserve nature in some form or other. In this one example we can see that people may want to abolish capitalism for different reasons. Moreover, just as moral argument may be made difficult in the world of politics through interest dependency, it may also be condition-dependent. Saving nature may be technically and economically more feasible in certain periods than others, just as Marx suggested in *The Critique of the Gotha Programme* that the principles regulating work and distribution were dependent on the level of the development of the productive forces. Finally, with regard to those Marxists who call for a restatement, rather than a revision, of Marx, the question of concreteness arises. An 'open', practice-orientated Marxism, or the development of a materialist dialectic within the context of a global capitalist framework, are worthy theoretical aims. However, specific matters of social and political agency, strategy and objectives also warrant consideration.

CONJECTURING THE FUTURE

So far various partial attempts to deal with Marxism's crisis have been evaluated. To couch Marxism's political future in a more comprehensive, if tentative, fashion, it depends among other things on the possibility for growth of explicitly or potentially anti-capitalist movements: this would seem a reasonable assumption to make since many of the problems created by capitalism, already mentioned by commentators considered above, appear irremedial within the system itself. They include the growing ecological crisis, whether in terms of resources or devastation of the environment, the international debt crisis, global inequality, trade wars and many other forms of international and domestic conflict generated by difficulties within the accumulation process, which involve attacks on working-class living standards and moves towards more authoritarian state structures. Furthermore, the greater the globalization of capital the greater are the possibilities of an international socialist movement through the creation of a 'world' culture, meant in the broadest sense of the term, and increased contradictions, which are obviously global and require global solutions. In addition, there has been an actual growth, at least in absolute terms, of the industrial working class on a global scale.[84] And in the advanced capitalist countries, as indicated in Chapter 14, although the industrial working class has declined, the working class as such has been 'reconstituted' in the sense of becoming increasingly 'white collar'. There is also the question of how the working class is to be defined. If we take Marx's notion of the 'collective worker', then managers, technicians, etc., would be included, and these could become a significant force if capitalism went into not merely crisis but 'meltdown'. Finally, the possibilities of growth of a genuine international socialist movement may in the long term be enhanced by the demise of the Soviet Union, in the sense that such a movement would not be the tool of the foreign policy of a single state, as was the Third International. Thus, it would be more difficult for the employing class to combine nationalism with anti-socialism, as occurred during the Cold War.

The question of such an international movement, its actual success is of course another question, depending upon a variety of factors, such as the economic and political strength of international capitalism and the historical differences between national working classes, as well as the organizational forms that this movement would take. Whether these forms involve alliances between, or amalgamations of, new social movements, old socialist movements of a reformist or Marxist complexion is impossible to foretell. But any Marxist organization has to be attractive and viable, although it may have to have the utmost organizational flexibility determined by political circumstances, and would have constantly to bear in mind the intimate connection between ends and means. Thus, the Marxist aim of creating a democratic society superior to liberal ideals cannot be achieved through the leadership of an undemocratic party, something that Marx instinctively grasped when he agreed to join the conspiratorial League of the Just in 1847 on condition that it became an open and democratic organization.[85]

The bringing together of means and ends also requires a re-evaluation of the Marxist political tradition, involving an honest, if painful, accounting of its past. The either/ors of yesterday, demanded by political calculation and often involving choices between imperfect truths for the sake of action, are not the same as those of today. Even the lessons of history change. Vitally, this entails a re-examination of the Soviet experience. The Bolshevik revolution and its failure to achieve its international objectives wrought a double schism within Marxism, between the Second and Third Internationals and between the Third and Fourth.[86] This twin polarization did not allow the 'true' Marx to prevail in all his complexity. In terms of his original perspective and project, each side was the loser. Moreover, these polarizations obscured some of the problems lying at the heart of the Marxian project. In the Second–Third International polarity Kautsky, with his commitment to electoralism and belief in the ultimate neutrality of the state, lost Marx's anti-bureaucratic and class-based political radicalism. On

Lenin's side, the relation between ends and means was precarious. The principles of *The State and Revolution* were not put into practice and the question of transforming the working class into a ruling class was ignored. So was the strength of parliamentary democracy in the West and the complexities of the modern state, stemming from the division of labour, recognized by Kautsky, but not fully acknowledged by Marx even in his more realistic, empirical moments when embracing the notion of complexity.[87] In the process of socialist transition in *The State and Revolution* Lenin relied on the principle of simplification, vis-à-vis the state (it was a parasitic phenomenon) and workers' self-administration of the economy.[88] In any case, the impact of this split was the Third International's failure – with Gramsci as the notable exception – to bring parliamentary democracy in the West fully within its strategic frame of reference.

On the reform–revolution issues in the Bernstein–Luxemburg debate, which was a dress-rehearsal for the Lenin–Kautsky conflict, Bernstein's argument did not entertain the possibility of root-and-branch capitalist resistance to socialist change, of the precariousness of reforms, because they were gained through struggle and could be lost through struggle, or of the state as a *capitalist* state. What Luxemburg did not consider was the possibility that reforms were crucial, not merely in heightening working-class awareness and organization, but also in having an objective impact on the workings of capital and in promoting its cultural advance in the process of becoming a ruling class.

The second schism between the Third and Fourth Internationals, between Stalin and Trotsky and their followers, again blurred some of the features of Marx's perspective and project. Elements of internationalism became obscured as the Third International became an instrument of Soviet foreign policy, as Trotsky had argued. Yet Marx had insisted that strategic calculation was condition-dependent. Stalin and his followers, as well as Gramsci, had to confront the fact that in the absence of any signs of permanent revolution, a more evolutionary strategy had to be adopted.

Trotsky and his followers instead clung to the theory and practice of the October Revolution. That Stalin pursued a more evolutionary strategy, taking into account the strength of the bourgeoisies in the West, because of some wish to 'betray' the world proletariat is questionable. Such an interpretation assumes that proletarian revolutions in the West would not have been in Stalin's interest. Indeed, Trotsky, as noted in Chapter 8, had not advocated a strategy of permanent revolution in relation to China before his split with Stalin. The outcome of this split was two distorted forms of Marxist strategy: one abstract and politically ineffectual, the other concrete and excessively pragmatic.

Bound up with the Stalin–Trotsky schism is the question of Lenin or, more precisely, the relationship between Lenin and Stalinism. Was Stalin a true heir or a gross betrayer of Lenin's theory and practice? This either/or led to exaggeration. Clear connections between Lenin and Stalin existed: their interpretations of historical materialism, with its teleological inflection and as a certain kind of 'science', were potentially elitist, and gave the development of the productive forces priority over production relations. This 'productivism' was used to justify the Five Year Plans, with all the human misery that they entailed. Furthermore, Lenin's notion that dictatorship of the proletariat could be exercised by the party rather than the Soviets was crucial to the justification of a one-party state. And in practice Lenin supported the banning of opposition parties from the Soviets in 1918 and of factions within the Communist Party in 1921. There is little evidence that he discussed the need to restore Soviets and factions. This is not to suggest that Lenin was as 'bad' as Stalin, but rather to note a connection between the two men. This connection, while partly ideological, stemmed from the adverse circumstances in which they found themselves in attempting to construct socialism: economic dislocation, material poverty, cultural 'backwardness', a small and organizationally ineffective working class and Western encirclement. Hence, the fleeting unity of Marxist theory and proletarian practice – of proletarian self-emancipation – achieved in October 1917 was rapidly fractured by circumstance.

On the other hand, the similarities between Lenin and Stalin can be overstated. Lenin clearly disliked Stalin's personal rudeness and his approach to the national question as evidenced by his handling of Georgia in 1922. In Lenin's 'Testament', written in December 1922, he wanted Stalin dismissed from his post as party secretary. Moreover, towards the end of his life – he died in 1924 – he clearly became worried by the growth of party bureaucracy.[89] Finally, he was clearly opposed to any cult of personality, and whatever his own sense of political certainty, he was far more willing to engage in open debate than Stalin, who was not averse to using assassination and show trials as a means of settling political argument.

The upshot of this discussion is that Lenin's theory and practice have to be contextualized, rather than fetishized or demonized, and understood as the application of Marxism to specifically Russian and existing global political and economic conditions. This entailed a good deal of practical and theoretical improvization. Marxism had to be adapted to circumstances not of Lenin's own choosing, but 'directly encountered, given and transmitted from the past'.[90] His undoubted strength lay in his capacity to make theoretical adjustments in the light of existing and changing circumstances. Yet such adjustments, as already noted, led him to equate the dictatorship of the proletariat with the dictatorship of the party. He provides us with a cautionary tale: the need to distinguish the explanatory and analytical power of Marxism from the ideological Marxism of power.

Equally crucially, the need to contextualize Lenin also points to the danger of attempting to generalize a theory and practice that derived from a specific situation. Indeed, the need to take specificity seriously (this was Lenin's point) lay at the heart of Gramsci's Marxism and was his fundamental strategic insight: the contrast between the 'East' and the 'West'. While the desire for proletarian revolution was as intense for Gramsci as for Lenin, he fully acknowledged the fact that the terrain of political combat in the West, with its strong and dense 'civil society', involved far more complex political manoeuvres than in Russia.

This brings us to a consideration of present global circumstances. An October 1917 scenario may be possible in such countries as Brazil, South Korea and South Africa, which possess well-developed proletarian movements and where parliamentary traditions are not firmly rooted. But there remains the rest of the world, with different types of working class and different state forms. Any attempt to construct an international socialist movement would involve acknowledging these differences. Strategically in the West, where parliamentary traditions are strong and social structures complex, this may entail, as Miliband has suggested, working within parliament while exposing its limitations. The question of a dual power scenario, as already indicated, is an empirical one. Obviously, in moments of extreme class contestation, fostering illusions of parliament as a vehicle for socialist transition can be disastrous, as in Chile in 1973. Yet the most effective form of transition may be articulated, first, by parliamentary and extra-parliamentary forces working in tandem and, second, by a pluralistic alliance orientation, combining unity and difference, which allows for situational differences stemming from job occupation, race, sex and gender.

All this entails rethinking the relation between ends and means, or goal and process, within Marxism, so that the pursuit of power is not separated from its objective: the maximization of social, economic and political equality. The practical linking of end and means could imply breaking with some of the primary taboos in Marx's own work, notwithstanding his own valid insights on this question: his denial of moralism and 'blueprintism' stemming from his overly materialist teleological assumption. Such an assumption enabled him to avoid moral prescription and 'recipes for the cookshops of the future', because he could point to a historical process that was already in train. However, a self-denying ordinance on the provision of any 'recipe', however broad and tentative, in a revolutionary situation could be viewed as an abnegation of 'leadership'. Indeed, Marx himself could not resist the temptation to speculate about the nature of communism in his *Critique of the Gotha Programme*. Similarly, as Geras has noted, a 'repressed' theory of justice existed in his work.[91] Again, some form of normative theory, grounded in self-interest and practical, material possibilities, would be crucial to any agenda of transition. While Gramsci, in discussing the party's role in the process of 'moral reform',[92] did not specify what this entailed, such a programme would have to appeal not merely to the industrial proletariat, but also to other wage earners and potential allies from other social strata, who were in either 'contradictory class locations', to use E. O. Wright's term, or oppressed minorities. The refusal to consider the importance and validity of moral argument by orthodox Marxists is based upon an inconsistency. Moral outrage against capitalism prompts them to make the self-sacrifices involved in revolutionary activity. To alter the meaning of one of Marx's criticisms of the utopian socialists, they divide 'society into two parts, of which one is superior to society'.[93] In other words, they see the working class as interest-driven, while they themselves are morally motivated. And usually collectivities engaged in social transformation are prompted by anger deriving from a sense of injustice.

The weakness of Marx's discussion in part derives from the parallels and contrasts made between bourgeois and proletarian revolutions. There is the question of class capacities. Marx in *The Communist Manifesto* saw the bourgeoisie as attaining first economic and then political power. In other words, its ruling-class capacities were developed over time. The working class was expected generally to develop these capacities in the revolutionary process itself. Any realistic theory of socialist transformation needs an expanded notion of the working class and possibly the winning over of sections of the middle class, recognizing that a socialist society, although its ultimate objective is the increase of free time, will be built on a complex division of labour and on sophisticated technical expertise.[94] Second, the implication of Marx's contrast between the previous ruling classes (including the bourgeoisie), which subjected the rest of society to their 'conditions of appropriation', and the proletariat, which, when coming to power, would abolish their 'own previous mode of appropriation',[95] warrants closer examination. The former task merely entails extending what exists, while the second demands some conception of what forms of collective control of the productive forces and distribution would be desirable after class exploitation had been abolished.

Whether such revisions still allow the appellation 'Marxist' to be applied to the resultant theory and practice is a difficult question, since the problem of definition has to be resolved. Marxism is a house with many mansions, with Bernstein, Kautsky, Luxemburg, Lenin, Trotsky, Stalin, Mao and Pol Pot all claiming to be Marxist. If we reject their claims on the grounds that they were not 'true' Marxists, then a definition of 'true' Marxism has to be offered. Certainly, if Marxism is taken to be the 'theory and practice of proletarian revolution', as suggested earlier, then the revisions could be viewed as operating within, rather than against, the Marxist tradition, which allows for theoretical modification in the light of new knowledge derived from working-class experience, new forms of social struggle, changing state forms and processes of capital accumulation, attempts to resolve the tensions in and omissions from Marx's own thought and, indeed, 'bourgeois' sources.

Yet even this line of reasoning begs an important question: how valuable is the attempt to maintain a theoretical and practical fidelity with Marx? Should not Marx be viewed as a major pioneer within the socialist tradition, rather than its prophet? Is it not better to follow the example, rather than the letter, of Marx? As a child of the Enlightenment he had an intense passion for freedom and knowledge in equal measure. He pursued knowledge in the name of freedom. This involved the destruction of any form of mystifying consciousness that sustained humanity's self-oppression, and the development of ideas that would be of practical use to the struggles of the oppressed and exploited. He would not have enjoyed the prospect of future generations looking to him not for inspiration, but for legitimation. Marx and the movement he created offer all those struggling for freedom and equality a treasure house of practical and theoretical wisdom – negative as well as positive. This movement is a constant reminder that the theory and practice of human freedom are always unfinished business.[96] As long as capitalism remains in business, Marxism as a movement and doctrine, in whatever form, is likely to remain obstinately relevant.

NOTES

1. K. Minogue, 'Ideology after the collapse of communism', in A. Shtromas (Ed.), *The End of 'Isms'?* Blackwell, Oxford (1994), 11.
2. A. Callinicos, *Against Postmodernism: a Marxist Critique*, Polity Press, Cambridge (1989).
3. C. Norris, *What's Wrong with Postmodernism: Critical Theory and the Ends of Philosophy*, Harvester Wheatsheaf, Hemel Hempstead (1990); N. Geras, *Solidarity in the Conversation of Humankind: the Ungroundable Liberalism of Richard Rorty*, Verso, London (1995).
4. J. Derrida, *Specters of Marx*, Routledge, New York (1994), 88, 94.
5. F. Fukuyama, *The End of History and the Last Man* (hereafter *EH*), Avon Books, New York (1992).
6. *EH*, xii.
7. *EH*, 110, 205.
8. *EH*, xix.
9. *EH*, 93.
10. *EH*, 288.
11. M. Rustin, 'No exit from capitalism?', *New Left Review*, 193 (May/June 1992), 107; F. Halliday, 'An encounter with Fukuyama', *New Left Review*, 193 (May/June 1992), 94.
12. P. Anderson, *A Zone of Engagement*, Verso, London (1992), 353.
13. Rustin, *op. cit.*, 98.

14. *Ibid.*, 107.
15. Anderson, *op. cit.*, 350.
16. Rustin, *op. cit.*, 100.
17. Halliday, *op. cit.*, 94.
18. Anderson, *op. cit.*, 356.
19. Halliday, *op. cit.*, 95.
20. Rustin, *op. cit.*, 103. See also Halliday, *op. cit.*, 93.
21. Rustin, *op. cit.*, 106.
22. *Ibid.*, 98; R. Miliband, 'Fukuyama and the socialist alternative', *New Left Review*, 193 (May/June 1992), 111.
23. Rustin, *op. cit.*, 107.
24. J. McCarney, 'Shaping ends: reflections on Fukuyama', *New Left Review*, 202 (Nov/Dec 1993), 43.
25. Anderson, *op. cit.*, 349.
26. McCarney, *op. cit.*, 51.
27. Milibrand, *op. cit.*, 112.
28. Anderson, *op. cit.*, 360.
29. *Ibid.*, 361.
30. L. Wilde, 'Farewell to Marxism?', *Red Letters*, 26 (1990), 7.
31. D. Singer, 'Prometheus rebound?' in W. K. Tabb (Ed.), *The Future of Socialism: Perspectives from the Left*, Monthly Review Press, New York (1990), 19.
32. A. Callinicos, 'Stalinism falls in line with theory', *Times Higher Education Supplement* (12 July 1991), 14.
33. A. Callinicos, *The Revenge of History*, Polity Press, Cambridge (1991), 17 (hereafter *RH*).
34. P. Sweezy, 'Postscript on post-revolutionary society', in Tabb, *op. cit.*, 292.
35. *RH*, 19.
36. M. Burawoy, 'Marxism is dead! Long live Marxism!', in Tabb, *op. cit.*, 161; Wilde, *op. cit.*, 7.
37. *RH*, 45-50.
38. *RH*, 3; Burawoy, *op. cit.*, 161.
39. R. Blackburn, 'Fin de siècle: socialism after the crash' in R. Blackburn (Ed.), *After the Fall*, Verso, London (1991), 178. See also Sweezy, 'Postscript on post-revolutionary society', in Tabb, *op. cit.*, 292.
40. I. Silbur, *Socialism: What Went Wrong?* Pluto Press, London (1994), 246-66.
41. Tabb, *op. cit.*, 2, 8; *RH*, 106; G. Therborn, 'The life and times of socialism', *New Left Review*, 194 (July/August 1992), 32; E. Hobsbawm, 'The crisis of today's ideologies', *New Left Review*, 192 (March/April 1992), 64.
42. C. Chase-Dunn, 'Socialism and capitalism on a world scale', in Tabb, *op. cit.*, 68.
43. *RH*, 81.
44. Hobsbawm, *op. cit.*, 62; S. Amin, 'The future of socialism' in Tabb, *op. cit.*, 106.
45. A. Nove, *The Economics of Feasible Socialism*, Allen and Unwin, London (1983).
46. C. Harman, 'The myth of market socialism', *International Socialism* (second series), 42 (Spring 1989), 10-34.
47. E. Mandel, 'In defence of socialist planning', *New Left Review*, 159 (Sept/Oct 1986), 11.

48. G. A. Cohen, 'The future of a disillusion', *New Left Review*, 10 (Nov/Dec 1991), 18-19.

49. P. Devine, 'Self-governing socialism' in Tabb, *op. cit.*, 197.

50. *Ibid.*, 199.

51. Harman, *op. cit.*, 39; Mandel, *op. cit.*, 32.

52. Mandel, *op. cit.*, 26-8; Devine, *op. cit.*, 198.

53. P. Devine, *Democracy and Democratic Planning*, Polity Press, Cambridge (1988).

54. *Ibid.*, 22, 235-58.

55. D. Elson, 'Market socialism or the socialization of the market?' *New Left Review* (Nov/Dec 1988), 30-5. See also Blackburn, 'Fin de siècle,' 218. For a clear and balanced discussion of the issues see H. Breitenbach, T. Burden and D. Coates, *Features of a Viable Socialism*, Harvester/Wheatsheaf, Hemel Hempstead (1990).

56. *RH*, 118.

57. P. Anderson, *In the Tracks of Historical Materialism*, Verso, London (1983), 79.

58. 'Reflections on the crisis of communist regimes' in Blackburn, *op. cit.*, 12-13.

59. R. Miliband, 'The plausibility of socialism', *New Left Review*, 206 (July/August 1994), 13.

60. Miliband, 'Reflections … ', 13.

61. Miliband, 'The plausibility … ', 13.

62. J. McCarney, *Social Theory and the Crisis of Marxism*, Verso, London (1990), 163.

63. G. Arrighi, 'Marxist century, American century' in Blackburn, *op. cit.*, 153; Blackburn, 'Fin de siècle', 238; Chase-Dunn, 'Socialism and capitalism on a world scale', in Tabb, *op. cit.*, 82; Tabb, 'Where we are in history', in Tabb, *op. cit.*, 10.

64. McCarney, *op. cit.*, 192.

65. Blackburn, 'Fin de siècle', 238-9.

66. See e.g. *Capitalism and Social Democracy*, Cambridge University Press, Cambridge, 1986, Chapter 1 *passim*.

67. *Modern European Socialism*, Dartmouth, Aldershot (1994), 113.

68. E. O. Wright, 'Class analysis, history and emancipation', *New Left Review*, 202 (Nov/Dec 1993), 35.

69. G. Therborn, 'Vorsprung durch rethink' in Blackburn, *op. cit.*, 306-8.

70. B. Kagarlitsky, *The Dialectic of Change*, Verso, London (1990), 8.

71. P. Auerbach, 'On socialist optimism', *New Left Review*, 192 (March/April 1992), 10.

72. S. E. Bronner, *Socialism Unbound*, Routledge, New York (1990), 178-80.

73. *Ibid.*, 147. See also J. Larrain, *A Reconstruction of Historical Materialism*, Allen and Unwin, London (1986), 124.

74. K. Marx and F. Engels, *The Holy Family*, Progress Publishers, Moscow (1975), 110. See also R. Gottlieb, *Marxism, 1844-1990: Origins, Betrayal, Rebirth*, Routledge, New York (1992), 40.

75. E. O. Wright, 'Class analysis, history and emancipation', 24. See A. Callinicos, *Theories and Narratives*, Polity Press, Cambridge (1995), 41-3, 102-4, on the distinction between 'philosophies' of history and 'theories' of history, and on

how a Marxist theory of history based upon 'directionality', supplied by the growth of productive forces, could be defended.

76. J. Habermas, 'What does socialism mean today? The revolutions of recuperation and the need for new thinking', in Blackburn, *op. cit.*, 34; Blackburn, 'Fin de siècle', 239.
77. A. Przeworski, 'Material interests, class compromise, and the transition to socialism' in J. Roemer (Ed.), *Analytical Marxism*, Cambridge University Press, Cambridge (1986), 181–8; A. Gorz, 'The new agenda' in Blackburn, *op. cit.*, 295.
78. Bronner, *Socialism Unbound*, 155.
79. Habermas, 'What does socialism ... ', 43.
80. Anderson, *In the Tracks of Historical Materialism*, 82. See also E. O. Wright, A. Levine and E. Sober, *Reconstructing Marxism*, Verso, London (1992), 100, on the moral corollary of a 'weak historical materialism'.
81. McCarney, *Social Theory and the Crisis of Marxism*, 184.
82. See, for example, W. Bonefeld, R. Gunn and K. Psychopedis (Eds), *Open Marxism*, Vol. 2, Pluto Press, London (1992), 1–34.
83. *EH*, 330.
84. P. Kellogg, 'Goodbye to the working class?', *International Socialism* (second series), 36 (1987), 10.
85. D. McLellan, *Karl Marx, His Life and Thought*, Macmillan, London (1973), 172–3.
86. Perry Anderson calls for the need 'to come to terms with the historical experience of the Second and Third Internationals': *A Zone of Engagement*, 362.
87. K. Kautsky, *The Social Revolution*, Kerr, Chicago (1913), 29.
88. See Blackburn, 'Fin de siècle', 180–2, for a discussion of simple–complex tension in Marx's work.
89. M. Lewin, *Lenin's Last Struggle*, Pluto Press, London (1975), Chapter 6 *passim*.
90. K. Marx, 'The eighteenth Brumaire', *Selected Works, Vol. 1*, 247.
91. N. Geras, 'The controversy about Marx and justice', *New Left Review*, 150 (March/April 1985), 47–85.
92. *SPN*, 132.
93. K. Marx, 'Thesis on Feuerbach', *SW, Vol. 2*, 404.
94. See P. Meiksins, 'Beyond the boundary question', *New Left Review*, 157 (May/June 1986), 116–20, for a discussion of the problems of class identification and alliance strategies.
95. *CM*, 65.
96. A. M. Jagger, *Feminist Politics and Human Nature*, Harvester Press, Brighton (1983), 6.

Further Reading

GENERAL SURVEYS

T. Bottomore (Ed.), *A Dictionary of Marxist Thought*, 2nd edn, Blackwell, Oxford (1991).

J. Braunthal, *History of the Internationals, Vols 1-2*, Nelson, London; *Vol. 3*, Gollancz, London (1966-80).

L. Kolakowski, *Main Currents of Marxism*, 3 vols, Oxford University Press, Oxford (1978).

G. Lichtheim, *Marxism*, Routledge and Kegan Paul, London (1961).

D. McLellan, *Marxism after Marx*, Macmillan, Basingstoke, (1979).

R. Miliband, *Marxism and Politics*, Oxford University Press, Oxford (1977).

C. Wright Mills, *The Marxists*, Penguin, Harmondsworth (1962).

CHAPTER 1

S. Avineri, *The Social and Political Thought of Karl Marx*, Cambridge University Press, Cambridge (1968).

R. Blackburn (Ed.), *Revolution and Class Struggle*, Fontana, Glasgow (1977).

H. Draper, *Karl Marx's Theory of Revolution, Vols 1-4*, Monthly Review Press, New York (1977-90).

A. Gilbert, *Marx's Politics: Communists and Citizens*, Martin Robertson, Oxford (1981).

R. N. Hunt, *The Political Ideas of Marx and Engels, Vols 1-2*, Macmillan, London (1974-84).

J. M. Maguire, *Marx's Theory of Politics*, Cambridge University Press, Cambridge (1978).

K. Marx, 'The class struggles in France: 1848 to 1850' in *Surveys from Exile* (Ed. D. Fernbach), Penguin, Harmondsworth (1973).

K. Marx, 'The civil war in France' in *The First International and After* (Ed. D. Fernbach), Penguin, Harmondsworth (1974).

K. Marx, 'Critique of the Gotha programme' in *The First International and After*.

K. Marx, 'The eighteenth Brumaire' in *Surveys from Exile*.

K. Marx and F. Engels, *The German Ideology*, Lawrence and Wishart, London (1965).

K. Marx and F. Engels, 'Address to the Central Committee of the Communist League' (March 1850), in *The Revolutions of 1848* (Ed. D. Fernbach), Penguin, Harmondsworth (1973).

K. Marx and F. Engels, *The Communist Manifesto* (Ed. F. L. Bender), Norton, New York (1988).

J. Molyneux, *Marxism and the Party*, Pluto Press, London (1978).

CHAPTER 2

E. Bernstein, *The Preconditions of Socialism* (Ed. H. Tudor), Cambridge University Press, Cambridge (1993).

L. Colletti, *From Rousseau to Lenin*, New Left Books, London (1972).

P. Gay, *The Dilemma of Democratic Socialism*, Collier Books, New York (1970).

N. Geras, *The Legacy of Rosa Luxemburg*, New Left Books, London (1976).

J. Joll, *The Second International*, Routledge and Kegan Paul, London (1974).

K. Kautsky, *The Class Struggle*, Norton, New York (1971).

R. Luxemburg, *Selected Political Writings* (Ed. Dick Howard), Monthly Review Press, New York (1971).

J. Nettl, *Rosa Luxemburg*, 2 vols, Oxford University Press, London (1966).

C. E. Schorske, *German Social Democracy, 1905-1917*, Harvard University Press, Cambridge, MA (1955).

H. Tudor and J. M. Tudor (Eds), *Marxism and Social Democracy*, Cambridge University Press, Cambridge (1988).

CHAPTER 3

J. M. Blaut, *The National Question: Decolonising the Theory of Nationalism*, Zed Books, London (1987).

J. Breuilly, *Nationalism and the State*, Manchester University Press, Manchester (1982).

I. Cummins, *Marx and Engels and National Movements*, Croom Helm, London (1980).

H. B. Davis, *Nationalism and Socialism: Marxist and Labor Theories of Nationalism to 1917*, Monthly Review Press, New York (1967).

H. B. Davis, (Ed.), *The National Question: Selected Writings of Rosa Luxemburg*, Monthly Review Press, New York (1976).

H. B. Davis, *Towards a Marxist Theory of Nationalism*, Monthly Review Press, New York (1978).

B. Franklin (Ed.), *The Essential Stalin*, Croom Helm, London (1973).

N. Harris, *National Liberation*, I. B. Taurus, London (1990).

E. J. Hobsbawm, *Nations and Nationalism since 1780*, Cambridge University Press, Cambridge (1990).

V. I. Lenin, *The Right of Nations to Self-determination*, Progress Publishers, Moscow (1967).

R. Munck, *The Difficult Dialogue: Marxism and the National Question*, Zed Books, London (1986).

E. Nimni, *Marxism and Nationalism*, Pluto Press, London (1991).

J. Schwartzmantel, *Socialism and the Idea of the Nation*, Harvester/ Wheatsheaf, Hemel Hempstead (1991).

CHAPTER 4

A. Brewer, *Marxist Theories of Imperialism: A Critical Survey*, 2nd edn, Routledge, London (1990).

N. Bukharin, *Imperialism and World Economy*, Merlin Press, London (1972).

R. Hilferding, *Finance Capital* (Ed. Tom Bottomore), Routledge and Kegan Paul, London (1981).

K. Kautsky, 'Ultra-imperialism', *New Left Review*, 59 (Jan/Feb 1970), 41-6.

S. F. Kissin, *War and the Marxists, Vol. 1*, André Deutsch, London (1988).

V. I. Lenin, *Imperialism, the Highest Stage of Capitalism*, Progress Publishers, Moscow (1966).

CHAPTER 5

A. Ascher, *Pavel Axelrod and the Development of Menshevism*, Harvard University Press, Cambridge, MA (1972).

E. H. Carr, *The Bolshevik Revolution, Vol. 1*, Penguin, Harmondsworth (1966).

T. Cliff, *Lenin, Vols 1-2*, Pluto Press, London (1975-6).

I. Getzler, *Martov*, Cambridge University Press, Cambridge (1967).

L. H. Haimson, *The Russian Marxists and the Origins of Bolshevism*, Harvard University Press, Cambridge, MA (1955).

N. Harding, *Lenin's Political Thought, Vols 1-2*, Macmillan, London (1977-81).

M. Leibman, *Leninism under Lenin*, Merlin Press, London (1975).

V. I. Lenin, 'The state and revolution', *Selected Works*, Lawrence and Wishart, London (1967).

V. I. Lenin, 'The April theses', Foreign Languages Printing House, Moscow (1970).

L. Trotsky, *The Permanent Revolution* and *Results and Prospects*, New Park Publications, London (1962).

CHAPTER 6

N. Harding, *Lenin's Political Thought, Vol. 1*, Macmillan, London (1977).

M. Leibman, *Leninism under Lenin*, Merlin Press, London (1975).

V. I. Lenin, 'One step forwards, two steps back', *Collected Works, Vol. 7*, Progress Publishers, Moscow (1965).

V. I. Lenin, *What Is to Be Done?* Progress Publishers, Moscow (1969).

R. Luxemburg, *The Russian Revolution and Leninism or Marxism?* University of Michigan Press, Ann Arbor, MI (1961).

L. Trotsky, *Our Political Tasks*, New Park Publications, London (n.d.).

CHAPTER 7

H. Draper, *The Dictatorship of the Proletariat from Marx to Lenin*, Monthly Review Press, New York (1987).

J. Ehrenberg, *The Dictatorship of the Proletariat*, Routledge, New York (1992).

K. Kautsky, *The Dictatorship of the Proletariat*, University of Michigan Press, Ann Arbor, MI (1964).

V. I. Lenin, *The Proletarian Revolution and the Renegade Kautsky*, Progress Publishers, Moscow (1967).

M. Salvadori, *Karl Kautsky and the Socialist Revolution*, New Left Books, London (1979).

CHAPTER 8

R. B. Day, *Leon Trotsky and the Politics of Economic Isolation*, Cambridge University Press, Cambridge (1973).

M. Lowy, *The Politics of Combined and Uneven Development: the Theory of Permanent Revolution*, Verso, London (1981).

J. Molyneux, *Leon Trotsky's Theory of Revolution*, Harvester Press, Brighton (1981).

J. Stalin, 'The October Revolution and the tactics of the Russian Communists', *Selected Writings*, Greenwood Press, Westport, CT (1970).

L. Trotsky, *The Permanent Revolution*, New Park Publications, London (1962).

L. Trotsky, *Revolution Betrayed*, New Park Publications, London (1967).

L. Trotsky, *The Third International after Lenin*, Pathfinder Press, New York (1970).

CHAPTER 9

D. Beetham, *Marxists in the Face of Fascism*, Manchester University Press, Manchester (1983).

E. H. Carr, *The Twilight of Comintern, 1930-1935*, Macmillan, London (1982).

F. Claudin, *The Communist Movement: from Comintern to Cominform*, Penguin, Harmondsworth (1975).

J. Degras (Ed.), *The Communist International, 1919-1943, Vol. 3*, Frank Cass, London (1971).

D. Hallas, *The Comintern*, Bookmarks, London (1985).

N. Poulantzas, *Fascism and Dictatorship*, New Left Books, London (1974).

L. Trotsky, *The Struggle against Fascism in Germany*, Pathfinder Press, New York (1971).

L. Trotsky, *The Spanish Revolution*, Pathfinder Press, New York (1973).

L. Trotsky, *Whither France?* New Park Publications, London (1974).

CHAPTER 10

P. Beilharz, *Trotsky, Trotskyism and the Transition to Socialism*, Croom Helm, London (1987).

P. Bellis, *Marxism and the USSR*, Macmillan, London (1979).

T. Cliff, *State Capitalism in Russia*, Pluto Press, London (1974).

E. Mandel, *Marxist Economic Theory, Vol. 2*, Merlin Press, London (1968).

E. Mandel, *The Inconsistencies of State Capitalism*, International Marxist Group, London (1969).

D. Purdy, *The Soviet Union: State Capitalist or Socialist?* Communist Party, London (1975).

L. Trotsky, *Revolution Betrayed*, New Park Publications, London (1967).

CHAPTER 11

A. Brewer, *Marxist Theories of Imperialism: A Critical Survey*, 2nd edn, Routledge, London (1990).

R. Debray, *Revolution in the Revolution?* Penguin, Harmondsworth (1967).

R. Debray, *A Critique of Arms*, Penguin, Harmondsworth (1977).

A. G. Frank, *Capitalism and Underdevelopment in Latin America*, Monthly Review Press, New York (1967).

E. Guevara, *Guerilla Warfare*, Monthly Review Press, New York (1961).

D. C. Hodges, *The Latin American Revolution*, William Morrow, New York (1974).

L. Huberman and P. Sweezy (Eds), *Régis Debray and the Latin American Revolution*, Monthly Review Press, New York (1969).

J. Larrain, *Theories of Development*, Polity Press, Cambridge (1989).

P. Limqueco and B. McFarlane (Eds), *Neo-Marxist Theories of Development*, Croom Helm, London (1983).

J. Quartim, *Dictatorship and Armed Struggle in Brazil*, New Left Books, London (1971).

H. Ramm, *The Marxism of Régis Debray: Between Lenin and Guevara*, The Regents Press of Kansas, Lawrence, KS (1978).

I. Roxborough, *Theories of Underdevelopment*, Macmillan, London (1979).

B. Warren, *Imperialism: Pioneer of Capitalism*, Verso, London (1980).

J. Woddis, *New Theories of Revolution*, Lawrence and Wishart, London (1972).

CHAPTER 12

C. Boggs and D. Plotke (Eds), *The Politics of Eurocommunism*, South End Press, Boston (1980).

S. Carrillo, *'Eurocommunism' and the State*, Lawrence and Wishart, London (1977).

J. Femia, *Gramsci's Political Thought*, Clarendon Press, Oxford (1987).

A. Gramsci, *Selections from the Prison Notebooks* (Eds Q. Hoare and G. W. Smith), Lawrence and Wishart, London (1971).

J. Hoffman, *The Gramscian Challenge*, Basil Blackwell, Oxford (1984).

R. Kindersley (Ed.), *In Search of Eurocommunism*, Macmillan, London (1981).

E. Mandel, *From Stalinism to Eurocommunism*, New Left Books, London (1978).

G. Napolitano, *The Italian Road to Socialism* (interview with Eric Hobsbawm), Journeyman Press, London (1977).

N. Poulantzas, *State, Power and Socialism*, New Left Books, London (1978).

R. Simon, *Gramsci's Political Thought*, Lawrence and Wishart, London (1982).

P. Thomas, *Alien Politics*, Routledge, New York (1994).

CHAPTER 13

V. Bryson, *Feminist Political Theory*, Macmillan, Basingstoke (1992).

Z. Eisenstein (Ed.), *Capitalist Patriarchy and the Case for Socialist Feminism*, Monthly Review Press, New York (1977).

F. Engels, *The Origins of the Family, Private Property and the State*, Penguin, Harmondsworth (1985).

B. Fox (Ed.), *Hidden in the Household*, The Women's Press, Toronto (1980).

R. Hamilton and M. Barrett (Eds), *The Politics of Diversity*, Verso, London (1986).

A. Kuhn and A. M. Wolpe (Eds), *Feminism and Materialism*, Routledge and Kegan Paul, London (1978).

E. Malos (Ed.), *The Politics of Housework*, Allison and Busby, London (1980).

J. Mitchell, *Women's Estate*, Penguin, Harmondsworth (1971).

S. Rowbotham, L. Segal and H. Wainwright, *Beyond the Fragments*, Newcastle Research Centre and Islington Community Press, London (1979).

S. Walby, *Theorising Patriarchy*, Blackwell, Oxford (1990).

CHAPTER 14

A. Callinicos and C. Harman, *The Changing Working Class*, Bookmarks, London (1987).

A. Cottrell, *Social Classes in Marxist Theory*, Routledge and Kegan Paul, London (1984).

N. Geras, *Discourses of Extremity*, Verso, London (1990).

M. Jacques and F. Mulhern (Eds), *The Forward March of Labour Halted?* Verso, London (1981).

E. Laclau and C. Mouffe, *Hegemony and Socialist Strategy*, Verso, London (1985).

N. Poulantzas, *Classes in Contemporary Capitalism*, New Left Books, London (1975).

P. Walker (Ed.), *Between Labour and Capital*, Harvester, Hassocks (1979).

E. M. Wood, *The Retreat from Class*, Verso, London (1986).

E. O. Wright, *Class, Crisis and the State*, New Left Books, London (1978).

E. O. Wright, *The Debate on Classes*, Verso, London (1989).

CHAPTER 15

P. Anderson, *A Zone of Engagement*, Verso, London (1992).

P. Anderson, *In the Tracks of Historical Materialism*, Verso, London (1983).

R. Blackburn (Ed.), *After the Fall*, Verso, London (1991).

C. Boggs, *The Socialist Tradition*, Routledge, New York (1995).

S. E. Bronner, *Socialism Unbound*, Routledge, New York (1990).

A. Callinicos, *The Revenge of History*, Polity Press, Cambridge (1991).

P. Devine, *Democracy and Economic Planning*, Polity Press, Cambridge (1988).

F. Fukuyama, *The End of History and the Last Man*, Avon Books, New York (1992).

R. Gottleib, *Marxism, 1844–1990: Origins, Betrayal, Rebirth*, Routledge, New York (1992).

J. McCarney, *Social Theory and the Crisis of Marxism*, Verso, London (1990).

B. Magnus and S. Cullenberg (Eds), *Whither Marxism?* Routledge, New York (1995).

J. Roemer, *Future for Socialism*, Verso, London (1994).

I. Silbur, *Socialism: What Went Wrong?* Pluto Press, London (1994).

W. K. Tabb (Ed.), *The Future of Socialism: Perspectives from the Left*, Monthly Review Press, New York (1990).

L. Wilde, *Modern European Socialism*, Dartmouth, Aldershot (1994).

E. M. Wood, *Democracy against Capitalism*, Cambridge University Press, Cambridge (1995).

E. O. Wright, *Interrogating Inequality*, Verso, London (1994).

E. O. Wright, A. Levine and E. Sober, *Reconstructing Marxism*, Verso, London (1992).

Index

Page numbers in bold denote chapter/major section devoted to subject.